ENGLISH RECUSANT LITERATURE
1558–1640

Selected and Edited by
D. M. ROGERS

Volume 216

LUCA PINELLI
*The Mirrour of
Religious Perfection
1618*

LUCA PINELLI
The Mirrour of
Religious Perfection
1618

The Scolar Press
1974

ISBN 0 85967 200 x

Published and printed in Great Britain by
The Scolar Press Limited, 59-61 East Parade,
Ilkley, Yorkshire and
39 Great Russell Street,
London WC1

1825253

THE
MIRROVR
OF RELIGIOVS
PERFECTION

Deuided into foure Bookes.

Written in Italian by the R. F. *Lucas
Pinelli*, of the Society of
IESVS.

*And tranſlated into Engliſh by a Father
of the ſame Society.*

Pſalm. 138. Verſ. 15,
Imperfectum meum viderunt oculi tui.
Permiſſu Superiorum. M. DC. XVIII.

TO THE RIGHT
R EVEREND, AND
RELIGIOVS LADY,
BARBARA VVISEMAN,
ABBESSE OF THE
ENGLISH MONASTERY
OF SION
IN LISBONE,
OF THE HOLY ORDER
OF S. BRIGIT.

AND
TO THE REST OF THE
RELIGIOVS SISTERS
OF THAT HOLY HOVSE,
AND FAMILY.

* 2

RIGHT
REVEREND LADY,
AND
RELIGIOVS
SISTERS,

D I D

DID not the abundance of my Respectfull Affection to your holy House and Family, ouercome the distance of Place, or my small Acquaintance; I should not commend this little Treatise of RELIGIOVS PERFECTION to a Patronage so far remote from our Natiue Countrey: but rather seeke a Protectour neerer home. But seing so much Land, as lyeth betweene, doth not hinder the Fame of your Ver-

tuous

tuous Example & austere Life, from passing into these parts: so neither shall the seas drowne my Desires of your continuall Progresse, nor stay them from aduenturing with this Present, to make them knowne vnto you.

In this R E L I G I O V S M I R R O V R, you may behould rare Vertues, and accordingly draw in your selues the forme of highest Perfection. Heere shall you find whatsoeuer may help to the spirituall Aduancement of your soules: and by reading attentiuely, reape condigne fruites of your deuout Labours. The Method is easy, the Stile plaine, the Treasure

thereof

thereof infinitely rich, and the Author well knowne through the world by his worthy Treatifes of Piety, and Deuotion: Wherof this One may feem, by Gods fpeciall Prouidence, appoynted for fuell to increafe the fire of Deuotion in your Brefts; thereby to inflame the Harts of many Worthy Perfonages, to an holy Emulation of your Example.

I will not trouble your Ladiship, nor the reft of your vertuous Family with a longer Epiftle; but end, with many harty wifhes of fpirituall Light to your foules by this refplendent MIRROVR, and of Happines to our afflicted Countrey

＊ 4   by

by your returne to your Ancient S ı o n, now forlorne and
desolate by your Absence. At
least, that I may meet with you
in the Heauenly S ı o n, with
all Respectfullnes I craue your
holy prayers. This feast of the
Glorious Virgin S a ı n t B r ı-
g ı t, resting euer,

Your La. deuoted
seruant,

I. VV.

THE PREFACE

OF THE AVTHOR TO

THE RELIGIOVS
Seruants of God.

I*T is my intention Religious Reader, in a simple and perspicuous stile to write a Treatise no! like vnto that which is intituled,* The Imitation of Christ, *composed by that learned and Religious seruant of God* Thomas à Kempis *; but yet very fit and profitable to the profession of Religious Persons. Wherin certaine wholsome Admonitions, and Documents are by* Christ our Lord *prescribed vnto euery Religious person, as well for the knowledge of his owne defectes, as the attayning to that*

perfection

perfection of spirituall life, whereunto by obligation of his vocation he is bound to aspire.

This little Worke of myne, whatsoeuer it is, as I haue compiled it by Gods assisting hand: so haue I thought good to dedicate the same to the seruants of God, to the end they may be the more incited & stirred vp to the reading therof. And though I must confesse, that there be already extant no small store of Bookes of this kind: yet I trust this of myne will be neither vnprofitable, nor vnpleasant. And as there is not one and the same gust of all, in reading and handling such spirituall affayres; so is it conuenient, that oftentymes the same matter be handled diuers and sundry wayes, that therby euery one may read, and affect what shall best agree with his tast. Almighty God vouchsafe of his infinite goodnes to communicate vnto vs all so much of his Grace, as both by this, and other spirituall Treatises we may reap that fruit, which may preserue vs from all sinne in this life, and from all punishment in the next. Amen.

THE TABLE
OF CHAPTERS.

THE FIRST BOOKE.

THE TABLE.

THE SECOND BOOKE.

THE TABLE.

THE TABLE.

THE THIRD BOOKE.

Chap. 3.

THE TABLE.

THE FOVRTH BOOKE.

Chap. 5.

THE TABLE.

THE

THE
MIRROVR OF
Religious Perfection.

THE FIRST BOOKE.

Wherin is treated of Vocation to Religion, and of the End thereof, which is Perfection.

Of the End which God requireth of those, whome he calleth to Religion.

CHAP. I.

MY Sonne, I am the Authour and Creatour of men, and therfore haue I a singular care of them al: & to euery one do I suggest such a manner of directing his life, as by the conduct wherof, in louing & seruing me his Lord and Maker, he cannot erre in attayning his eternall saluation. But some

A   haue

haue I selected and chosen out in particular,
amongst which number thou art one, and
called from the world to Religion, that is,
to a state far more excellent & more perfect
then the secular, that thou mightst know,
loue, and serue me after a more perfect manner, and with more facility and ease attaine
to Heauen, enriched with the merits of
good Works. Neither haue I ordayned the
Offices and exercises, which thou hast found
in religion wherto I haue called thee, to any
other end, then that by the help therof thou
shouldst labour more or lesse to the perfection of a spirituall life. For if there be iust
cause, that more be exacted of them, to
whome more hath been giuen, for the like
reason also a greater loue and desire of Perfection is required at the hāds of the Religious
vpon whome I haue heaped, and with munificent hand bestowed so singular gifts and
priuiledges.

2.　　So did I before time deliuer my
most beloued people of *Israel* out of their
sore seruitude of *Ægipt*, that being brought
into the most pleasant *Land of Promise*, they
might there attend to the seruing of me in a
more quiet, and perfect manner. Therfore
did I by *Moyses* giue them a Law, & appointed them Ceremonies to obserue and keep.
　　　　　　　　　　　　　　　　All

All were indeed exempted,& set free frō the miseries of *Ægipt*, but all entred not into the *Land* of *Promise*. For they who out of an hard hart became rebellious to my precepts, were as vngrateful persons deseruedly punished & taken out of this life:for he is not worthy of pardon , who contemneth his Lord and Maisters commaund .

3 . O how much are those Religious persons deceiued, who thinke they haue satisfied their vocation , if they charge not, nor staine their conscience with mortal sins, and when they do any the very least good worke,they thinke I am cōtented ther with, and therupon, without further care or desire of ariuing to Perfection, they languish and become carelesse in my seruice. But the cause standeth not so:for I haue deliueredthē from out the snares of the world, and out of the daunger of more grieuous faults,not for any other end, then that they may the more readily attayne to the perfection of a spirituall life, by seruing of me truly, and deseruing my grace by the continuall exercise of holy actions.

4 . Certes, that man who out of a certaine carelesnes neglecteth to attaine to the perfection that I require of him, besides this going backward , and fainting, pleaseth me
nothing

nothing at all . For as I haue said by my Prophet , it is not inough to haue declyned from euill, but he must further do what good he can, cōformably to the state whereunto he is called. He sustayneth a great detriment, who when he may with his commodity, by carelesnes neglecteth the abundant gaine of spirituall things. And therfore no meruaile, though some religious persons neuer come to those inestimable treasures, that I haue prepared for them in the Land of the liuing . And more then this, it is no wonder, that some do leaue their vocation , and returne to the flesh pots of *Ægipt*, that is vnto the world, sith I do most iustly permit it for their negligence, carelesnes, & ingratitude vnto me . For he is worthily spoiled of his goods, who either knoweth them not or vseth them not according as he should do.

5. If I had freed you but from the worlds calamities, miseries, and deceits, I had done you a great good turne;but I haue besids this called you to Religion , haue admitted you as it were into myne owne family, and bestowed all manner of commodities vpon you, that you might the more perfectly serue me. Go to, tell me whosoeuer thou be, that hast not a will to labour to come to that Perfection of louing and seruing me, but thinkest

it

it inough, if thou offendeſt me not with a
mortall ſinne, whoſe is the greater hurt,
myne, or thine? ſurely it is thine alone, and
that much greater then thou conceiueſt. A-
gaine tell me, if thou enioyedſt al commodities in the world, and wert freed from all
daungers of life, and wert further aſſured of
thy ſaluation, wouldſt thou not hold it for a
ſingular benefit to ſerue me thy Creatour &
Lord? doubtleſſe thou wouldſt.

6.   Now then ſeeing I haue exempted
thee from all miſeries and troubles of the
world, and haue deliuered thee from the
daungers both of body and ſoule, that thou
maiſt be able the more commodiouſly to
ſerue me the King of Glory, iudge thou thy
ſelf whether it be not fit & requiſite for thee
to ſhake off al drowſines & negligence. Doſt
thou peraduenture thinke, that I require of
thee more pure, and more perfect loue and
ſeruice, then of ſecular perſons, becauſe any
commodity may therby accrew vnto me?
It is not ſo : for I need not thy ſeruice, ſith al
the fruit therof redoundeth not to me, but
vnto thy ſelfe.

7.   Beſids, the ſtate of thy profeſſion requireth, that thou ſerue me withall the perfection that poſſibly in thee lyeth, ſith Religion is nothing els, but the Schoole of Per-

fection . Neither is it any other thing to be
religious, then to enter into a course of life,
wherin a man may labour to the perfection
of louing me, and imbracing of vertues.
Wherfore vaine is the Religion of those,
who in the exercise of good works neglect
this way of perfection. For this is that,
which I require of all Religious Persons;
this is my will, and for this very cause haue
I drawn them out of the worlds snares, and
placed them in the paradise of religion. The
tree may not continue long standing in the
orchard, that shal not bring forth fruite, for
which it was there planted, set, or graffed.

*Wherein consisteth the Perfection of the loue
and seruing of God, wherunto a Religious Person is bound : and what
God requireth at his hands.*

CHAP. II.

SOME religious persons do performe
great matters. If they do them not moued
out of a pure loue to me, they neither please
me, nor am I bound to any remuneration for
them : but if they do them for loue of me,
yet with a languishing, and imperfect loue,
they do not satisfie their profession and
vocation. So when I called thee out of the
world

world, thou dideſt deliuer thy ſelfe wholy
vnto me, and dideſt promiſe to do all for my
loue, and I accepted this thy promiſe, receiued thee into my houſe, as one of myne,
gaue thee my Liuery, prouided thee of all
neceſſaries, and intreated and vſed thee as
one moſt deare vnto me. And if thou now
ſhalt haue a will to let ſome other enter
into, and poſſeſſe thy hart, or to make this
part common to another beſides me, thou
ſhouldſt not indeed diſcharge the office and
part of a perfect louer, ſith thou muſt not
giue that to another, that thou haſt giuen to
me already. For he who receyueth and taketh vnto himſelfe the thing againe, that he
hath once giuen to another, either for himſelfe or to giue to another, is a theefe and
worthy to be puniſhed.

2. Haſt thou a deſire, my Sonne, to know,
what religious perſon loueth me perfectly?
Truly he doth it, who in all things, as well
little as great, ſeeketh to do what pleaſeth me:
who delayeth no tyme of executing my will
ſo ſoone as he ſhall vnderſtand it: who doeth
not only willingly obey my commandmẽts,
but alſo manifeſteth a promptitude and readines in himſelfe, at the very leaſt ſigne or
becke of my will. A perfect louer hath one
and the ſame hart, and the ſame will with

A 4   the

the beloued, and therfore both hateth, and
loueth what the beloued hateth or loueth. A
perfect louer spareth no paynes nor trauaile,
all wearines is sweet vnto him, that he may
accomplish, what is pleasing to the beloued,
The perfect louer is not only wary and vigilant not to displease the beloued in the
very least thing, but also is exceeding carefull to please him more and more. He that
laboureth not to affect and loue a thing as it
deserueth, either knoweth it not, or is otherwise iniurious vnto it.

3.   That religious man is far from perfection, who when he shall haue set his affection & care ouermuch vpon things of litle
regard, is much troubled, and lamenteth if
I at any time procure, or cause the same to be
remoued, or taken away from him. This is
a signe of an imperfect louer, who loueth
me more in words then in deeds. He doth
indeed confesse in words, that he hath giuen
himselfe wholy vnto me, but his hart intangled with dissembled loue, holdeth him so
fast tyed, as if I would vse myne owne right
in wholy enioying it, & thrust out of it the
loue of the very least thing of all, it would
eftsoones bee in trouble, and rise against me.
Many say, and brag that they loue me, but I
only regard them, who loue me in works &
verity

verity. The tongue maketh no true and fincere louers , but the works that haue their
fourfe and fpring from a pious and deuout
mind.

4. It remaineth now, that I fhew vnto
thee, what religious perfon ferueth me perfectly. He I fay perfectly ferueth me, who ferueth me of pure loue, though he fhew it not
by fo great works : for what euer is done for
loue of me, I efteeme much , and will abundantly requite it . I make a greater reckoning of a good worke, though very litle, proceeding from a burning loue, then of a great
worke, accompanied with a meane meafure
of loue . Some weary themfelues out with
taking exceeding great paynes , but with
very little, or no profit at all to themfelues:
for that the actions , though neuer fo good,
which be not fealed vp with the feale of charity, be not gratefull to me, and therfore they
receiue not their hire: and if they be fealed
vp with a little fcale, their reward is alfo
little. Others in feruing me feeke after their
owne commodities , wherof when they
fhall fee but a little hope , they pull their
hand backe from their accuftomed labours
of feruing me, & do excufe the fame through
weaknes of body or of mind : but indeed
there is nothing that maketh them afraid,

but

but their owne. will, and the absence of
those commodities they had hoped for.

5. He serueth amisse, who in seruing
seeketh to profit himselfe : for such an one
serueth not me, but himselfe, & therfore he
doth in vaine expect any reward frō me. He
that will not for loue of me discommodate
himselfe, neither is my seruant, neither do I
hold him worthy the name of a seruant . A
good seruant is nothing afraid to suffer aduersities for his Lord and Maister, and this
is to be truely a seruant . My Ghospell de-
nounceth, that a seruant ought to be not
only faithful, but also wise: for he is boūd to
accommodate himselfe to the will, & manners of his Maister, and he must not seek, that
his Lord accommodate himselfe to his will.
He cannot possibly serue another, who hath
a will to liue at his owne pleasure, and as he
listeth himselfe .

6. Many religious persons liue discon-
tended with their lot in religion, and that
they must not impute to me, but to themselues. For being blinded with the ouermuch loue of themselues, they will liue
where they list, and exercise those functions
and offices that like them best, and not what
the Rule, or Obedience shall assigne them :
& if they be not pleased in their desires, they
fall

fall into paſſion, and leauing the narrow
way, they enter into the broad way of this
world, and do lay the cauſe of their inconſtancy vpon others. It is not the part of a ſubiect in religion to make his choice either of
place, or of office, but it is in him to obey
the Superiours ordination, will, and commaundement.

7. A wiſe ſeruant only aymeth at this,
that he may well and rightly conceiue his
maiſters will, and willingly and diligently
execute the thing that ſhall be commaunded
him. And he is not ſo hardy, as to ſay, this
or that office is not for me, this or that place
liketh me, this exerciſe and not any other
pleaſeth me: for that were to vſurp the office
of the maiſter, and not of the ſeruant, to ſeeke
trouble and diſquiet, not peace and quiet-
nes. For how knoweſt thou, whether this,
or that exerciſe be for thy ſoules good, or the
ruine of it? How canſt thou tell, that in the
place thou haſt choſen, thou ſhalt not meete
with any tentation? Therfore a wiſe ſeruant doth with more conſideration expect,
vntill he vnderſtand from his maiſter,
where, and in what it ſhal pleaſe him to vſe
his induſtrie, paynes, and ſeruice. And
though ſometimes he may haue a thought,
that this or that office will do him good, yet
he

he desireth not, that it should be cast vpon him, because he knoweth not whether he be a fit man to discharge it. For it appertaineth to the Superiour, & not to the subiect to iudge whether he be fit, or no. For it is not inough, that the office be good and fit for thee, but there is further required, that thou be good, and fit to exercise the same.

That a Religious person ought to make great reckoning of his vocation.

CHAP. III.

LORD, I should be euer foolish, willfull, and vntoward, if I should not esteeme of my vocation, which I doubt not, but is to be numbred amongst the heauenly gifts, proceeding from thine endles clemency. I should also be very vngratefull, if I should not continually render thy diuine maiesty thanks, for that without any desert of myne thou hast vouchafed to cast thy merciful eyes vpon me, and among so many millions of men, to receiue me into an holy family of Religious persons.

2. So it is, my Sonne indeed, thou art to make an high esteeme of thy vocation, not only because it is my gift, but also becausethou art admitted vnto it, not deseruing

it

it, but rather worthy of my wrath and indignation, procured by the peruerſe conditions and manners of thy forepaſſed life. And if thou make no reckoning of ſo great and ſingular a benefit of loue, beſids the puniſhmẽt which is due to ſo extreme an ingratitude, thou makeſt thy ſelfe worthy to be ſpoiled of all the gifts, and graces beſtowed vpon thee · For he is vnworthy of all benefit, who either acknowledgeth it not for ſuch, or altogeather refuſeth it.

3. Beſides that, ſith it is vndoubted & certaine, that among all things which thou haſt, nothing is more precious thẽ thy ſoule, and that amongſt thy greateſt affaires, that is the moſt important, which concerneth the euer ſauing therof; it manifeſtly followeth, that, that vocation is eſpecially to be eſteemed, wherby a man commeth to ſaue his ſoule. And he maketh a great accompt of his vocation, who loueth it, admireth it, and moſt inwardly affecteth it. Neither is this inough (for he may not eſcape the note of an vngratefull perſon, who though he maketh a great reckoning of the benefit, doth neuertheles forget the benefactour) but to take away, or preuent the blot of an vngratful mind, there needs both an hart, a tongue and deeds to requite the good turne, and benefit

nefit done thee.

4. If againe thou confider, whence I haue called thee, thou fhouldft do thy felfe an iniury, if thou fhouldft little regard fo great a benefit : for by calling thee out of the world, I haue deliuered thee out of an intricate and dangerous labyrinth, into the turnings and windings whereof the further a man fhall put himfelfe, the harder maketh he his owne getting out . For we fee the miferable louers of this world being puffed vp but with a little fmoke of ambition, and vayne glory, to hunt & range after honours and dignityes, as though they were put forwards, and driuen by the very furies of hell. And as often as this fmoke drineth towards them, they pleafe themfelues, and become proud, but when it declineth them, their courage falls, they haue no hart at all, and giue themfelues to forrow & languifhment . And yet all this fmoke doth nothing, but fill the eyes of them who gape after it, with tears and weeping, and their mind vvith bitternes.

5. Others taking the way of carnall pleafures, do precipitate themfelues into fuch a madnes and frenzy, as they make no reckoning at al of either foregoing life, foule yea their fupreme and only good, which is

God

God himfelfe, fo they may enioy their cōtenment of a moſt fliting and baſe pleaſure. A carnall and fenſual man hath neither knowledge, nor taſte of matters appertaining to God, & therfore is ready and apt to exchang them for a ſhort and little pleaſure of the ſenſes, in ſo much as no meruaile it is, though a blind man be deceiued. Others not finding a way how to forſake their honours and humane reputation, if they be once fruſtrated of their deſires in that kind, tranſported with wrath and indignation, become more fierce and raging, then the very wild beaſts, whils for reuenge of the very leaſt iniury, they come to kill one another, and ouerthrow both families and cittyes.

6. VVhoſoeuer is cruell towards his owne ſoule, is alſo cruell to others: for none hurteth his neighbour, who firſt hurteth not himſelf Others ſore oppreſſed with the yoke of wedlocke, are ſo ſore afflicted, as they wiſh rather to dye, then to lead a life among ſo many and dayly moleſtations, troubles, & cares of children and family. An vnfortunate choice hath an vnfortunate concluſion. Others walke vp and down in a labyrinth, but yet fettered in a golden chaine, that is, with riches & wealth of this world, which torments them, as poore bond-ſlaues, both
night

night and day, without giuing them any true rest at all. To be fast bound with a cord is a very sore punishment, whether it be of silke, or gold. He is a foole, who casteth all his affection vpon things, that in his life time cause trouble and care, and at his death sorrow and griefe. Riches that are possessed with loue, be forgone and left with grief.

7. Vnderstand further, my Sonne, that the world, out of which I haue called thee, is a Schoole, wherin humane lawes made by men giuen to passions, are more regarded then be the laws diuine. For in it is taught, that the transitory and brittle goods, that passe away and perish vnto vs with death, are more to be esteemed, them be those, that accompany vs to the other life, and do neuer dye. In it the more fouly a man is deceaued and offendeth, the more prone is he to sinne still, and the lesse acknowledgeth he the greeuousnes therof. In this schoole the good and vertuous are laughed at, the wicked and reprobate be commended, and therfore it is worse then hell it selfe, where al the wicked are reproued, and tormented.

8. Now if thou consider, in what place I haue put thee, thou shalt find many causes of yealding me thanks for the benefit of thy vocation. I haue placed thee in a religious

state,

ſtate, that is, in myne owne houſe, the fóndations wherof ſith they be laid in Humility, all thoſe that dwell in it, for the knowledge they haue of their owne weaknes and vtility, do reioyce in the contempt of themſelues, and had rather liue in obſcurity, then be knowne; rather to be reprehended then commended . They reueng not themſelues of iniuries done to them, but they willingly forgiue them. There they liue in a moſt pleaſing tranquillity, and peace : there, *Myne* and *Thyne*, that is the origen and fountaine of all diſſentions, hath no place at all . All there do labour for the common good, al help one another : he that can do more, doth more : and all ſerue one another, & all againe ſerue God . There be many togeather without confuſion, great variety of nations and of manners without difference of opinions & iudgments; functions and offices ſo diſtributed, as one troubleth not another, and yet all ordayned for the glory of God, to the good of ſoules.

ꝑ.   The keepers of this houſe be three ſiſters, moſt inwardly conioyned by fayth, fidelity, and the faſt band of loue; whoſe office is to defend , and keep all thoſe who dwell therin, from all calamityes of this preſent life, and to ſecure them from the incur-

sions of enemies, both visible and inuisible.
For voluntary pouerty exempteth a religious man from all trouble of procuring, conseruing, & increasing worldly riches, which
are wont so to molest, and paine the rich
mens minds and harts, as they leaue not vnto them a moment of quiet and repose. A-
gaine Chastity deliuereth them from infinit
desires of the flesh, whose tyranny oftentims
groweth so great and outragious through
the contentments of carnall pleasures, as it
maketh the soule (Reason being brought in
subiection to the lust of the flesh) a meere
bond-slaue.

10.   Finally Obedience exempteth a Religious man from daungers, whereinto they
do cast themselues, who out of a certaine
secret pride, desire to do all things by their
owne will and iudgment, refusing to be aduised or counsailed by others, and by so doing cast themselues into the Diuels snares,
who is the authour of all pride. He that
hath vertue to guard him, hath security on
earth, and is not without his reward in
heauen.

11.   Therfore vnderstand my Sonne, that
the Schoole of religion is directly repugnant
to the schoole of the world. For in that, is
deliuered the manner and way of seruing
God,

God, by the obferuation of his precepts and
counfailes : in it is fhewe d vnto thee a moft
compendious and fecure way of comming
to the end whereunto thou art created. In it
are difcouered and laid open the frauds, and
fnares of Sathan, fet by him for the intan-
gling of foules, and thrufting them downe
into hell. Of this fchoole I am the chiefe
maifter, and gouernour, who do by inward
infpirations fhew vnto all men the way of
perfectiō. In the inftruction of the fchollers
of this Schoole, I obferue no difference of
perfons : for I haue no more regard of a Gentleman then of a Clowne, of a rich man then
of a poore ; though I loue and affect thofe
more, who do practically by their works
manifeft, how well they haue learned their
leffons of humility, meeknes, obedience, and
the reft of the vertues, which I both declared by example of my life, when I liued
amongft you, and alfo dictated after my de-
parture to my Euangelifts, who did faithfully write them for the vfe of pofterity. He
is no good fcholler, who endeauouréth not
to imitate his maifter.

*How greatly a Religious man offendeth God,
who maketh light reckoning of his
Vocation, and Religion.*

CHAP. IIII.

WHITHER soeuer, Lord, I turne
my selfe, I find causes of feare. For
if I examine the benefit of my vocation to
Religion, I conceyue it to be so noble and
excellent, as I must confesse my selfe far vnable to render thanks for it. If I looke into
my selfe, I find so great an imbecillity, and
dastardy, as I am afraid least I should be deemed most vngratefull. Againe the greatnes
of thy maiesty confoundeth me, being such
and so great, as no satisfaction can possibly
be made vnto thee, but by a certaine infinit
loue, and seruing of thee, which is more then
I can, or am able to do. Who then would
not be afraid?

2.   Out of question my Sonne, I bestowed a great benefit vpon thee, when I tooke
thee out of the stormy Ocean of the world,
and placed thee in the quiet harbour of Religion. It is also certaine, that of this benefit
there ariseth an obligation, and that by so
much the greater, by how much the benefit
was great. But for this thou hast not any
                                   iust

iuſt cauſe to feare : ſith I am he, who do communicate to all, competent grace and forces, towards the ſatisfying of their obligation, ſo they be not ſlacke and negligent of themſelus, but do put to their owne helping hand, as much as they are able. And it is my máner of old to be rather more franke and liberall in beſtowing of benefits, then ſeuere in exacting obligations and debts.

3. Neither is there cauſe, that the greatnes of my Maieſty ſhould put into thee any feare, or confuſion , ſo thou be not wanting on thy part in louing and ſeruing me; not ſo much as my worthines requireth , but as thine owne forces be of ability to beare, ſith I haue neuer exacted more of a man, then he can well do. That perſon hath indeed iuſt cauſe to feare, who when he is able doth not what he ought, and is required of him to do.

4. There is but one thing for thee greatly to be afraid of, and that is , that thou offend not me thy benefactour by ſome greiuous ſinne, who of my ſingular grace haue raiſed thee vp to ſo high an eſtate of holy life, and am ready to raiſe thee higher, if thou be not a let therunto thy ſelfe . That religious man offendeth me moſt of all, who thinketh that he may liue a more holy life in the world, then in religion, & that is the cauſe he
B 3   maketh

maketh so light esteeme of the benefit of his
vocation. For he who affoardeth me little
honour, respect, and seruice in myne owne
house, will not doubtles yeald me greater
where my enemies haue to do. This is a
manifest and notable abuse and deceit, and
the very origen of all perturbation. For if a
man could serue me more perfectly in the
world, I would neuer haue inuited him to
religion. All good proceedeth from me: I
wish and counsaile true and solid perfection
to all, and I know best, what most profiteth
and is necessary for euery one towards the
attayning of his saluation.

5. A religious man must not cast his eyes
vpon that which best pleaseth him, and
highly preferre it before another thing, as
more excellent; but what shall please me.
Those also offend me sorely, who when in
religion they obtaine not all things as they
list, or haue their part in some discommo-
dities, do easily murmure, and as it were
sorrowing and grieued that they haue forsaken the world, do thinke a religious life
hard, and painefull. So were some of the
children of *Israel* affected, when they were
out of *Ægipt*. For so soone as they began to
want their former commodities, and to endure the troublesome labours of trauayling,
they

they murmured; & reflecting vpon the flesh-
pots of *Ægipt*, they wished themselues a-
gaine in their former bondage. I did not call
them out to rest, but to take paines ; neither
did I appoint them recreations, and great
commodities of life, but from the very beginning diligently inculcated, that many
things were to be endured for Christ, & that
the flesh is to be mortified, togeather with
the desires therof : and this condition they
accepted, and vndertooke to performe.
What cause then haue they to complaine?
And though none of all this had happened,
yet if their Lord suffered so great matters for
them, what great thing shall they do, if they
also being seruants, shall suffer somewhat
for their Lord?

6. A religious man, who is afraid to
suffer any thing, looseth his reward, and because a man must needs suffer many things,
if the labour and affliction be doubled, it
maketh the burden the more intollerable.
Others make light esteeme of Religion their
Mother, for that they thinke themselues not
bound to their religion, but their religion
to them. But they are deceyued. For if they
examine the matter well, they shal find that
they haue receyued very many benefits of religion, and religion none at all by them. For

to

to be religious and Gods seruant, is so noble a gift of God, and of Religion, as it ought worthily to be preferred before all the good works, that are done for religion. For there is not any earthly dignity in the world, that may enter into comparison with the dignity of religious life. It is an argument of a base and vnthankeful mind, if a religious person busy himselfe rather in thinking vpon the commodityes that he hath brought to religion , then those that he hath receyued from it.

7.   Againe that religious man displeaseth me not a little, who careth not how he imployeth the talent he hath receyued of me: for by that he manifesteth, what small reckoning he maketh of it, and hath no will to satisfy his office, when he may, & is able. How many be there, who being able to my great pleasure , do vndergoe some exercise for the good and helping of soules, but because they see they be not able to do them with so great applause , as some others can, they giue them cleane ouer. Is not this an ambitious prid? Is not this to hide the talent vnder ground , which I gaue him to make his gaine therwith ? I cannot be ignorant, what is good and healthfull for euery one, and therfore I giue fiue talents to some, two

to

to others,& but one to another. And though
to negotiate with one talent, doth not cary
so great applause and credit amongst men, as
to negotiate and trafficke with fiue, yet it is
not so with me. For I consider not, how
much euery one negotiateth, but how well
and carefully. And if to negotiate with the
help of many talents, should redound to the
soules good of many, and to the greater glory
of my name, it would be a worke worthy
of commendation.

8. But this is that which I find fault
withall, that many haue a desire to haue
many talents, and much negotiation, that
they may be the more admired at, and the
better esteemed of men, whiles to me, the
authour of all good, they leaue either no
place at al, or very litle. My beloued seruants
did not so at other times, who ascribed the
imperfections and lapses to themselues, and
the fruit of their good works to me, & that
they might transfer the praise and glory of
all their labours to me, they would be said
to be vnprofitable seruants: for the commendation of an excellent worke returneth not
to the instrument that wrought it, but to
the craftesman himselfe.

9. Sonne, of the contempt of thy vocation, or religious profession, there groweth

B 5   another

another euill, and that is a negligence, or carelesnes of attayning the end of thy vocation, and a neglect of obseruing the rules of thy proper Institute. And this vice offendeth me so highly, as I am forced euen to punish such persons in this present life. I abundantly affoard them health and strength of body, witt, and all helps both naturall & spirituall, that they may cheerfully hold on in the course of vertue which they haue begon, and at length come to their prefixed end. And if they by neglecting and contemning all this, reape no fruit of their good works at all; what meruayle, though like vnto the accursed fig-tree, that did indeed beare leaues, but yet no fruit at al, they somtimes decay, and wither away. The trees that I haue planted in a religious garden, ought continually to yeald the fruite of good workes; els as vnprofitable, they are to be accursed, and being once withered are to be throwne into hell fire. For whosoeuer worketh not well, whiles he is able, shall not escape vnpunished, when he would.

of

*Of the tentations, and daungers of
leauing ones Vocation.*

CHAP. V.

Sonne, the gift of thy vocation to a religious life, is a precious iewell, which hath no place on Earth, nor is it procured by friends, or obtayned with money, but commeth downe from Heauen from the Father of lights, and is of so great a price & worth, as nothing in this life may be compared to it. The property of this precious iewell is most worthy of admiration. For by it owne bright shining light it sheweth vnto religious persons all the down-falles and daungers, that be in this present life: which because secular men, who are destitute of the light of this diuine gemme, cannot see or discouer, they otherwhils stumble and fall very sore. It further layeth open al impostures, tentations, and trecheryes, that the enemy of mans saluation vseth for the intrapping and vndermying of soules.

2. Againe this light is so cleare, as it maketh entrance euen into Gods hart, and vnto Religious men layeth open Gods will touching their owne state: and in the execution of this will of God, Religious Perfection consisteth. Who vseth not the benefit of this

light

light in his way to saluation, walketh not in security, and though he fall not, yet he must needs many tymes tryp & stumble. The vertue also of this noble Gemme is of no lesse reckoning, the is the brightnes. For it giueth great courage & force to those, who labour towards heauen (whence it also commeth) against the enemy both visible & inuisible, who seketh to stop vp the way thitherward. For it animateth the Religious to ouercome al difficultyes that occur in the spiritual way.

3. This gemme hath yet another condition, that the longer it is worne & vsed, the fayrer and perfecter it becommeth. It can neuer be taken from a Religious man, to whome it is once giuen. It cannot be lost vnles he hath a meaning of himselfe wilfully to cast it away. If then a Religious man should make light esteeme of this iewell, should he not be worthy seuerely to be punished? And should he not deale iniuriously with his benefactour, if he should forbeare to vse the vertue and efficacy of it? For he is accompted no lesse vngratefull, who vseth not the benefit bestowed vpon him, then he who acknowledgeth it not, or disteemeth it. This gemme as it is defended with three vowes, that guard and keep it; so is it beseeged by three cruell enemies, who seeke continually

tinually to fteale and take it away. The firft
is the World, who putteth man forwards to
feeke after riches and vanities. The fecond
is the Flefh, togeather with the defires, and
the whole route of fenfuall pleafures. The
third is the Diuell with his proud fuggeftiõs
proceeding of felfe loue.

4. My Sonne, that thou mayft not loofe
fo great a Treafure, thou muft needs haue
three things. The firft is Vigilancy or Cir-
cumfpection, for that whiles a man fleepeth
in the field, cockle is eafily fowne amidft the
good corne: and he that is not confiderate
and wary, eafily falleth into the enemies
fnares. The fecond is a fingular affection towards the iewell of this thy Vocation, that
thou mayft loue it more hartily then thyne
owne life: for the better it is loued, the more
carefully is it kept. And becaufe it is fo excellent, as it bringeth thee to God, and to e-
ternall felicity, nothing ought to be more
deare vnto thee then the fame, as there is not
any thing found in heauen or in earth, that
is more excellent then God, or euerlafting
faluation. The third thing neceffary, is that
thou place this Iewell fo faft in thy hart that
thou fuffer it not to be taken from thee by
any aduerfity, or pleafure, or for the refpect
of any creature whatfoeuer, & if any fhould

go

go about to fpoile thee of it, that togeather with it he mutt take away thy hart alfo.

5. Befids thefe, there be fome other things that hurt a Religious man, and difpofe and prepare him to the ouerthrowing of Gods calling in him. In the firft place thou mutt earneftly endeauour to mortify and roote out the bad habits thou haft brought out of the world, before they thruft thee from the ftate of religion. For like vnto bad plants in the ground, they fticke faft in the moft inward parts of the mind, and become to be fo ftrong in time, and fo great, as they in conclufion choake vp the good feed of thy vocation, that they may obfcure, and take away the bright fhining of this heauenly margarite. Whofoeuer in religion retayneth his peruerfe habits of the world, fufficiently manifefteth, that he hath not wholy abandoned the world. The horfe running out of the ftable, and carrying his halter with him wherewith he was tyed, by often ftumbling is eafily taken, and brought back againe into the ftable: euen fo a Religious man, running out of the ftable of this world, if he draw his old manners & cuftoms with him, by often ftumbling eafily yealdeth to tentations, and is brought backe againe into the ftable of the world, out of which he had runne.

ruune. He profiteth nothing by his running away, who runneth away haltred or tyed.

6.   It also much hurteth a Religious man, and in tyme throweth him downe from the state wherein I haue placed him, to make little reckoning of lighter faults & defects, which do by little and little quite ouerthrow him, and bring him into a certaine loose, & hurtfull liberty of life, wherewith the true spirit of Vocation cannot haue coherence, which in all things both little & great requireth obseruation. He can neuer be secure, who whiles he may, freeth not himselfe from his enemies, though they be neuer so little. An house before it falleth giueth some little signes of the future ruyne, which if the owner preuent not in time, it soone after quite falleth to the ground: So a religious man, if he do not in the very beginning prouide a remedy against little faults & defects, that are found and obserued in him, will in time shake and weaken all his vocation: and bound fast in such kind of bands, wil leade a miserable life out of Gods house. Who healeth not vp his wounds in good tyme, when need is, repenteth himselfe with his owne greater hurt afterwards.

7.   Those also suffer great detriment in their vocation, who discouer not their tentations,

tations, nor defects to their Superiour. The theef flyeth away as soon as he is discouered, but whiles he is not knowne, he neuer giueth ouer, till he hath stollen some thing: Euen so a Religious man, as long as he concealeth from his Superiour, what it were fitting for him to know, giueth an occasion to the infernall theef of robbing him of the precious Iewell of his vocation. He that discouereth not vnto the Phisitian the quality of his disease or sicknes, either vnderstandeth not the greiuousnes therof, or maketh light reckoning of any cure.

8. O how much deceyueth he himselfe, who ouer confidently thinketh himselfe secure in his vocation. This presumption ariseth of nothing but this, that he doth not sufficiently examine and consider his owne imbecility, and who he is. For the more exactly a man looketh into himselfe, the more he feareth, and the lesse confident is he in his owne ability. And this is an excellent remedy for the procuring of strength and courage against all tentations. But he that is more confident in his owne industry then is meete, easily turneth his backe in the very beginning of the encounter, and abandoneth the Colours of his Religion. The more a Religious man presumeth of himselfe, the

lesse

leſſe he doth , becauſe preſumption is the daughter of pride. But he who feareth, doth the more, becauſe holy feare is the daughter of Humility, which euer moueth vs to worke well.

9. Moreouer a Religious man is deceiued, and is not far from daunger of leauing his vocation, who thinketh, that he may be able to do more good in the world, then in Religion. For who is not good amongſt the good, & amongſt ſo many examples of good perſons, and in an holy place, how will he do good in a bad world amongſt the bad, where ſo many bad examples will be preſented euery day vnto his eyes, and where ſo many occaſions be of liuing naughtily? With theſe fraudes the diuell vſeth to draw the vnwary Religious man into his net. For when he ſhall once haue perſwaded him, that he may do more, and more excellent works in the world, he forthwith ſuggeſteth that no great reckoning is to be made of the ſtate of Religion, and ſo in concluſion dryueth him from his vocation. It is the Diuels property to deceyue vnder pretence of good, who neuer caſteth out his hooke, but that it is euer bayted to catch Religious perſons.

10. Neither be they in leſſe daunger, who by a certaine careles drowſines waxe

by little and little cold in spirit, and in my
seruice, and though they well find and perceiue this in themselues, yet they neglect to
put it away. When a sick mans feet, or hands
become so cold, that they cannot recouer
heate, it is a signe, that he is in extremity
and neere vnto his death : So a cold Religious man, if he take not paynes to recouer his
heate and warmth of spirit, is not far from
dying spritually, & from daunger of loosing
his religious life. Who will not be holpen,
when he may and can , how can he be secure of obtayning help at all times?

That it is not inough for a Religious man , to
be called of Goa to Religion, but he must
earnestly labour to the perfection
of his Vocation.

CHAP. VI.

LORD, I giue thee most harty thanks for
this precious stone, that thou hast vou-
chsafed to send me downe from heauen,
when as pittying me, thou calledst me to
holy Religion ; and I ascribe all the ioy and
spirituall comfort, which I receiue heerby
in consecrating my selfe to a Religious state,
to thy goodnes and clemency .

2.   My Sonne, if thou dost this, and no
more

more befids, thou commeſt too ſhort of thy
duty. For vnles befids theſe things, thou endeauour by good and holy actions to arriue
to the perfection of thy vocation, inſteed of
being rewarded thou ſhalt be puniſhed. To
be called to religiõ, & to weare the habit, increaſeth the puniſhmết, vnles not by words,
but by works thou anſwere ſo many and ſo
great benefits of myne beſtowed vpon thee.
He that after benefits receiued of me, neglecteth to profit in vertue, doth not only incurre the note of ingratitude, but doth further, as it were, bind my hands faſt, that I
giue or beſtow no more vpon him. Men do
ordinarily make a coniecture by the outward
habit and cloathing, whether one be Religious or not; but I iudge by the inward.

3. O how many do dwell in Monaſte-
ries, and weare a religious habit, and be not
indeed religious, as be al thoſe who haue not
wholy giuen themſelues to the exerciſe of a
religious life, and of ſolid vertues, but do
partly ſerue God, & partly the world. Contrariwiſe there be many in the world, who
weare a ſecular habit indeed, but yet in affection be truly Religious, and do exerciſe
vertue; in ſo much, as it is not the habit, nor
the place, that make a true Religious man,
but the inward hart and mind, and the ex-

C 2   ternall

ternall works which do manifest the same.

4. What doth it profit a man to be notably well armed, if at the time when by commaundement of his Captaine Generall he were to fight with his enemie, he should not vse them? The tree that yealdeth no fruit, is to no purpose suffred to stand in an orchard, sith it is for no other end planted there, then for the bearing of fruite. I haue taken vp all religious persons to serue me in my warre, & haue giuen them weapons and armes, that they may vse them, as I would haue them. And therefore whosoeuer glorieth in the name of a Religious man, and sheweth not by deed his loue towards me, nor doth conformably to the spirit of his vocation yeald me spirituall fruite, he doth not the office & part of a Religious man.

5. O how far are they deceiued, who thinke themselues to haue discharged their duty well, for that they haue entred into the state of religion, and continued therin, often reckoning the number of the yeares, which they haue liued in it, & not examining how negligent they haue beene in the exercise of pious works, and how little fruit and profit they haue reaped by their labours & paynes. The number of yeares maketh not a Religious man happy, but his good works, and the

exercise

exercife of vertues. To glory of the great
continuance in religion, and to be deuoid of
vertue, and the perfection therof, is no commendation at all, but a reproach and con-
demnation.

6.   The fcholler, that hath frequented
the Schoole for many years, is not to be therfore praifed, but he that hath profited in the
fchoole, and is become excellent for his learning. If thou wouldft confider that thou
art to giue an accompt of all the tyme thou
haft mifpent in religion before my Tribunal,
thou wouldeft not brag of thy felfe, but la-
ment rather, for hauing, like a fruitles tree,
occupied the place of another, who might
with greater profit haue yealded me much
fruit.

7.   In like manner he alfo deceyueth himfelfe, who being entred into the gate of religion, thinketh it inough, if he tranfgreffe
not Gods commaundmends, and is not of-
fenfiue, or fcandalous to any. But he is
wholy deceyued, neither am I content therwith alone: for he who thinketh he may
make a ftand heere, doth not a little offend
me. He ceafeth to be a true religious man,
when he beginneth to haue a will not to be
better.

8.   A good religious perfon neuer thinketh
C 3   himfelfe

himselfe to haue ariued to perfection, nor
euer sayth, *Now it is inough.* For he knoweth
that in the spirituall life, not to go forwards
is to go backwards . It is my will, that a religious man mortifie himselfe conformably
to his Institute, and exercise himselfe manfully in all those things, that be therby prescribed or commaunded . This if he do , he
answereth his vocation , and for this end
haue I called him to a religious state . And
who seeth not that he performeth very little
or nothing at all, who when he hath means
to do much good for his owne soule, and for
Religion, doth of set purpose let all alone?
Who againe seeth not, that he is far out of
the way, who thinketh himselfe to satisfy
his vocation & institute, if he find himselfe
to haue a will to do no euill ?

9.   Tell me, I pray thee, what that mar-
riner meriteth, who being hyred to help in
the time of nauigation, should thinke that
there were no more for him to do, thē not to
be troublesome to any in the ship ? or when
there were occasion to hoise vp the sailes,
or let them downe, or to fight with pirates,
should sit still & looke vpon others ? Should
not he deserue, as an vnprofitable seruant; I
say not , to be only thrust out of the ship, but
also to be cast headlong into the sea? Euen so
                                    should

should it be with a religious man, who being admitted into a religious ship, vpon no other condition, then that he should exercise himselfe in the functions of religion should giue way, or place to idlenes, which in all Congregations hath euer been a thing scádalous. Neither can it be said, that an idle person doth no euill, because he doth euill inough, who doth not what he ought. This man then if he be not thrust out of religion, nor be cast into the sea of this vnhappy world, as he well deserueth, cannot yet 'escape the finall sentence of Gods seuerity and iustice. The punishment that is differred, is not taken away, or lessened.

That a Reli ious man must attend, and haue an eye to those things, which be proper to his owne Reli ion, and not of another.

CHAP. VII.

SONNE, I am he who haue from the beginning gouerned my Church, and still do, because it cōtinually fighteth & standeth in battaile for the mayntenance, and defence of my honour and glory. And though it consist of diuers parts, yet haue I so knit them togeather in one body, as they make a well ordered army, seruing happily vnder

C 4   my

my Croſſes ſtandard. And in this my Churches army the ſquadron of Religious men
marcheth in the vanguard, whoſe charge it is
with the inuincible help of ſpirituall arms
to gayne & make a conqueſt of the kingdome
of Heauen. This battalion according to the
diuerſity of Religions, hath differēt colours,
and yet all haue their directions from me
the Generall of the whole Army. Euery Religious man alſo muſt ſerue vnder thoſe Colours, and in that Company wherin he was
firſt enrolled, euen vntill his death, and muſt
exerciſe himſelfe in thoſe armes that are
proper to his order, or religion. It helpeth
much, if he be well affected to his owne
Order. For the ſouldier that is well affected
to his colours, doth not eaſily chang or forſake them, but when need is ventureth his
life alſo for the defence therof.

2.　Though all Religions commonly
ayme at this, that they may make their ſubiects perfect in my ſeruice, yet euery one
hath certaine proper and peculiar exerciſes,
wherby to become perfect in their one:
and this is the ſpeciall end and ſcope, that
all thoſe who imbrace the ſame, ought to
propoſe vnto themſelues. For example: they
who imbrace the religion, that profeſſeth a
ſolitary life, remoted and retired from conuerſation

uerſation with men, as is that of Ermites,
ought to labour to become perfect in cloathing, in dyet, in contemplation of heauenly
things, and in the praiſing of God. And ſuch
as haue entred into a religion that profeſſeth
an actiue life, that is, to help their Neighbours both ſpiritually and corporally, ought
to profit in the exerciſe that is proper to an
actiue life, that is, in exerciſing charity to
their neighbours, with as much paynes and
care as they are able, without any the leaſt
regard of their owne cōmodity, but meerly
for my glory, knowing that whatſoeuer
they ſhall do to their neighbour for loue of
me, they ſhall do it to me, and that I will be
their reward for it. The ſame muſt they alſo do who imbrace a religion that attendeth
to Contemplation, that they may the more
entirely vnite themſelues with God their
maker; and that alſo which mixeth Contemplation with Action, ſuch as be commō-
ly Religious of the begging Orders.

3.   And theſe particuler exerciſes can
neither be well done, nor continued long,
vnles they that practiſe them, endeauour to
that perfection of life, that is common to all
religious perſons; that is, vnles they ſeek and
labour to deny their owne will, to mortify
their ſenſes, and to contemne themſelues.

For of thefe vertues, as of foundations, the
fpeciall and proper exercifes of euery Religion do confift, and are by them fupported.
He that is good, & perfect in himfelfe, may
eafily help othersto become good alfo, which
he cannot wel do, if he fhal not be good himfelfe. For he, who hath no care of his owne
perfection, cannot wel promote it in others.
Who is naught to himfelfe, to whome will
he be good ?

4.   O how ill doth that Religious man
vnderftand the forme of his Inftitute, who
pleafeth himfelfe rather with the exercifes of
another religion, then with thofe of his
owne. Therfore to different ftates of Religious I haue imparted different gifts & graces,
that euery one may execute his owne function and office aright. Whence it is, that
he, who hath not receiued, or hath not the
true fpirit or free gift of his owne religion,
cannot fatisfy the office he beareth in it. If I
would haue had a religious perfon tyed to
another exercife, I would alfo haue called
him to another religion, and would haue
giuen him the proper gift therof. But if I
haue called him to this Religion, it is nothing fitting, that he meddle with another. For he, who leaueth the functions of
his owne religion, and taketh vpon him
                                         thofe

those of another, shall not satisfy the one nor
the other.

5. He that professeth a solitary life, doth
no little matter if he attend to himselfe, and
he doth wisely, if he leaue the care of helping
his neighbours to others. Wherfore that religious man much pleaseth me, who addres-
seth all his thoughts, and all his paynes to
the scope he hath proposed to himselfe, and
to the functions of his owne religion, and
for the compassing therof laboureth to ouercome all difficulties, by auoyding those
things, that may hinder him, and by imbracing againe those things that may help him
to the obtayning of the same end. He doth
much, who laboureth to do what he is boud
vnto, & which agreeth with his profession.

6. There is an other errour also obserued
in some Religious persons, who from the very beginning of their conuersion determine
and assigne vnto themselues some peculiar
end, but yet little conforme to a Religious
estate, and that is, that they may become
great Philosophers, Deuines, or Preachers,
and therunto directly and indirectly they
imploy all their cogitations and studyes. It
cannot be said, how hurtfull this intention
is, seing it bringeth in the obliuion of a good
and religious life, and the contempt of his
owne

owne rules and inſtitute, and which to ſay
in one word, is the Seminary of infinit vanityes and troubles. For if the ſuperiour commaund any thing to ſuch kind of men, who
hath little correſpondence with their end,
they inſtantly refuſe to obey, they murmure,
complaine, and are afflicted therfore. Againe
if the Superiour, becauſe he would not
contriſtate them, ſuffer them to hold on the
courſe they haue intended, behold there forthwith followeth the breaking of a moſt excellent order, & therwith the ruine of themſelues and their Religion togeather. For nothing in a religious life is more pernicious,
then to leaue vnto ſubiects the power of doing their owne will. Where there wants o-
bedience and ſubordination, there neceſſa-
rily followeth contuſion, and diſorder.

7. I haue often ſaid already, that he cannot be my ſcholler, who mortifieth not himſelfe by the abnegation of his owne will. I
am the way, I am the guide : who followeth
not me, the further he goeth, the further is he
off from the marke. This way held all thoſe
ancient Religious men, who do now enioy
the ſupreme felicity in heauen. For they in
the beginning imbraced that which was
proper to their vocation, and in other
things they ſuffred themſelues to be be directed,

&ted and gouerned by their Superiours, my
Subſtitutes, and Vicegerents heere on earth.
And he that doth otherwiſe, deceiueth and
ruyneth himſelfe.

8. Finally they are deceyued alſo, who
ſeeke to accōmodate the proper inſtitute of
their religion, the end , and miniſteries therof, to themſelues and their owne will, & do
not, as they ought, rather accōmodate themſelues ynto it . Such be they, who will needs
exerciſe theſe or theſe functions, both when
and how they ſhal themſelues deeme fitting,
and beſtow as much tyme, or as little in thē
as ſhall beſt pleaſe themſelues . This is not
the direct way : for ſeeing they be the members of Religion, is it fit, that they accō mo-
date themſelues to the whole body, that is ,
to the Riligion, and not contrarywiſe the
Religion to them . Arrogancy and Pride
will in concluſion, when he leaſt thinketh
ther of, ouerthrow that religious man, who
accommodateth not himſelfe to his Superiour.

Wherein doth it conſiſt, to be a true and
perfeƈt Religious man.
CHAP. VIII.

L ORD, as often, as I conſider the many
good purpoſes, I haue made of louing
thee

thee withall my hart, and of seruing thee
with my whole affection al the dayes of my
life, I thinke my selfe to be religious, & that
truly, though I am afraid I may be deceiued.
For when I call to mind, what my forefathers haue done, what great things they
suffered for the loue of thee, what paynes
they tooke for the purchasing of vertue: and
and on the other side considering with my
selfe how little I haue hitherto done, for the
gayning of the same, and how little I haue
endured for the glory of thy name, I seeme
not to my selfe to be a perfect, or true Religious man.

2.   Sonne, there be many who in their
owne opinion be religious, and that true
& perfect also, but there be very few indeed.
For perfection is a certaine vniuersality of
all vertues, which in truth is found in very
few. Some there be, who thinke they haue
gotten the name of Perfection, if they dayly
say so many Psalmes, or so many payre of
beads, if they fast some dayes in the week, if
they punish their bodyes with haire-cloath
or disciplines; and if they should omit al this
they thinke themselues to come far short of
perfection. Good and laudable be all the
said actions, but yet in them consisteth neither the summe of spirituall life, nor a religious

gious mans perfection, but in true and solid
vertue, inherent in the seule.

3.   These externall actions be in some, as
it were the meanes and instruments, apt for
the attayning of spirit and true deuotion,
so they be vsed with moderation, such as is
agreable to beginners. In some againe they
be the effects and fruit of the spirit, or of spirituall perfection, as in the Proficient and
Perfect, who by that seuerity of pennance
do subdue the rebellion of the flesh, that it
may not rise against the spirit, and by frequent prayer they stir themselues vp in
the loue of God, that they be euer conioyned,
and vnited to him : though in some also
those outward mortifications of the body
(if the perfection of vertue should be wholy
placed therein) may giue an occasion of ruine, as whiles they proceed so far in mortification of the outward man, as they neglect
the inward, that is, the restrayning of the
motions & perturbations of the mind. And
it comonly happeneth, that such manner of
men be willfull and stiffe in their owne iudgment, and such as would seeme to teach all
men. And where humility is not, there can
be neither a true spirit of God, nor true deuotion and piety , and therfore a most rare
thing it is, for such to be amended : seing he
is

is hardly brought into the right way againe,
who thinketh himselfe all this time to haue
runne in the same. And a manifest sinner is
with more facility conuerted, then a secret
one, who hideth his indiscret actions vnder
a cloake of vertue..

4.   Know this my Sonne, for certaine
that, that Religious man is more deare to me
who restrayneth, and mortifyeth all his bad
desires, then he who giuing the raynes to his
inordinate appetites, continually fasteth;
weareth haire-cloath, disciplineth himselfe
to the bloud. He can neuer recouer his health
who applieth not a remedy to the place
where the euill resideth. Wherefore to ease
thee of the doubt, which thou hast in this
matter, I will giue thee a most cleare looking
glasse, wherein the forme and proportion of
a true and perfect Religious person is to be
seene, wherewith if thou wilt compare thy
selfe, thou maist easily ghesse, whether thou
best like it, or no, & shalt vnderstand withall what is wanting in thee.

5.   The Poesy of a perfect Religious man
is *To do*, and *To suffer* : for in these two words
is comprised all the perfection of a Religious
man. *To do*, signifieth nothing els, but that a
true religious man ought so to order his life,
as he may satisfy the charge & function he
oweth

oweth vnto God, his Superiours, his Religion, his Neighbours, to himselfe, and to other things created. And *To suffer*, all the actions of a religious man do manifest, whether he exerciseth them for the increase of my glory, or for the promotion of his owne cōmodity : whether they haue their beginning from a true spirit , or rather from humane prudence.

6.　That Religious man satisfieth God , who louing his Creatour aboue all things, diligently obeyeth his precepts, and Euangelicall Counsailes , magnifieth him withall his hart ; prayseth him in aduersity as well as in prosperity : accepteth al things from Gods hands, as gifts from heauen ; would choose rather to dye a thousand deaths , then to offend his Creatour in the very least thing, or in any thing to go against the prescript of his diuine will. Finally whatsoeuer he doth, he doth it for the amplifying of my glory and honour .

7.　A perfect Religious man satisfieth his Superiours, who at the very least signe of their will, doth promptly and cheerfully obey them, as if it were the voyce of God, not as men, but as Gods Vicegerents. Them he reuerenceth and loueth as the fathers and pastors of his soule, by me appointed ouer him,

D　　　　　interpreteth

interpreteth all their ordinations & actions
in good part, and modestly defendeth and
purgeth them, if he heare any murmurations
against them.

8.   He also satisfieth his religion, if he
do what a good sonne performeth towards a
most deare Mother, who doth not only honour and loue her, but also as often as he perceiueth her to require his paines and seruice,
is ready at hand, & willingly offereth himselfe to beare the burden, whatsoeuer it shall
please her to lay vpon him. He is glad if men
report, and speake well of her, if they report
ill, he laboureth with modesty to defend her
good name. Finally he hartily wisheth, and
beseecheth the diuine Maiesty, that she may
euer proceed, and hold on in the spirit of
Humility, and Deuotion.

9.   Againe he declareth himselfe to be
well affected towards his brethren, and religious persons, whome he loueth from his
hart, and reputeth their good, or euill to be
his owne. He thinketh and speaketh well of
all : he pittyeth the defects of euery one : he
seeketh to edifie them also euen in the very
least things, and in what he is able helpeth
them, especially in matters appertayning to
spirit.

10. The obligation of a perfect religious
man

man extendeth it felfe alfo to the men of the
world, whome he fatisfieth when he truly
wifheth vnto them, as to his neighbours e-
ternall felicity, and loueth them as himfelfe.
And if he fee the bad example of religious
men hurtfull vnto them, he vfeth all meanes
that no occafion or example of fcandal be giuen vnto them by himfelfe, and in all his
conuerfation laboureth to be exemplar, and
ouerflippeth not any occafion of doing them
good for their foules health.

11.   A good religious man is bound to
performe fomething towards himfelfe alfo ,
as he is Religious: and this debt he fatisfieth
if he diligently beat downe his owne defirs
contradicting reafon: if he mortify the wan-
tonnes of his flefh, if he contemne the world
togeather withall the vanities therof : if being moued out of a loue to me, he mortify
himfelf in al things, & feek not after his own
glory, but myne . For if he haue no regard
of his owne eftimation, he is then come to
a perfect and abfolute victory ouer himfelfe.
Againe if he keep his body in fubiection to
the vnderftanding, and yeald it nothing but
what is neceffary : for fo doing he fhall leaue
the foule a free paffage of mounting vp to
heauen . To be fhort, being dead to himfelfe
and to the world , he fhall liue to me, his

Creatour alone.

12.   Lastly a perfect religious man satisfieth other created things also, if he conuert
them to his owne vse, so much only as is requisite, and no more. And because he cannot be ignorant, that God hath committed
them vnto vs, as far as they may be an help
vnto vs for the attayning of our end, let him
only loue those for his owne vse, that may
further him to his said end, and reiect the
rest, that may hinder him. For by so doing a
true religious person may of the creatures
make himselfe a ladder to clymbe vp into
heauen.

13.   The other word appertayning to a
religious mans poesy, was *to suffer*. Al men at
their first entrance into a religious state, do
promise willingly to suffer, but few there be
that discharge the same truly, and for that
cause come not to any perfectiõ. And by this
word of *suffering* is meant, that a religious
man is by suffering purged, and perfected,
and that none can be perfect in religion, but
by suffering much. Therfore in holy Writ
perfection is compared to an Hill, to the top
wherof none can come, but by labour and
difficulty.

14.   A perfect religious man murmureth
not against God, if he send him sicknes, persecutions,

secutions, or other calamities, but giueth the
father of mercies thanks for them, as for gifts
comming from heauen. Neither complay-
neth he againſt creatures, ſaying : This man
hath done me a great iniury, that other hath
ſued me againſt all equity, right or reaſon,
another man exerciſeth his malice and hatred towards me: but as one deſirous to ſuffer
when any aduerſity hapneth, he accepteth it
for a ſingular fauour of Gods benignity towards him. And this is the way of drawing
forth and getting good out of euery euill.
Whiles a religious man taketh any thing in
ill part for me, it is a ſigne, that he caryeth
a greater reſpect of loue towards himſelfe,
then to me.

Of the inward defects, that be impediments
to Religious Perfection.
CHAP. IX.

SONNE, after the wound giuen to thy firſt
parent *Adam* long ſince in the terreſtriall
Paradiſe by Sathan, all the powers and faculties of the ſoule became ſo languiſhing,
faint, weake and decayed in his poſterity, as
that euer ſince they haue diſpoſed man
rather to lapſes and vices, then to the loue of
vertue. Hence haue proceeded all the difficulties, imperfections, and impedimentſ,
D 3   which

which we dayly find in the spirituall life, which doth so molest and trouble vs in the way of perfection, as they either disturbe & hinder it quite, or at least lay a barre against it, that it succeed not so well.

2. Wherfore that we proceed more slowly to mount vp to the perfection of vertues, wheron is placed the seate of Religious Perfection, in the first place this is the cause, that we do not seriously resolue with our selues to haue a will to vse all our forces to get vp to the top of this mountaine: and this proceedeth of nothing els, then that we do not effectually labour to get perfection. He that effectually desireth health, careth not what medicine be giuen vnto him: This defect is such, as it cutteth off cleane all hope of arryuing to perfection. For he that hath not made a firme purpose to hold on in the way to perfection, will hardly begin to pace towards it: and he who beginneth not, how is it possible for him to come to his prefixed end? And he that is so affected in mind, when he neglecteth the occasion of doing well, will either do no good at all, or will fall to what is worse.

3. O how great a losse of spirituall gaine sustayneth that religious man, who prolongeth his iourney in the way of perfection!

He

He will no doubt at the houre of death better vnderstand this errour then now he doth:
for in that exact and last examen of his conscience, he shall more clearely see, that he
had no iust cause of differring the exercise of
vertues, but that it was pretermitted of him
through his owne meer carelesnes and negligence. And his grief and confusion will at
that time be the greater, the more he had his
part in my inspirations, wherby I did so
often inuite him, stir him vp, and sollicited
him to perfection.

4. There is another impediment also to
a Religious man, that maketh him with the
more difficulty to labour to perfection ,
becaufe he apprehendeth it for an ouer great
difficulty to obtaine victory ouer himselfe,
and to ouercome the bad affections of his
mind. But as delay made without caufe, de-
iecteth the mind , and very much hurteth a
man: so an effectuall, and cheerfull resolutio
of vndergoing a thing , greatly helpeth towards the ouercomming of any difficulty.

5. Son, if thou wert the first of those who
should enter into the way of this warfare,
thou mightst haue some caufe & excufe, but
since there haue been so many, who though
sometimes ouercome , did yet in the end
victoriously get vp to the top of the hil, thou
canst

canst pretend no cause of excuse at all, or of pardon. For the obtayning of a victory and Crowne it is not inough to fight, but a man must go away also with the victory.

6. There is yet another vice, that hindreth vs from getting vp to the mount of perfection, for that we are fettered in fast bands at the foot of the hil. And whosoeuer is so tyed, he may indeed moue himselfe a little, but mount vp he well cannot. That Religious man is much deceiued, who preposterously affected to some humane thing, thinketh that he may ariue to perfection. For whereas he holdeth his hart, fast tyed with the cord of affection to some thing created, he must needs either mount vp the hill without an hart, which is not possible, and would not be pleasing to God; or els without life with the thing created, to which he cleaueth fast, which God would neuer indeed tolerate, who hath neuer suffred any thing to be beloued togeather with himselfe. For sith he is of himselfe, & of his owne nature good, his wil is also to be beloued alone by himself. The Creatour cannot loue him, who against his will transferreth his loue to a creature.

7. An impediment also to the same ascending, is the ouer sore burden, that a man layeth vpon his owne shoulders. For wheras

as

as he muſt go an hard and painefull way, the
more he is ſurcharged and loaden, the leſſer
and ſhorter iourneyes maketh he, and otherwhiles he is ſtayed in the midde way , and
cannot go any further. Wherfore a religious
man, who intangleth himſelfe in many affaires and imployments that norbing concerne his vocation, will either trauaile ſlow-
ly towards the mount of perfection, or will
be forced to ſtay in his way thitherward, becauſe the ſtrength of his ſpirit is weake, the
way painefull and vneuen , and the diſpoſi-
tions of his mind eſtranged from ſuch a iourney, or rather inclined to the contrary . A
Religious man hath inough to carry his one
burden, which if he ſhal increaſe with other
mens cares, no meruaile though he yeald and
fall vnder the burden , and oftentimes come
to that miſery, that he is not able to beare his
owne, and much leſſe anothers.

8.   Finally it is not the leaſt impediment
of getting vp to the top of the hill, for a Religious man to be moued with too much cō-
miſeration of himſelfe. If one haue a dull
horſe, and out of pitty dareth not giue him
the ſpurre, probably he will not come to the
end of his iourney . I like not of a religious
man, that is ouer nice and delicate, who leaſt
he ſhould put his body to ſome paines, laboureth

boureth not to perfection, as he should do.
The souldier, who hath ouer much care of
sauing his life, and an horrour of the daügers
of war, doth ordinarily but make vp the
number, & giueth no increase to the strégth
of the army at all: for when there is occasion
presented him of shewing his valour & courage, he runneth away for feare.

9. The Religious, who are now crowned in heauen, did not so. For though they
were of a weake body by nature, and had
accustomed it to all manner of ease and delicacy, yet after they once became Religious,
for the attayning of perfectiō, they punished
it with fasting, pennance and mortification,
and so with commendation and merit arriued to that which they sought for. That religious man, who fauoureth his body more,
then meete is, loueth it too much, because he knoweth not how to loue it truly,
like vnto an ouer mild Phisitian, who by
his curing increaseth the sicknes.

Of other outward defects, and imperfections,
that be impediments to Perfection.

CHAP. X.

SONN, in some Religious persons there be
found other imperfections and defects,
which as they do no lesse hinder Perfection,
then

then the former, so be they no lesse displeasing vnto me. The first is, that they will not
labour to perfection by the common and ordinary way, but do bethinke and deuise another new way, vnknowne to their forefathers. But they erre very sore in the matter:
for where it is of it selfe very hard & pain-
full to get vp to the mount of perfection, the
paine would be doubled, if a new way besids
the ordinary be to be taken: neither doth the
crafty enemy seeke any other thing, then to
hinder a mans endeauour of climing vp, by
adding a new labour and paine in doing it.
Who goeth on in the beaten way, trauayleth securely: for that they who went before, by their example shewed the security of
it, and of this security he hath no signe at al,
who goeth and seeketh out a new way.

2. O in how great an errour be those
Religious persons, who reiecting and neglecting the ordinary spirit of their owne Religion, do follow and imbrace another particular, & strange spirit. This is to go a new
way, both with more labour, and lesse profit.
For it commonly hapneth, that such men
whiles they find not an end of their way, being ashamed of themselues, are forced to go
backe againe, or els do fall headlong into
some pittfall or other. That religious man
cannot

cannot be guided by Gods spirit, who refuseth to keep the way, which all those that went before him held. I haue appointed to euery religion a certaine and determinate way, ordayning to that end peculiar laws & constitutions, declaring the manner and meanes, how euery man may come to his iourneys end. He therfore, who shall neglect his way, and go another, doth plainly giue to vnderstand, that I haue not instituted euery religion wisely inough to content him. And heere is to be seene a notable deceit, and tricke of the Prince of darknes, who leadeth the negligent and vnwary religious persons out of the common way of their owne institut, that when they are once wearyed in it, he may cast them downe headlong to their further ruine.

3. A second defect is, that they will not vse the guide, whome I haue giuen to direct them in the way without errour. For that trauaylour is not without cause deemed temerarious and rash, who goeth his iourney without a guide, which he knoweth, by reason of the many turnings and by-wayes, to be subiect to many daungers & strayings out of the way. I am the guid, who to al religious men do shew the right way to perfectiō. And I do it by Superiours, & spiritual

Fathers,

Fathers, whome I haue appointed in euery
religion. Wherefore it is ho meruaile though
they, who will not suffer themselues to be
gouerned and directed by their Superiours
and ghostly fathers, but follow their owne
iudgment, stray out of the way, be spoiled
by theeues, or fall into misery and ruine. So
hapneth it vnto those, who before they be
schollers, do professe themselues to be maisters, and so by a secret pride, wherby they
contemne their superiour whome I haue de-
signed for their directour and maister, become schollers of the Diuell, who is the captaine and chief leader of all the proud.

4.　A third defect there is, arising of humane respect; namely, that some be ouer sol-
litous to gaine the good will and fauour of
all. Is the care of a religious person to please
men, and not to displease the world ? Vpon
what true ground, or reason can he seeke after the worlds fauour, who hath once so earnestly abandoned and giuen ouer the world?
I called him therfore out of the world to religion , that he might not seeke any thing ,
but to please me alone, & in that way to hold
on towards perfection . If by the help of this
world a man might be brought to a perfect
state, a religious man might also vse the benefit and help therof: but it is not so . For

the

the world followeth a far other profession,
and intertayneth other manner of cogitations, then those of attayning spiritual perfection. Who studyeth, and hath a care to
please men, is no disciple of mine, neither
pleaseth he me, nor do I intertaine him for
my seruant.

5. A man can serue but one maister,
with true loue. And if he would deuide his
hart into two parts, let him not determine
to offer me the one of them: for I will in no
sort accept it. If thou hast so great a desire to
please men, wherfore didst thou leaue them?
O miserable religious man, who when thou
liuedst still in the world, didst not only not
hunt after the fauours of men, but also didst
not any thing that might obscure thy good
name and estimatiō; but after the time thou
hast imbraced a religious estate, thou burnst
with a desire of pleasing men, in so much as
thou art not ashamed to do many things, vnworthy thy vocation and condition, and
which is worst of all, grieuously also to offend me, least thou shouldst perhaps offend
men. Wherfore then, my Sonne, doest thou
vaunt, that thou hast trodden the world vnder foot, if thou hast so earnest and longing a
desire to please it? Seest thou not, that by the
care of gayning the grace of other men, thou
                                        loosest

loosest the peace and quiet of thy mind? This is not, I must tell thee, the way to the mount of perfection, but to the downe-fall, & pitt of eternall damnation.

6. There is yet another impediment in attayning to the perfection of vertues, to wit when a religious man obserueth no order or good proceeding in his spirituall actions. An army, though neuer so great, complete, and prouided of all necessaryes, if it be not well ordred, either when it marcheth, or when it ioyneth in battaile with the enemy, shall neuer get the victory: So a religious man, who must contend and fight for the getting of Perfection, that is seated vpon an high hill, and compassed with all complete armour of vertues, if he obserue no order in all his spirituall exercises and actions, which be as it were so many souldiers, shall neuer go away with the victory.

7. There be some, who before they haue layd the foundation of humility, begin to raise their spirituall building. Others againe before they be past the Purgatiue way, think they may be most inwardly conioyned, and vnited with me. But this is not the way & course of comming to perfection. Humility must be procured in the first place, and from it a passage must be made to pennance, and
by

by it the mind and conscience is throughly
to be cleansed. It is not inough for him, who
falleth into the myre, to rise out of it, vnles
he also wash away all the durt : euen so it is
not inough, that a religious man hath renoū-
ced, and forsaken the world, and to haue
gotten out of the sinke of sinne, but he needeth further to extirpate his bad inclinatiōs,
and hurtfull affections and propensions,
which remayne as staynes behind in the
soule, and in place of them by the help of my
illuminating grace to plant most beautifull
vertues: so doing he may aduenture to become most inward, and most familiar with
me.

8. Lastly, an Inconstancy in spirituall
life stoppeth vp, and debarreth the entrance
not only to perfection, but also the meanes
of compassing any vertue at all. For there be
those, who endeauour often to get vp to the
mount of perfection, but they still fall down
againe into the valley that lyeth vnder it,
because they are more prone to abandon and
giue ouer the thing they haue once begon,
then they be manfull to go through with it.
O how much shall they be afflicted for this
their inconstancy, when the houre of their
death shall be at hand, when the Diuell shall
vpbraid them with this, that they did
indeed

indeed with great feruour wrest from their Superiours , frequent exercise and vse of prayer, fasting, disciplines, and other mortifications for their profit of spirit, & for their helps to perfection ; but afterwards they did none of them at all, or very little .

9. If a Religious man had as great loue to perfection, as he should haue, he would euer aspire and labour to it, neither should there occur any difficulty, that might terrify him from compassing it . But because his loue languisheth in the thing it selfe, whence that inconstancy groweth , he easily relenteth, and recoyleth. A Religious man, doth not only suffer the losse of time by trysling thus, but also becommeth worse euery day, then other .

How Perfection is finally to be attained.
CHAP. XI.

LORD, if it be so hard and painefull a matter to arriue to perfection , by occasion of so many defects & impediments, that stop vp the way ; I see not how I, that am most weake, can come thither, or ouercome so many difficultyes with my most slender forces. Sonne, he that resolueth seriously & hartily to labour to perfection, doth most certainly arriue vnto it. So many Religious

E   men

men in former times most perfect, who now enioy their euerlasting felicity in heauen, were mē like vnto thee, & had the same difficultyes that thou hast, and much greater, & yet they manfully and constantly ouercame them, and thou mayst do as much, if thou wilt. Neither shalt thou want my grace and help, as they neither wanted, so thou resolue vpon some thing, as they did. Neither must thou be discouraged and recoyle for feare of the difficultyes that will encounter thee, especially seing there be as many and more meanes, wayes, and remedyes for the remouing and taking away of those difficultyes, and procuring of perfection.

2. The first remedy is, with an inward affection to imbrace perfection, & earnestly to labour therin, sith for the ouercoming of all the rockes of this mountaine there is nothing better, or more effectuall then the affection of loue. Neither is there any thing that inciteth a Religious man more to continue on his way, and to labour to perfection, then the same. Of loue there then followeth a desire, and care of vsing and frequenting those meanes, that be necessary or profitable towards the attayning of perfection. And study, care, & diligence do help very much towards the more speedy compassing

paſſing of what is deſired or loued . Of the
ſame loue groweth conſtancy and perſeuerance, wherby ſpirit, life , and hart is giuen
a religious man to hold on, and to proſecute
his labours, and of this next followeth the
victory, and crowne . To him who loueth
nothing is hard, no not the ouercoming and
gayning of heauen, and the getting vp to the
top of the mount of perfection

3 .   A ſecond remedy, and meanes to the
attayning of perfection is, to haue a conſideration and regard euen of our very leaſt imperfections . Some are wont, when they fal
into ſuch manner of imperfections, to breake
forth into theſe, or the like words: It maketh
no matter, it is a thing of little moment, it is
nothing : and theſe men be the very bane of
religion . For of this contempt they become in
time bold, temerarious, raſh, & by their own
bad example they draw others to a certaine
pernicious and diſſolute liberty. That muſt
not be held in light eſteeme, that diſpleaſeth
me : neither ought it to be thought a ſmall
matter, which I cōmaund, or forbid, though
it be not great indeed in it ſelfe. And know
thou, my Sonne, that the very leaſt imperfections pleaſe me not, & for that cauſe I haue
forbidden them . Know thou further , that
the religious man who maketh a conſcience

E 2   to

to transgresse or offend in the very least
things, is deliuered from greater imperfections. For all the great ruyne, and breaches
of good order and discipline, that are found
in religion, haue receiued their beginning
of smaller faults. Who shutteth his eyes at a
light fall, will also shut them at a greater, because that prepareth the way therto, that is,
a smaller to a greater.

4. A Third, and very good means also
is, for a man to mortify himselfe in the very
least things. For religious perfection com-
prehendeth all vertues; all which a man cannot be possessed off, vnles he get a full & absolute commaund ouer his passions & senses.
And a man commaundeth his passions, if he
restrayne them so soone, as they raise themselues against the reason, or against the laws
of religion : neither must he also yeald vnto
the senses euen in the least matters, more then
is fitting to his religious estate. For he who
condescendeth to his senses, beyond the mediocrity of vertue, soone findeth them rebellious; and he who doth not resist his inordinate passions in the beginning, becometh a
slaue vnto them in the end.

5. A fourth meanes and way to perfection, not only auaylable, but also necessary,
is, that a religious mans mind euer conspire,
and

and accord with his Superiours will and desire in all things. For all helps haue their origen from me, which are needful towards the
attayning of perfection, & them I ordinarily
communicate by the Superiours, by whom
I do enlighten and gouerne my subiects.
Whereupon such a one as is separated from
his Superiours, wanteth such kind of gifts,
and helps. And more then that, he is separated from me ; and therfore no meruayle
though hefall often, be troden vnder other
mens feet, be contemned, and pyne way and
languish, because he is a dead member cut off
from the head. It little auayleth the scholler
to go vnto the schoole, if he be not one with
his maister, by whome he may be directed
in his course of learning and studyes.

6. Finally, it helpeth not a little to perfection, if these wayes be practised, not with
a tediousnes, & heauines of mind, but with
promptitude and alacrity. For this alacrity
profiteth much to the ouercoming of difficultyes, which the body apprehendeth and
feeleth in the attayning of vertues: it confoundeth the enemies that oppose theselues
in the way of perfection ; and maketh the
paines of the iourney the lighter, and more
easie to be endured. And which is more, this
promptitude and alacrity, wherewith a religious

ligious man serueth me, pleaseth me much, because it hath the beginning of loue also. And to conserue this spirituall ioy and cheerfullnes in mounting vp to this hill of vertues, a man must haue companions in his iourney. It cannot be said, how much vtility and profit a religious man receyueth by the company and conuersation of the good, by whose speach, and example he may be excited and stirred vp to deuotion, sith nothing there is, that in humane life hath more force to moue a man to perfection, then the example of good vertuous companions.

7.   Wilt thou, my Sonne, be wise? Conuerse with the wise. Wilt thou be perfect? Liue with them, who loue and seeke after perfection. Therfore I haue prouided, that in euery state of my Church there should euer be some holy and exemplar men, who by their examples, as by lights set on high in a candelsticke, might giue light vnto others. Whereupon a religious man, whiles he compareth their life with his owne, easily perceyueth, how little he hath profited in the spirituall life, and by a certaine holy emulation stirreth vp himselfe, to vse more diligence for the time to come in the exercise of vertues. If good examples haue more effect

to

to moue then words, whosoeuer profiteth not by them, doth manifestly declare that he hath a will ouermuch propense, prone, and addicted to euill.

Of the spirituall ioy which accompanieth a religious man, that attendeth to perfection.

CHAP. XII.

SONNE, the spirituall ioy, and content-ment, that a good Religious man hath after he is entred into the narrow way of perfection, is no doubt great, and singular, as on the contrary, the grief and heauines of hart that oppresseth a bad religious man, holding on in the broad way of imperfections, is hard, disgustfull, and bitter. Where-upon the one and the other beginneth in this life, to haue a taste of that which is pre-pared for them in the other, either punish-ment, or reward. Lord, I know not, what I may answere to this: for I see many Religious men to imbrace the broad way, & not to labour greatly to come to perfection, and yet to be very iocand, cheerfull, and merry.

2. Son, thou art deceiued. For in the way of liberty, and where no obseruation of dis-cipline is in practise, there is not any true or solid ioy, though it may seeme to be such. A

Religious

Religious man who liueth at his owne wil
and as he pleaseth, displeaseth others, and he
oftentimes is cast downe with grief, & pen-
siuenes, because he cannot haue what contenteth him. True ioy hath the seate in the
mind, and ariseth of the peace and tranquility of conscience, which is felt within;
which cannot be in the religious man, who
leadeth a free and dissolute life, because his
mind is day by day, as a sea, tossed and tum-
bled with the surges and waues of perturbations & passions. Woe be to a religious man,
reioycing in his imperfections.

3. There be others in religion, who
runne the way to perfection after their own
will; neither vse that moderation in mortifying themselues, that were to be required.
These men do often stumble in their way,
because they preiudice, and hurt their health,
and yet they ariue not to that holines of life,
whereunto they labour. And whereas they
be destitute of ioy and comfort, both from
within and without, all the fault is ascribed
to ouermuch deuotion, which is no such
matter. For it is not deuotion, that causeth
either infirmity, or anguish of mind, but indiscretion, and that more is done and vndertaken, then reason dictateth, or I require.
None can be either his own guide, or iudge.
4. But

4. But true peace and ioy, is to be found in those religious men, who do with due moderation attend to perfection, & practise the meanes of coming vnto it, by the aduise, direction, and prescripts of Superiours, and spirituall Fathers. For what way soeuer they turne themselues, they euer find occasions of being glad, and of reioicing spiritually. If they conuert themselues to me, they haue no want of consolation, because they know wel inough, how much it pleaseth me to see a religious man, labouring earnestly towards perfection. And if there were not any thing els in this life, it were and ought alone to be inough for a religious man, to passe ouer his life in an exceeding ioy. For a seruant cannot haue any greater pleasure and contentment, then to vnderstand, that all his offices, and seruices be pleasing vnto his Lord. And if they turne their eyes to their Superiours, they experience the same by tranquillity of mind. For seeing they be studious and desirous of perfection, they must needs be quiet, peaceable, obedient, most obseruant of Religious discipline, and consequently in high esteeme and beloued of their Superiours ; which if they once get knowledge off, they cannot but reioyce greatly.

5. Now if we looke vpon others, with
whome

whom they liue & keep company, they haue
no cause of griefat al. For seeing they attend
to the exercise of vertue, they hinder or hurt
none, but haue a care to do good to all, as to
themselues, and therefore they intertayne
peace with all : and where peace is, there is
true ioy. And more then that, vertue maketh
them amiable, not only to their friends, but
to their enemyes also. For the vertuous are
beloued, honoured, and respected of all, in
so much that a religious man can neuer
want internall consolation and comfort.
Againe if they consider themselues, they cannot be without consolation also. For it is
proper to vertue, wherein they exercise thé-
selues, to worke with pleasure and taste, and
therfore needs it must be, that true Religious
persons reioyce in all their actions: yea they
find consolation in their tribulations, and
persecutions, when they be ready for loue of
me, euen to suffer and endure the paynes of
hell, if it could be without their owne fault
and would be for my glory; and not only
that, but all the aduersities and miseries of
this world besids.

6.   Finally the meditation of death,
which strickeh a feare and horrour into o-
thers, to good religious men is an occasion
and matter of ioy, not only for the reward,
that

that they expect, but becaule they fhall then
haue their part of that exceeding and furpaf-
fing confolation, which they attend for at
the houre of death, tor the care and defire,
they had in arriuing to perfection. For the
foule will at that time be exceedingly glad,
neither fhall fhe be able to find an end of rendring thanks for receyued benefits.

7. There is but one thing, that can make
a good Religious man fad, & that is, if he fal
into fome imperfection. But this forrow
cannot be of continuance, becaufe it is inftantly taken away by the vertue of pennace,
and the fault cancelled by contrition, and
vpon this the mind is put againe in poffeffio
of the former tranquility. Tell me now my
Sonne, who peraduenture makft but little
efteeme of perfection, in what other thing
mayft thou find fo great and vniuerfal a contentment of mind? What thing can fecure
thy mind more, or better, then the defire of
of perfection? Confidereft thou not, that
to labour & attend to perfection, is nothing
els, then before hand to take an eſſay, & that
of eternall felicity? Thou muft needs be vn-
wife if thou robbe and fpoile thy felfe of fo
great a good, that thou need not take any
paines in reftrayning and conquering the
defires of thy flefh, and fenfes. And this
madnes

madnes will appeare the more euident vnto
thee, when there will not be oportunity for
thee to do that, which now thou shouldst
do. Happy is he, who shall in that last ago-
ny be able to say: Whatsoeuer good I could,
or ought to do, that, by the fauour of Gods
grace, I haue done in my life time.

Of the great paynes, and myseries, that Reli-
gious men do suffer, who forsake and
leaue the way to Perfection.

CHAP. XIII.

LORD, if the discomending of a bad religious man be in the same measure, that
is the commending of a good one, I make no
doubt, but he liueth in very great affliction
of mind, for abandoning and giuing ouer the
way to perfection. So it is, my Sonne, and
so much the worse, because they acknowledge not their owne infelicity. Euery euill
is wont to be the more dangerous, the lesse
it is knowne: for if it be by carelesnes neglected in the beginning, it increaseth, & by
little and little gathereth so great force and
strength, as in the end it exerciseth a commaund ouer all. O how much doth a bad
religious man hurt himselfe! who transported, and carryed away by an ouer great liberty of liuing, looketh not into himselfe,
that

that he may vnderſtand, whence ſo ſore perturbations & afflictions which he endureth
in religion, haue their beginning .

2 . If he turne himſelfe to me, he is aſhamed: for he knoweth, that he was called out
of the world, to lead a ſeparated, retyred, and
perfect life : and he knoweth how many
benefits I haue beſtowed vpon him; & how
great cōmodityes I haue giuen him towards
the proſecution and practiſe of vertue. And
that by neglecting them, he hath left off all
cogitation of labouring to perfection , and
ſeeketh alwayes to liue at more liberty , and
to ſatisfie the alluremēts of the ſenſes. He offendeth me as much , as his ingratitude is
hatefull vnto me, whence ſuch a life proceedeth . Theſe be not thoſe pious and good
purpoſes, that he made, and gaue teſtimony
of, at his firſt entrance into religion: neither
is this the way that I taught him, & wherin I walked my ſelfe . Neither can he but
know in his own cōſcience, that this his life
(which is far from that of a religious man)
diſcōtenteth me greatly. And therfore he is a-
gainſt his wil, inwardly tormēted with moſt
bitter ſtings of conſcience, though outwardly he ſhew it not ; and when time cōmeth ,
ſhall receiue his deſerued puniſhment . The
ſeruant, who is priuy to his maiſters will, &
doth

doth it not whiles he is able, if he be not a
very foole, meriteth seuerely to be punished
for it.

3.   If he hath to deale with his Superiours, he is much afflicted, and troubled. For
fith ne is neither obedient, nor loueth religious difcipline, it is not in him to keep
common peace with them, and therfore it
muſt needs be, that many things be in like
manner done, that be one while difconten-
ting to himſelfe, and otherwhiles to the Superiours. Befides that, the poore & compaſ-
ſionate Superiours be grieued, not knowing
how they may deale with him, that he may
be holpen. For if they deale fauourably & after a indulgent maner with him, he being
accuſtomed to liberty, abuſeth their gen-
tlenes, and becometh the more proud. If
they handle him with more ſeuerity, by forcing him to do his duty; then as one impatient of ſo hard difcipline, he ſhaketh off the
yoake therof, and troubleth the Religion. If
any thing be commaunded him, he refuſeth
to do it : if pennance be inioyned him, he
complaineth and murmureth. That he liue
ſo ſtill amongſt the reſt after his owne will,
is nothing expedient: for the longer the cuſtome of doing ill is continued, the worſe
it maketh the man, and by his bad example
                                                        he

he hurteth & misleadeth the more. Whence
it followeth, that a Religious man, who
contemning the desire of perfection, liueth
disorderly, and maketh no reckoning of intertayning peace with Superiours, must
needs be troubled with a continuall heauines, and bitternes of mind. Certes, he cannot but be bad, & become euery day worse
then other, who contradicteth and resisteth
his Superiours and betters.

4.   Againe, if he turne himselfe to other
Religious persons, amongst whome he liueth, he findeth no comfort at all. For if he
perceiue, that the wise & spirituall brethren
make very little reckoning of him, & shun
his conuersation and company in what they
can, he cannot but be much troubled & moued in mind, and therfore is forced to keep
company with his like, who be desirous
of a more free and disordered life. Neither
can he yet receiue any solide comfort from
them, for that where the spirit of deuotion
is not, there neither peace nor ioy can be of
continuance. The friendship of the bad is
not long lasting, and is euer suspected: and
where suspition raigneth, the mind is euer
in suspence and doubtfull, and therefore he
cannot possibly be truly merry.

5.   Finally, if a bad religious man turne
his

eyes vpon himselfe, he hath no cause of reioicing, but of lamenting. For sith he hath no
part in true vertues at all, he hath none to
direct him in his actions, nor who may defend and help him in his temptations, and so
he becometh prone to fall, yea & to apostasie
also. Againe, what ioy can he haue, who
must take great paynes without hope of spirituall profit? As long as he is in religion, he
must needs exercise himselfe in the ordinary
offices of the same; which because he doth
vnwillingly, or with loathing, murmuring,
and other imperfections, he looseth all his
merit. Besides that, what comfort can he
haue, who receyueth a tormēt in wholsome
and meritorious actions? Who wanteth spirit, and cannot be holpen? if he be to pray, he
is in paine; if to heare a sermon, or some pious, and spirituall talke, he loatheth it; if
discourse about the purchasing of vertue, he
may not endure to heare it. O miserable religious man who drinketh gal, when others
tast of most sweet hony! It is a signe of death,
when the sick person becometh the weaker
by receiuing a medicine.

6.   Moreouer in enduring tribulations, he
is so much the more afflicted, by how much
lesse he was armed, & prepared against them;
like vnto a little boate, when a sore tempest
                                        ariseth,

ariſeth, wanting both oares & ſterne. By one
thing alone he may ſeeme he may be eaſed of
all his troubles and miſeries, and take ſome
poore refreſhment and quiet, and that is by
death. But death, vnles he want the vſe of
reaſon, will rather increaſe his feare, and ter-
rour. For the ſooner it ſhall come, the ſooner
ſhal he be preſented to my Tribunall, to giue
an accompt of euery moment ſpent in religion without ſpirituall profit. For death is
to the bad & wicked the beginning of more
heauy puniſhments.

That a Religious man ought with great con-
fidence to labour to the attayning
of Perfection .

CHAP. XIIII.

LORD, if I ſhould mount vp to the tree
of vertue, to gather of the ſweet fruit of
Perfection, I find not where I may ſtay my
ſelfe. For the tree is very high, and my forces
very weake, my nature is afraid, my body
conceyueth an horrour of it, and if it be preſ-
ſed forwards, it kicketh and refuſeth, and
therfore I am forced to ſtay vpon the ground
beneath, becauſe it is impoſſible for me to
get vp higher. But tell me, Son, how I pray
thee, can it be ſaid to be impoſſible, when as
all religious, as many as be now in heauen,

F   and

and many more, who be still liuing on earth, haue not without their exceeding great commendation, mounted vp to it, and gathered of the wished fruite of perfection. Yet I must confesse, that some came to the height of it more speedily, and some more slowly, some with more merit, & some with lesse. And therfore for euery one that hath a will, it is neither impossible to follow them, nor very hard: if thy forces be not sufficient, thou hast my help at hand: if thy industry and cooperation be not wanting, my grace shall not fayle thee.

2.　To get vp to the height of this tree, and to gather the fruit of perfection, is to get the victory: and to obtaine the victory, a man must needs carry himselfe manfully. To statuaes and pictures may a scepter & crown be giuen, though they neuer come to the battaile, but not to a reasonable creature, and free, to whome the crowne of vertue is his reward, and the reward is not giuen without merit, nor merit without encounter precedent and gone before. If then thou aspirest to the crowne of vertue & the perfection of it, thou must needs prepare thy selfe to the pains, & to the fight, as others haue done before thee. He knoweth not what a reward is, who expecteth it without labour & paines.

Seeing

Seeing then the hope and confidence of obtayning perfection, relyeth not only on the
help of my grace, but on thine owne cooperation also, thou must of necessity on thy
part performe the conditions, that I am now
to set downe.

3. First, necessary it is, that thou haue a
true and sincere desire of labouring to perfection: for this desire is not only the foundation of the aforesaid confidence, but also
helpeth to the furthering of thy progresse &
going forwards, to the ouercoming of difficultyes that euer and anon occur vpon the
way, and to the mitigating and easing of all
the paines. Sonne, experience sufficiently teacheth, that he who hath not a desire, seeketh
not, and that he who hath a great desire of
a thing, seeketh it earnestly. Againe putting
thy confidence in me, begin thou with courage to exercise the actions, now of this vertue, now of that; for by so doing thou shalt
extirpate all thy bad inclinations, and in
place of them plant in thy mind all the most
beautifull slyps of vertues. And though I
am accustomed to lend my helping hand in
this busines; yet know thou, that I otherwhiles try a Religious man by the with-
drawing of my help, that so his constancy
may appeare, and how great a confidence he

F 2   hath

hath in me.

4.   O how much is a Religious man deceiued, who if he peraduenture stumble in
the middest of his course, intended to the attaining of perfection, by falling into some
imperfectiõ, or finding himselfe not to profit so much in vertue as he desireth, fainteth,
and is quite discouraged: & diffident of being able to arriue to perfection, neglecteth to
hold on, or to proceed any further : and of
this it cometh to passe, that after that he giueth himselfe far more free scope to runne a
disordered course of life, then euer before.
This is not the way to get the victory , neither is it an argument & signe of a valiant &
noble mind, but of a faint & cowardly hart .

5.   Certes, that way-faring man should
be deemed mad who would not hold on the
iourney he had begon, or should go backe a-
gaine, because he trypped and stumbled once
vpon a stone, or had had a fall: for that were
nothing els then of a small euill to cause a
greater. But the wise & wary trauayler doth
not so, but if peraduenture he slippe, or haue
a fall, he presently riseth againe, & continueth his iourney forwards : and of this fall he
learneth to be more wary and heedfull for
the time to come, that he fall no more. The
very like hapneth amongst religious men .
                                                                For

For when one vnwary and vnprouident
falleth into any imperfection, he neither
hath a care or desire to rise againe, neither is
he vigilant to preuent a fall against another
time. But when a prudent & spirituall man
falleth, he sodainly getteth vp vpon his feet
againe, and if he should fall an hundred tims
a day, he would rise vp againe an hundred
times, and would be sorry for his falls.
Whence it is, that he is not only not dismaid
but he also doth with greater earnestnes, care
and endeauour by the exercise of vertues,
hold on his way to perfection. And this is
of euill to draw out good.

6. Those Religious men be also deceiued, who thinke the exercise of vertues to be
laborious, painefull and hard, and therefore
for feare of preiudicing and hurting their
health of body, they let courage fall, become
pusillanimous, or like vnto skittish horses
will not go forwards with spurring, but do
resist, & kicke. These men would (forsooth)
runne on to the reward of vertues without
any their owne paines taking, and with the
enioying of their accustomed recreations:
but truly the nature of man is not so fruitfull
a ground, as to yeald forth fruit of it selfe
without husbanding & manuring: neither
is the condition of vertues so comtemptible,

F 3   as

as a religious man ought not worthily to renounce his owne commodityes, and the
pleasure of his senses, that he may attayne to
the perfection of them. It is selfe loue, that
thrusteth a man into this deceitfull conceit,
that he haue a greater regard of the temporal
commodities of his body, then of the spiritual ornaments of his mind. Who fauoureth
his body ouer much, thrusteth vertue headlong out of his owne soule.

7.　There be found other Religious persons, who forbeare to profit in the study of
perfection, because they haue a conceit, that
I will not affoard them so much help and
assistance, as is to be required to this study:
and this opinion is worse then the former.
What is this els, then for them to offend me,
and to deceiue themselues? For not to put
their confidence in me, is to do me an appa-
rant iniury, as if I knew not how to help
them, or could not, or would not. It is nothing so, I desire nothing more then to help,
neither do I euer withdraw my internall inspirations, or other meanes, for the stirring
vp of them to perfection, and for this end I
haue taken & drawn them out of the world.
How then can any be destitute of my help?
How can he be diffident of my grace, sith I
continually stand and knock at the doore,
　　　　　　　　　　　　　　　　that

that I may be let in, and help euery ones necessity? If they will with this cloke couer
their cowardize and slouthfullnes, they are
deceiued, because they lay it much the more
open. He that layeth his owne fault vpon
others, sinneth double.

8.   So it is, Lord, it is not thine, but our
fault, that we go not on to perfection. For
sith thou art most wise, thou knowest the
wavs of helping vs, because thou art omni-
potét, thou art able also to do it, neither art
thou vnwilling, because thy wil is goodnes
it selfe, and therfore all the fault is entirely
and absolutely ours.

That nothing in the world should diuert a
Religious man from pursuing after
Perfection, and getting therof.

CHAP. XV.

SONNE, a faint harted and fearefull souldier will neuer set his flagge vpon the e-
nemies walls, for that ouer much feare causeth him either to keep himselfe aloof off, or
if he be neere, to turne his backe, and therfore he deserueth not any reward, neither
is held in any esteeme with his Generall; and
more then that, is contemned for a coward,
& one without hart, of his fellow souldiers.

I would not haue my seruant ouer bold or temerarious, and rash, nor yet ouer fearefull. I desire he should be magnanimous, and constant, and not be afraid where no cause of feare is. Let a religious man, who sayth that he will not hold on in the course of perfection, tell me, what it is, that causeth him to make a stand, and to giue ouer: not for that his paines and endeauours be to no purpose, sith we haue said already, that many haue arriued to perfection, & I am ready at hand to help all with the assistāce of my grace. Truly if Religious persons were as ready to imbrace and lay hold on the help, that I offer them, and by their owne industry to cooperate with my grace, as there is desire in me to affoard it, there would be a far greater number of perfect persons, then now there be.

2. Neither is the power of the enemy so great, as it may hinder, or draw a Religious man from the way of perfection. For though the enemy be powerfull, yet if the Religious man haue a will, he may not only be not ouercome or hindred by him, but it is in his power also easily to ouercome him, sith his power and might consisteth only in tempting, and not in ouercoming and hindring, vnles a man would willingly of himselfe

felfe be hindred or ouercome by him . The
enemy is weak inough, who hath no power
giuen him of ouercoming, but of fuch as be
willing to be ouercome , and therfore it ar-
gues a bafe mind in a man , who fuffereth
fuch a one to preuaile againft him . And he
who tempted by the enemy, falling not, maketh a great gayne in fpirit, for that by fuch
exercife he becometh the more couragious,
ftoute, and the more conftant ; and trufting
to the help of greater ftrength, he proceedeth
on to perfection , which is nothing, but to
gayne perfection it felfe . For the more often
a fouldier hath tryed his manhood in handling his weapons, and in the more warres he
hath ferued, the better fouldier is he reputed,
and the more experimented .

   3.   Neither muft a good Religious man ,
for the mockings, & taunts of the imperfect
or negligent, ceafe to hold on, & continue in
the way to perfection : for that were to regard more the fpeaches of the bad , then my
infpirations, that are intended for his foules
good . O how much do they difpleafe and
offend me, who with their peftilent tongues
do bite, and detract thofe Religious perfons
who take exceeding great paines about the
attayning of perfection , and fay, that they
make ouer much haft to the height of fan-
       ctity,

ctity, or ayme at ouer high matters that they may haue the greater fall after. And there want not those, who be not afraid to say, that for a man to giue himselfe to deuotion, is nothing els, then to hurt his health, to surcharge his head with melancholy, and to make himselfe quite vnable for the seruing of God. Meruaile it is, that such men do not consider and see, how much hurt they do by these their poysoned speaches, though the same may seeme to be vttered in iest. And whiles they do not well themselues, nor suffer others to do well, they do seeme to performe the office of the Diuell. These be truly enemies, false brethren, the ministers and instruments of hell, whose help Sathan vseth about either the hindring, or quite ouerthrowing of the pious endeauours of other religious men.

4.   He that hath a desire to kill his enemy by poyson, vseth the help of one of the same house, or familiar with him. O vnhappy and miserable seducers, who do neither discharge their owne office, nor yet suffer others to satisfie theirs. O how vnlike be they vnto those, who first serued me in religion: for they exhorted and encouraged one another to the study and practise of vertue; and by example of life, and pious talke stirred vp

to

to the loue of God, & animated one another
to the mortification of their passions, and to
the contempt of themselues, that so they
might come to that perfection, which they
proposed vnto themselues, and sought for.

5. But suppose, that a religious man, after counsaile, by the iudgment of his Superiour, or of his ghostly Father, giuen about
exercising vertue with discretion, become
sicke therby, how great an hurt is this? What
hurt should therof come vnto him? I, that
am his Lord, will haue it so : and what if I
by this way thinke to deliuer him from a far
more soare sicknes of soule? Do these men
thinke, that if a pious and good religious
man fall sicke, I am forthwith displeased
with him? None do displease me but the imperfect, who the more healthfull they be in
body, the more grieuously do they oftentims
offend me. A sicke Religious man, so he be
deuout, is more gratefull to me, then one in
health if he want deuotion, for as much as
he giueth good example in sicknes, and exerciseth vertue, neither wherof is to be found
in the whole vndeuout person : and therefore a religious man desirous of perfection,
when he is sicke, before me sustayneth no
losse of any thing, because I pay my souldiers
their ordinary wages alike, both in time of
sicknes

ſicknes and of health.

5.   A ſpirituall diſeaſe, growing of imperfections, bringeth great hurt, & not that
ſicknes of the body, of which good religious
perſons oftentimes make a ſingular profit to
themſelues. If when the body were ill and
ſicke, the will ſhould be infirme and ſicke alſo, ſo as the ſicke man could not merit any
more, his hurt ſhould be ſomewhat, & none
could but haue iuſt cauſe of flying from ſuch
a ſicknes. But it is rather the contrary, and
therfore my Apoſtle ſaid, *That when he was in-*
firme, he was the ſtronger: and that vertue was perfe-
cted in infirmity. My Sonne, wilt thou do a
thing that may do thy ſoule good, and be
pleaſing to me? Auoid theſe ill meaning de-
tractours, as thou wouldſt do venemous ſer-
pents: and know thou, that if thou contemne what they maliciouſly calumniate, and
attend to the loue of perfection, thou ſhalt
increaſe thine owne glory; becauſe I, for
loue of whome thou doeſt this, will in moſt
liberall manner reward thee.

6.   Some againe will not follow the way
of perfection, becauſe they ſee but few to
walke therein: but this is no iuſt cauſe, that
a buſynes ſo fruitfull, and laudable, ſhould
be omitted. What skilleth it, whether thou
haſt many or few companions in ſo moſt
                                                        pleaſant

pleasant a iourney? Ought it not be inough
for thee, that the way is good, secure, and
bringeth to a most happy end? Not to haue
many companions in walking the way of
perfection, doth rather increase thy comme-
dations and merit, then diminish it: yea thou
oughtest to reckon it for a singular benefit
in that it hath hapned to few. There be also
few elected, though many be called: and
many runne in the race, & but one wynneth
the prize. If thou canst be one of the number of those few, & merit a precious crowne,
why forbearest thou to runne?

7. He that laboureth out of loue, is not
sollicitous about the company of others, but
it is inough, that he be not wanting vnto
him, for whose sake he taketh the paynes. I
am he, for whose sake all religious persons
runne the race of perfectiō. I am their guide
captaine, and companion. I help, ease, and
defend them, & this alone should be inough
for them, to continue their iourney with a
stout, able, and willing mind. Neither must
thou meruaile, that this way is traced of few,
because they be few, who mortifie themselus
in earnest, who restraine their desires, and
contemne the flattery of the senses, & many
there be, who suffer themselues by delight-
full allurements of this world to be carryed
away

a way into the spatious & broad way, which no man, but knoweth how repugnant it is to a Religious estate.

8.   Moreouer there be some, who permitt themselues to be with-held from the commendation of this perfection for human respects, and the commodities of fortune, which is nothing els then to be notably iniurious to vertue, whose property is to be an ornament to a religious man: whereas contrariwise human respects, and all temporall commodities are to be troden vnder his feet, and contemned. He then who leaueth those for these, doth necessarily put vertue vnder a religious mans feet, and raiseth humane respect vpon his head.

9.   Againe he that more regardeth the worlds estimation, and riches therof then perfection, whereunto I daily exhort all religious persons, doth me an iniury, and himselfe hurt. For all know, that he who shall be ashamed of me before men, I will also be ashamed of him before the Angells of God. But what absurdity, and folly is this? They, when they liued in the world, out of a desire of following perfection, did forsake the world, the temporall comodities therof, and all humane things besids: but now hauing imbraced religion, they will giue ouer perfection,

perfection, to follow the world . Is not this
a manifest folly ? And sith humane respect is
nothing els then a certaine vaine feare, least
a man be discōmended in some one or other
of his actions; how is it possible , that a religious man , desirous of perfection can be
discommended? Can there any greater glory
befall him in this life, then if this may be affirmed & said of him ? And what new thing
can happen to a religious man, if he be contemned of the world ? Doth he expect any
reward or recompence from it ? Or is he a-
fraid, least it would censure him by a con-
demnation ? It maketh no matter, whether
a religious man be loued or hated of the
world; but it auayleth much, if he be deare
to me .

10.   To conclude, others forbeare to tread
this way of perfection, by reason of the repug-
gnance that mans nature findeth in practi-
sing the meanes , and for the difficulties that
the body maketh trial of, in tracing the same
way . But these men misse the marke : for to
be a true Religious man, or to walke on to
perfection, is nothing els but to mortifie the
desires of the flesh , and the perturbations of
the mind . And therfore, if thou forbeare the
exercise of vertue , least thou incommodate
or hurt thy body , thou louest thy selfe too
                    sensually,

senſually : neither do I ſee, what difference there is betweene thee, and a delicate ſecular perſon . Remember Sonne, that theſe be not the promiſes thou madeſt at thy entrance to religion : for then thou didſt purpoſe with thy ſelfe to ſuffer many things for me, to chaſtiſe thy body, to ſerue me, and for loue of religious perfection to depriue and ſpoyle thy ſelfe of all humane conſolation.

That a good Reliʒious man muſt not content himſelfe with whatſoeuer degree of Perfe- ction ; but muſt labour, and aſpire to a greater .

C H A P. XVI.

SONNE, thoſe religious men do not ſatiſ- fy me, that aſpire to a mean degree of re- ligious perfection, vnles they alſo ayme at the higheſt . For ſo I declared vnto my diſ- ciples, when I exhorted them to be perfect , not as the Patriarcks, and Prophets were , nor as the Seraphims, and other the Angells, but as my Father in heauen . O how doth that Religious perſon pleaſe me, who like the couetous man is deſirous of true vertue, and perfection . The couetous man hath ne- uer his fil : for the more he hath, the more he deſireth . And I would haue religious men ſuch

such followers of spirituall couetousnes.
For it is a signe of a base mind, if a man,
when he hath meanes to attaine to greater
perfection, do propose vnto himselfe, and
thinke vpon lesser. But I desire to haue my
seruants valiant, and generously minded,
who aspire to great and hard matters. For
if I haue created them to an end, the most
excellent in the world, & haue raised them
vp to so high a state, that is, to be Religious;
why should they not with all their possible
forces labour to perfection, that would be
most contenting to vs both? Who coopera-
teth not conformably to the benefit receiued, is iniurious to the Benefactour.

2. Let him tell me, whosoeuer hath
no care to arriue to any great perfection,
but thinketh it inough to haue had a tast
therof, whether he would so deale with his
body? Is he contented it should enioy a
mediocrity of health, when he may haue it
perfectly strong, sound, and lusty? Would he
wish but a poore meanes of lyuing, and not
the best? If then of all earthly things, which
serue the body we choose the best, most perfect, and all in great quantity, number, and
quality the most excellent, why should we
not also for the souls good, which is the mistresse of the body, wish and make choice of

G   the

the most perfect, and most absolute vertues?
That family is nothing well gouerned,
where the handmayd is better treated, then
the mistresse of the house.

3. Who would deny, that it is a fowle
and shamefull thing for a Religious man, to
stay in the lowest degree of vertue, when he
seeth secular men neuer to make a stay in
their degree of state of life, which they haue
once imbraced, but euer to aspire to an higher, vntill they come to the highest?
Hence it is, that a vulgar person first seeketh to raise himselfe to be a Gentleman,
then a Baron, next an Earle, a Marques, a
Duke, vntill in conclusion he lay hold on
the Scepter and Crowne: and when he is
come to this, he is not contented with an
ordinary Crowne, but he seeketh a more
rich, more potent, & a more noble Crown,
and consequently the greatest that can be
had in this life. And shall a Religious man
be of so dastardly a mind, as not to labour to
obtaine a most noble spirituall Crowne?
Should he stand in the first degree of perfection, when he may with his great commendation, and no lesse profit mount vp to
the highest? Is not this a strang kind of sot-
tishnes, and folly? Is not this to make a light
esteeme of my will, and to refuse the help of
my

my grace, by the benefit wherof he might
compasse an higher degree of perfection ?

4. Vnderstand my Sonne, that a Religious man is more deare vnto me, who endeauoureth for my greater glory, to arriue to
the highest degree of perfection : and this
ought not without cause to be inough vnto
him, not to stay in his course, but stil to hold
on. Go to, tel me, what seruant is so contép-
tible & vile, who is contented to be in litle
grace and fauour with his Lord, when he
may be in very great? Why then, thou Religious man, who art for so many respects
bound vnto me, as my seruant, why I say,
when by labouring to perfectió thou mayst
deserue my extraordinary fauour, thou de-
layest to do it? What paynes doth the poore
seruant take to gayne his maisters grace? and
how much is he afflicted, whé he seeth, notwithstanding all the diligence he vseth, he
cannot get into his maisters fauour? wherefore then dost thou make a stand in the very
entrance to perfection, when thou mayst
easily get into the innermost parts of it, &
gayne thy Lord vnto thee? To please me, is
not my gayne, but thine.

5. O of what worth is but one degree
of glory in heauen, and how glorious is he
in heauen, who hath deserued it! The Reli-

G 2   gious,

gious, who now triumph in heauen, do
make so great an esteeme euen of the least
increase of glory, which they had merited,
whiles they laboured to perfection heer on
earth, as they do not only yield their Creatour immortall thankes, but had rather also,
if there were need, spend their bloud a thousand times, then not to haue obtained that
glory. Wilt thou therfore, who mayst without spilling of thy blood, or losse of life,
increase thy glory and crowne in heauen
from day to day by profiting towards perfection, stand still in the dore, contented
with a very small measure of perfection?

6.   Take heed, my Sonne, least that befall vnto thee, which I told my disciple of:
That to him who hath, shall be giuen ; and from him
who hath not , shall also be taken away that he hath.
Neither is that wont to be done only for a
punishment of ingratitude, but ordinarily
also it hapneth to all things more or lesse
affected with some quality. For example:
Wood not much kindled, easily forgoeth the
little heat that it hath, not so if it had been
well kindled. So a Religious man, who
hath gotten but little perfection, doth very
easily loose it; but he, who hath got many
degrees of it, doth not easily forsake it, but is
like a tree, that hath taken deep roote, and
strongly

ftrongly refifteth both winds, and tempefts.

7.   Thete be alfo fome, who affeᵭed to
a more free life, do for purging of themfelus
fay, that the ftudy of perfeᵭion is only proper to Nouices . But they be miferably deceiued ; for as much as all religious perfons
be bound to labour to perfeᵭion , and the
more ancient a man is in religion, the more
diligent ſhould he be in furnifhing himfelfe
with vertues, as he, who ought to haue both
a greater vnderftanding and knowledge of
his owne obligation, and hath a longer tri-
all and experience of the fweetnes of perfeᵭion, He that is not hungry, is foone filled:
and it is an ill figne in a religious man, if he
receiue no pleafure in the ftudy of vertues .

8.   Others contrariwife haue an ouer
hafty defire to get vp to the higheft degree
of perfeᵭion, and if they happen peraduenture to fall into fome defeᵭ, they be eftfoons
difcouraged, and loofe their courage . But
this is not my will, neither is it the way of
labouring to perfeᵭion . For the greateft
perfeᵭion is in the viᵭory & ouercoming
of all vices, and in the purchafing of all vertues , & for the effeᵭing of this, there muſt
be fome continuance of tyme . Wherfore to
feeke euery day more perfeᵭion then other
(which we fpeake of heere) is nothing els

but

but to ouercome the paſſions, or to reſtraine
the perturbations of the mind, & the inordinate deſires therof. And to be abſolutly
perfect, is nothing els, then after the victory
ouer our ſelues to be dead to the world, and
to liue to god alone.

9 .   He that hath enemies and aduer-
ſaries, can neuer be ſecure, vnles he cut them
off cleane, and deſtroy them : but neceſſary
it is not , that he take them a way at one
time, & all togeather . So á Religious mans
enemyes be the paſſions, which dayly rebell
againſt him, and though he cannot ouercome the all at once at one & the ſame time;
yet let him labour to extirpate one after an-
ther, and ſo doing, he ſhall hold on to greater perfection . In like manner an whole
Kingdome is not ſet vpon all at once , but
now one caſtle is taken from the enemy ,
and then another, or ſome Citty brought in
ſubiection, and ſo one after another, vntill
he become poſſeſſed of the whole Kingdome : Euen ſo doth a religious man, who
hath a deſire to inuade & ſet vpon the kingdome of perfection , whiles he muſt now
gaine one vertue, and then another : & this
is euery day to labour to greater perfection .
And therefore he muſt not in any ſort be
diſcouraged , though he become not very
                                        perfect

perfect by one or two actions, He goeth
well onward in his iourney, who stayeth
no where vpon his way .

That a Religious man must conserue and
keep the perfection he hath gotten :
and of the manner of keeping it.

C H A P. X V I I.

SONNE, little profiteth the good health
of body to be recouered, if it be after
hurt againe by any intemperance of eating,
or other carelesnes, since the relapse into
sicknes is more dangerous, then the sicknes
it selfe. The same is the consideration of
spirituall Perfection, which once being
had, profiteth little; if we forgo it againe,
through default of our owne vigilancy and
wary keeping of the same. And if the relapse into corporall sicknes be a matter of
so great consideration for the daunger towards the body ; much more is to be feared a
relapse into the old imperfections, that in-
danger the spirituall life.

2. Sonne, desirest thou to be freed from
the daunger of dying spiritually ? Then
shunne those things, that be dispositions to
that death. For we learne by dayly experience, that they, who once languish in the
study

study of perfection, do fall into a thousand defects, and into so great leuity and inconstancy of manners, liberty of conuersation, and imprudency of mind, as not only all shame laid aside, they do nothing worthy of prayse, but do furthermore glory, & reioyce in their owne errours and defects. And in this they be not vnlike to those Angells, who fell from heauen, and togeather with their most greiuous ruine, lost also all their spirituall gifts, and procured to themselues most extreme euills. For looke how much more excellent they were in dignity then all creatures, so much more by their fall from heauen they became worse, and more contemptible then them all. My Apostle also, who betrayed me, from his dignity of Apostleship fell into the downfall of desperation. The same hapneth to the Religious men, who from the higher degree of perfection they fal, be the more sorely bruized and crushed by their fal, and become worse. And as he is called happy, who declineth from euill, and imbraceth good: so contrariwise miserable and vnhappy is that man, who forsaking the way of perfection, traceth & holdeth on the way of licenciousnes and liberty.

　3.　But to conserue the degree of perfection

&ction thou haft gotten, there be two vertues
that may help thee, and those be *Loue* , and
Humility . Loue will make thee vigilant to
auoid the daungers growing from theeues ,
and robbers. Humility will conceale and
hide thee, that thou come not within their
view or fight. And how profitable & auai-
lable Loue is for this purpose, it is no hard
matter to demonftrate. A rich and wealthy
man , who is not in loue with his riches ,
foone loofeth them . For he that loueth not
any thing , efteemeth it not : and he that
efteemeth it not, hath no care of keeping it :
and euery one knoweth, that a thing negli-
gétly kept, is eafily loft. Euen fo as neceffary
it is for a Religious man to be greatly affe-
&ted to the perfe&tion he hath once got: for
of loue there is caufed a feare of loofing it :
of feare a follicitude & diligence in keeping
it: &folicitude againe cauleth him to find,
and fearch out meanes and wayes,neceffary
& profitable for attayning to the end.

4.   Whofoeuer hath a care to keep his
corporall health, asketh aduife of expert &
learned Phifitians, eateth good and whole-
fome meats, keepeth his fet times of eating,
negle&teth not requifite exercifes of body ,
choofeth an habitation in a healthfull
place, and ayre approued of the Phifitians ,

keepeth himselfe out of the rayne, winds, and from other outward incommodities; and in few words, is very carefull not to exceed in any thing, that may peraduenture any way hurt him. The same causeth sollicitude in a Religious man, if he haue a desire to conserue Perfection, and seeke his soules health. For first his care is not to order his owne life according to his owne will, or by the counsaile of more loose and free companions, but rather by the direction of Superiours, and spirituall Fathers. Secondly, to eate of good meats, namely those that I vsed my selfe, when I liued on earth, that is, to do the will of my Father, who is in heauen, whose will is our soules sanctification. And therfore whatsoeuer God giueth vs for the sanctifying of the soule, is the best meat, as contrariwise whatsoeuer maketh to the defiling therof, such as be sinnes, is the worst poyson of all. Thirdly, he neglecteth not the vse and exercise of vertues. For sith perfection is founded in Charity, which is like vnto fire, whereunto if wood be cast, it increaseth, if it be remoued and taken away, it goeth out: Even so, the more, Religious men, who haue their part in Charity, do exercise themselues in vertue, the more they profit in perfection : and the lesse they be

exercised

exerciled in them, the lesse they get of perfection : And therfore all exercise of vertue
ceasing, perfection ceaseth also.

5. And as touching an healthful place,
where the soule is to dwell, I know none
comparable to Religion, where I haue placed the religious man : but if we consider
particular places, the best is that, that his spirituall Phisitians or Fathers assigné him.
And if he would fly all occasions of falling
into any imperfections, he shal so very well
arme and defend himselfe against all outward difficulties . Finally he committeth
no excesse , because in all doubtfull matters, he repaireth to his spirituall Father, &
seasoneth all pennances and mortifications
with the salt of moderation and discretion.

6. The other way that conserueth perfection, is by humility . He that is become
possessed of a rich and pretious iewell , is
very wary three ways, that he loose it not at
any tyme . First he layeth it vp in a secret
place, that it may not easily be seene, discouered, or found of others . Secondly , he
letteth not euery owne see it, neither doth
he openly brag, that he hath such a Iewell .
Thirdly, he taketh it not from the thing ,
whereat it hangeth . For example, the heat
of water dependeth of the fire, and if you
remoue

remoue it from the fire, it looseth the heate.
Humility in a Religious man, whose precious stone is the study of perfection, remedyeth all these three daungers. First it causeth him to conceale, and hide his vertues, and perfections from the sight or knowledg of others. Secondly, not only not to vaunt and brag of his spirituall riches, but also to thinke himselfe vnworthy of them, and withall to acknowledge and confesse himselfe poore, a beggar, and an vnprofitable seruant. Thirdly, to acknowledge, that the Iewel of perfection dependeth of my grace, knowing that it is lost, if it be separated frō it. For as I resist the proud, so giue I grace to the humble. And therfore if thou hast a desire to haue thy perfection not only conserued, but to increase also, attend thou diligently to the exercise of true humility.

The end of the first Booke.

THE

SECOND BOOKE
of Religious Perfection.

Wherein is treated of the three Vowes
of Religion, and the perfect obseruation thereof. And first of the
three Vowes in generall.

---

*Of the dignity, and excellency of the three
Vowes, that be made by Religious persons.*

CHAP. I.

O N, when any thing, though
otherwise of great worth is
not knowne, it is not much
esteemed, because the excellency & worth therof is obscured
by the darknes of ignorance, and therby the
due estimation is taken away. And this is
the cause, wherefore the three Vowes, that
be

be made in Religion, be not so esteemed of some, euen Religious men themselues, because they vnderstand not the worth, excellency, & profit therof. He cannot be free frō fault, who vnderstandeth not what in regard of his state he both may, and ought to know. Wherfore know thou (my Son)that the excellency of these vows is greater then many conceiue, neither are they of litle consequence. And vnder the name of *Vow*, is vnderstood an obligation of a Religious man made to God his Creatour, of performing and doing some better good . And sith this obligation is very noble, spirituall, and diuine, euery religious man ought not without cause, diligently to ponder, reuerently to esteeme, and exactly to obserue the same.

2 .   That it is most noble, it cleerly appeareth by this; for that the will bindeth it selfe , which amongst the faculties of the soule holdeth the principality, & first place, and hath a commaund ouer all the rest of the powers. Againe, it is most noble, because it is made to God, whose maiesty is infinite, & who is the authour of all true excellency. Moreouer because it is made for a most noble end, namely the glory of Gods Name, which is the more amplified, the more exactly that obligation is kept . There is added
further,

further, that the vertue of Religion among all morall vertues excelleth for noblenes & dignity. Seeing therfore a Vow is an action of that most noble vertue that giueth light to all other vertues, it manifestly followeth, that a Vow is a most noble vertue. For what the tree is, the same be the fruits therof.

3. And that this obligation is spirituall and holy, is out of controuersy; both because it is directed to a spirituall good, namely to holines of life, and because it is the very entrance and beginning of the spirituall life of Religious men. Whereupon as the life of the body dependeth on the hart as the beginning: so the religious life, and to be a religious man hath the dependance of this holy obligation. And as by the least hurt of the hart, the life of body receiueth great hurt also, and the hart being taken away, the life is taken away togeather: euen so by the very least default in the obseruatiõ of this obligation, the Religious life is much preiudiced, and that againe ceasing, or taken away, a man ceaseth to be Religious. The nearer the euill cometh to the hart, the more dangerous it is.

4. That this obligation is diuine, is also certaine, because it is of the holy Ghost, who by his diuine inspiration moueth a
mans

mans mind to the making of such an obligation. Secondly, because the person, to
whome it is made, is diuine, that is, God
himselfe. Now let a Religious man consider and see, how much he ought to loue
it, with what regard to keep it, and with
what deuotion, and care to obserue it in
all things that he is able, because it is made
to him, who penetrateth and entreth into
the most inward secret of the hart, and well
knoweth, who hath iust cause to obserue it,
and who not.

5. But now I would desire to know of
those to whome it causeth some trouble and
difficulty, that they be tyed in so noble and
holy a band, what the cause is, that secular
men haue them in so great regard, and veneration? They will say perhaps, because they
be religious and my seruants. And, what
made them religious and my seruants, but
these three Vowes? Many secular persons
liue at this day in the world, far more learned, more holy, and more perfect then many Religious, and yet be they nothing so
much honored, as religious men be; and the
cause is, because they be not tyed to me by
these holy bands of Vowes. Secular men,
when they behold Religious persons, doe
consider them, as wholy mine, by three
Vowes

Vowes confecrated to me, & what honour
they do them, they thinke they giue to me.
But this they do not to men of the world,
though otherwise eminent for their vertue:
and therfore to be tyed in these bands, is no
contemptible matter, but moſt honorable,
and moſt noble, euen to the world, ſith the
Religious be in ſo great veneration with
the great men of the world.

6. Theſe three Vowes againe be of very
great regard, for that they cauſe the Religious to triumph victoriouſly, and to go away
with victory ouer their three deadly enemies. For whils they exerciſe *Pouerty* againſt
the vanity of the world, *Chaſtity* againſt the
tentation of the fleſh, and *Obedience* againſt
the frauds of the crafty diuell, they go eaſily
away with victory. But thoſe Religious,
who vſe not theſe kind of armes, are oftentimes ſhamefully ouercome. Let not him be
a ſouldiar, who will not take a weapon in
hand, neither let him go to the battaile, who
refuſeth to fight.

7. And now tell me, my Sonne, what
thoſe Religious men deſerue, who make but
light eſteeme of ſo holy, and godly an obligation, and what they alſo deſerue, who
keep it not, when they may, & ought to keep
it? What puniſhment attendeth them, who

H   do

do not only breake it, but further contemne
it also? O how straite an accompt are they
to make, not only of their owne transgressions, but also of those of others, that is, of
those, who by their bad example were induced to violate and breake their Vowes
they had before made vnto me. For promise by Vowe is not made to men, but to
the diuine maiesty: it is not made vnwillingly, but voluntarily. Neither is the obligation therof concerning any light or temporall matter, but touching a great and spirituall matter, that is, the saluation of the
Soule. He that lightly regardeth what he
hath once promised to God, shall againe be
as little regarded of God.

Of the vtility and profit that Vowes bring,
and cause to Religious persons.

CHAP. II.

LORD, our Nature is so sore depressed &
surcharged with the weight of our
owne miseries, as I know not, whether it
were good and profitable for a man to bind
himselfe by Vowes, sith to me it seemeth
nothing els, but to adde one burden to another, and consequently much to be feared,
least in conclusion, seeing it is very weake,
it

it fall vnder the burden. And more then this there be so many obligations, and bands of precepts imposed partly by thee, partly by thy Church layd vpon vs, as it is almost impossible for vs to satisfy them; therefore it seemeth not good to surcharge our selues with new bands of Vowes. Neither doth there appeare so great vtility likely to redound vnto vs by the benefit of Vowes, but that there is presented a greater daunger by transgressing, and breaking them. I add further, Lord, that free and voluntary offices of deuotion are more accepted off by thee, then be the forced. But whosoeuer shall make a Vow, is forced to stand to his promise, and therfore I see not, how great a vtility there is of Vowes.

2.   Thou art deceiued, my Sonne. For Vowes be burdens that load not, but rather ease, & help nature it selfe to the exercising of all more noble works. The feathers and wings of byrdes carry a shew of a burden, and yet they help to raise them aloft, and without which they cannot fly. Besids, experience teacheth, that they be religious, who do most promptly & most exactly obserue the commaundments of God : whence it appeareth, that by the benefit of Vowes they are holpen to obserue the precepts of

God, and of the Church, after a more exact, and perfect manner.

3. Thou art wide, if thou thinkest that any profit returneth to me by thy Vowes. It is not so. There is no sowing, nor mowing for me heere. Promises made to men, redound to the profit of them to whome they be made, but the merit of the Vowes that are made to me, remaineth to the vtility of him who voweth : yea the honour & glory that of Vowes arise to me and my seruice, appertaineth also to the good of them that vow. For I do abundantly reward them, as I do seuerely chastise the bad workes, that be dishonorable to piety, and to the seruice of God.

4. And where thou sayst, that by Vows all liberty is taken away, in so much as the Religious do all things of necessity, & therfore haue no merit of their works at all, thou art deceiued. For there be two necessities; one naturall, and this taketh away all liberty, merit, & commendation of all good works, such as is the falling of a stone downwards. The other is voluntary, or procceeding of the will, or of a promise voluntarily made, and this doth not only not take away the merit of the good worke, but also much increaseth it : for that both the worke, and
the

the promiſe be voluntary and free . And
this is the neceſſity ſo highly commended
of the bleſſed in heauen; becauſe it did driue
them to the exerciſing of the more noble ,
and more excellent workes . Happy is that
neceſſity , which compelleth to what is
better .

5.   Moreouer thou muſt know, my Son,
that the grief, & difficulty, which we otherwhiles find and feele in executing our promiſe of Vowes, doth not take away nor di-
miniſh in the Religious their merit, but rather increaſe it : for in fullfilling our Vows,
there is not only done a good worke, but
that heauines, repugnance, and difficulty is
further ouercome, which indeed is a matter
of no little conſequence . Howbeit to fullfill a good worke promiſed by Vow, though
there occurre no difficulty in doing it, is
more meritorious, then to fulfill it without
any precedent Vow . For as I will declare
after, the Vow it ſelfe is meritorious, which
merit he hath not who doth a good worke ,
which he before promiſed to do without
making a Vow .

6.   There be other vtilityes , which
vowes do bring to the Religious. For firſt
vndoubted it is, that the tree , the deeeper
roote it ſhall take within the earth, brin-

geth forth the better fruite: Euen so mans will, the more stable it shal be in good, produceth the more noble works. And among the effects of Vowes one is, that it maketh the will more firme in good works. Who knoweth not, how various, and mutable mans will is: now it is willing, & within a while it is vnwilling, and what pleaseth to day, displeaseth to morrow. And doubtles it would be better, if the will were constant and stable in imbracing good, and that it may be stable and immutable, is effected by the benefit of Vowes. For so soone as a man shall haue made a Vow, he must performe it, neither may he reuoke it without sinne: & that he may not go backe, is both profitable and good, and deriued from the very nature of a Vow. And of this it followeth, that a good worke proceeding from a will grounded in good, is better then other good workes, and deserueth a more ample reward. As contrariwise a bad and hurtfull worke, comming from a peruerse and obdurate will, is more detestable then other ill works, and meriteth a more sore punishment. Would you haue a Lunatike person to do no hurt? Then bind him fast vpon the first occasion.

7. Another vtility nothing inferiour

to

to the former, is this. Euery man will confeſſe, that it moſt profiteth a man, if he be
moſt inwardly vnited to God Almighty.
And this is effected by Vowes: for whiles a
man by Vowes bindeth himſelfe to me, I
am in like máner tyed againeſaſt vnto him;
and therfore if the Religious do by theſe ſa-
cred bands bind themſelues faſt vnto me, &
ſo become mine, how is it poſſible, that I
ſhould not deliuer my ſelfe vnto them alſo?
That I ſhould not help them, not defend
them, not conſerue, & keep them, as a thing
moſt deare vnto me? I ſhould not be what
I am, if my creature ſhould go beyond me in
liberality. Wherfore it is very agreable to
reaſon, that ſeeing they háue moſt firmely
conioyned themſelues to me the fountaine
of Grace, I ſhould alſo communicate vnto
them the flowing ſtreames of my grace, and
my heauenly gifts, and take ſo great care of
them, as neither the Diuell, nor any other
creature may do them harme. The Religious liue ſo much the more ſecure, the more
potent, and powerfull is their Lord, and
Maiſter to whome they haue conioyned
themſelues.

8. There is yet another vtility, that al
good workes done by Vow, do merit more
with God, then thoſe that are not done by

Vow. He that keepeth chastity for loue of
me, doth well, and meriteth: but he that
forloue of me maketh a Vow of chastity &
keepeth it, doth better and meriteth more.
For the former exerciseth but one vertue,
that is, Continency: but the later exerciseth
two, namely Continency and Religion, the
noblest of all morall vertues. Moreouer to
promise a good worke, is a good thing: and
to performe a promise is also good, and therfore for them both a man is held worthy of
commendations and thanks. Let him then
be more deare vnto thee, who bestoweth
more spirituall good vpon thee.

9. Seing so many benefits redound vnto vs by Vowes, as the stability of the will,
the coniunction with God, and the merit of
workes, I would be now glad to vnderstand
why some, when they should most of all re-
ioice, be sory that they haue tyed themselues
by Vowes? What cause of grief should they
haue? For if these sacred bands should depriue them of some great commodity, they
might haue iust cause of sorrowing. But
indeed they loose none by it. For as a vine
fastned to a tree, or to a post, and therefore
lesse obnoxious and exposed to the iniury
of the winds, bringeth forth better and
more abundant fruite, then if it were loose
                                          and

and vntyed : Euen ſo be Religious perſons,
by the benefit of theſe Vowes, are more
ſtrong, and ſtable, and more free from tentations, and do yeld greater increaſe of good
works, & therefore why ſhould they afflict
themſelues with grief?

10. Euill muſt needs pleaſe him, who
is ſorry for good, or complaineth therof.
When good meate is hurtfull to a man, it is
a ſigne that his ſtomake is infected and ſurcharged with bad humours, and therfore it
is to be purged with ſome antitode, if he
meane to preuent the hazard of his life. In
like manner if the making of Vowes, which
is good and holy, be to ſome Religious perſon troubleſome, it is a ſigne, that his mind
is infected with ſome bad diſpoſition,
which muſt be taken away and remoued by
the ſpirituall Phiſitian, that the hazard of
his ſpirituall death may be auoyded.

How acceptable and pleaſing to God the
three Vowes of Religious perſons be :

CHAP. III.

SONNE, how ſhould not the Vowes of
the Religious be accepted by me, when
as they be made for my honour and glory?
How is it, that they ſhould not be deare to

me, when as they be the meanes of attaining perfection, which I do so earnestly desire at their hands? O how much should some earthly Lord glory, if his seruants should make him any such promise, he would no doubt exult for ioy, though he should not be assured, whether they had done it in earnest, & from their hart, for the loue of him their Lord, or in regard of their owne commodity. And should not I, who am assured, that the Religious do from their hart make these Vowes, and only for loue of me bind themselues to the performing of good and holy workes, reioyce, and be glad? Should not I make a demonstration, how much they please me?

2.   For there be three things, that do in particular please me in Vowes. First the deuotion, wherewith the Vowes be made. Secondly the diligence, wherewith they are obserued. Thirdly the ioy, that the Religious conceiue by occasion of the making of their Vowes. Deuotion groweth of the consideration of the excellency of the oblation, that is made in the Vowes. For the Religious man by a benefit of his three Vowes offereth himselfe wholy in sacrifice, without reseruation of any part to himselfe. And if the sacrifices of the old law, which

were

were of bulles and calues, were so pleasing
vnto me ; how much shall these content me,
which Religious men do voluntarily offer
vnto me ? And if I made so high esteeme of
Abrahams only will, when he was ready to
sacrifice his only. Sonne vnto me , what a
reckoning should I make of the sacrifice,
that a Religious man maketh of himselfe,
by offering me his will, soule, body and all?
Againe , Diligence ariseth of the loue they
carry towards me . He that loueth , cannot
expect, or of slouth put of till another time,
or prolonge that which he knoweth to be
very pleasing to the beloued . And in Religious life nothing pleaseth me more, then
the obseruation of Vowes . Finally ioy
for the Vowes made, groweth of this , that
the Religious man considereth, how pleasing this his oblation was vnto me. O how
sorely should a Religious man offend me,
if he should be troubled , and grieued for a
thing very well done, and most acceptable
to me . It is no lesse a sinne to be sorry for a
good work, then to be glad of a bad one .

3.   There be also other things , that
make this Religious oblation most pleasing
to me, and cause me to make an high estimation therof, and that is, because it hath
the beginning of sincere loue towards me .

For

For firſt the Religious do by theſe three Vowes, as with three nayles, voluntarily nayle themſelues to the Croſſe for loue of me, not for three dayes alone, but for al their life. They do not only crucify their body with the nayle of Pouerty, and the ſenſes with the naile of Chaſtity, but their vnder-ſtanding alſo, and their owne iudgment with the naile of Obedience, by obeying their Superiours will rather, then their owne. The theeſe that confeſſed me on the Croſſe whereon he did hang a very ſhort time, where he ſpake vnto his companion but one word in fauour of me, taſted ſo a-bundantly of my beſt loue towards him, as I made him that very day an inheritour of paradiſe. And why ſhould I not loue a Re-ligious man hartily, who in regard of his Vowes made for loue of me, is bound to continue vpon the Croſſe all his life long? Why ſhould not his oblation be moſt plea-ſing to me, who for the amplificatiō of my glory expoſeth himſelfe to all dangers, that he may preach my Ghoſpell, not by word alone, but, which is more, by example of life alſo?

4. Another cauſe, why I hold the obla-tion of a Religious perſon amongſt the things that be moſt deare vnto me, is, be-

cause by these three Vows he doth wittingly and willingly giue me whatsoeuer he can
giue. For whereas he doth by Vow yeald
himselfe wholy to my seruice, he giueth me
not only the workes, but also the worker of
them. Certes, a secular man neuer giueth me
so much : for by doing well, he giueth me
nothing but the fruite, and not the tree,
whiles a Religious person giueth me the
one and the other. This further pleaseth me
that the Religious in making their Vowes,
make protestation, that they will not loue
any other besides me, nor serue any but me,
and this not for a certaine time, but for all
eternity. Moreouer the Religious consecrate vnto me all their owne right & power
of doing any thing contrary to their Vow
once made, and this pleaseth me very much.
A secular person, for example, who doth
without making any Vow for loue of me
renounce all his riches, doth indeed well,
yet he reserueth to himselfe an interest and
right of gathering riches togeather againe
when he shall please : But a Religious man
by making the Vow of Pouerty, depriueth
himself not only of riches, but also of power
of heaping or gathering of riches for the
time to come, and of all propriety thereunto
foreuer.

5.   **The**

5. The third thing that in the obligation of Vowes pleaſeth me; is, that the Religious do by it not only giue all, but do it after the beſt and moſt perfect manner, that is, that I ſhould haue ſuch a comaund, power, and right ouer them, as I may vſe their ſeruice in whatſoeuer thing, where, when, and as much as ſhall pleaſe me. And hence it is, that the Religious ought not to vſe himſelfe, as a thing of his owne, but as mine, and conſecrated to me. Neither muſt he vſe his owne iudgment, where & when he liſteth, but at my pleaſure, becauſe I am his Lord, and not himſelfe. Wherefore know thou my Religious child, that he ſhal commit a grieuous ſacriledge, who would either take from me that which had beene formerly conſecrated & deliuered vnto me by Vowes, or vſurpe and vſe it at his owne pleaſure. The leſſe thou haſt, and the leſſe thou doſt after thine owne will, the leſſe will thy errour be, and the leſſe accompt thou ſhalt yield to God.

6. The fourth and laſt cauſe is, why I moſt of all approue and allow of the Vows of Religious perſons, is, for whereas the world which is a deceyuer of ſoules, is hatefull to me, I am very glad, if the iuglings, frauds, and vanityes of it be diſcouered and
laid

laid open . And seing the Vowes of the Religious be cleane opposite to the world (for by vertue of them all the riches, pleasures , honors, & other the worlds vanities be contemned) they cānot but be most acceptable. But consider, my Child, that this contempt of the world is not to be manifested by an externall shew, or by words alone, but by facts and workes, and therefore it is not inough to haue made Vowes, but thou must further of necessity obserue, and keep them. It is good to proclayme a defiance to thine enemy , but better it is to ouercome him . While, a Religious person performeth his Vowes , he declareth himselfe an enemy to the world, but when he dischargeth his promise made by Vow , he ouercommeth and vanquisheth it quite.

How conuenient it is , that Religious men bind themselues to God by three Vowes .

CHAP. IIII.

SONNE, it is very agreable, that the Religious be furnished and prouided of the armes of three Vertues, which he hath promised by Vowes, to wit, Pouerty, Chastity and Obedience . When the souldier desireth to imitate his Captaine, and to arme himselfe

selfe with those weapons which he doth, that he may manfully, according to his Captaynes pleasure, fight with his enemy, he is worthy both of praise and reward. I am the Captaine and Generall of all the religious warfare who haue marched in the vanguard with these three Vertues, and haue shewed all my followers, how they should fight with these armes I ouercame myne enemies, & triumphed ouer them; & therfore meet it is, that the Religious, who serue vnder my colours, and be to fight with the same enemyes, should vse and handle the same weapons, which if they do as they ought, they cannot but go out of the field victorious. The souldier, who endeauoureth to imitate his General, though he arriue not to his great strength and courage, is neuertheles worthy of his reward.

2. It is further requisite, that the Religious man cast of all things, that may be of power to hinder his profit of spirit. A scholler is to do three things, that may make to his profit in humane literature. First, he must remoue all the obstacles and impediments of his studyes, such as be the pleasures of the flesh. Secondly such things, as may hinder his true progresse in his studyes, and those be the cares of temporall goods, and
helps.

helps. Thirdly, he muſt make choice of the
moſt effectuall and beſt meanes for the taking of his maiſters leſſons, and that is, diligently to obey his maiſter, and the law of
the Schoole . Theſe three obſtacles the Religious alſo remoue and take away by the
benefit, and help of their Vowes . For by
the Vow of Chaſtity they cut off all carnal
delights: by that of Pouerty, the ſollicitude
of temporall things : and by that of Obedience they fulfill the laws of their inſtitute
and their Superiours precepts . To remoue
the impediments of this ſpirituall way, is
to walke on, and profit in ſpirit .

3. Sonne, ſith thou art abſolutly reſolued
to renounce the world, and all the vanities
therof, meet it is, thou giue it ouer, and forſake it in the perfecteſt manner that is poſſible . Some leaue it in affection, as do thoſe
that haue no deſire of vanities at all, and
they do well : Some forſake it indeed, as do
they who imbrace a Religious ſtate, and
theſe do better . Some againe leaue it both
wayes, and they renounce it after a moſt
perfect manner, and this do my Religious,
when they vow Pouerty, Chaſtity, and
Obedience . The further thyne enemy is
from thee, the leſſe can he hurt thee .

4. The world vſeth three ſorts of nets,

I   wherein

wherein many be caught. The first net is of gold and siluer, that is, of terrene riches, which because it delighteth the eye, is loued of them who are within it, and is desired of them who are out of it. This net the Religious escape by Vow of Pouerty. For pouerty, the veyle of concupiscence being taken out of sight, causeth, that though the net be made of gold and siluer, it seeme nothing but a net, and a sore prison to be in.

5.   Another net is knit of the birdlime of pleasures of the flesh, wherein those that be caught, the more they stirre, the more be they intangled and woone in it. From out of this net the Religious be deliuered by the Vow of Chastity, by the pure and milke white wings whereof they be raised aloft; and freed from the cleauing glew of carnall contentments, they become like vnto Angells.

6. The third net is rather an imaginary and phantasticke one, then a solide & true net, wherein they be caught who presume of themselues, aud seeke after the vayne honours and estimation of this world. The Religious auoyd this net by the Vow of Obedience, who as they subiect themselues vnto others, so thinke they not of imbracing any other thing, then humility and
                                    contempt

contempt of themselues. To liue in the world, and to haue beene caught in one of these nets, is no great matter; but to liue in in Religion, and to haue fallen into the worlds snares and nets, is a case to be exceedingly lamented.

7. There is yet another cause of congruity, that the Religious make the aforesaid three Vowes, because I haue chosen, and called them out of the world for the doing of some noble, great, and generous actions, & therfore they need a great, and stout courage, which they must declare and manifest by their worthy deeds : and the height & excellency of the Religious state, wherein I haue placed them, exacteth no lesse. For a man to be affected to these transitory and passing goods, argueth an abiect and base mind: in like manner to take a contentment in the pleasures of the flesh, is rather of beasts then of men. Therfore agreable it is, that Religious be most far from both, and this they effect by their Vows, whiles they giue demonstration of their generous mind, and by exercise of vertue auoyding that whereunto both nature & al the senses do incline.

8. But Lord, I see not, what generosity is manifested by the Vow of Obedience, by which the Religious do wholy subiect

themselues

themselues vnto others. Neither do I well conceiue, how contemptible a matter it is to be affected to riches, and pleasures of this life, and is not a base thing also to obey, and serue another in the very least, and most abiect things.

9. Sonne, thou easily discouerest thy self neither to vnderstand, nor indifferently to examine matters. For if thou thinke, that the Religious by the Vow of Obedience be subiect to others, then to me, thou art greatly deceiued. And if thou thinke, that to serue in base things for loue of me, or to be subiect to others by ordination from me, is an abiect thing, thou art much more deceyued. There is a far different manner of liuing in my Court, from that of the World, where the dignity is taken of the office that is exercised, and not of the end or scope that is aymed at, and therfore all seeke rather to haue a power and commaund ouer others, then to be commaunded, and in subiection; and all aspire to dignityes and honours. And because these be of greatest regard with mé, therfore they also who be possessed of these honours, are in greatest estimation, and be held for great men.

10. But the case is far different. For if the end for which any thing is done, be vile and

and abiect, the actious must needs also be
abiect, and of the same nature . And where
the louers of the world do all for an abiect
end, as for the gaine of money, the estimation and opinion of a good name , vaine
glory, reuenge, and the like, it consequently
followeth, that all their trauayles & actions
must also be held most base. But in my court
the eye and intention is especially bent to
the end, which am I, and from me all humane actions receiue and borrow their
worth, and dignity. And where I reward
all the actions, that my Religious friends ,
and children do for loue of me with euerlasting glory, none of them ought to be reputed either little or abiect, but great and
noble . And he who for loue of me subiecteth himselfe to another, giueth an euident
signe of a generous and great mind, because
he omitteth nothing , that may be pleasing
to me his Lord .

11 . Wherfore thou must not my child,
accompt that base and vile, which is done
for loue of me, and for my glory, because a
consideratiō is to be had not so much of the
thing, as of the affection, & end for which
it is done. It is not vile and abiect , that
maketh an entrance into heauen, and is recompensed with an heauenly reward : but

that is truly vile, which creepeth vpon the earth, cleaueth fast vnto it, and receiueth what is terrene & earthly, for a compensation and reward.

How Religious Perfection consisteth in the three Vowes.

CHAP. V.

LORD, if Religious Perfection consist in perfect charity, and the coniunction with the supreme Good, which thou art; what need we to busy our selues in other vertues, and leaue that which is our end. Thou knowest Lord, that charity is the Queen and Lady of all vertues, and of it dependeth all the law of grace, and therfore if we conuert all our cares, studyes, and cogitatiōs to the purchasing therof, we should not labour much about the procuring of other vertues : for if we haue but that one vertue, we can want nothing.

2. It is true my Child, that the end & scope of Religious perfection is perfect charity, & vnion with me thy Creatour, but how canst thou be able to attaine the end without the due meanes vnto it? How wilt thou be vnited with me, vnles thou remoue all the things that hinder thee? Wherfore vn-

derstand

derstand thou, that, to that most inward v-
nion with thy Creatour, that is, with me ,
in which perfect charity consisteth , thou
must come by internall affections of mind ,
conspiring with the spirit of Religion ,
whereunto thou art called by me. And three
things there be, that may hinder the humane affection , that it be not conioyned
with me .

3 . The first is the desire of riches, and
of other goods of Fortune , which when
it shall once haue seazed vpon a part of a
mans harts, suffereth not the whole man to
come vnto me. Whereupon that yong man
to whom I said, that if he would be perfect,
he should sell all that he had, and giue it to
the poore , and then come and follow me ,
went his way sad, because he was ouermuch
deuoted to his possessions , which he had,
many and great . This affection is taken a-
way by the Vow of pouerty, whereby the
Religious renounceth all that he possesseth
in the world, that he may with all his affection, and loue vnite himselfe with his
Lord.

4. Another impediment and bar, is the
loue of carnall and sensuall pleasures, that
he cannot see to vnite himselfe with me ,
which consisteth in spirituall loue. Where-

I 4   upon

upon in a parable of the Ghospell a certaine man being inuited to a wedding, answered, that he could not come, because he had married a wife: and this carnal loue is quite taken away by the Vow of Chastity.

5. The third thing that hindreth, and is lesse acknowledged, is the inordination of mans will, which as it is propense to comaund others, so doth it with much ado subiect it self to the will of another. And this inordination is such, as it separateth a man from me, and therfore I said in the Ghospel: He that will come after me, let him deny himselfe, that is, his owne will, and renounce as it were himselfe. Neither is it any other thing to be vnited to me, then to forsake himselfe, & to yeald himselfe wholy to me; but he laboureth in vaine to vnite himselfe to me, who doth not first of all depart from himselfe. This third let is taken away by the Vow of Obedience, by benefit whereof the Religious by subiecting himselfe to others, suffereth himselfe to be gouerned by the will of others. Seeing then Religious perfection consisteth in perfect charity, and an inward coniunction with me, and these Vowes be the means of obtayning it, and ordained for remouing the impediments thereof, it is not without
cause

cauſe affirmed, that in theſe three Vowes
Religious perfection conſiſteth.

6. Moreouer, ſith theſe three Vows be
the very foundations of a Religious life, it
is not without congruity alſo ſaid, that the
perfection therof hath it dependance of the,
euen as the perfection of a materiall edifice
dependeth of the foundations. And there be
three things in the foundations neceſſary.
The one is, that in laying them, there be a
ſpecial care & conſideratio had: for the ſurer
the foundations be, the more ſtable will be
the building. A ſecond thing is, that they be
kept whole and ſound, and be not remoued.
For by the very leaſt mouing of them, there
follow great cracks and ruines in the walls.
The third is, that the edifice retayneth not
the name of a building, or of an houſe, if the
foundatio be wanting, but is called a poore
cot, wherinto the ordure and filth is wont
to be caſt.

7. Seing then the three Vowes be the
foundations of Religion, theſe three things
alſo ought to be obſerued in them. And firſt
that a Religious mans principall care be of
his Vowes, for that of them dependeth the
life and eſſence of his vocation: and if
the Vowes be ſure and ſtable, all the frame
of a Religious mans ſpirituall building will

ſtand

stand sure and immoueable also . Secondly,
that the Vowes be conserued and kept vnstayned : for the very least default in the
Vowes, causeth a notable hurt in Religious
discipline. Finally, as when the houses foun-
datiō being taken away, the house forgoeth
and looseth it name : euen so the Vowes
being away, the Religious is said no more
to be Religious, out an Apostata, who being once fallen from his state, is easily stayned with the filth and dirt of this world.
When the rootes of the tree , which are the
foundations therof, be hurt, the tree doth ca-
sily either wither away, or is little worth .

8.   Besides, certaine it is, that Religion
is a state, and a place of rest for the mind ,
where a man freed from dangerous stormes
and tempests of this world, reposeth as in a
quiet and secure harbour, and leadeth a spirituall and peaceable life . And Religion
most of all compasseth this by the help of
the Vowes , which intertaine and defend
the Religious tranquillity and quiet, by deliuering a Religious man from the sollici-
citude , care , and trouble of this world :
and for this cause also it is said, that Religious perfection is cōprehended in the three
Vowes .

9.   Wherefore the Vow of Pouerty first
is

is in cause, that a Religious man is exempt from the care of keeping, or increasing, or also of dispensing temporall goods. Next, the Vow of Chastity freeth him from the care of house, of wife, of children and family, which is otherwhiles so combersome and tedious, as it bringeth many to desperation. Finally, by the Vow of obedience there is taken from the Religious the anxiety, & care, where with most men are wont to be vexed, whiles they be not able to determine and resolue by themselues, whether they should do this, or that, whether it would more profit to lead this manner of life, or that. But the Religious, who hath by Vow of Obedience left himselfe in all things wholy to the directiō of Superiours, is most free from such kind of superfluous anxietyes, perplexityes, tentations, and doubts.

10. Sonne, thou must haue a speciall regard to thy tranquillity and peace of mind, for that of it dependeth thy soules weale. Where trouble and disquiet is, there can be neither spirit nor deuotion. And know thou, that as long as in Religion thou keepest thy Vowes, they will in like manner keep thee in peace and quiet.

11. To conclude, Religious perfection is
attributed

attributed to the Vowes, becaufe it perfe-
cteth the holocauft, that the Religious offer
of themfelues to God. In the old law the
holocauft was all confumed with fire for an
odour of fweetnes, and the oblation of it
was foone ended. But the holocauft of the
Religious continueth for life, & the nearer
it is to the end, fweeter is the fent thereof,
and therfore is to me made a Vow of perpe-
petuall Pouerty, perpetuall Chaftity, and
Obedience for euer. In the holocauft of Pouerty are offered me all the externall and
temporall goods: in that of Chaftity, the
goods of the body: & in that of Obedience,
the goods of the mind. For in that the will
is offered to me, all the faculties and powers
that be in fubiectiō to it, be offered withal,
and becaufe nothing more remayneth behind to be offered, by the Vowes a whole,
entire, and perfect holocauft is not without
caufe offered.

12.   The ftate of Virgins is perfect in
it felfe, and very acceptable to me, but the
Religious ftate is much more perfect, and
more pleafing to me, becaufe the Virgins do
for loue of me only depriue themfelues of
the pleafures of the flefh, but Religious further fpoile themfelues of their owne will,
and giue me whatfoeuer they haue. He giueth

ueth not little, who giueth all he hath;
neither shall he receaue little in beauen,
who shall for his remuneration and reward
receaue me my selfe.

13. Now I would haue all to be themselues iudges in this matter, of how great
reckoning the Vowes of Religious ought to
be, sith they be the foundations and ground-
worke of Religious life, the conseruers of
the minds tranquillity and quiet, so much
desired and sought for of men, and the most
effectuall meanes towards the attayning of
perfection, & the offering of a perfect sacrifice to the Creatour. A souldier maketh a
great reckoning of his horse and armes, by
the benefit whereof he may be able to maintaine his temporall life, and triumph ouer
his enemyes. And shall not a Religious man
esteeme of his Vowes, by help whereof he
conserueth his spirituall life, and goeth a-
way with victory, not only ouer his enemyes, but ouer himselfe also?

14. O how great will the splendour of
these three Vowes be in Heauen, when like
vnto three most precious stones they shal be
set in a crowne of glory? For if the same
now couered, concealed, and hidden as it
were, do neuertheles giue out so great a light
on earth, as the very great and mighty ones
of

of this world admire them; how great wil the brightnes therof be in heauen, where all things shall be seen, and appeare? doubtles their ioy and peace of mind will be exceeding great, who shall transport these iewells with them into heauen: as contrariwise great will be their grief and confusion, who whiles they liue, had them not in the esteeme that they ought to haue had. If thou contemnest those precious stones, which haue a vertue to raise thee vp to greatest honour, what is it that thou makest any great reckoning of?

Of the perfect obseruation of Religious Vowes.

CHAP. VI.

SONNE, in the world a great regard is had by euery man of his own honour, and renowne of his family, and therefore there raigne so many hatreds, and enimities so many slaughters committed, families brought to extreme pouerty & ouerthrown, and which is worst of all, many soules run to vtter perdition. And all this euill and mischief ariseth of this, that they labour only to fullfill the worlds foolish lawes, and yet to the performance therof Christians be neither bound, nor tyed by any Vow, but
be

be rather by my contrary lawes forbidden
to do them , vnder paine of eternall damnation. And if the men of this world do
with so great an hazard of their fortunes ,
life, soule, and all , so diligently obserue so
pernicious Lawes: certes, a Religious man
hath much more reason to be very studious
diligent, and exact in obseruing the lawes
of his vows, which be the statutes & laws of
the Holy Ghost , that concerne the good of
soules, and my glory . And in truth he who
preferreth the decrees of the world, his enemy, before the lawes of God, his Creatour,
fighteth against himselfe .

2. Sonne, it is true, that a man is by the
world reputed vile & dastardly, who vseth
not the law of reuenging an iniury : but if
for loue of me he remit & forgiue an iniury,
he is with me, & withall vertuous persons
censured for magnanimous & wise, because
he ouercometh himselfe , and regardeth
more the lawes of God, then of the world.
But he who in Religion transgresseth his
Vowes, is contemned of the world , is held
infamous to the Religious , is of all other
men condemned for ingrate, for that by benefit of Vows he was raised vp vnto so high
an estate , namely of Religion, and by the
the same enriched with so many gifts and
spirituall

spirituall graces. And who seeth not, that
to violate his Vowes, is nothing els then
not to stand to his promise, nor satisfy his
band? Who perceiueth it not, that it is as
much as to contemne his benefactour and
setter vp? And therfore the saying of the
Ghospel ought not to seem harsh vnto thee,
which I pronounced against them, when I
said, *That he is not apt for the kingdome of heauen*,
who after putting his hand to the plough, looketh back
againe.

3. The beginners are not crowned in
heauen, but the perseuerers in good euen till
death. It is also said in my Scripture. *That*
an vnfaythfull promise doth greatly displease God : &
not without cause. For he that dischargeth
not his word in keeping promises made by
Vow, goeth on next to this, that he cōtemne
Religion, & consequently the same is contemned also, if it keepeth in it such as discharge not their duty. For it is no little scandall vnto men of the world, if they see
the Religious to be defectiue in euery principall point, in which consisteth the essence
of Religion it selfe. And the least reproach
doth not redound to me also: for sith I haue
accepted their promises made by Vow,
if they be not performed as is requisite, I
am vnworthily iniured by them, whome I
haue

haue fo tenderly loued, and whome I fo inwardly affected. Befides the greateft hurt
of all lighteth vpon the tranfgreffors themfelues, becaufe they caft themfelues into manifeft hazard of Apoftafy, and into the enemies fnares , neuer likely to get out againe.
And what meruaile if fometimes in this life
alfo I bend the bow of my indignation a-
gainft them. He that can fatisfy the debt
that he oweth , and vfeth coufenage that he
may not pay it, is worthy neither of remiffiõ
or pardon , nor of commiferation. It is a
leffer euill to vow, then to reuoke the vow
a man hath once made.

4. The Diuell the capitall enemy of
Religious perfection is not ignorant, how
much good cõmeth to a Religious man by
the exact obferuation of his Vowes. For nothing bringeth him fooner, and with more
fecurity to the height of perfection, then the
mortification of carnall defires . And what
is it els, in a perfect manner, to performe
the Vowes, then for a man to mortify himfelfe ? The Vow of Pouerty mortifyeth the
defire of heaping vp riches : The Vow of
Chaftity the tentation and contentments
of the flefh ; and the Vow of Obedience the
facultyes of the mind, the will, and proper
iudgment. And this is the caufe, why the
K   Diuell

Diuell laboureth so much to perswade the
Religious to make no conscience, or scruple
in transgression of their Vowes, not only
that he may so diuert them from the seeking
of perfection, but also for this, that when
the foundations be once shaken and weakned, it is no hard matter for him to ouerthrow the whole house. And an euill signe
it is, when the beginning of the euill is giuen and occasioned by the principall part.

5. O how deare be those Religious to
me, who seeke out diuers meanes, and helps
for the attayning of the perfect obseruation
of their Vows, both for the better strength-
ning of the foundation of their spirituall e-
difice, and for the making of more sharp
warre vpon the Diuel, by manfully resisting
him. Some there be, who do euery day to
themselues renew the Vow they haue once
made to me, and do humbly craue my grace
for the perfect obseruing of them. And this
much pleaseth me? for they easily declare &
make knowne, how great an inward desire
they haue to auoyd all defects, and to performe their Vowes exactly. By this double
desire of perfect obseruation of the Vowes,
and of crauing grace, the soule maketh as it
were the first step to the obtaining of what
it desireth. Often to renew the Vowes once
made,

made, is nothing els, then often to driue
in the nayles faster, wherewith the Religious be nayled vpon the Croſſe with me,
in ſo much as if they begin peraduenture to
be looſe, they may be made more faſt. And
by this help the Religious be made more
ſtrong, able, & more conſtant in obſeruing
their Vowes.

6.   There be others alſo, whome I loue
as well, as the former, who when any tentation ariſeth againſt their Vowes, do not
diſpute with themſelues, whether it were a
great fault or a little to do that which the
tentation ſuggeſteth, whether it could be
done without mortall ſinne, or no; but ſo
ſoone as they perceyue it to be contrary to
their Vowes, they eftſoons reiect it: no o-
therwiſe then he, vpon whome when peraduenture a ſparke of fire falleth, examineth not, whether it would burne him litle
or much, but he inſtantly ſhaketh if off, and
putteth it out with his hand, or foot. He
that contemneth a little imperfectiō, which
he might eaſily auoid, doth in time diſſemble great ones. Giue eare my Sonne. Didſt
not thou make thy Vowes for loue of me,
and that therby thou mighſt do me ſeruice?
Doeſt not thou keep the ſame, that thou
mayeſt gayne the greater fauour at my

hands? Sith then thou art assured, that the
very least defects, committed against thy
Vowes, do displease me, wherfore doest
thou not forbeare to commit them? If in
things appertayning to the body, thou do
not suffer any fault, neither great nor smal,
why permittest thou any defect in obseruation of thy Vowes, then which nothing in
Religion is more excellent? To do any
thing that displeaseth me, though it be very little, is not of a zealous louer, such as I
desire euery Religious man should be.

7. There is yet another meanes, by
help wherof the Religious man may come
to an exact obseruation of his Vowes: and
this commonly doth he vse who is feruent
in spirit, imitating the vse and manner of
such as be very hungry. For they most carefully seeke what to eate, and they do without any difference eate whatsoeuer they
find, whether hoate or cold, well or ill prepared, rosted or sodden. Euen so the feruent
Religious be lead with a great desire to exercise those vertues which they haue promised by Vowes, and this both in great
matters and in little, as well in hard and
painefull, as in easy and pleasant. And for
one to exercise himselfe often in his Vowes,
& in the often actions of Pouerty, Chastity,
and

end Obedience, maketh the obseruation of the Vowes very easy. For the frequentatiõ of such acts prepareth a Religious man to the getting of an habit. And habit of it owne nature maketh a man agile, prompt, and ready to the exercising of Vertue, and consequently to the obseruing of his Vowes perfectly. We haue a plaine example in the skill of musicke, for the more a man frequenteth the exercise therof, the more readily, and the more cunningly is he accustomed to sing, or play.

8. By this it may be vnderstood, how greatly and daungerously they be deceiued, who care not for light transgressions in the obseruation of their Vows, not considering or marking, that the essence of a Religious man is in his Vowes, that they make or marre, to the good or hurt of their soules, that of the same depends al the good or euill of religion, scandall or edification, and my glory also, because the promises be made to me; and finally the merit it selfe of the three principall vertues, that be comprehended in the Vowes. Wherfore if there be not need of great care, and vigilancy that we fayle not in our duty, I know not in what there will be need. And if a man will not shew a feruour and zeale in this thing, I see not

K 3   wherein

wherein he should declare and manifest the same.

Of the three Vowes in particuler: and first of the Vow of Pouerty, *how agreable and requisite it is, that the Religious be louers thereof.*

CHAP. VII.

SONNE, meete it is not, that the seruant should refuse what his Lord & Maister hath imbraced, neither beseemeth it the scholler to learne another lesson, then that which his maister hath appointed him. Whiles I liued on earth, I chose, and willingly imbraced Pouerty. The same I taught and proposed to all that followed me, and now againe I earnestly recommend it to all, who aspire to the perfection of spirituall life. For I was borne so poore, as there was not a corner found in any house, that would intertaine and receiue me, when I was to come into the world. And therefore my poore Mother was forced to retire her selfe into a stable, wherein I was both borne, & layd in a maunger. I was borne of a poore Mother, brought vp as poorely, conuersed amongst the poore, and liued poore till my dying day ; and at my death I was much more

more poore, becaufe I had not whereupon
to reft my pierced head, and gaue vp my life
at laft vpon the hard bed of the Croffe.

2. Let the Religious now confider, whether it be not agreable, that they fhould be
well affected to Pouerty by the voluntarily
promifed, and fo highly efteemed and beloued by me. Let them ponder, whether it
be meet, that members fo richly adorned
and fet forth, lye hid vnder fo needy an
head. The feruant deferueth not to ftay in
the houfe, who is not contented to vfe the
fame meate, drinke, and cloathing that his
Lord vfeth. Neither was I a louer of Pouerty alone, my Apoftles imbraced the fame,
who befides that they were poore fifhermē,
when I called them out of the world, did
further leaue that little which they had and
poffeffed for loue of me, moft affectuoufly
imbracing Pouerty, as a true and faithfull
companion. O how much did it pleafe me,
when being called by me, they did without
further lingring, or delay forfake parents,
fhip, nets, & whatfoeuer they had, or might
haue in this life. And though this action
of Pouerty were great & heroicall in them,
becaufe they forfooke all; yet I ftayed not
heere, but would further haue thē exercifed
in the fame Pouerty, by liuing with with
me

me of the almes of other men, and therfore
I sent them to preach abroad from one place
to another, without purse or scrip, prouided
of nothing which was necessary, that they
might repose all their hope in Gods prouidence.

3. The Religious man the lesse he hath,
and the lesse desire he hath of temporall
things, is the more apt for the helping of
soules. And when I did after send them forth
to preach the Ghospell all the world ouer,
did they go loaden with baggage, or atten-
ded vpon by great traynes of seruants, or
did they aduertise the citties, whither they
went; of their comming, that they might
find all manner of thinges prouided and
made ready for them? No such matter. But
they went full of the holy Ghost, loaden
with the weight of my doctrine, and incensed with a burning desire of conuerting
countryes to the fayth: they did like poore
men enter into the Citties and Townes,
where whiles they made their stay, by preaching me poore, and naked, dead vpon the
Crosse, they caused exceeding motions in
their hearers minds. Whome when they
saw, neither to seeke, nor to accept of gold
or siluer, meruailed much. And when they
further saw them to take so long iournyes al
                                                        the

the world ouer in extreme penury, and
want of things, only for the gayning of the
foules of others, and alfo to loue want and
pouerty; they were almoft aftonifhed with
very admiration, and for that caufe they
were more ready, and more eafily induced
to put their neckes vnder the yoake of the
Ghofpell. Thefe two things do not well
fuite, to gaine foules, and to attend withall
to our priuate commodityes and pleafures.

4. If againe, my Sonne, thou turne thy
felfe to the founders of Religion, thou fhalt
find that they were fo great louers of Pouerty, as they would not fuffer the words *Myne*
and *Thine* to haue any place amongft them,
thinking that by thefe two words, is de-
ftroyed all the force of Pouerty : and if they
found any Proprietary amongft them, they
inftantly banifhed and thruft him out, as an
infectious perfon from their Company.
Let them now fpeake, who be fo much a-
fraid of the name of Pouerty, whofe difci-
ples, and followers they be : What rule permitted them to haue goods and prouifion of
their owne ? Wherfore do they take paynes
to get money togeather, whether to couert
it to their owne vfe, or to leaue it to others ;
howfoeuer they do it, euen fecular men haue
not care to gather riches for any other caufe.

K 5   What

What difference then is there betweene the Religious men, and those of the world? This is not for a man to beare heauen away by violence, but to afflict and vexe himselfe for the gathering of earthly trash togeather. The doctrine that I haue deliuered is not so, neither be they the followers of their founders and forefathers; and seeing they trace not the same steps with them, they will neuer come to the same degree of perfection that they did.

5. Lord, if thou giuest vs not some sput to put vs forwards to loue Pouerty, it will easily be abandoned and forsaken: for sith it carrieth an outward representation of ignobility, contempt, and basenes, and of being next vnto misery, no esteem is made therof. Sonne, thou art very much deceiued, because thou viest not a distinction. In forced Pouerty, & that which commeth of necessity, is contemptible, and hated of the world: but voluntary Pouerty, sith it is a noble and heroicall vertue, how can it be ignoble and base? If it treadeth vnder foote, & contemneth all precious stones, and the worlds treasure, how can it be miserable? To the loue of it what may moue vs more, then to vnderstand, that I the Sonne of God, and Lord of Maiesty, when I liued on earth, betroathed

troathed Pouerty vnto my felfe, and loued
and intertayned it till my dying day. And
fhould not this alone worthily induce euery
Religious perfon to loue and honour it? For
in all Courts, he is in greateft honour and
regard, whome the Prince loueth moft.

6.　But wilt thou vnderftand my Son,
who is a true louer of Pouerty ? He it is,
who moft delighteth and reioyceth in it,
who commendeth, and defireth it more
then other, who thinketh not to offend it
either by worke, word, or by any figne; who
finally imbraceth and loueth it, as an heauenly margarite, that maketh the foule moft
fayre, and beautifull in the fight of the creatour. O how much did the Religious before
tyme to pleafe me, who were fo affected to
Pouerty, as they held all the riches of this
world for toyes and ordure, if they were
compared with it. And for a declaration of
their exceeding great affection vnto it, they
called Pouerty their Lady and Queene, and
for fuch they efteemed and vfed it. Neither
did they this in the firft feruour of their con-
uerfion only, but the elder they waxed in
the feruing of God, the more they loued,
and reuerenced it, and for that caufe they
were very earneft and defirous, that they
might giue vp their laft breath to God vpon
the

the bare ground.

7. On the contrary side, I am not a litle displeased to see some Religious so little deuoted to Pouerty, as those, who discommend it, haue an horrour to it, as a thing to be detested, and by deeds also go against it. Hence it is, that in their meate and drinke, in their cloathing and habitation they will be intreated commodiously and daintly, yea & that better and more commodiously then they intreated themselues in the world; and if they haue not euery thing as they list, they be troubled, and can take no rest at all. And what an infelicity is this? They giue ouer the world to serue me, they leaue all their riches, neglect their commodityes, and of themselus vow Pouerty, that they may euer lead a quiet life, and after they be once entred into Religion, they suffer themselues to be disquieted and troubled for the things that they forsooke in the world. This is nothing but to sing a song of recantation, and to reuoke their Vow of perpetuall Pouerty. For what difference is there, whether thou desire earthly riches, or superfluous commodities and recreations, when as the one and the other be repugnant to Religious Pouerty?

8. But it displeaseth me more, that there

there be some, who not finding in Religion
all abundance of things, as they had in the
world, do looke backe, and craue their cō-
modities firſt of one ſecular man , and then
of another, and make themſelues their vaſ-
ſalls and ſlaues . And if ſo to do for their
owne vſe and commodity, be bad ; how
much worſe it is then, to exact ſuch things
of ſecular men, that they may be giuen to
others ? Is it poſſible , that any Religious
man ſhould be found, who ſhould bind
himſelfe to ſecular men, for the doing of
good turnes to others? O infamous madnes
of ſuch a Religious perſon, who for ſo baſe
a thing maketh himſelf a vaſſal to ſo many !
Of this bad fountaine doth ſpring for the
moſt part all that looſeneſſe, diſſolution ,
and breach of good order, and Religious diſcipline, which we ſee (a thing to be lamented) in many Religious with our own eyes.
Woe be to that Religion , the Religious
wherof be no louers of Pouerty, for that by
their ouermuch liberty of manners and life
they become the ruiue and ouerthrow of
Religion .

Of

Of the dignity, and commendation of Religious Pouerty.

CHAP. VIII·

SONNE, I haue not without cause in my Ghospell amongst the Beatituds giuen the first place to Pouerty, and bequeathed the Kingdome of heauen to the poore, for without Euangelicall perfection it is impossible to come to blisse. Seing then Pouerty is the first foundation of Euangelicall Perfection, of good right it meriteth the preheminence of the first place. For which cause I haue sent all those, whome I haue inuited to follow me, or haue been desirous of perfection, it they did not of their owne accord renounce the riches of the world, or did not voluntarily become poore, to the first foundation, that they should first forsake all, and then follow me. Perfection would not haue men bound, but free and loose.

2. Lord, if the kingdome of heauen be for the poore, very great will the number of the blessed be, because there be more poore in the world, then rich. True it is, my Sonne, that the Kindgdome of heauen is for the poore, yet all the poore be not for heauen,

heauen , but only those, who make an election to be poore, and such be very few .
Some there be, who indeed be not possessed
of any thing in this life, yet they haue it in
desire, and this pouerty is not only no vertue
nor worthy of praise, but also spoyleth many of their eternall felicity, both for that
it taketh not away the exceeding desire of
hauing, which is the roote of all euills ; and
also for that it setteth it on fire so fare, as it
maketh a mans mind denoyd of all manner
of peace and quiet : Whence it is, that many
become robbers, theeues , and do not admit
any cogitation of heauen at all .

3. Some be possessed of great store of
riches, but they tye not their affection vnto
them, yea they be ready, when it shall please
me, and when I shall thinke good, to leaue
them: and of such poore in spirit there be
found very few in the world . Finally some
there be, who that they may be the more
free in the exercise of true vertue, do contemne and forsake all earthly riches, not
only out of an affection of mind, but by effect of workes also . So did my Apostles, &
many other Religious, who be now in present possession of the riches of heauen. And
this is Religious Pouerty, whereunto I
haue promised the kingdome of heauen ,
                                    where

where all the Religious shall be crowned with the most noble crowne of glory: but the number of these is very small.

4. If the kingdome of heauen could be bought with money, or exchanged with kingdomes and riches of the world, great would be the excellency and dignity of the goods of fortune, and euery one might loue them, as his owne soule. This excellency I haue imparted to Religious Pouerty, which of terrene riches maketh a ladder, whereby it may mount vp to heauen. Contrariwise the rich of the world dig the earth for the getting of gold and siluer out of her bowels, and therein they place and fixe their hart, and bury it with the renouncing of heauen togeather with the true felicity therof. But the poore Religious man, because he directeth his hart to heauen, maketh himselfe worthy of an heauenly reward. What manner of way a man shall enter into, such shall he find the end of it.

5. Besides, a Religious man by the Vow of Pouerty becometh superiour to the whol world, and aboue it. For whereas he desireth not to possesse any thing in this life as his owne, he hath no dependance on the world, or the things therof, but as one aboue it, he contemneth all, that is within the compasse,

compaile, or power of it. The contrary hapneth to such as be addictedto the world, who be at the commaund of so many maisters, as be the things that they desire to haue and possesse.

6.   Moreouer Religious Pouerty manifesteth a certaine power and might against the nature of man it selfe. For nature desireth and inclineth a man to desire riches, and the commodities of the body, as the delicacies of meats, niceness of apparel, sports pastimes, and recreations; but Religious Pouerty withdraweth all these from it selfe for my sake, and therfore ouercometh Nature. And how then should not I highly esteeme them, who wittingly and willingly, moued out of loue of me alone, do depriue themselues of al these lawfull commodities, and whereunto Nature of it selfe inuiteth them?

7.   Heare also, my Sonne, another excellency of Religious Pouerty. If any needy or poore man become rich by his owne industry, or by any other occasion, the world meruayleth not: but it wondreth much, if a rich man become voluntarily poore, and such a one indeed, as doeth not only make away his riches, but also depriueth himself of the power and ability of possessing them

L   for

fore euer after. And at this the world is astonished the more, for that it selfe hath nothing in more esteeme then riches of the
world, & shunneth nothing with a greater
care, then Pouerty. All this proceedeth of
nothing els, then that it vnderstandeth not
the dignity and excellency of Religious
Pouerty. Let the world tell me : Can it
withall it owne riches, and pleasures satiate
and fill a mans hart, so as it may be at quiet?
Nothing lesse : for that as many as be louers
of the world, the more they haue, the more
desire they to haue, and whiles they cannot
be satisfied with what they haue got, they
neuer arriue to any true peace and quiet of
mind. But the Religious, who neither haue
any thing proper, of their own, nor desire
to haue, liue content with very little. Is not
this a certaine participation of euerlasting
felicity, that a man, as he shall one day liue
content in heauen with the glory therof, so
liueth now on earth content, & quiet with
his Religious Pouerty?

8. Neither is it the least commendation
of Religious Pouerty, that it not only conserueth, and keepeth the Religious, but
hath further beene the foundresse of all Religions, as many as haue beene, and still be
in Gods Church. The monasteries indeed,
and

and the Cloisters be erected and built with
money, and the goods of fortune ; but the
Religious be not founded by them . For the
first founders, who had store of riches, for
the consecrating of themselues to my seruice
did giue away their riches, as impediments
to a better course of life . And after a good
foundation layd of the spirit of Pouerty,
and of mortification , I vsed them as di-
rectors and guids for the drawing of others,
and by this means Religions were founded.
Stones, and tymber be laid and rayfed by riches, but vertues are built & raifed by Pouerty of spirit .

  9 . But suppose, that there were not any
thing worthy of comendation, or excellent
in Pouerty; is it not a great dignity, that it
is loued of me, and esteemed of me ? That it
was to me an inseparable & fast companion
during the whole course of my life ? That I
vsed the help of it in the worlds conuersion,
not by sending the rich, mighty, and wise ,
but the poore ignorant & rude for the ouercoming of the wise & mighty of the world?
That I wrought so great miracles by men
poore and abiect for the good of soules? Do
not these seeme vnto thee any commendations and renowne of Religious pouerty ?
And if they be great prayfes; haue not I, my

Sonne, most iust cause to complaine of thē, who do not only not loue Pouerty, but do also without cause contemne it? That it is contemned of the world, is no meruayle, because the profession & scope therof night and day is to attend to the heaping vp of riches, and increasing of honours: but that there should be any religious found, who by deeds refute the same, and vnder hand practise it, is a thing that highly displeaseth me, whiles I behold that Lady and Queen promised me by Religious and solemne Vow, which should haue a commaunding hand with them, so impudently and shamefully thrust out. Spiritual things cannot be loued without a spirit.

Of the vtility and profit, that voluntary Pouerty bringeth to the Religious:

CHAP. IX.

LORD, what good and profit can Religious Pouerty bring, sith it hath nothing, wherby it may ease mans necessities? And more then that, in regard of the incōmodityes that be adioyned therto, it seemeth preiudicial, not to the body alone, but to the soule also. For the body being ill handled therby, easily falleth into sicknes, and

and being ill dilpoled, cannot ferue and attend to the fpirituall actions of the foule,
neither can the mind it felf vfe the ordinary
exercife of prayer, and meditation. Befides
it is no little impediment to the Religious,
who towards the helping of their neighbours, do profeffe an actiue life. For if they
want things neceffary, they are not able to
go through with their labours, in helping
their neignbours. Therfore it feemeth to me
that Pouerty is an impediment to much
good, and contrariwife promoteth what is
ill, as is ficknes and other infirmities, yea &
haiteneth death it felfe.

2.   Sonne, thou art far wide of thy
marke: for thou thinkeft that Religious
Pouerty is a feuere and cruell Miftreffe that
withdraweth from the Religious thinges
neceffary towards their meate, drinke and
cloathing, according to a requifite proportion required in their inftitute. It is not fo.
Pouerty by frugality is good, both for the
foule & body, & profiteth a man more, then
do the riches and pleafures of the world.
For in the firft place the defire of tranfitory
honours doth fo torment a mans mind, as it
depriueth him of all quiet, pricketh him
forward to fucke vp the bloud of the poore,
and bringeth him to fo great a blindnes, as

L 3   it

it bereaueth him of all feare of God & men, without any regard had of his owne foules good. Neither do men defirous of getting more, make a ftand heere.

3. He that is once become rich, eftfoons raifeth vp his head, becometh arrogant and proud, vndertaketh to patronize the wicked, and out of a madnes runneth headlong into all naughtines. From thefe euills, and many more, voluntary Pouerty freeth the mind, whiles it doth take from him not only the riches that he hath, but alfo the hope & defire of hauing, which is the beginning of ruine both of body and foule, and procureth fuch tranquility and peace, as it maketh the mind fit and difpofed to the contemplation of heauenly things, and to all manner of fpirituall actions. Whence it is, that a Religious man, fo foone as he is become poore, confequently becometh humble, modeft, meeke, a friend of the good, and of vertue, and an enemy of the bad, and a contemner of vices.

4. That Pouerty alfo profiteth the body, is out of queftion. We do not defire any thing more earneftly for the body, then good health: and we haue an horrour of nothing more then of ficknes: for there is not any who would not be rather poore and
                                        whole,

whole, then rich and ficke. And dayly experience manifeftly teacheth, that the frugality of pouerty conferueth the good health of body, prolongeth and continueth mans life more yeares, then doth all the ftore of riches and pleafures. Who feeth not, that the poore be more healthfull, & go through with more labours, then do the rich? A poore man is as well content with a fimple, ordinary, & meane dyet, as be the rich with dainty and delicate fare. The poore man cōmeth euer hungry to his meate: the little that he hath he eateth with a good appetite: whē he is a thirft he refufeth not a draught of watter: after labour he feeketh not for a foft bed, but he fleepeth, lyeth downe, & taketh his reft where it hapneth at aduentures: and in the morning he rifeth early with meate difgefted, found, and healthfull and without loathing.

5. On the contrary, the rich man, feruing the time ordinarily, fitteth downe to the table with a full ftomake, taketh very little taft or pleafure in his meate, fcarce fleepeth by night, but turneth himfelfe euer and anone, now to one fide of the bed now to another: & therefore the Phifitian muft euer be at hand, and drugs prepared in his chamber ready to take vpon euery occafion.

L 4   Loe

Loe thus be they turmoiled, who liue in delicacies : they liue badly, and dye soone. My
seruants did not in times past liue so in the
wildernesse, who professed so great Pouerty,
as some when they besprinckied their herbs
with a little salt, or oyle, thought they had
made a feast ; and yet these men neuer vsing
the benefit of Phisitian, or of philicke,
liued to very old age, and therfore Religious Pouerty is not (as thou thinkest) the
cause either of infirmities or of hastning thy
death . Nothing hurteth ones health so
much , as the variety and abundance of the
meate .

6.   Religious Pouerty bringeth another
commodity with it , and that is security ,
voyd of all suspition, and sinister thoughts.
He, that aboundeth in wealth, is afraid of
theeues, not only from abroad , but of his
own house also. An I not without cause:for
many, whiles they see they cannot come to
the riches they desire, do first spoyle them of
life, and then of their riches . How many
sonnes haue killed or poysoned theirParents
that they might the sooner come to enioy
their inheritance ? How many treasons, &
treacheries haue there beene wrought a-
gainst most deare friends, for the spoiling
them of their treasures ? But the poore sleep
                                                    in

in security, they trauayle night and day out
of all feare, they are troubled with no suspitions, because they haue nothing to loose.
Adde to this also, that Pouerty hindreth
none in his trauayle, nor bringeth in, or
causeth any forgetfulnes of the Kingdome
of heauen, which is occasioned by riches,
but rather vrgeth and forceth vs to thinke
more often vpon the beauty of our heauenly
country, and vpon the great treasures there
prepared for vs.

7. Lord, at the day of iudgment thou
wilt make them only partaker of the Kingdome of heauen, who for loue of thee shall
haue afforded meate and drink to the needy
and shal haue holpen them in all their other
necessities: and what soeuer shall be done
vnto them, thou wilt haue reputed to be
done to thy selfe. If it be so, what reward
shall come to the poore Religious, who
when in their entrance to Religion, they
haue renounced all their possessions, haue
not wherewith to relieue them? Wherfore
it seemeth they might haue done more wisely, if they had relerued some part of their
goods to giue afterward to the poore.

8. Sonne to giue almes to the poore,
is a good worke, and meritorious of life
euerlasting: but it is a far more excellent

L 5   worke

worke for a man to forsake both all his posselsions & the world also, & to follow me. Hence it is, that I did not counsaile that rich yong man in the Ghospell, who asked me, what was needfull for him to do to attaine to a perfect life, to stay in the world, and to giue much almes to the poore, but that himselfe after distribution of all his goods vpon the poore, should become also poore, & so follow me in my Pouerty. And therefore the Religious need not to feare in the day of iudgment: For seeing they haue for the loue of me forsaken not only all that they had, but all they might haue had in the world also, they exercise a most noble, and perfect worke, which in that day shall be recompensed and payd with a most abundant reward of euerlasting felicity. He is not bound to giue almes, who hath distributed all that he had to the poore at once, and hath nothing left him to giue.

9. Seeing then by the so great commendations, and vtilityes of Religious Pouerty it may euidently appeare, that secular men be greatly deceiued, who seeke with so great a desire to heape vp riches ; how great an errour, thinke we, doth a Religious man commit, if he should in like manner study to get money togeather, who by Vow of Pouerty

uerty hath renounced it for euer? What folly and madnes would it be for him, whiles
he forsaketh the world, to haue a will to go
out naked, that when he were to fight with
the Diuell, he might not haue wherewith
his enemy should take hold by, to throw him
to the ground, and now to haue a will to be
clad in Religion, that he may be with the
more ease laid hand on, & ouerthrowne by
the enemy? The Diuell, when he findeth
not whereon to fasten, or to lay any hold,
goeth his way ouercome, and vanquished,
or leaueth of to molest and trouble.

How God, euen in this life, rewardeth the
Religious for their Vow of Pouerty.

CHAP. X.

SONNE, I am he, who affoard necessaryes to the whole world : I commaund
the Sunne to shine as well vpon the good,
as the bad: I send downe raine in tymes and
seasons: I cause the earth to bring forth
fruits, plants, and all liuing things, and the
Sea to abound in fish, to the end euery kind
according to the condition of their nature
may haue helps agreable therunto. Neither
doth it beseem me, the Creatour of all, to be
ouercome of man, that he should giue me
more

more, then I giue him. And therefore sith
the Religious do by Vow of Pouerty giue
themselues, and whatsoeuer they haue in
the world, and to the end they may serue me
the more readily, and the more at ease, they
renounce all their possessions, honors, commodities and recreations otherwise lawful,
and further bind themselues by band of perpetuall Vow, that they may not at any time
be able to go backe from the profession of
Pouerty; meet it is, that I in like manner
promise to affoard them all necessaries for
their sustenance.

2. First then I requite this their so feruent loue and liberality towards me in such
sort, as I consecrate my selfe wholy vnto
them, as I did vndertake long since in the
person of *Aaron* to do, to whome I said, *That
I would be his inheritance*, vnderstanding and
meaning in this figure all the Religious.
Thus I make my selfe their procuratour &
dispenser. Neither do I hold it inough for
my selfe to sustayne the person of a good
Lord towards his faithfull seruants, but I
further reckon them, as doth a most louing
Father of his dearest children. And if the
birds and fowles of the ayre be so carefull
to seeke and prouide for necessaryes for the
feeding of their yong ones; wilt thou haue
me

me to forget my Religious children, who
do in their Monasteryes, as in their neasts,
expect their sustenance? Wilt thou not haue
them clad with necessary cloathing, who
haue for my sake spoiled themselues of all
their commodityes of body, retayning nothing as their owne? He standeth in need
of nothing, of whome God taketh a care.

3. Wherfore know thou, that I haue
prouided, and still dayly do, necessary helps
for all, because neither there be the same
functions of all, neither do all follow the
same manner of liuing. For I haue caused
those, who liue seperatly, and, as touching
their owne person, depriued of al dominion
of their possessions, that they may serue me
in this degree of Pouerty, to be prouided of
possessions in common, wherof euery one
may haue the meanes to entertaine life.
Againe, I help others, who haue imbraced
the lawes of a more strict Pouerty, in so
much as they will not euen in cōmon inioy
any stable or certaine rents, by mouing the
harts of the faithfull, now one, then another
to be willing and ready to prouide for euery
one conformably to his rule, and vocation.
Be not thou on thy part wanting vnto God,
and God will not be wanting vnto thee.

4. And that we may come nearer to the
remuneration,

remuneration, that I make to the Religious
in this life alſo, for the recompence of the
Vow of Pouerty, tell me, my Sonne, wherfore when any one of thy order cometh frō
ſome foraine part to thy monaſtery for his
lodging, all come running to giue him all
things neceſſary? For what cauſe is this
done? In very deed for no other, then for
the Vow of Pouerty, & that is a part of the
compenſation, that is due to Religious Pouerty. If that gueſt ſhould haue any proui-
ſion of his owne, whereof he might liue,
euery one would forbeare to help him, neither would there want murmurers, who
would ſay, this man is rich inough at home,
no doubt but he commeth hither to ſpend
what is ours, that he might ſpare his owne.
But it is nothing ſo. For ſeeing none can be
ignorāt, that he by reaſon of his Vow of Pouerty, neither hath, nor can haue any thing
of his owne, therfore al neceſſaries be with
charity and good will affoarded him.

5. Againe, with what a company of cars
is a ſecular man troubled and turmoyled for
the prouiding of his family with ſuch
thinges, as peraduenture as appertayne to
meate, drinke, and cloaths : how often paſſeth he whole nights without ſleep, taking
care and ſollicitude, where, how, and what
way

way he may remedy his present want? how
often lamēteth he & weepeth, while he findeth not the meanes to help himselfe, or others? Doth not he seeme, my Sonne, vnto
thee happy, who is exempted from all such
sollicitude ? Holdest not thou him much
priuiledged, who deuoyd of cares, hath others to procure him all necessaryes? And
whence haue the Religious this priuiledge
but by me, in regard of the Vow of Pouerty.

6.   Consider also, my Sonne, that a Religious man, if it be his happe to trauaile
through other countreys, and to come to
the houses of his order, is very kindly and
louingly intertayned, and welcomed with
much Charity, allthough they neuer saw
the man before; offer themselues to do him
seruice, for this respect alone, that they vnderstand him to be their brother, & a child
of the same mother, that is Religion, with
them. When he cometh thither, all thinges
be there as common vnto him, as they be
vnto those, who make their habitatiō there,
and therefore for one house that he left in
the world for the loue of me, he findeth a
thousand other better then his owne. And
this is to haue nothing, and yet to possesse
all.

7.   There is not a Prince so commodiously

ously treated as he is when he is out of the
territoryes and lymits of his owne gouernement. For in his Inne he is courteously
wellcomed, and intertayned by the host of
the houte for no other cause theior the gaine
he hopeth from him; and whosoeuer bringeth not necessary prouifion with him, is
wont to make great expenses, and to beare
with many incommodiryes, because he
taketh not vp his lodging in his own house
as the Religious doth, and whatsoeuer fer-
nice is done him, it is done for his money,
and not for loue, as is done in Religion.
Thou now seeft, how much better in this
kind the condition of a poore Religious
man is, then is that of the mighty & rich,
& this for nothing els, but for the Vow of
Pouerty, through the benefit wherof he enioyeth many priuiledges, and commodities
whereof he was not the authour or cause
himselfe.

8. It is indeed true, that the manner of a
Religious mans liuing and intertayning is
meane and slender, but if thou diligently
consider the conditions of it, thou wilt not
doubt to preferre it before the tables and
diet of great Princes. For firft, all that a Religious man eateth, is bestowed vpon him
for the loue of m: : all is prepared and
                                        dressed

dreſſed of loue: and all out of the ſame loue
of my ſeruants brought to the table afterwards: and whatſoeuer is ſet before him,
he eateth and drinketh without any ſuſpition at all. But what Prince is there in the
world, who is ſerued meerely, and purely
for the loue of God? In what Princes court
be things ſerued in ſo great peace, as in Religion? Whence come ſo many foretaſts in
Princes tables, but of the ſuſpition of poy-
ſon? And who ſeeth not, that a greater
eſteeme is to be made of loue and ſecurity
wherewith the Religious are ſerued, then
of all the magnificall miniſteryes & ſeruices
of Princes?

9.   The Religious alſo be not depriued
of their wonted attendance, euen in their
old age. But he that hath done ſeruice to
temporall Lords, when he once commeth
to be old, when he is ſcarce of ability to do
his wonted offices of ſeruice, though he be
not thruſt out of the houſe, is neuertheleſſe
hardly endured in the ſight of others, neither is vſed according to his deſeruings,
though he haue ſpent his whole life in his
Lords ſeruice, but is held for an vnprofitable perſon, not fit for any ſeruice. Contrariwiſe a poore Religious man, the more he is
aduanced in yeares, the more reſpect is had

M   of

of him, and the more commodiously is he treated: neither is there considered in him, what he doth for the present, but what he did before time, and all cast their eyes vpon him, as vpon my seruant, and a man consecrated to me. Not old age, but an vntoward and peruerse will causeth the Religious to fall from my grace and fauour. A spirituall Religious man, and aged, who can take no longer paynes, serueth me more profitably, then many strong and able yong men, and those voyd of spirit. I in my seruants consider not so much their forces and strength of body, as their will, and spirit, which waxeth old, and dyeth not through the fault of age, but of a peruerse custome.

10.   Finally, a Religious poore man is tended more carefully, more faythfully, and more louingly in sicknes, then be secular Lords. For they obserue the Phisitians prescriptions most exactly, and there be euer both day and night at hand those who attend them in their sicknes. If there be any daunger of life, they be admonished and put in mind in good time to prepare themselues to their death. At his dying many of my seruants are about him, with their prayers, and good exhortations, assisting him in his happy passage to another life. Certes, if a
    Religious

Religious man were to haue none other reward in this life, this alone ought to seeme vnto him inough, being so singular and excellent a thing, as many Princes, and great men of the world haue much desired it, and yet could not obtayne it. For how many of them haue ended their liues without any preparation going before , for that they were not put in mind of their danger? And how many againe, togeather with their temporall life haue lost the eternall? And if the reward of my Religious be such in this life, what wil that be, that is prepared for them in the next? What manner of crowne shall be giuen them in my Court for the Vow of Pouerty? How many great Lords astonished at their excesse of glory, will say : We esteemed their Pouerty nothing but madnes, but we were mad, and they wise indeed?

Of the necessity of the obseruing the Vow of Pouerty.

CHAP. XI.

IN my Ghospell I resembled riches vnto thornes, & worthily. For thornes hinder and let trauaylers in their way, that they cannot go on with expedition, because they

are

are afraid of the pricking of the thornes. In like manner the thornes taken in hand do pricke, and being pressed, they draw the bloud, and put a man to payne. Therefore great is the priuiledge of them, who haue left them beind, and whiles they are vpon their way, haue them no more in sight. For to handle the pricks of the thornes, & not to be prickt, if it be not impossible, at least it is very hard, and it profiteth little whether the pricks be great or small, many or few, because all do pricke, and euer pricke: Euen so riches do greatly hinder such as trauayle towards heauen, and do weary a man much with the bearing of them.

2. To haue any thing proper, and not to be affected vnto it, is not graunted to many, much lesse to all. The affection is that, which bringeth forth the thorns of cogitations, suspitions, & cares of gathering riches togeather, whereunto the more a man shall giue his mind, the more shall he be prickt and bebloudy himselfe. Wherfore not to abound in riches, or to be bound to leaue them, is an exceeding great benefit, and in it consisteth the Vow of Religious Pouerty.

3. But it is not inough, Sonne, to make Vowes, if they be not performed; for that the end of a Vow is to obserue it by deeds & actions.

actions. Remember therfore, that thou art bound of thyne owne accord to perpetuall Pouerty (which amongst the morall and religious vertues is the principall) and that the obligation was made in my sight. But by contrary works to exempt thy selfe from thy Vow, is nothing els, then to denounce war against the chiefest vertue of al, which thou hast chosen for thy Lady, and Patronesse, and therby so to incurre the punishment of violating thy obligation, that is, euerlasting damnation, & to offend me thy Creatour and Benefactour, who accepted thy Vow. And now iudge thou, how necessary it is for thee to stand to thy promises once made to me, which as they profit to saluation when they be well kept, so being broken they damne eternally.

4.   Lord, seeing riches be so troublesome and dangerous, and yet a man needeth meate, drinke, and cloathing necessary to the sustentation of life, it should be inough for thee, if we should at least be in the number of those poore, whome holy writ commendeth in these words: *Blessed is the man, who hath not gone after gold, nor hath put his hope in the treasures of money:* For so we might be possessed of some necessary things, the affection being remoued from the money, without

M 3   preiudice

preiudice or breach of the Vow of Pouerty.
It is true, Soune, that *Blessed is he who is not gone
after gold*: but the Scripture addeth by and
by after: *VVho is he, and we will prayse him?*
Who is he that desireth not gold? Who is
he that desireth not to keep it, after he hath
got it, and also to increase it? if thou go not
after gold, gold will come after thee, and
will like vnto thorns cleaue fast to thy cloathing, & though it pricke thee not, yet will
it hinder thy going. Wherefore the Vow of
Pouerty quite debarreth all possession of
ones owne, whether it be much or little.
Neither must thou be sollicitous about thy
meate, drinke, and cloathing: leaue that
care to me, let thine endeauour only be to
satisfy thy Vow of Pouerty, and I will prouide other necessaries. Who putteth his
hope in any other then God, he doth God
an iniury, and shall find himselfe deceiued.

5. Remember that Pouerty is called the
wall of Religion, and the mother of the Religious. As long as a Citties wall is found
and whole, it is easily defended and kept
from the incurfion of theeues, and enemies,
but if it be broken downe, or be decayed, the
enemy easily breaketh in, and spoyleth it.
Euen so Pouerty, which is the wall of Religious discipline, if it be either contemned

or

or neglected, so as some propriety be admitted, becometh obnoxious and subiect to the enemyes spoyle. And therfore need there is, thou keep and defend the wall, if thou desire to keep and gard thy selfe.

6. Who in time of warre watcheth vpon the walls, must haue two conditions. One that he watch, the other that he suffer not himselfe to be wonne with bribes. These two conditions be in a Religious man, that voluntarily imbraceth Pouerty, who liuing sparingly, is not molested, or ouerpressed with troubles in his sleep, and becaufe he is not a proprietary, his enemys do not eafily corrupt him with brybes. Wherfore there is not a more vigilant keeper, nor a more stout defender of the wall of Religion, then a truely Religious poore man. Besides, neceffary it is, that the City walls be often looked vpon, that where and when need is, they may be repaired, and strengthned. For if they shall begin once either to decay, or to bend and incline to one part, a remedy will hardly be found. So the Pouerty of Religió must often be examined, and looked into, that it be not in any part loofened, and if it happen to be, that it be repayred againe. For so Religion will be more strongly fortified, and the state therof the more secured. For

as

as the firſt drift of the enemy is to vnder-
mine and ouerthrow the walls of ſome bulwarke; ſo the greateſt care of them, who
defend it, muſt be, that the walls be conſer-
ued and kept.

7. It is alſo called the mother of the
Religious, becauſe Pouerty is that which
firſt communicateth to a Religious man his
very eſſence and nature, and nouriſheth and
bringeth him vp. True it is, that ſhe is ſom-
what ſeuere in the educatiō of her children,
not for that ſhe withdraweth frō them ſome
commodityes neceſſary, but rather ſuperflu-
ous: yet ſhe doth it for a good end, namely,
that her children may become valiant ſoul-
diers, and fight manfully againſt all kind of
vices. For ſhe well knoweth, that a man
brought vp in delicacy, and nothing accuſtomed to the enduring of labours, cannot
be a good ſouldier. Amongſt the conditions
of this mother one is, that to her children
that loue her, ſhe is deare and gratefull, and
to them that loue her not, ſeuere and ſterne;
and whoſoeuer is bound to be vnder the
gouernment of ſuch a Mother, if he ſhall refuſe to accommodate himſelfe vnto her, he
ſhall not be without a continuall affliction
all his life long.

8. If it diſpleaſe thee, Sonne, to haue
ſuch

such a Mother, remember that Pouerty hath
not chosen thee for her Sonne, but contrarywise, that thou hast chosen her for thy
Mother, & she accepted thee for her Sonne.
Thou also in regard of thy Vow art bound
perpetually to lead thy life with such a
Mother, and therfore it is not any longer in
thy power to leaue her off, thou being
bound to loue, honour, and defend her. Tell
me, should not that Sonne sinne grieuously,
who should handle his Mother ill & rudely,
or should thrust her out of her house? And
what other thing is it for thee to enioy and
vse some little thinges for the satisfying of
thyne owne desire, but wickedly to handle
thy Mother, Pouerty? And nothing to regard her, what is it els, then to driue her out
of thy hart, which is her habitation, and
house to dwell in? Take heed, my Sonne,
what thou dost, because all the hurt returneth vpon thine owne head, sith it is certaine, that she needeth not thy seruice, but
thou needest her help; neither canst thou
lead a Religious life without her : she is not
bound to thee, but thou to her. The Kingdome of heauen belongeth to the poore, but
he that will not know Pouerty for his
Mother, shall neither haue part in that inheritance which is the kingdom of heauen.

M 5   9. Lord

9.   Lord, I know and vnderstand wel, that to make the Vow of Pouerty, is nothing els, then to promise to thy maiesty, that I neither will haue, nor haue a will to haue any thing proper, and will lead my life in Pouerty. But I long to know, whether I can satisfy my Vow of Pouerty, if I possesse nothing of myne owne, and yet all things are pleasing vnto me, and agreable to my manner of doing.

10.   Sonne, as it pleaseth me, that euery one be prouided of thinges necessary : so it displeaseth me, if a Religious man either haue, or procureth to haue superfluityes. But what is necessary, or profitable, it is not for thee to iudge (for we be easily beguiled by our senses, or our owne affection) but thy Superiour. It is for the Superiour to iudge, what is conuenient for Pouerty. He is not poore who wanteth nothing, neither liueth he after the máner of the poore, who hath all things, as he listeth.

Of the defects, that are committed
against Pouerty.

CHAP. XII·

SONNE, he that is prouided of rents after the manner of poore, & yet will, like
vnto

vnto the rich, make great expences, goeth
greatly awry: for he shall within a while
find himselfe so sorely engaged, as he must
be forced to lye in prison, and there be punished, vntill he shall haue payed the very
last farthing. Whatsoeuer thou hast in Religion, is giuen thee by me, and for me, and
I haue giuen it thee, as to a poore man for
thy vse, and necessary for thy Religion.
But if thou wilt vse, and spend the thinges
of Religion, after the manner of the rich, at
thyne owne will, as though thou wert an
absolute owner thereof, it will fall out ill
with thee, because thou art one day to giue
a strait accompt of all. Thou hast forsaken
all that thou hast in the world, and that
thou mightest not vse them at thyne owne
will, thou art spoiled of them: Why then
doest thou in Religion thinke to vsurpe a
dominion vpon another mans goods, and
to dispose of them at thy list? This, certes,
is neither conuenient, nor pleasing to me.
Wherfore thou must needs resolue to vse the
thinges of Religion, as my things, and consecrated to me, and what is transferred to
thy owne vse, thou art to handle not as
thine, but as myne, allowed of me tothee by
thy Superiour, and that to serue thy vse as
long as it shall please me, so as it is in my
                                                    will

will to take it from thee, when it shall to
me seeme good.

2 . It doth displease me much, when a
Religious man is transported with so great
a desire to something that is permitted him
to vse, as he can hardly forgoe it againe,
when reason requireth. For what manner
of beast should that be, who being hired to
beare burdens, would not haue the instruments afterward taken from him, that were
fit to beare the burden with ease? Whatsoeuer Religion assigneth to euery one, it doth
it for my seruice, & whether I would take
something away from any, or permit him
to vse it still, he must not be therefore grieued, or troubled. An ouer great affection to
thinges lent, maketh them to become anothers.

3 . O how much do those Religious
offend me, who be ashamed to be poore, &
to weare a poore garment, or to vse a slender
dyet. For how can it be they should be a-
shamed for that, which is to them a glory,
by the benefit whereof they are raised to so
high a state, and maketh them like their
Lord and Maister? Could they be forgetfull
of their promise made of Pouerty? If they
haue not forgotten it, wherefore do they so
lightly esteeme it? What man is there in the
world,

world, who would be afhamed of his profeffion? And fith the Religious man hath
made a profeffion of Pouerty, and that publiquely, what is the caufe, that he is afhamed of it? Some feruants of myne did not fo
who now enioy eternall felicity in heauen,
who were rather confounded, if they found
any more poore then themfelues. Who is
afhamed of vertue, plainely declareth that
he loueth it not. An euill figne it is to hate
Pouerty, which is a principall vertue, and
proper to Religious life.

4. There be others, who are afhamed
of their parents pouerty; and fome againe
who brag and boaft of their riches, and
both of thefe be affections of a Religious
man ill mortified. That the Parents be rich,
is not a vertue, wherfore then fhould a Religious man glory of them? Yea the richer
they be, in the greater danger be the Religious, leaft they one day looke backe, and for
that caufe they haue greater matter of feare,
then of glorying. And that thy parents be
poore, was it through any fault of thyne? &
if not, wherfor fhoul lft thou be afhamed, or
afflicted for it? If to be poore in the world
fhould be a crime, thou fhouldeft haue a iuft
caufe of confufion: but it is not. Or if Pouerty fhould make the way to heauen more
hard,

hard, thou mightst worthily be fory, and complaine: but it is more then certaine, that the coming to it is made hard, not by Pouerty and want, but by riches. Wilt thou haue thy Parents rich? Procure then that they may be vertuous, & content with their estate: for so they shall be in Gods grace and friendship, which by many degrees surpasseth all the riches and honours of this life. The Religious man that hath a desire his Parents should be great and honorable in the world, and laboureth not that they be prouided of spirituall riches, sheweth himselfe to haue very little charity, and no spirit at all.

5. It is also a fore defect in the Vow of Pouerty, if a man thinke he hath done inough, when he possesseth nothing as his owne, and in the meane time is sollicitous, that he may want nothing. Certes, I see not how there can be any coherence betweene these two. To make a Vow of Pouerty, and not to haue a will to make a tryall of Pouerty: To be poore, and not to be willing to try the effect of it: To loue Pouerty, & yet to haue a will to be far off from it. I was my selfe poore, for that in the whole course of my life I experienced the effects of Pouerty, by suffering hunger, thirst, heat, cold, wearines,

wearines, nakednes, and a thousand incommodityes . I loued Pouerty, and therefore
I would haue it to accompany me to my
Crosse , where I was nayled naked vnto it.
My Apostles also , and some of my disciples
and followers suffred many incommodities
of Pouerty, euen vntill their dying day. But
thou not only seekest no occasion of suffering any thing, after the manner of poore
persons, in thy meate, drinke, & cloathing,
but further most carefully, and importunely
thou seekest for what is best, and more commodious, and if thou haue it not, thou art
troubled, and murmurest for it, and which
is worse, thou oftentymes pretendest necessity and health, when it is thy meere sensuality . He is not poore, who shunneth the
incommodityes of the poore . O how did
those Religious please me, who notwithstanding they were destitute of ordinary
things, and of necessary sometimes also, yet
complained not , nor were sory for it , but
with ioy sayd : This is to be a poore one of
Christ, his name be euer blessed for it .

6. Those also, who are not content with
the common entertainment of Religion ,
but without iust cause desire either some
particularityes, or not necessaryes, do sorely
weaken, yea and ouerthrow their Vow of
Pouerty

Pouerty. For in the one there is meere super-
fluity; in the other there be made expenses
without necessity, and both of them be repugnant to Pouerty, whereof it is commonly sayd, *As much as is inough, and no more*.
To vse parsimony in the things of Religiō,
and to spend them but when necessity requireth, is not misery (as the haters of Pouerty will haue it) but an act of vertue, because Pouerty exacteth it.

7. It is also a vice and fault, repugnant
to Religious Pouerty, both to take thinges
without the Superiours leaue, and to giue
them vnto others. For whatsoeuer is giuen
to a Religious man, is the Religious, not
the mans, who cannot haue any thing proper, and therfore if he accepteth of gifts, he
sheweth himselfe a proprietary: so if he giueth any thing to another, he maketh a shew
that himselfe is the owner therof, and both
the one and the other, that is, propriety, &
dominion be repugnant to Religious Pouerty. Neither is that Religious man altogeather free from fault, who accepteth, or
giueth things of very little value, sith in
the Vow of Pouerty there is not any excep-
tion made of things little or great, but he
hath absolutly promised, that he will not
vsurpe any propriety in any thing, either
little

little or great, nor take any dominion to
himselfe therein. An errour in little and
light things, doth not forgo the name of an
errour.

8. Finally Pouerty is an hurt, when
the expenses be superfluous, and the thinges
that be bought, be rather curious and faire,
then profitable and necessary. He that is
truely poore, and imbraceth Pouerty with
sincerity, laboureth to do what it required
and no more. For what difference is it for
a religious man to haue a faire guilded book
or a garment sowed with silke; when as a
booke not guilded might serue him as well
as guilded, and a garment sown with common thrid, would be as good for him, as
sowne with silke? And if the one consor-
teth more with Pouerty, then the other,
why will he not conforme himselfe to Pouerty? In like manner tell me, I pray thee,
what is the cause, that a Religious man retayneth and keepeth other mens things in
his chamber, that do him no good, and yet
might profit others? Is not that superfluous,
that hindreth anothers good?

9. Sonne, thou hast a desire to be receiued into the number of the poore, either in
earth or in heauen. If in earth, it is inongh
that thou hast made a Vow of Pouerty, and

N   be

be reckoned amongst the poore, and if in
heauen, it is not inough , but further there
is required thou be poore in deed, that is,
that thou cut off all superfluityes, and exercise thy selfe continually euen till death in
the acts of Pouerty ; and this is to be a true
Religious man. He is not to be numbred in
the company of my poore, who will aboūd
in superfluityes, neither shall he come to the
reward of the poore, who shall not haue
made a tryall of the effects of Pouerty.

*Of the Vow of Chastity , and what Religi-
ous Chastity is, & the proper office therof.*

CHAP. XIII.

SONNE, if the vertue of Chastity were
not, it would be greatly amisse with man
sith the concupiscence of the flesh is of that
nature and condition , that if it were not
restrayned in time , it would make a man
(otherwise indued with reason and vnderstanding) in a short time like a brute beast.
For the pleasure and itching of the senses do
so obscure and blind a mans mind, as they
draw it into all manner of filth and vncleanes: whence it cometh to passe, that when
the will is abandoned of iudgment and aduise, a man runneth in a miserable manner
headlong

headlong into all wickednes . Hence it is ,
that a man giuen to the pleasures of the flesh
is spoyled of all courage & power of doing
well, speaketh & thinketh not of any other
thing, then of lasciuiousnes and carnality ,
nor wisheth any other thing, then that he
may al his life long haue hisfill of such kind
of delights and pleasures, and for this cause
he also hateth the other life . Neither doth a
carnall mans madnes stay heere, but his hatred further extendeth it selfe to his Creatour, who hath by his law prohibited those
foule pleasures of the flesh, and condemned
them . In a sensuall man the sense fayleth ,
and the fault increaseth .

2.   Another condition of concupiscence
is, that there is no good which a sensual man
contemneth not, nor any euill that he committeth not, so he may enioy and compasse
what he vnlawfully desireth . He hath no
regard or consideration of riches , which
for the satisfying of his lust and sensuality ,
he wasteth not : he exposeth his life to a
thousand daungers : he hath no care of his
health at all : he respecteth not the doing a-
gainst his conscience, and to hurt his owne
soule, so he may enioy his desires . Finally
he preferreth his carnalityes before all that
is both in earth and heauen . He becometh

sensuall

senſuall and beaſtly, who exerciſeth beaſtly actions.

3. A third condition of concupiſcence is, that it is neuer ſatisfyed, but increaſeth more and more by ſenſuall pleaſures, and ſetteth the body ſo on fire, as no feuer though neuer ſo burning and hoate, ſo ſore tormenteth a man, as doth the concupiſcence ; nor any fury of hel is ſo turmoyled, or in ſo great torments, as is a luxurious man, whoſe burning and raging heate is ſo great, as it may ſeeme not poſſible to be extinguiſhed, but by death . The fleſh firſt tyeth a man faſt, next it blindeth him, and laſtly it tormenteth him. Who hath no will to be thus handled, let him not put himſelf into the fleſhes tormenting hands.

4. With this peſtiferous, and vnruly wild beaſt the vertue of Chaſtity is to make warre, who being called on for her ayde, willingly preſenteth her ſelfe, & greatly repreſſeth the fury of this beaſt, and abateth the concupiſcences heat. Wherfore it is the generall office and charge of Chaſtity to moderate and direct all the deſires of the ſenſes according to the rule of reaſon, by yealding vnto euery degree of Continency what is conuenient and no more. And becauſe there be diuers degrees of Continency, there

there be also diuers permissions and prohi-
bitions therof which she prescribeth. In the
first and lowest degree is the continency of
the married, who are only forbidden
vnlawfull pleasures. In the second is that
of widowes; in the third that of the single
and vnmarried, who do not only renounce
vnlawfull pleasures of the flesh, but also the
lawfull which they might enioy without
sinne, if they had a will to marry. In the
fourth degree is Continency of Virgins,
which as it is more perfect then the aforesaid, so deserueth it a greater reward, the
perfection wherof consisteth not only in a
firme purpose of contayning from all manner of venereous pleasures, but also in the
perpetual conseruation of virginal Chastity.
In the fifth and highest degree is placed the
cōtinency of religious, which though it be
not sometymes Virginall, is yet in perfectiō
more excellent then the rest, for that it is
by Vow consecrated vnto me, which because it is an act of excellent Charity, and
of the greatest of all the morall vertue, namely of Religion, causeth greatest perfection, and excellency to Religious Continency.

5. Now the law of Chastity comman-
deth Religious Continency to exercise three

offices worthy of it selfe. The first is, to conserue the purity of the flesh, whereunto is
required a great courage. For sith the flesh
of it selfe is prone to incontinency, and impurity, a great alacrity and courage of mind
is necessary towards the keeping of it vnder,
that a man, who naturally loueth and fauoureth his owne flesh, nor easily suffereth
it to be afflicted, giue it not the bridle ouer
much, nor plunge himselfe into the myre &
puddle of carnall pleasures. A second office
is to keep a gard ouer the senses, and therunto needeth vigilancy, and diligence. For
seing the senses be wandring and slipery, &
present a thousand occasions of such pleasures, vnles a Religious man shal be very diligent in keeping them, they will easily
breake out beyond their bands. The third
office is to conserue the purity of the mind
vnstayned, wherein circumspection is very
necessary for the considering & examining
of what is admitted thereunto. And if there
be any thing that may stayne or infect, it
must be kept out, for that it is more easy to
keep it from entring, then to thrust it out,
after it be entred.

6.   Sonne, this is the law of Religious
Chastity, and these be the offices thereof.
If thou desire to be holpen thereby, seeing
for

for that end thou requirest the ayde of it,
thou must also needs fauour it, and not deny
it thyne help, that it may discharge it
owne office. If thou shouldst deny this thou
shouldst do, as if thou calledst a Phisitian
home-vnto thee, but wouldst not haue him
to touch the sicke mans wound for feare of
the payne, or loathing that would follow.
This is not the way of curing the sicke body, but of increasing his sicknes rather. The
body inured to pleasure, is wont to complaine, that Chastity is euer exact and seuere in
executiō of the precepts of her laws, which
forbids many things and permits few. But
these be the complaints of the nyce, delicate
and sensuall sicke, who ordinarily desire &
long for the things that be most hurtfull
vnto them, which if they be yealded vnto,
do hurt them, and therefore such things be
more discretly denyed them. Suffer the Phisitian my Sonne, to put his hand to the yron;
for the loathsome sore of carnall concupiscence, vnles it be launced in tyme, will easily grow to a festred, and pestiferous impo-
stume. He that will not with a very little
payne be cured as he ought, shall be els
where eternally tormented, as he deserueth.

of

CHAP. XIIII.

SONNE, man consisteth of two parts,
the owne called the inferiour and sensuall, appertayning to the body: the other
the superiour and reasonable, appertayning
to the soule. When he was created in the
terrestriall Paradise, as long as he continued
in his state of innocency, he enioyed great
peace also, because the inferiour part was in
perfect subiection, and obeyed the superiour
part, neither was it so hardy as to resist.
But after that man did by sinne make resi-
stance against his Creatours will, he fell
from that happy and peacable state of innocency, & the inferiour part began to rebell
against the superiour, that is Reason : and
hauing also, out of a pride, a will to vsurpe
her authority, it fell also shamefully; for
that reiecting the counsaile of Reason, it
began to attend wholy to pleasures . Hence
arose the warre, that is now made between
the Sense, and Reason. By this, man became
spoyled of his former peace and tranquility
& for that cause he was driuen to gard himselfe with the help of vertues for the bringing of sensuality vnder the subiection of
Reason. And amongst these vertues Chastity

ftity hath a principall place , which if it
once find an entrance into Reafons kingdome , and into the fuperiour part of the
foule, like a prudent and wife Lady fhe cō-
mandeth the fenfuall part to hold it felfe
within it owne bounds , and to yeald foue-
raignity to reafon. Hence it is, that the firft
excellency of Chaftity is to reftore man, as
much as may be , into his former ftate and
poffeffion of innocency wherein he was
created, and to honour him with that ornament of purity, which he did weare before
in the terreftriall Paradife.

2 . Chaftity is alfo called an Angelicall
vertue, becaufe it maketh man like vnto an
Angell, while it caufeth him to lead an Angels life. For though man of his own nature
be in the middeft between Angels & beafts,
for that the conditions of both haue place
in him ; though he be fuperiour to thefe, &
inferiour to thofe, yet is he fomtymes beaft-
like, fometimes againe Angel-like. Beaft-
like, when the fenfuality in the encounter
with the fuperiour part, goeth away with
victory , and hath a commaunding hand
ouer Reafon, and caufeth a man to plunge
himfelf fo deep in the boggs of terrene pleafures, as he maketh himfelfe vncapable of
the heauenly, & as a brute beaft, reciueth no
taft

taſt of ſpirituall matter at all . But when
Chaſtity is once got into the kingdome of
the mind, the warre commeth to a far different concluſion . For Chaſtity in the firſt
place layeth hand vpon ſenſuality, impri-
ſoneth her, and ſetteth Reaſon in her owne
place and authority of gouernment and
commaund. Next it prouideth that the ſpirit hold the fleſh vnder, and in ſubiection ,
and this is to be Angell-like . And though a
man be agreably to his nature faſt tyed to his
fleſh, and whiles he is in this baniſhment,
trauayleth vp and downe in fleſh , yet becauſe through benefit of Chaſtity he liueth
not according to the fleſh, he is ſaid to lead
an Angells life . And he that on earth liueth as an Angell, ſhall in heauen ſhine alſo
as the Angells do .

3.   Againe, Chaſtity raiſeth a man vp to
the performing of great and wonderfull
thinges : contrariwiſe the intemperance of
the fleſh abuſeth him to abiect & moſt contemptible things. Experience teacheth, that
ſuch as purſue the fleſhes pleaſures, do not aſpire to the effecting of noble and heroicall
matters, and more then that, whiles they ſee
themſelues faſt tyed and caught in the fleſhs
ſnares , they drowne themſelues ouer head
and eares in the puddle of luſts . This vice
                                                            alſo

also so dulleth mans wit , as it doth not only lay a bar and impediment to his progresse and profiting in discipline and arts , but also bringeth in a forgetfullnes of those thinges that were learned before . On the contrary side, Chastity as it is an Angelicall and celestiall vertue, so doth it rayse a man to the execution of generous and most noble workes .

4.   The founders of Religions, if they had not lead chast liues , had neuer gone about so great, and hard matters, as the foundations of new Religions be : neither could the Apostles, when they preached the Ghospell, haue moued the world, or haue done other great matters, which they did, if they had been cumbred with wiues & children . Those therfore who imbrace purity both of mind and body, be more apt to receaue the cleare light of my grace , to contemplate matters of heauen, the mysteries of the Diuinity, the blessed Spirits, the greatnes and excellency of the eternall felicity, and of the goods prepared for the vertuous in heauen . Whence it is, that man also, though still liuing in a mortall body , if he conserue his integrity of body and mind, doth euen now in part begin to enioy the pleasures of Paradise.

5 . Neither

5. Neither is this the least of Chastities excellencyes, that it so beautifieth and setteth forth a mans soule, as it maketh it most gratefull to myne eyes. For though all vertues adorne the soule, and euery one giue it a particuler ornament, yet Chastity, becaufe it conferueth it from all stayne of the flesh, maketh it most pure and most beautifull: as contrarywise the vice of the flesh maketh it so fowle and vgly, as though it be prouided of all other moral vertues, yet may it hardly be endured. The externall beauty of times is an occafion of the foules perdition: but Chastity, which is the foules beauty, befides that, that it is most acceptable to God, procureth both the foules and bodyes good togeather.

6. Finally Religious Chastity, though it be of it felfe noble & excellent, receyueth yet greater splendour and perfection from many other thinges. For first it is greatly ennobled by Vow, by vertue whereof a Religious man hath renounced all kind of pleasures, whether the fame appertayne to the body and fenfes, or to the mind and internall facultyes therof. Againe it boroweth no fmal excellency from the very fountaine and origen thereof, which is a fincere and perfect loue of me. For a Religious man

moued

moued not of any neceffity, or hope of commodity, nor for any other human refpect is
induced to forfake all pleafures of the flefh,
but only for the pleafing of me. And therefore Religious Chaftity is the more commendable for this, becaufe it is endued
with moft perfect Charity, which is the
nurfe and mother thereof. No little fplen-
dour and perfection alfo is added vnto it by
the end and fcope that Religious Chaftity
hath propofed : and this end is nothing els,
then my honour and glory, and therfore the
Religious bind themfelues to perpetuall
Chaftity, for that by it Gods feruice is in a
wonderfull fort amplified, and fo it is no
meruayle, though Religious Chaftity chal-
lengeth the firft place amongft all the degrees of Chaftity. The more excellent and
perfect Chaftity is, the more it communicateth to them that loue it.

7.   Wherefore, Sonne, feeing Chaftity is
fo noble & excellet, I do not hold it inough
if thou imbrace it after a meane manner, or
haue an earneft defire vnto it, as to a moft
precious Iewell ; but I could rather wifh,
thou wouldeft alfo confecrate thy felfe therunto, as to a thing, that did moft of al pleafe
me. And know thou, that I do aboue all
things loue a pure and chaft hart, and loue
it

it so affectuously, as I not only with a singular ioy repose therin, & enrich it with sundry gifts, but also nothing can be required of me, that I do not gratiously impart vnto it. And this alone should set euery Religious mans mind on fire to desire this heauenly gemme, wonderfully shining, not only in the company of vertues on earth, but also in heauen amongst the company of the blessed. The more tenderly thou shalt loue Chastity, the more thou shalt be loued of God, and if thou canst not loue it, as much as it deserueth, at least loue it in what thou art able.

How greatly conuenient it is for a Religious man to be chast.

CHAP. XV.

LORD, I well vnderstand, that it is very conuenient, that he be chast, who attendeth to thy seruice, considering by the benefit of his Vow he is consecrated and bound to thee, the fountaine of all purity. It is nothing agreable, that vnder a cleane and pure head the members should be filthy and fowle. But I know not how I may long defend my Chastity, sith I haue at home a capitall enemy, who trusting to both in-

ward and outward helps, becometh so stout
& hardy, as I almost despaire of the victory.
Now thou knowest, o Lord, how sore this
insolent and proud flesh persecuteth the purity of my soule. Thou art not ignorant,
how many assaults it maketh night and
day vpon it. And yet this doth not make
me afraid. Another thing perplexeth and
troubleth me much more, that is, that both
the wantonesse and rebellion of the senses
within, and the most cruell enemy Sathan
without, do minister helps vnto it.

2. Sonne, what thou sayst is most true,
but thou must not be dismayd for it : for the
greater that the enemies boldnes & power is,
the more glorious wil the victory & crown
be that followeth after. Neither shalt thou
want my help, only play thou the man, and
vse all thy forces for the maintayning of
Chastity, and no enemy from within or
without shall get the victory from thee.
And seeing thou acknowledgest, and con-
fessest also, that it is conuenient, that my
Religious seruants be chast, as I their Lord
am ; know thou that I was euer so harty a
louer of purity, as myne aduersaries, who
calumniated me in very many things, durst
not accuse or condemne me of the very least
defect against Chastity. And that the Religious

gious ought to be such their state exacteth,
sith they make a profession to be my followers, & imitators of my life . Wherfore
seing I was exceedingly affected to this
vertue of Chastity, and regarded it as the
guid of a spirituall life, requisite it is , that
they also imbrace and take it for their Lady
and Mistresse.

3. And because I make so high an esteem
of purity, and am in the highest degree a-
uerted from the vice of concupiscence, why
wouldst thou haue me to entertayne a dis-
honest seruant within my house? or that I
should endure him in the same? How should
I suffer, that any seruice should be done me
by him, whom I know to haue an vncleane
mind ? The seruant that accommodateth
not himselfe to his Lord and Maister, or neglecteth to procure his loue and good will,
either will not be long stable in his office,
or if he continue in it, will make very little
profit therby, and will put himselfe in danger of being thrust out , to his owne great
hurt, and no little shame and confusion. Do
I require at my seruants hands any thing
vnfitting, vnseemly, or impossible? I require
purity, which is a principall vertue: I require of him, that he suffer not himselfe to
be supplâted or ouercome by his sensuality,
and

and this is honorable . I exact of him, that
which he hath promised, and that is to liue
chastly, which is a point of iustice.

4.   Further, I long to kno w , wherein
consisteth to leaue and forsake the world ?
Not that a man giue ouer to liue vnder heauen, or to dwell on earth, or to draw this
ayre (for all these be necessary, and as common to secular men, as to Religious) but
that he lead a life far different from that
of the world . Amongst the euills of this
world one is, to neglect spirituall things, &
to seeke after the pleasures, & contentments
of the flesh . The Religious therfore , who
forsake the world in sincerity, must lead a
life in conuersation and manners contrary
to the world, by mortification of their desires, by a renunciatiō of the senses delights,
and by a contemning of whatsoeuer this
blind world loueth and imbraceth : and in
brief, their conuersation must be in heauen .
But nothing so much contradicteth the desire of heauenly things, & nothing is so preiudiciall to the tast of spirituall matters, as is
incontinency: whiles on the contrary , nothing promoteth a Religious man so to the
leading of an heauenly life, as doth Chastity
alone, which as it conserueth the mind pure
so doth it rayse a Religious man to the con-
O   templation

templation of heauenly thinges. The furrther thy life is off from that of the world, the more secure shall thy Chastity be, and vpon earth will sooner further thee to the leading of a celestiall life.

5.   Sonne, doest thou conceiue the cause why any vnchast man, euen amongst the heathens, neuer came to so great impudency as he durst publiquely in the presence of others commit any lasciuious act, but rather confounded in himselfe, would seek about for corners, and hidden places, wherby to hide and couer his fault. Naturall light hath taught him, that all acts of vncleanes be vnworthy the sight of men, and therefore he seeketh corners, and hideth himselfe, fearing least he should attempt, or do any thing against his honour, and the rule of reason. Wherefore if an act repugnant to Chastity be vnworthy an heathen, how much more vnworthy a Christian, in whose law the vice of concupiscence is condemned. And much more vnworthy be they in a Religious man, who hath professed Chastity, and bound himselfe by solemnity of Vow also to liue chastly. And though a man in committing any foule act of carnality auoydeth to be seen of men, yet shall he not escape the sight of God, who is euery where, and beholdeth

holdeth all thinges.

6.   That one man subiecteth himselfe
for loue of me to another, his inferiour, de-
pending vpon his will, and obeying him in
all things, is both honorable, and very meritorious, for that whatsoeuer is done for the
loue of me, is done to me, and it is my part
to remunerate & reward it. But that a man
placed in a high estate, should to his owne
great hurt and reproach subiect himselfe to
a vile thing, and inferiour to himselfe, is repugnant to my will, who am Lord also
of man. Go too now, tell me my Son, whether it be more conuenient, that a Religious
man subiect himselfe to the sensuall part,
namely to the hand-mayd, or to permit,
that reason, as the mistresse commaund him.
And if this be more conuenient, & not that,
it is more meete also, that a Religious man
make an esteeme of Chastity, by help wherof he may bring the hand-mayd *Concvpiscence*
in subiection to *Reason*, her lawful mistresse.
He that putteth himselfe vnder 'him that he
should not, is also handled in the manner
that he would not.

7.   Sonne, he that hath enemyes, hath
need of a guard for his person. And as he,
who hath them within and without his
hold, is in the greater danger, so needeth he
greater

greater help, especially if both sorts of enemyes, both within and without, shall conspire togeather. But what should he deserue,
who by putting his enemyes into prison,
had deliuered his castle from danger? He
should deserue, no doubt, to obtayne of the
Gouernour of the Castle whatsoeuer he
would.

8.   Sonne, thou hast one domesticall &
troublesom enemy within, namely thy flesh,
and two without, to witt, the world and
the diuell, who are ioyned in a confederacy
togeather, and seeke to inuade & breake into the fortresse of thy hart. How much then
may Chastity deserue at thy hands, which,
by the ouerthrow of thy flesh, and beastly
desires, thy domesticall enemyes, exempteth thee out of so great a danger? Iudge
thou, how great esteeme thou oughst to
make of Chastity, which is both thy faythfull friend, and a capitall enemy of thyne
enemyes? Consider if it were not thy part
to fauour her, sith she so greatly fauoureth
and helpeth thee. Thou must needs be ingrate, if thou forbeare to choose her for the
gouernesse of thy hart, that she may conserue it free from all impurity, and defend it
from the guiles of crafty concupiscence.
Who acknowledgeth not his owne misery
                                                and

and danger, is nothing follicitous about any to help him.

How profitable and neceffary it is, that a Religious man be chaft.

CHAP. XVII.

IN euery white and pure thing, the very leaft ftayne appeareth, and the whiter it is, the more plainly doth the fpot difcouer it felfe. Euen fo in a Religious life, be-caufe it is moft white & pure, the very leaft defect of purity is obiected to the eyes, and offendeth them that fee it. Secular men haue Religious for certaine fpectacles of vertues: but a looking-glaffe difpleafeth, vnles it be all cleare and fhining. In other vertues a light default neuer offendeth fo much, or doth fo great hurt in a Religious man, as doth a defect in Chaftity. A Reli-gious man doth not eafily incurre the loffe of his good name, if either he tranfgreffe fomewhat againft meeknes, becaufe he is by nature cholerike, or be not very franke and liberall, or feeketh after a little vayne glory, or be not perfectly humble, or fall into fome like defect. But if he commit but fome very little matter againft Chaftity, he forthwith obfcureth the opinion of his good name.

For euery wise man iudgeth that a Religious man, though he be neuer so hard, and fast handed, may yet be an holy man. In like manner one by nature cholerike, or somewhat curious, may yet be pious and deuout: but when they come to Chastity, the contrary is conceyued, namely, that there cánot be any holines, where incontinency is, nor that the deuotion can be sincere, where the perturbations of mind beare sway: neither can there be spirit, where the flesh commaundeth. Besides, the defects of other vertues be easily excused, either for that they grow of a naturall complexion, as choller, or for that they proceed of a good end and intention, as is sparing and frugality: but a defect of carnall concupiscence is condemned of all, and excused of none.

2.   All thinke Religious men to be as it were the Salt of the Earth, and the Light of the World, as my Scripture speaketh, and therfore they need to take paynes, that the true propertyes of salt and light may concurre in them. Salt with the sharpnes drieth vp the humors, and preserueth from putrifaction, but if it be not pure, or be mixed with earth, it not only not preserueth, but also causeth putrifaction the sooner. So if a Religious man be pure, and sincere in his

words,

words, & counsailes, he will easily conserue
others, but if he be vncleane & stayned with
a little stayne of carnal desires, he will by his
bad example easily marre them . Light also
serueth to giue light, and to shew where the
dangers and downfalls be, but if the candles
weeke be either foule, or moist , it yealdeth
more of smoke then of light. So a Religious
man, if he haue not a pure and cleane hart,
will not only not enlighte, but also obscure,
and darken the way , that both himselfe, &
all that do accompany him, may shamefully
stumble , and so giue a greater stincke and
smell, then light . He shall haue much a do
to conserue & enlighten others, who neglecteth to keep and giue light to himselfe.

3 . Moreouer the Religious life is so tender and delicate, as not only the defect of
purity, but the very least suspition of incor-
tinency also hurteth a Religious man much.
Who would esteeme that matrone for wise,
who should for help and counsailes sake go
to a Religious man , suspected of incontinency? Is it not an extreme misery , that a
Religious man consecrated to me, should be
ill reported of ? Certes , the Religious person, that should make no reckoning of his
good name with his neighbour, receyueth
no good by him neither. O how grieuously
do

do thofe Religious men finne, who do not
beware of falling into the occafions of being infamed by fuch a vice, but perfwade
themfelues, that it is inough, if they commit
nothing that is euill by deed, whatfocuer
men fay and report of them. They are not
without fault, if they giue but the occafiõs
of fuch obloquies and detractions : for they
are bound not only to fly from the vice it
felfe, but alfo to take away all fufpition
therof· He that hateth the Diuell, will not
eafily endure to fee him painted.

4.   It is nothing conuenient to thruft a
man againft reafon out of his owne houfe,
neither can it be done in confcience. Remember, Sonne, that thy hart is my Temple
and my houfe. I haue layd the foundations
of it, raifed and perfected the building, and
whatfocuer is faire and precious in it, hath
come from me. And that this houfe might
be euer beautifull, & that I might ftill make
my aboad and habitation therein, I deliuered it to the keeping of Chaftity, a trufty &
vigilant keeper. But if thou wouldeft now
thruft me againft all reafon out of it, thou
canft not do it without moft grieuous fa-
criledge. And if thou haft a will to driue
Chaftity out of the houfe of thy hart, that
concupifcence may commaund in it, thou
                                              mayft

mayst not do that also without a great crime. He that thrusteth out him, of whome
he is holpen and honoured, will easily fall
into the hands of some one, who will handle him according to his desertes.

5. Tell me, I pray thee, when thou
vowedst perpetuall Chastity, what didst
thou promise to God ? Didst thou not promise, that thou wouldst from thenceforth
make warre against all carnal pleasures both
of body and mind ? Didst thou not promise
to perseuere chast to thy liues end? Dost thou
not therefore thinke, that thou art bound
necessarily to performe thy promise, sith
thou canst not look any more backe? Knowest thou not, what my Apostle sayth : Who
shall violate, or defile Gods Temple, God
will destroy him? And if thou for some litle
carnall pleasure driuest me out of thy hart,
with what right canst thou challeng of me
to be receiued into the kingdom of heauen?
And if for a little pleasure of the senses ; by
defyling thy hart, thou abusest Chastity,
wherefore shouldst thou exact her to bring
thee to the vision of God, promised to the
cleane of hart alone? Vnderstand therefore
that it is no way good for thee in the very
least thing to offend against Chastity, because thou hast by Vow of Chastity promised

mised no way to preiudice her purity, neither in great matters, nor in little.

6. It is further necessary that a Religious
man aspire to the perfection of Chastity for
this, for that he hath made a profession of
leading a spirituall life, which sith it hath
not a more sworne enemy, then the concupiscence of the flesh, cannot possibly liue a
spirital life, vnles the flesh be first brought in
subiection to the spirit. For the Religious
who is truely spirituall, must not only be a
stranger to the vice of the flesh, but also be
auerted from all those, that haue their origen from the flesh, or haue any dealing with
it at all. And therfore he must diligently, &
carefully exclude and keep out all bad cogitations, & impure suggestions. In his talke
he must be circumspect, that any words fall
not from his mouth, that may seem against
honesty. He must not cast his eyes vpon
lasciuious acts, though they should be done
without sinne. And these be helps for the
mortification of the flesh. But I would haue
thee, Sonne, to consider and obserue, that the
flesh sometyms faigneth it selfe dead, when
it is not, & pretendeth it selfe to be in most
great subiection to the spirit. But then a
wise and spirituall Religious man must be
most of all vpon his gard; for it is accustomed

med to diſſemble the matter vpon hope of
commodityes, and of greater liberty, and in
tyme it perſwadeth the Religious man to
withdraw ſomewhat of his former rigour,
ſith it was ready to yeald moſt prompt ſeruice to the ſpirit. But he that will not be
deceiued, or beguyled by the crafty fleſh,
muſt vſe the counſaile of his ſpiritual father.
There is no truſt to be had to a diſſembling
enemy, becauſe by his faigning he diſco-
uereth himſelfe.

Of the vtility of Religious Chaſtity.
CHAP. XVII.

SONNE, when I did in my Ghoſpel vnder the name of Eunuches commend
them who do for the loue of me voluntarily
make the Vow of perpetuall Chaſtity (for
this is to make himſelfe an Eunuch, and
to geld himſelf for the kingdom of heauen)
I did intend that very thing, becauſe a man
by ſuch a Vow, as it were with one ſharpe
cut of a knife, cutteth off all power, and occaſions of vſing carnall pleaſures. For what
is not any longer lawfull, is truly ſayd to be
impoſſible. And hauing commended theſe
my chaſt Eunuches, I added, *He that can take,
let him take.* For I knew, that all would not
vnderſtand

vnderstand the most great vtilityes, that perpetuall continency bringeth to the Religious. I omit to mention heere, how by the
benefit of it they are freed from infinit molestations and troubles, and the reprochfull
insolencyes of the flesh, which if it get once
but the least commaund, casteth headlong,
euen wise men into the bottomles gulfe of
vices. And if the care of outward riches be
troublesome for the sollicitude they bring
with them, much more cumbersome is the
concupiscence, which because it is home-
bred, woundeth more sorely, and therefore
the wounds therof be the more deadly.

2.   I say nothing that they be eased of
many afflictions, and carking cares of gouerning their house, which be otherwhiles
so troublesome, as they bring men to desperation. It appertayneth to the maister of the
family to prouide for his wife, for the good
bringing vp of his children, for the placing
of his daughters in marriage, to take care
that no necessary thing be wanting, that
the seruants of both sexes do their duty. And
if all in that family be good and modest and
well ordred, and yet there is no want of
troubles; what will there then be, if many
of them be peruerse, vntoward, and vnruly?
I pretermit, that the Religious by the benefit

fit of the fayd Vow be deliuered from the
fufpitions of wife and children, which are
wont otherwhiles fo to torment the huf-
bands, as therby they become almoft mad,
and out of their wits. Finally I forbeare to
remember other infinite incommodityes, &
vnluckly euents, which happen vnexpe-
cted in families, and are wont wonderfully
to vexe and trouble the maifters of the family. Wo be to thofe Religious men, who free
from fo many impediments and fnares, do
not labour to the perfection of their ftate.

3. Religious Chaftity then cutteth off
all thefe troubles, and vnquiet thoughts, &
caufeth the Religious man, as a Cittizen of
heauen, content with his vocation, to attend only to the cotemplation of heauenly
things, and to the procuring of his owne
foules good. And how healthfull and profitable this is, thofe Religious know well,
who farre remoued from the fayd bufines
of imployment, do liue a fingle life. The
afflicted men of the world alfo are not ignorant therof, who to their great hurt, and
griefe haue a dayly experience of thofe troubles and miferies. And if there were nothing els, then to thinke how to pleafe their
wiues, how to appeare the before world,
how to content their kins-folks & friends,
this

this were a crosse heauy inough to beare as long as they liue. But the chast Religious need not to thinke vpon any other thing, then how to please me. O how much more ealy it is to please me, then the world, and how much sooner the Creatour is satisfyed, then the Creature. Whosoeuer in this life pleaseth God most, shall haue the higher place of honour in his court of Heauen.

4. Againe the secular man, tyed in marryage, hath no power of his owne body, but the wife hath a commaund ouer it. For so writteth my Apostle, & it is most true, that the law of Matrimony requireth it. And is not this a kind of seruitude to beat the commaund of a Woman? and seing it is not for one yeare, nor for ten, but for the whole life is it not a continuall seruitude? It is indeed to be confessed, that the tribulation is the lesse, if the man happen vpon a vertuous wife, and yet it looseth not the name of seruitude. But when he lighteth vpon a vayne impuder, quareling, or scolding wife, what is it but an hell? How great is the husbands misery? What bound sloue is worse handled then he? But a chast Religious man hath to do with Chastity, that is, a benigne vertue, he hath to deale with me, who though his Lord and Maister, yet a most louing & kind Father.

Father. And to serue me by Vow of Chastity, is nothing els, then to heap vp store of merits, and to increase them. Vnhappy is the man, who by his seruing others profiteth himselfe nothing: but more vnhappy is he, who sustayneth detriment also, and losse of the things he hath.

5. Moreouer, he that is forced to keep company both night & day with a cruell & enuenimed wild beast, is in a manifest hazard of his life, either by his byting or impoysoning him. But if a man could be able to stop vp the beasts mouth, that he could neither bite him, nor spit out the poyson at him, he could not but profit and do himselfe good. Senne, no wild beast is more cruell, nor more full of venime, then is our flesh, rebelling & venime wherof destroyeth & killeth the soule. And seing we be forced to haue the continuall company thereof with vs, no doubt our soule must needs be in great perill, from which Chastity deliuereth it. For whiles by the band of Vow it bindeth the concupiscence, which is the beasts mouth, it so prouideth that it can neither byte, nor cast forth it poyson. He is not worthy of commiseration and pitty, who suffreth himselfe to be bitten of a beast chayned and tyed vp: neither deserueth that man pardon,

who

who contemneth the helps prefented vnto him.

6. When any tumult or ftyr arifeth in a common wealth, for the quietting thereof neceffary it is, that he who firft caufed it, be forthwith laid hold on : for when the vulgar and common fort want their Captaine on whome to relye, they eftfoons difperfe themfelues, and the tumult endeth . In a religious man, who is like a Commonwealth well ordred, there is a tumult rayfed, when the inferiour part of the mind ftirreth and rebelleth againft the fuperiour, and therfore for the appeafing of the ftirre, and bringing of the common wealth to quiet, it muft imprifon the flefh , which is the Captaine of the common people, and rayfeth vp the paffions againft the foule, and the defires of the fenfes againft reafon . And Chaftity is that, which by help of the Vowes, putteth the flefh in prifon , and by well guarding and manning the hart , which is a Religious mans caftle, preferueth and maintayneth the common wealths tranquility and peace . And this vtility, caufed by Religious Chaftity , is fo important, as a Religious man without it , differeth nothing from a certayne Babylonian confufion .

7. Of this there arifeth another vtility, nothing

nothing inferiour to the aforesaid ; that a
Religious man, because by the help of Chaftity he hath procured peace and quiet of
mind within , may alfo go away with victory ouer them that be enemyes without.
The generall of an army, who hath his fouldiers, though few, agreeing and confpiring
togeather, and obedient vnto him, hath not
any difficulty in obtayning the victory . So
the Religious , if he can keep the inferiour
or fenfuall facultyes fubiect and obedient to
the fuperiour , may fecurely ioyne battaile
with the aduerfe part , and go away with
an vndoubted victory. A vnited fmal number in an army is farre better then a difagre-
ing or iarring multitude , and therfore the
Generall of the warre muft make much of
thofe in the army , who be the authors of
peace and concord in others ; Euen fo in the
fpiritual warre, the Religious who is as the
Generall, muft make an high efteeme of
Chaftity, which promoteth and furthereth
the peace of the fouldiers . He is eafily ouercome, who before he commeth to encounter with the enemy , hath not drawn his
fouldiers into a firme peace amongft themfelues .

P   *of*

Of the daungers of loosing Chastity.
CHAP. XVIII.

SONNE, thou knowest well, that Chastity is a gemme of great price & worth, no lesse pleasing to me, then profitable to thy self. But thou must further know, there be many theeues and enemyes, who seeke to spoyle thee of it, or at least to destroy and marre it, out of malice they beare vnto thee, & therfore thou needest to be very vigilant, and well armed against their assaults. Neither must thou be ouer confident, though thy flesh be tyed by Vow, sith it is so crafty & insolent, that though it cánot breake out by breaking the bands, which it euer laboureth to do, yet after her old manner, though she be neuer so fast bound, she maketh stirres & tumults, hoping therby either to worke her owne liberty, or to giue some deadly wound to Chastity her enemy. Neither be thou so confident, that Chastity, because it hath for a tyme seated it selfe within the castle of thy hart, is therfore secure, & out of danger: for most strong fortifications many times are surprised & taken on a suddane, & ouermuch security it cōmonly hurtfull, because it is the mother of slouth, & carelesnes.

2. The

2 . The first danger imminent is of treason: for seeing Chastity is round beset with
enemyes, both domesticall and forayne , it
may easily be betrayed , and therefore the
religious must stand vpō his guard, that his
domesticall enemy, namely his flesh, be not
seconded, and backed by enemyes from a-
broad. Sonne, if thou wilt be intertayned
delicately with meate and drinke, and sleep
at thy pleasure, and yet thinke thou mayst
preserue thy Chastity vnstayned against the
assaults of the flesh , thou art greatly deccy-
ued, because by that thou effectest nothing
but this, that thou giuest weapons & armes
vnto the flesh. And what meruaile, if it after rise against the spirit ? What meruaile if
it go about to breake the bands of Vow, and
to thrust Chastity out of her possession,
though she hath long stayed therein ? Wilt
thou haue thy flesh not to be wanton? Chastize it then with hard dyet . Wilt thou not
haue Chastity betrayed, nor to be thrust out
of her house ? Put a guard vpon her : fasting
and watching be two good keepers , who
do not only keep and defend her, but do also
spoyle the enemyes of their weapons, that
they may not rise against her. The more thou
flatter, and fauour thy flesh, the more strongly it fortificth it selfe against Chastity .

3. Lord,

3. Lord, for the suftayning of life, and for the feruing of thy diuine maiesty, a man needeth meate, drinke, and sleep, and if the flesh waxe thereby proud, and rife a-gainst the spirit, or Chaftity, it is not our fault, becaufe it is not the end propofed by vs. Sonne, I find no fault with thofe things that be neceffary for the intertayning of life, and the fuftayning of trauayles and labours for my fake (for whatfoeuer is directed to my feruice and glory, is bleffed, good, and laudable) but I only improue what is fuper-fluous. Meate and drinke not neceffary, but immoderate, ferteth the flefhes concupif-cence on fire, and bringeth the Chaftity in daunger. Who eateth ouer much, ferueth not me, but his owne appetite and defire. Thofe pleafe me, who eate that they may liue and ferue me, and contrarywife they difcontent me much, who feem to liue that they may eate. Many of my moft deare fer-uants, did not fo, to whome it was a payne to eate, and a loathing to fleep: and in thefe men Chaftity raigned, as in her owne king-dome. Moderate diet profiteth body and foule, & contrarywife exceffe hurteth them both.

4. Another danger groweth from the fenfes, which becaufe they be the gates of

the

the hart, where Chastity resideth, need a
strong guard, because both good and euill
make their entrance thereby into the hart.
He that hath not a diligent and carefull eye
to the keeping of the gate of his house, shall
oftentymes find something missing, & taken
away, or within it shall find something that
he would not, and would wish away. For
doores are made, that they may be shut and
opened: they are shut against men vnknown
and that may do hurt; they are opened to
men knowne, & to friends who may help.
A Religious man must not permit any one
to enter into his house of Chastity, without examining him first.

5. So do they in Frontiere places, and
townes of kingdomes, and there most of all
where there is feare, or suspition of treason
from enemyes, where not only be examined
those that desire to enter, but their packes
also, letters, and weapons are viewed and
searched that nothing hurtfull be brought
into the Citty. And this vigilancy is not
discommended, but commended. And yet
this care and diligence oftentymes doth not
remedy all inconueniences, sith experience
teacheth that, notwithstanding the watching and warding at the gates, there be
many treasons committed. Wherefore then

should

should not a Religious man stand vpon his
guard in keeping the gates of his hart, wherin he hath all his good, and whercon dependeth both his saluation, and his eternall
damnation. Who will say, that the vigilancy and diligence is ouermuch, where there
be so many enemyes? Who keepeth the
gates of his senses negligently, shall find
death entred into his houle.

6. Moreouer to conuerse and keep company with lasciuious persons, or such as be
not chast, is to cast ones selfe into a manifest daunger of loosing his Chastity. For
as experience hath taught, more chast persons haue been by the lasciuious drawn to
intemperance, then haue lasciuious been by
the chast induced to Chastity. For such is
the nature of the condition of man, as after
the losse of his integrity of life, he is more
prone to euill then to good, and as the sick,
rather desireth those things that delight the
tast, then profit the health. But if the conuersation with such kind of men arise peraduenture of an inordinate affection, there
is greater danger imminent. For if the only company with vnchast persons be daungerous, of how great daunger will it be to
keep company with carnall affection? He
that is prouoked by the obiect from with-
                                        out,

out, and put forwards by an affection from
within foon falleth, though he be fpiritual.
And therefore my feruants, who were in
loue with Chaftity, fo foone as they perceaued themfelues to be by any inordinate affection drawn to daungerous company, forthwith left it, as an enemy to Chaftity. For
he eafily learneth to halt, who often con-
uerfeth, and keepeth company with the
halting.

7.   The fame is the daunger of reading of wanton bookes, which be repugnant to Chaftity. I know not, how that
Religious man can be excufed, who keepeth
fuch an infectiõ within his chamber. Poyfon, though it be put into good and whole-
fome meats, ceafeth not to be poyfon, or to
kill them who take it: euen fo vnchaft matters, whether expreffed in pictures, or inter-
laced in the bookes of found doctrine, do
neither forgoe the name of difhonefty, nor
ceafe to hurt the beholders, readers, or hearers. And if vnto fecular men the reading of
fuch bookes cannot in good confcience be
permitted, how fhould it be permitted to
the Religious, that profeffe Chaftity? What
is read in books, is reflected vpon in hart, &
what is ruminated in mind, is eafily retay-
ned in the affection.

8. There

8.   There is another enemy of Chastity
the more to be feared, the more hardly he is
knowne and discouered, and that is an ouer
great security and confidence of a Religious
man in his owne continency . For this hath
drawn many into their ruine : and what
maruell, sith it is prides daughter. Who hath
a will to be chast, and shunneth not the dangers, presumeth ouermuch of himselfe . My
lowly and chast seruants did not so, but diffident of their owne forces, they ranne diligently from whatsoeuer might set the desires and appetites of the flesh on fire . And
though security maketh not a Religious
man rash, and ouer bold, yet it maketh him
negligent and carelesse, a id both the one &
the other doth endãger Chastitỳ not a litle.
Who trusteth ouermuch to himselfe , easily
exposeth himselfe to perills, and therefore is
often beguiled, & sustayneth a greater losse
then he would haue thought .

Of the meanes to conserue Chastity .

CHAP. XIX.

SONNE, in the battayles that are fought
amongst men, it profiteth sometymes to
come before the face of the enemy, & sometymes to skirmish with him , for as much

as

as boldnes is wont to abate the enemyes courage, and to cause him to fly. But in this spirituall warre, where we are to fight with the flesh, the victory is obtayned rather by flying from the enemy, then encountring him. For he, who seeketh to set vpon his enemy, putteth himself into very great danger to be ouercome, and ordinarily his losse is greater then is the gaine. Neither ought this to seeme strang vnto thee, for that in the conflicts of this world, whiles an assault is made vpon the enemy, the souldiers courage is set the more on fire, and the enemyes harts begin to faint; but in this encounter the contrary happeneth. For the more manfully thou shall resist thy concupiscence, the more it rageth, and the fire of it increaseth; in so much as it either striketh and woundeth, or pricketh, and therefore more wisdome is shewed in flying from it.

2. Thou art not wiser then *Salomon*, who because he flying not from the occasions, fell so shamefully, as he did. S. *Iohn Baptist* my precursour, though he were sanctified in his mothers wombe, did notwithstanding for the auoyding of all occasions of sinning, hide himselfe being but a child in the desert: and wilt thou, who neither art sanctified, nor so vertuous, thrust thy self

into

into the middeſt of occaſions, & make head
againſt thyne enemy to fight with him?
This is a manifeſt ſigne, that either thou haſt
not got any knowledge of thy ſelfe, or thou
makeſt little reckoning of Chaſtities gift.

3. Another meanes is, moſt ſpeedily to
repell & ſhake off the foule ſuggeſtions that
the Diuell preſenteth to the mind. For they
be like little plants, which if they be not
fortwith pulled vp out of the ſoules garden,
do ſoone take roote, grow, & bring forth
thornes, that pricke the mind, and choake
vp Chaſtity. A Religious man, who putteth not away vncleane thoughts after he
hath once perceiued them, doth declare his
liking of them: and if they pleaſe him, how
can he loue the purity of mind, that is ſtay-
ned with ſuch manner of thoughts? Againe
if foule cogitations hurt, as ſoone as euer
they put out their heads; how much more
will they hurt, if they ſhall by delay gather
more ſtrength? Little coales, though they
lye but a little tyme vnder cloaths, do not-
withſtanding both cauſe a bad ſmell, and
burne the cloath. If the Religious would
conſider, from how great incommoɗ s
and troubles they ſhould free themſelues, if
they ſhould in the very beginning ſhake of
the foule cogitations of carnality, there is
                                                    none

none, who would suffer the little ones of Babylon to grow to any bignes within his hart, but would instantly dash them against the rocke. Our cowardize, and daftardy in putting away impure cogitations, maketh the Diuell diligent and bold in tempting vs against Chaftity.

4. It helpeth also to chaftityes conferuation, to be otherwhiles blind, deafe, and mute. For if it be true, that it is not lawful to fee, or heare what it is not lawfull to defire, what caufe hath a Religious man, when he goeth abroad, to caft his eyes vpon the countenances of all that he meeteth? Let him leaue that office to the Painters, who for the true expreffing of mens countenances, muft needs haue their eyes fixed vpon them. A good and chaft Religious man rather taketh vpon him to conteplate the countenaunces, fuch as they fhall one day be after death, then as they be in life. For what profiteth it to behold thofe things that be nothing good, but be rather impediments to the meditatio of heauenly things? The leffe thou fhalt fee, or heare of thinges of this world, the more fecurely fhalt thou enioy the comfort of Chaftity.

5. Another foueraigne help for the conferuing of the minds purity, is the auoyding

uoyding of ydlenes, which as it is moſt
comberſome to Chaſtity, ſo it is moſt contenting to the fleſh, which is accuſtomed to
grow wanton by ydlenes, & cóſequently to
become more fierce againſt Chaſtity euery
day then other. To liue idly, is to ſet open
the doore for theeues and robbers to enter
into the houſe. For he, who careth not for
the looſing of his own goods, doth nothing
but giue vnto theeues oportunity of robbing him of what he hath. Who is well
buſyed, is not wont to lend his hearing to
any one, but in neceſſary matters: but one
that is ydle, and giuen to his recreations, is
ready to heare all, whether the talke be ſecular, or ſpirituall: if it be ſpirituall, it inſtantly paſſeth away, if it be ſecular and carnall, it taketh increaſe by ydlenes.

6.   Conſider thou now, whether it be
conuenient that thou be idle, who art
come to Religion for no other end, then to
ſuffer many labours, and much paynes, for
Chriſt. And whether it be meet by ydlenes
and eaſe to patronize the fleſh againſt Chaſtity, when as thou haſt by Vow promiſed
thy Chaſtity to God? Some caſt the fault
vpon the Diuell, that they be ouer ſore troubled with impure cogitations, who are rather culpable theſclues. For he by tempting
ſecketh

seeketh to put occupations vpon them who haue none, that they may satisfy their duty: and therefore if they should be euer busy in some pious action or other, the Diuell should not haue any place, and the Chastity might be the more safely kept. To haue a desire and will to be ydle, and not to haue a will to be tempted, cannot agree togeather, for that nothing inuiteth the Diuell sooner to throw his darts of tentations, then ydlenes, and ease.

7.   My seruants, who now raigne happily in heauen, for the mantayning of their Chastity on earth, exercised themselues in two vertues aboue the rest, to witt, humility and pennance. Humility of hart, like a pious mother, seeketh most carefully to conserue Chastity, as her deare daughter. For those my seruants vnderstood very well, that it was a very hard matter for a proud, and arrogant person to keep & preserue his flower of Chastity. Againe Pennance is the conseruer of Chastity as touching the body, and therfore they were much giuen to the mortifying of their flesh, some to fastings, others to disciplines, watchings, and to other afflictions of that kind, knowing that they were the preseruatiue antidots of purity. And when these remedyes will not help,

let

let them vſe more effectuall. Whence it is, that ſome for the extinguiſhing, and putting out the heat of luſt did caſt themſelues into moſt freezing cold waters, ſome into ſnow, others caſt themſelues naked into nettles & thornes, ſome did burne off their owne fingers. By which acts they declared themſelues to be great enemyes to their fleſh and faythfull conſeruers of their Chaſtity. The body cannot be brought vnder ſubiection, but by vſing ſome ſeuerity and rigour to it: and a body vntamed and vnruly can not away with Chaſtity, and in concluſion either cleane abandoneth it, or preſerueth it not long vnſtayned.

Of the Vow of Obedience, and wherein Re-
ligious Obedience conſiſteth.

CHAP. XX.

LORD, though I deſire much to imbrace this courſe of life without falling and erring, yet I fall & erre ſo often, as I am aſhamed of it. In ſomethinges I make ouermuch haſt, in others I am ouer ſlow, neither can I well reſolue, what I ſhould do. I doe further attempt many thinges, but yet with an vnfortunate euent.

2. Sonne, in this life none is ſufficient
of

of himselfe, that he may liue as he ought, because none hath euer come to that perfection of knowledge; that he should be free from all errour. Thou knowest not, what will be to morrow: the harts of men be to thee vnknown and inscrutable, neither dost thou well know thy selfe. How then canst thou without falling or errour either conuerse with others, or gouerne thy selfe? Who trauayleth by night and in darknes, though he fal not, yet he stumbleth at least or goeth out of his way. And though thou mayst be prouided of knowledg & of light, yet where be thy forces, and helps necessary for the ouercoming of the difficultyes that often occur? For so violent be the perturbations of the mind, as they carry away euen those who seeme to haue gone beyond the condition of mans nature, neither be the forces of nature of ability to keep them in. And if in the naturall life, wherin the light of reason shineth to all, there be so many errors, how many will there be in the spirituall, wherein there is both lesse light & vnderstanding, and greater difficultyes do occurre?

2. So it is Lord, but shall we continue in this darknes, depriued of all helps and remedies? Sonne, in this necessity the vertue of Obedience is able to giue thee both

an

an help and a remedy, of which it is a common saying: Suffer thy selfe to be ruled. He that taketh a iourney, and cannot well see his way before him, standeth in need of a guide, & of one well sighted, & that knoweth the way. The vertue of Obedience is that which deliuereth a Religious man into my hands, that I may guide and direct him. And seeing I am skillfull of the way, and know the windings, turnings, and difficultyes, let euery Religious man be secure and assured, that I will faithfully direct him in the way that shall bring him to life euerlasting, so he suffer himselfe to be for his owne part gouerned, and brought to his iourneys end.

4. All Religious, whiles they renounce the world, begin to follow me, but many thinking themselues not to stand in any need of my conduct, leaue and forsake me, not to any hurt of myne, but their own. It is not inough to haue begon. If there should be no difficultyes, but in the entrance into the way, they might haue some cause of excusing themselues, but seeing the same to be dangerous all the way, and in the whole course of their iourney, they must not leaue their conductour. He, that not knowing the way contemneth a guide, manifesteth
that

that he maketh little reckoning of his going
aftray.

5. In the world I adminifter, and gouerne all : by me Kinges raigne, and Princes commaund : by me the Law-makers determine what is iuft, and the Iudges do iu-
ftice. And where I haue commaunded obedience to be giuen to temporal Lords, whofoeuer refifteth their commaund, refifteth
me, and my ordination. The fame is done
in the fhip of Religion, wherein I am the
chief Maifter, and Pilot : I direct it, and
bring it fafe into the harbour : I affigne euery marryner his office and charge, and to
whome they and others muft be obedient.
And wheras I am in euery one of them, and
determine what euery fubiect is to do, to
obey them is nothing els, then to obey
me, and to contemne them, is to contemne
me.

6. All Religious be indeed in a fhip,
but all haue not good fpeed and fucceffe in
their nauigation. He that fuffereth himfelfe
to be gouerned, fayleth on without danger,
and hath not any caufe to be troubled or
afraid, and therfore, as the common faying
is, goeth his iourney fleeping. But he, who
fuffereth not himfelfe willingly to be gouerned, ftayeth not within the fhip, one

Q   while

while grieued that he entred into the ship,
an otherwhile wishing to leape a shoare,
and out of a discontent and pusillanimity of
mind he taketh no pleasure of any thing at
all. And whence cometh this? because his
desire is, that the ship should be directed, as
himselfe liketh best. And this is to haue a
will to gouerne, and not to be gouerned.
Woe to that Religion which accomodateth
it selfe to the propension, and will of euery
subiect. Who passeth in a ship from one
place to another, must accommodate himselfe therto, and not contrary wise. It were
no good trauayling, neither would the
ship euer get into the hauen, if the nauigation should be directed as euery one listed.
That Religious man cannot liue in peace,
who refuseth to do the will & commaund
of another.

7. Doest thou long to know what
Obedience is? It is nothing els, then a
Burying. Wilt thou vnderstand, wherein
it consisteth to obey? It consisteth in the
buryall of the owne will. O happy is that
Religious person, who can truely say, and
affirme: Now I haue buried myne owne
will, and vnwillingnes: Now haue I satisfyed the liberty of myne owne will, because
he hath cast off whatsoeuer might haue
                                    hindred

hindred his entrance into heauen. None can take vp his croſſe and follow me, vnles he ſhall firſt haue buryed his owne will, and denyed himſelfe. A Religious man, retayning his owne will, and doing as he liſt, is not dead to the world, and therfore appertayneth not to Religion, which is but one, and ought to be gouerned by one will, namely of the Superiour, and all the reſt of the wills of the ſubiects muſt be buryed : if they be not, as a body, that lyeth vnburyed, they will yield forth an intolerable bad ſent.

8. Tell me, I pray thee, my Sonne, if a man ſhould without any cauſe, induced by his own will and pleaſure alone, take vp a body, that had beene ſome monethes ago buryed, would it not ſtrike an exceeding great horrour into all that ſhould ſee it, & cauſe them to laugh at his folly, & madnes? And what other thing is it, not to obey the Conſtitutions of the Order, or the Superiours commaund, then to take vp againe thyne owne will, and nill, that were before buryed, both which bodyes thou buriedſt at thy entring into Religion, with a firme purpoſe neuer to vnbury them, or to take them out of the ground againe? Thinkeſt thou to be excuſed before me, while thou

now

now callest them, I can, and I cannot? That
I cannot, which thou hast sayd to thy Superiour, thou didst not say to me. I know,
what euery one is able to do, or not able. I
see also what a Religious man hath in his
mouth, and what he carryeth in his hart.
And I know againe, when not to be able, is
not to haue a will for the shunning of some
incomodity, or paynes taking. And though
the Superiour accepteth of his subiects false
excuse, neither examineth, whether he be
truely able to do the thing, or no, that is
commaunded, yet he hath no cause to be
therefore glad. For the whole matter consisteth not in that alone, it will at some o-
ther time be examined at my tribunal, wher
the last sentence shall be pronounced, that
will admit no hope of any future appeale.
For men in censuring and distinguishing
the truth of the thing, may be deceiued, but
God cannot, who hath a perfect knowledge
of all things, both within, and without.

How acceptable to God the Obedience of a
Religious man is .

CHAP. XXI.

SONNE, thou canst not be ignorant,
what was the end of thy first father *Adam*
and

and of his disobedience , namely, that not
only himselfe was exiled and banished out
of the terrestriall Paradise , but he was further togeather with his whole posterity
made thrall & subiect to malediction . The
labours on earth, the sweating in procuring
bread to eate, the paynes of women trauayling with child , and all other miseryes ,
wherewith man kind is afflicted , be the
punishments and maledictions of disobedience , which becaufe it is the daughter of
Pride , can yeald forth no other fruite ,
then it doth . Thou knowest also what followed of the Obedience of *Abraham* , that
not only himselfe, and all his family, but al
the nations of the world also be blessed in
his feed, of which was to be borne one, who
by his obedience should set open the gates of
heauen, that were by disobedience shut vp
before: in so much as it may be truly sayd ,
that all celestiall gifts, and all graces & vertues be the effects, and benedictions of O-
bedience .

2.   Againe, if Obedience, accompayned
with my expresse commaundment, which
seemeth in a manner to force man to do
what I commaund, be so gratefull and pleasing to me, as I abundantly reward it ; how
much more acceptable ought Religious

Obedience to be, in regard whereof a man ot himselfe moued not by the cōmaund of any, but for the sincere loue of God, though the contrary propension of his nature repugne, bindeth himselfe to performe my coūsayles? And where I know right well, that man is borne to high matters, and is propense to designe & vndergo heroical actiōs, yet when I see him for loue of me to abase himselfe, according to the iudgment of the world, to vile and contemptible functions (though in my sight they be honorable and excellent) when againe I see him not to seek glory and applause of men, but rather the contempt of himselfe: when I see, that he spoyleth himselfe of his owne will, which is the fountaine and beginning of all generous workes, by which a man may merit greatest honours before the world: & when I see, that to please me, he subiecteth himselfe to another man, his equall by nature, and oftentymes in Religion also to them, ouer whome he had authority, and a commaund in the world; how, I say, can it possibly be, that I should not be most inwardly affected to the Obedient? And that such Obedience should not be most pleasing to me, that exciteth the Religious to do so great matters for the loue of me? How
should

should I not rayse them to greatest dignityes, who that they might obey for loue of
me, abased themselues so farre, euen against
the inclination of nature? He can neuer receiue any losse, who doth much for God.

3. Obedience also pleaseth me, because it maketh the subiects tractable,
prompt, and ready at euery beck of the Superiour: and nothing comforteth and helpeth
the Superiours so much, as to haue tractable
subiects. O how do I like that Religious
man, who doth with ioy and alacrity go a-
bout the doing of whatsoeuer his Superiour
shall haue commaunded him, & if he should
be againe by his Superiour willed to cease
from the worke he had begon, he leaueth it
as gladly, and executeth as readily any new
worke, that shall be commaunded him. On
the contrary nothing troubleth, and afflicteth the Superiour more, and causeth him
more to groane vnder the weight of his
gouernment & office, then to haue subiects
stubborne, slacke, & hard to obey. An vn-
tractable beast doth not easily suffer burdens
to be layd vpon his backe, and after they
haue byn with much payne layd vpō him,
he either throweth them downe, or carryeth them with so ill a will, as a great care
must be vsed, least he cast them downe at

Q 4   length.

length. A Superiour, that hath hard, froward and stubborne subiects, cannot be confident in them, and therfore if any thing though neuer so little, be to be commaunded them, there needeth more circumspection, then if a man were to deale with an vnruly beast.

4. Hence it is, that where the subiect should otherwise respect, reuerence & feare his Superiour, through the default of disobience the quite contrary is done, that is, the Superiour feareth the subiect, whome, least he should giue him an occasion of leauing his order, with the offence & scandall of others, he leaueth to his owne will, neither commaunding him any thing, nor reprouing him. O misery to be lamented! In the world he liued as he listed, not at anothers charge, but at his own: but in Religion he hath a will to liue at his own pleasure, and with my cost, and my bloud, which as it cannot be done without iniustice, so neither can it go vnpunished. Wherfore should I not hate disobedience, which is so iniurious to Religion? Why should not the disobedient displease me, who be the ruine of their Religion? This is not the state of the obedient. For the Superiour liueth with the obediēt securely, without distrust, without

without ceremonyes, he is confident in thē, and if he commaund thē any thing, though very hard, they moſt readily do it. He obey-eth without difficulty, who imbraceth all commaunds without any excuſe : but he, who forced, yealdeth to the Superiours cō-maundment, either doth it not at all, or doth it ill. He indeed retayneth the rynd, that is, the externall act of his labour, but he looſeth the kernell, that is, the fruit of the merit of obedience.

5. Moreouer I adde, that Religious Obe-dience pleaſeth me alſo for this, that it com-prehendeth many other vertues in it ſelfe, and exerciſeth their actions. For when the Religious mā for obedience ſake ſubiecteth himſelfe to others his equalls, or inferiours, he exerciſeth the vertue of Humility. If the Superiours commaundement that he doth be hard, he exerciſeth the vertue of Forti-tude, becauſe he ouercometh the difficulty. If it be repugnant to the ſenſe, or to his owne nature, he exerciſeth Patience, be-cauſe he exerciſeth what he is auerted from. If he obey for loue of me, he exerciſeth Cha-rity : & ſo Obedience maketh the Religious mā like vnto me, becauſe my obedience had the company of theſe vertues. And ſeeing ſimilitude is the cauſe of loue and beneuo-

Q 5 lence,

lence, it manifestly followeth, that all obedient persons be most inwardly conioyned
with me: and the more vertues go in company with odedience, the more doth the o-
bedient merit.

6.   Sonne, the gift is the more accepted
to him, to whom it is giuen: the more noble
the thing is, in like manner it is the more
pleasing, when excluding all the vtility of
the giuer, it is only an argument and testi-
mony of the giuers inward beneuolence &
good will. Wherefore seeing Obedience is
the gift of a mans liberty, then which a religious man hath nothing more noble, or
more excellent; it cannot but be to me most
deare, and so much the more, for that to the
offering of this gift he was not moued vpõ
any human respect, nor for the vanity of the
world, but for the only loue of me. Though
this also maketh the giuer acceptable to me,
that for such a gift bestowed vpon me, he
remayneth not poore or imperfect, for that
the more a man giueth to God, the richer,
and the perfecter he becometh.

7.   Sonne, Religion is a deare and beloued vineyard to me, and the rules & constitutions of it be the branches of the vine,
and as it were trees planted therein by me,
not without my paine. The worke-men be
those,

those, whome I call out of the world, & do furnish with sundry tooles, and talents for the good husbanding of my vineyard. The keeper of it is Obedièce, which apointeth vnto euery worke-man what he is to do. All do indeed enter into the vineyard, but all be not profitable vnto it. The Religious who take paynes in husbanding the trees and vines, that is, obey my lawes and ordinations, be most pleasing vnto me, and I haue appointed them a singular hire, because they on their part do maintaine and defend Religion. But the disobedient, who spoyle my vineyard, cannot haue a mery or pleasing looke from me. For what is it els to forgoe and transgresse the rule, but to cut off some vine, or to transplant it to some other place? And what is this, but to dissolue and ouerthrow Religion? Wherefore as much as disobedience displeaseth me, which ouerthroweth Religion, so much Obedience contenteth me, which setteth it forth, preserueth, and increaseth it.

Of the Excellency and Dignity of Religious Obedience .

CHAP. XXII.

SONNE, hast thou at any time considered this saying of my scripture: A man obedient

dient speaketh of victories. Know thou,
that there cannot either a greater, or more
wonderfull victory be in this world obtayned, then that of ones selfe. Enemyes may
be ouercome by stratagems, and frauds, and
though they be ouercome by might & force
of armes, yet they are ouercome who be
inferiors, or be at least in fight become inferiors. But in the victory of ones selfe, the
victory is not obtayned by art, or fraud, but
by vertue, and he is ouercome who is equal
and euer remayneth equall. In other victoryes the higher the vanquisher is raised, the
more is the vanquished and ouercome depressed and humbled, but in the victory of
ones self the vanquished hath as high a place,
as hath the ouercomer. In other encounters
and fights enemyes are ouercome, and therein passeth hatred, ire, and indignation, but
he that ouercometh himselfe, ouercometh
one, to whome he is most conioyned in
loue and freindship. And this difficulty
maketh the victory the more glorious. Such
is the victory of the obedient, for that whils
he doth voluntarily subiect himselfe to anothers commaund, he ouercometh himselfe.
And this victory is so much the more noble
& glorious, with how much the more difficulty, namely against nature, it is ob-
　　　　　　　　　　　　　　　tayned.

tayned . And in this victory there are to be seene many other victoryes. For an obedient Religious man maketh the senses, appetites, add passions to be at reasons cōmaund, and reason it selfe againe togeather with her owne iudgment to be subiect to the will & iudgment of the Superiour . And this also is not the least victory to yield and deliuer vp the honour of the triumph to another. He that in battaile turneth his backe and runneth away, looseth the victory : but in obedience he turneth his backe, who refuseth to submit himselfe to another .

3 . Againe, Obedience is so stout a warriour, as it also fighteth for other vertues against all those, that oppose themselues against the Religious state, and perfection . If the concupiscence make warre against Chastity, Obedience commeth forth , and causeth the will to deny consent, and to remember the Vow that was formerly made of leading a chast life . If the desire of temporal things insult vpon Religious pouerty, Obedience riseth vp against it, and perswadeth pouerty to keep the promise of vsing no propriety in any thing . When the Diuel inciteth any to transgression of the rules of Religion, Obedience, as a faithfull defender of Religion, is in armes and stoutly standeth
against

against him. As often as the perturbations
of mind impugne reason, Obedience com-
poseth them, and causeth euery particular
faculty of the mind to shew obedience,
where it should. By all these most noble
victoryes a coniecture may be made, how
great an efficacy and glory is that of Obedience; and that a Religious man, as long as
he shall haue so noble a champion to defend
his quarrell, must needs fight with good
successe, and go away with many victoryes.
The Generall of the warre, if he desire to
haue good souldiers, and to ouercome his
enemyes, must haue a speciall consideration
and regard of them, who fight manfully
with the enemy.

4. After that the Diuell had by the sin
of disobedience supplanted *Adam*, he began
to make great reckoning of disobedience, &
vpon his flag, which he did set vp, and dis-
play in signe of victory, framed this word, or
poesy: Inobedience the daughter of Pride,
the mother of death, the worlds ruine, and
Religious bane and infection. By these he
triumphed long. But I againe raysed vp and
displayed the Crosses banner, wheron ending my life by obedience, I ouercame death
and repayred the hurts by *Adams* disobedience done to mankind. And therefore the

motte

motte, or poesy of my banner is this: Obedience Humilityes daughter, Spiritual lifes
mother, the worlds Redresse, and Religions Gouernesse. Of these commendations, which be most true, thou mayst vnderstand the excellency of Obedience. For
seeing it is humilityes daughter, whose proper office is to exalt the humble, it cannot
but haue a part in the same property, as
is to be seene in me, to whome it gayned a
most happy victory ouer all myne enemyes,
accompanyed also with a most glorious triumph. Sonne, none can continue stable and
perseuere in Religion, vnles he fight. He
that fighteth not vnder obediences colours,
must needs fight vnder disobedience, which
is Sathans banner.

5. It is out of question, that the excellency of the will, which is by a Religious
man offered and sacrified to me by the Vow
of Obedience, addeth great force to the sacrifice, sith the will is not only the noblest
part of man, but also the queene of al the facultyes of the mind. And the dignity and
worth of this sacrifice increaseth the more,
the more I esteeme of it. And how could I
not but highly esteeme of Religious Obedience, in which a Religious man offereth me
his liberty, which all the world maketh so
great

great reckoning of? Is not this gift such, as it should be held for great? For if I esteeme greatly of Pouerty & Chastity, I am bound to make much more of Obedience. For Pouerty offereth me the externall goods only. Chastity for loue of me only depriueth the body of corporall pleasures, which be the goods therof. But Obedíéce offereth me the internall goods of mind, which by how much they excell the goods of fortune and of body, by so much the oblation of them is more excellent, and more acceptable to me.

6.   It cannot be denyed, but that *Abrahams* obedience was most excellent, when at the first word I spake, he resolued to sacrifice vnto me his only and most louing sonne *Isaac*. Neither was *Isaac* his obedience lesse memorable, who to obey me in the person of his Father, suffered himselfe to be bound, and out of a most noble courage & hart, in the flower of his youth offred his head to be cut from his shoulders. But I make no lesse reckoning of a good religious mans obedience, which comprehendeth in it the perfection of the obedience of them both. Of *Abraham* indeed, because a Religious man doth loue himselfe as well, as did *Abraham* his sonne: and of his sonne, because a Religious man out of as great a fortitude of mind

mind bindeth himfelfe by Vow of Obedience, as did *Ifaac* fuffer himfelfe to be faft
bound by his father: Neither doth he with
leffe promptitude offer his owne will to be
cut off by the fword of fpirituall Vow, then
did *Ifaac* his necke by the materiall fword:
Moreouer by the difference between *Abra-*
hams and a Religious mans obedience, it appeareth, that this is to be preferred before
that. For in that, a cōmaundment was layd
vpon *Abraham*, in this it was but counfaile:
that was only in will, this both in will and
fact: his act endured but for a fhort fpace,
this mans fact for his whole life.

7. Sonne, wilt thou go beyond *Abra-*
hams obedience? Seeke prompt obedience
in all things, for that God is no leffe pleafed
with Obedience in little matters, then in
great. Further certayne it is, that no worke
though by the iudgment of the world it be
thought honorable, is of any accompt with
me, if it hath not a conformity with the diuine will. Let a man difpofe all his goods
for the behoof of the poore : Let him fuffer
perfecutions, and be contemned : Let him
dy for the fayth; if thefe and the like workes
be not done according to my will, they are
neither pleafing to me, nor meritorious at
all . But the vertue of Obedience, as alfo of

R   Charity

Charity her sister, causeth a Religious man to conforme his works to Gods will, and consequently maketh them meritorious. Adde, that a creature indewed with reason, is then said to be perfect, when it reposeth in the diuine wil, neither hath a will to any thing, but what the Creatour hath a wil to. And by what other vertue is the Religious man made prompt to obey Gods will, then by Obedience? Who forceth a Religious man to haue a will neither lesse, nor more then his Creatour in whom consisteth true perfection, but Obedience? O if all Religious men were so harty louers of Obedience, as the excellency threof deserueth, it would be much more reckoned of in Religions then now it is, and there would be great store of perfect Religious persons.

Of the profit and vtility, that Obedience bringeth to a Religious man.

CHAP. XXIII.

LORD, though a Religious man receiueth many, and very excellent vtilities by Obedience, yet I would thinke it much better, if thou thy selfe without the help of other Superiours, wouldst commaund, & ordayne all: for we would in a most prompt manner

manner obey thee, neither would there be
any place left for murmurations, neither
wouldst thou euer giue any occasion of
complaints; and in few wordes, thy gouerning would be most sweet. And if that
may seeme not to haue beene conuenient,
yet thou mightest haue done well, if thou
shouldest gouerne vs by an Angell, who as
he should be of more credit, and authority
with vs, so would we more reuerence him,
then men.

2. Sonne, all this that thou sayst, sprin-
geth out of the fountaine of selfe loue. If
Religious men were spirits, it would be
conuenient that they should be gouerned
either by me, or by some Angell, but because they be composed of a body, and a spirit, it is very agreable that they be gouerned
by a man, their like; and the same requireth
the sweet prouidence, wherby the whole
frame of this world is gouerned. When I
brought the world to the true fayth, I sent
not Angells, but men, & for men I gouerne
it. I did also found Religions, not by Angells, but by men, and therfore fitting it is,
they should be gouerned by them. If heere
an Angell were a Superiour, how often
would these, or the like wordes proceed
from mens mouths? If this Angell our Su-

R 2   periour,

periour, had experience of the troubles of
the flesh, the burdens of body, and the miseryes of this life, as we haue, he would
take more compassion on vs, then he doth.
How many excuses would not take place
with an Angell, which now haue place
with a man, Superiour? How many scruples would Religious men haue, if they
should be gouerned by an inuisible Superiour? And more then this, euery Superiour
ought to help his subiects rather by example
of life, then by word of mouth ; but if the
Superiour should be inuisible, he could not
giue any such example for imitation : and
therefore better it is, that the Superiour be
an Angell rather in conditions & manners,
then by nature. And where it is sayd, that
the Superiour, if he should be an Angell,
should be more loued and respected by his
subiects, then if he were a mortall man, is
not true. For whereas I am in the Superiour, he that loueth not me, nor obeyeth me
in a man, my Vicegerent, would loue and
obey me lesse in an Angell.

3. Call to thy remembrance, what
my beloued disciple *Iohn* wrote : If thou
louest not thy neighbour (quoth he) whom
thou seest, how canst thou loue God, whom
thou seest not? If thou obeyest not the Superiour,

periour whome thou feeft, how wilt thou
obey thy Superiour whome thou feeft not?
But how great humility would it be to be
fubiect to an Angell? For whiles the Religious do for loue of me fubieft thefelus to a
man, as to my fubftitute, and obey him, as
they do me, it is an act not only of great
Humility, but alfo of Fortitude, Magnani-
mity, Fayth, Hope, and Chariry, fo much
the more pleafing vnto me, the more vertues it goeth accompanyed with. He that
fubmitteth himfelfe to a man for my fake,
will leffe fubmit himfelfe to an Angell. It
is my will, that a Religious man muft do:
And it little skilleth, whether it be declared
by a man, or an Angell. A regard is not fo
much to be had of him who fpeaketh, or
commaundeth, as of him, in whofe name
he fpeaketh, or commaundeth. Neceffary
it is that water runne into the garden, but
it skilleth not, whether it be brought in by
conducts of lead, or of filuer.

4. Sonne, doft thou now defire to vnderftand the vtilityes of Obedience? Tell
me, if one fhould ride through daungerous
rockes, and downefall places vpon a wild,
and vnruly horfe, and one fhould be ready
to offer his help and paynes to lead his horfe
by hand, through all thofe fo many dan-

gers.,

gers, would he not thinke that a speciall
benefit were offered to him? No doubt, he
would esteeme it a most great one. And if
he should refuse to vse so great a benefit,
should he not shew himself a very mad man?
Our body, vntamed in regard of the disor-
dred passions, that raigne in it, is this vnruly horse. The errors that are wont in the
spirituall life to be committed, be those
downefalls and cragged rockes. Our Superiour is he, who is ready to guide and lead
our horses, that we fall not. Thinke then
how great the madnes of that Religious
man should be, who should refuse in so
great dangers to be gouerned by his Superiour? For them, that want the skill of
swymming, it is good to rest vpon others
mens armes. A Religious man, who obeyeth, and permitteth himselfe to be gouerned of another, swimmeth in his Superiours armes, and swimmeth securely in the
waues of spirituall daungers.

5. Another ytility is, that Obedience
freeth a religious man from an infinit number of molestations and troubles. Nothing
tormenteth a man so much, as do the anxious cogitations of mind, of which the miserable man, who lyueth in the world, is
meruaylously rent and gnawne, as is the vi-
per

per by her yong ones, which she carrieth in
her belly. And though he hath not care of
family , or of the administration of the
goods of Fortune , yet the very thinking
vpon his owne affayres and actions is too
comberfome. For he must not only confider, what is to be done , but also when,
how, and by what meanes. And this loathing, and croffe is againe increased by the
ouermuch follicitude about the good ending and fucceffe of the things that are to
be done.

6. But all this is nothing, & nothing
worth, if it be compared with the cogitations of spirituall actions. For those, that
they may be pleasing, must be conforme to
my will, and if they be not done with Charity, and diferetion, I make no reckoning
of them . And Obedience exempteth a Religious man from those and all other cares ,
and cogitations, commending this one
thing alone , that he obey, and lay all the
rest vpon his Superiours shoulders, whose
charg it is to fee, what, when, how, and by
what wayes euery thing is to be done . It is
in him to procure all things neceffary both
for the spirituall, and temporall : for he is
the Father, the mother, maister, prouider,
directour, guide, and all. What other thing
R 4   then

then is it to liue vnder obedience, then to cast his burden vpon anothers backe ? If you were entred into a wide wood, that almost had no way out, and dangerous for the cruell wild beasts therein, and were further very sore loaden, should not he do you a singular pleasure, who should not only bring you safe out of the wood, but also ease you of your burden, by taking it vpon his owne shoulders ? And what other thing is it to obey, thē to trauayle the more securely with a guide in the way, & without any burden to beare? He that acknowledgeth not a benefit, neither regardeth, nor maketh reckoning whence it commeth, or who is the authour therof.

7.   There is added another vtility of Obediéce, that the things which be good of themselues, it maketh more excellent; and what is of very little worth, it causeth to be had in greater esteeme. He that moued by Gods grace, doth of a free will exercise a good worke, doth well, and meriteth a reward according to the greatnes of the work and his pious affection withall: but he that doth of Obedience exercise the same workes, out of the same disposition of mind that the other did, meriteth much more by occasion of the vertue, & efficacy, which the

vertue

vertue of Obedience addeth to that worke.
And more then that, Obedience is so fruitfull, and of such power, as it maketh the
works that are of necessity, more noble also, and those that of themselues are not
praise worthy, as be the actions of eating,
drinking, sleeping, walking &c. if the
Religious do them by obedience, pleasing
vnto me, which I also reward according to
the measure of the pious affection & Charity they be done withall. And it sometimes hapneth, that the Obedient without
doing any worke, maketh more spirituall
gaine, then he who doth the worke.

8. The Religious, who hath a desire
to fast for the punishing of his flesh, for his
sinnes, and yet for Obedience sake forbeareth to fast, meriteth more before God by
not fasting, then doth another fasting of
deuotion. For this man hath the only merit of his fasting: but that man hath merited
not only the good of fasting, because he
was of his part ready to do it, but also the
merit of Obedience. Iudge thou now, whether that be not a priuiledg, both profitable
& healthfull, which I haue conferred & bestowed vpon the Religious, by the benefit
of Obedience. And how am I affected,
thinkest thou, vnto them, who are so little

deuoted

deuoted to obedience? O what a detriment
and losse sustayneth that man in his spirituall goods, who doth all of his owne will
that he might do by obedience. Euery good
worke, great or little, if it be signed with
the seale of Obedience, is of great esteeme
and price, as well in heauen, as in earth.

How it is conuenient, that a Religious man
be studious of Obedience.

CHAP. XXIIII.

SONNE, if thou be resolued with thy
selfe to imitate me, necessary it is, that
thou haue an earnest desire to imbrace the
vertue of Obedience, and make thy selfe
fit for the performing of perfect obedience.
Remember that I assumed, & tooke vpon
me the forme of a seruant, that I might sub-
ject my selfe to men, and obey them for thy
soules good. Neither did I propose alone,
and openly professe, that I wascome not to
do myne owne will, but the will of my
Father who sent me; but I began also very
tymely to obey the precepts of his law,
wherunto I was not yet bound, neither
might I be drawn from the obseruation of
the either by shame or confusion, or for any
daunger of life. And as my disciple and E-
uangelist

uangelist *Iohn* wrote, I called Obedience,
my Meate. And not without cause, sith
there was not any thing in this life, wherein I tooke so great a pleasure, as in doing of
my heauenly Fathers will, in so much as
whatsoeuer hapned bitter or sower, became
to me sweet thereby. For this cause the
Chalice of my passion, which was to my
humanity most bitter, was most readily accepted of my spirit, as a most sweet cup,
because it was offered me with the hand of
Obedience by my Father. What Religious
man then can with reason refuse obedience
which was meate to me? It is an ill signe
when the Lords & Maisters meate cannot
content the seruant.

2.   But what can it be, Sonne, that pleaseth thee not in Obedience? It is, because
thou seest thy selfe in subiection to a man?
or that thou art ashamed to be commaunded by another? I am the Lord of this vni-
uerse, I am the wisedome of my heauenly
father, and yet was I in subiection to men;
neither that, by the way alone, or for a few
tymes, but euen from the tyme of my comming into the world, vntill my most i-
gnominious death vpon the Crosse. Neither obayed I the good and iust alone, as my
Mother, and *Ioseph* my fosterfather, but the
vniust

vniuſt and wicked Iudges alſo , as *Annas,*
Caiphas , *Herode* , and *Pilate* , who though
they knew me to be vniuſtly accuſed , nor
that any thing of that which they wicked
ly obiected, could be proued againſt me, did
neuertheleſſe condemne me to be crowned
with thornes, to be whipped, and to the
Croſſe it ſelfe ; all which I tolerated with
patience, without making of any appeale,
or vſing any Apology for my ſelfe : & more
then that without ſpeaking any word at al.
I alſo obeyed their peruerſe ſeruants , who
did without cauſe buffet me, ſpit vpon my
face, and moſt ignominiouſly dragged me
vp and downe through the publike ſtreets.
And of all this I complayned not, & though
I might haue reuenged my ſelfe, and might
moſt iuſtly haue puniſhed the for the moſt
extreme iniury that was done vnto me, yet
I did forbeare, and did readily do all that
they commaunded me . Tell me now, whether it be yet any hard and painefull matter for thee to obey ? Thou art not for Obedience bound faſt to a piller, & there whipt
as I was. Thou ſtandeſt not with thy hands
bound at thy backe, and with a rope put a-
bout thy necke, drawne and haled through
the ſtreets of the Citty, as I did, and was .

3 . Can it be poſſible, that thou ſhouldſt

be

be aſhamed to obey in good things, that redound to thy glory and merit, when as thy
Lord obeyed in ill things, that made to his
reproach, torments, and ignominy? Reaſon
now, and conſider with thy ſelfe, whether
it be more conuenient promptly to obey the
commaunds of Superiours, or to refuſe, if
any thing be commaunded little pleaſing
thyne owne appetite. And though it be an
eaſy matter to do, yet the enemy will cauſe
it to ſeeme hard and paynefull, that thou
mayſt either not obey at all, or that thou
looſe the merit of Obedience. Thy parents
Adam and *Eue* may be produced for an example, to whom when as God had giuen a
cōmaundmēt to abſtaine from the fruit but
of one tree only in paradiſe, which was not
any ſore or hard commaundment, ſith there
were many other fruite-bearing trees in
place, the crafty enemy of mākind wrought
ſo in their minds, as it might ſeeme an ouer
hard commaundement, and thereby the
more eaſily draw them to tranſgreſſe it. It
ought not to ſeeme hard vnto the ſeruant
to go on that way, which his Lord & Maiſter went before him with much more difficulty and daunger : and though the way
ſhould be dangerous, ſo it be not impoſſible
to paſſe, yet meet it is, that he go through .
                                    4. Sonne,

4. Sonne, as long as the bird is loose, and vpon her winges in the fields, she doth what she list, but when she is caught, and put in a cage, she doth as it pleaseth the owner. When thou wert in the world, thou liuedst, as thou listedst, thou didst eate at pleasure, thou didst whatsoeuer pleased thee, because thou wert thyne owne superiour, which was then conuenient for thee, sith in the world all make profession to do and gouerne themselues as they please, and after their owne manner. But when thou renouncedst the world, thou didst choose to thy selfe another Superiour, who might supply my place, and thou madest professiō of directing thy life, not after thyne owne will and iudgment, but after anothers. He therefore, who beeing in religion continueth tō liue after his owne manner, as he did in the world, declareth that he is not yet gone out of the world to religion, or sheweth himselfe to be a Religious man indeed in outward habit, who inwardly is a man of the world, or rather neither the one nor the other. Where Obedience is not, there neither Religion can vse it owne name, because they cannot long continue subiects, sith they be not conioyned with the head.

5. The chiefest bulwarke and defence
of

of a Citty, is the concord, and vnion of the cittizens : so the vnion and coniunction of the subiects with the Superiour their head, which obedience causeth, is the safety of religion . Where Obedience is, there is consent, and consent conserueth and strengthneth euery congregation, though there be many in it . My Apostles were in number few, abiect, and contemptible in sight of the world, yet did they great matters, because they were concordant, and so obsequious to me their Superiour, as that they might not forgoe their Obedience, they chose to loose their liues . Therfore he that neglecteth to obey euen in small matters, knoweth not the worth of obiedience, as the Apostles, and their Maister did, who were more ready to loose life, then to leaue Obedience .

6.   In the warfare of the world, the Obedience of the souldiers towards their Generalls and Captaynes is so strict, and so straitely obserued, as they be hanged for the very least disobedience ; and yet those that serue in the wars, make no Vow of Obediece at al, but only promise vpon their oath to fight against the enemy, and to defend, and maintayne the Citty, or strong hold against him . If then the temporall

warrefare requireth so exact Obedience, neither permitteth any the least disobedience in tryfling matters to passe vnpunished; how great, vpon iust cause, should the spirituall and Religious warfare exact, whereinto none is admitted, vnles he bind himselfe vnto Obedience by a sollemne Vow ? And how may any disobedience be tolerated in it, sith it is so proper in this warfare to obey the Superiors, as it obedience be wanting, the spirituall warrefare must needs come to decay.

7. There be some who indeed refuse not a Superiour, but they would not haue any thing commaunded them by him, especially if it be hard, and troublesome. This is not the desire of a good, and true Religious man, labouring to perfection; but only to be willing to seeme Religious in name, and not indeed, and to wish that the Superiour were a Statua or Image, & not a liuing man. Others would haue a Superiour industrious and diligent in procuring necessaryes, appertayning to meate, drinke, cloathing, and like commodityes, and in all euents to take a special care in patronizing, defending, and helping them: but they with him not to be so vigilant in obseruation of Religious discipline, which dependeth of Obedience.

Obedience. And this defire is much worfe
then the former: for to wifh this, is nothing
els then to haue a will and defire, that the
Superiour make his fubiects, not good Religious, but idle and flouthfull, who may
haue care of their bodyes, and neglect to direct their foules in the way of fpirit; who
may be a good companion, and a bad Superiour. The fubiect who hath a defire, that
his Superiour fhould not performe the office
of a good Superiour, doth manifeftly declare, that he carryeth himfelfe not for a
good fubiect vnder him.

Of the firft degree of Obedience, which con-
fifteth in execution of any thing
commaunded.

CHAP. XXV.

SONNE, thou muft not thinke, thou
halt done much, if thou fhalt at any
tyme haue done what thy Superiour hath
commaunded thee: for this is the very low-
eft degree of Obedience, and common to all
kind of fubiects, whether feruants or bond-
flaues : yea it is found in the very brute
beafts, which go whither foeuer their keeper driueth them, and do whatfoeuer he
pleafeth who hath care of thē. He is a poore
&

& miserable religious man, who whiles he obeyeth not his Superiours will, doth lesse then the brute beasts . And though this first degree of Obedience, which consisteth in the execution of that which is commaunded, be of it selfe the lowest, yet if it be kept as it should be, it is very pleasing vnto me. Foure conditions and qualityes made my Obedience, that I performed to my Heauenly Father, the more gratefull, and these be, Promptitude, Entirenesse in all points, Fortitude, and Perseuerance . These make a Religious mans Obedience acceptable, and the more easy be they, the greater the will is of imitating me .

2.   Not to obey with promptitude and speede , is a defect, and nothing pleaseth me. If it grow of a cold & languishing will it is the more displeasing vnto me, because the effect is bad, and the cause worse . He that hath tyme to do what Obedience commaundeth and putteth it off, suffereth the losse of tyme, and putteth himselfe in danger of not doing what he should. And if the Religious differeth to obey, because he is busied in some particular matter of his owne, he displeaseth me more, because he preferreth himselfe, and his owne busines before the busines of his Superiour . The truly

truly obedient, that he may obey perfectly, leaueth his busines begon , and vnperfect. O how much do those Religious please me, who if but a signe be giuen to do any thing that the holy Rule, or Superiour shall appoint , do leaue off, euen pious works, they haue in hand, and come running to what is commaunded. And they gaine my singular fauour, who to do any act of Obedience interrupt the talke they haue begon with me in prayer .

3 . Consider thou now, how litle those are in my grace , who blinded with selfeloue , least they should be depriued of any their least commodityes or recreations, bee dull and slow in accomplishing the worke that is appointed them by the Superiour . And I am offended more , if they vse the same delay, when the bell giueth a signe to prayer, or other spirituall exercises. O how much do such manner of men hurt themselues, and the Community also , especially seeing that when they are called to thinges commodious for their body, as to meate, drinke, recreations &c. they vse no delay at all, but be diligent , prompt and ready. Certs, it were better for them neuer to shew themselues abroad : for where there occurreth not any iust cause of purging them ,

R 2   there

there is a manifest offence & scandal giuen.
Those that be condemned as slaues to the
Gallyes for their crymes, be so ready to o-
bey, as that a signe is no sooner giuen, then
the thing is done and dispatched: and they
are so quicke and speedy in execution therof
as whiles the thing is yet in doing they cry
alowd, That it is dispatched. And though
they be so diligent and quicke for feare of
blowes, yet the loue of God should make
the Religious more prompt in this kind,
sith loue is more strong, and more effectuall
then feare.

4.   Neither is this to be seene in the
Gallyes alone, where a man shall see the
chaines, and the marriners with whips in
their hands, but also in the Courts of great
Lords. For I aske of thee, what is it that
maketh the seruants so ready and quicke
at the very voyce, and call of their Lords?
Is it the hope of reward? But that is more
liberall with me. Is it the loue they beare
towards their Lord? But much greater loue
is due to me: for goodnes and bounty,
which is the cause of loue, is farre more excellent in me, and the reward which is expected from me, is without cōparison greater. Indeed the slownesse of the Religious
proceedeth of the want of loue. If the subiects

ieéts were better affeéted to their Superiour
they would allo be more diligent in fulfilling of Obedience. In which kind the
children of this world be more wife, and
more ready,then the children of light.

5. Another condition is, that Obedience be intiere : for fuch was my owne O-
bedience. It fhall be inough for Religious
men to loue this entierneffe, if they throughly vnderftand, that this is my will, and
fuch the Superiours intention, that what is
commaunded be entierly done. There be
thofe, who be only ready to obey in matters
of great moment , but not in little. To o-
thers it feemeth inough, if they do part of
the things by the Superiour commaunded ,
and leaue the reft vndone. I know not who
hath made them Iudges , or Interpreters
of Obedience. Neither do I know, whence
they haue learned, that it is not neceffary to
obey to all that the Superiour decreeth or
commaundeth.

6. Let them fay , when they vowed
Obediéce, whether they thought they were
to obey in all things, or but in fome? Whether they vnderftood, that they were all-
wayes to obey, or only for a tyme? And if
they vnderftood, that they were to obey
not in all thinges, but for a certaine tyme
only,

only , who will accept of such a vow? Surely I accepted not the vow of half , and mayned Obedience , but of that which is entiere and whole. If some seruant should do but part of those things that were commaūded him by his maister, when he could haue done the whole , he should not be kept long in the house, and though he were still kept, yet in giuing vp his accompts it would soon appeare, whether one did owe any thing to the other , the seruant to the maister, or the maister to the seruant. He is not worthy of reward, but of punishment, who serueth not at the will of his maister . Many liue in Religion , with whome an accompt shall in the end be taken, and then it will be vnderstood, whether they merit reward or punishment , who haue not performed the whole and entier Obedience .

7 . The third condition is, that obedience be done with Fortitude . The Religious man pleaseth me not, who manifesteth a fortitude of mind in obeying, when easy matters are commaunded , or obeyeth willingly whiles matters go well with him, & the Superiour commaundeth those things that be contenting vnto him . This is not true Fortitude, nor can a stout obedient person be well by this way tryed. Whiles

a faire gale of wind bloweth , euery ſhip
ſayleth away merrily : and an infirme and
weake man walketh in a plaine way . The
Fortitude of an obedient perſon is found
and diſcouered in painefull & hard things,
as when incommodityes, labours & paynes
be to be endured; when preſent afflictions
of body keep him not from doing the acts
of Obedience ; when the courage getteth
ſtrength in ouercoming of difficultyes .

8. O how imprudently doeſt thou ,
my Sonne, whiles to the end nothing may
be often commaunded thee , thou ſheweſt
thy ſelfe vntoward in performing Obedience, deceiued with this opinion, that he
is wont to be ſurcharged with many labours , and offices, who manifeſteth his
own promptitude, and facility in obeying.
For what other thing is this, then to condemne the Superiour of indiſcretion , and
imprudency ? Then to put away a moſt
rich crowne from himſelfe ? If I giue thee
health and ſtrength of body for the taking
of paynes , wherefore art thou ſo afraid of
labours? Art thou ignorant, that the more
thy paynes be increaſed, the more is increaſed thy merit? Wherfore then ſuffereſt thou
thy ſelfe to be ouercome of ſlouth & lazines?
This is not Fortitude , but malicious care-
leſnes.

lefnes. I did not fo, who, when I could haue brought thee to thy faluation by eafy meanes, did neuerthelesse choofe the most difficult and hard for thy greater good, as was death in the flower of my youth: neither chofe I any manner of death, but that which was most ignominious and bitter, before which there went fo many and fo great torments, not only contumelious and difgracefull, but alfo cruell.

9. The fourth condition is Perfeuerance, which if it be wanting, there is obtaynd no Crowne at all, nor is there any merit of Obedience. I did runne the way of Obedience till death, contemning and remouing all difficultyes and impediments that encountred me on the way. My Apoftles alfo perfeuered in the obferuation of my precepts to the very end: and therefore he who by his inconftancy either for fome commodity of his owne, or for other humane refpect, neglecteth to performe Obedience, is not a difciple of myne. To begin Obedience, and after without iuft caufe not to execute it, is a property of children, not of Religious perfons.

of

*Of the second Degree of Obedience, apper-
tay ing to the Will.*

CHAP. XXVI.

SONNE, thy will is a blind faculty and
power, and thou art further blinded by
thyne owne passions, and so thou canst not
be a good guide thereto, least both of you
fall into the ditch. It must therfore needs
rely vpon me, and vpon him who supply-
eth my place in gouerning. And this requireth the second degree of Obedience, namely, that thou not only subiect thyne own
will to that of thy Superiour, & conforme
thyne vnto his, but that thou make his will
thyne, which thou shalt effect, if thou imprint thy Superiours wil within thy soule.
Two slips sprouting out of this graffe, to
witt, the Will, and the Nill of the Superiour, are diligently to be conserued, and if
any other bud should peraduenture begin
to peep forth, it is presently to be cut off,
least it take away the vigour and strength
from the yong graffe.

2. Obedience, which appertayneth to
this second degree, requireth three propertyes, which make it pleasing vnto me. One
is, that it be voluntary; a second, that it be

merry,

merry; the third, that it be feruent. These
three propertyes haue one common enemy
which troubleth them very much, and is
named Repugnancy. The Religious that
ouercometh not this Repugnancy, is easily
ouercome, because he knoweth not to obey
cherefully and feruently: and if the Repugnancy proceed from the superiour part,
what is voluntary, is taken away also. But
tell me, my Sonne, whence groweth the
Repugnancy, that maketh thee so froward
and backward in the performance of Obedience? Is it peraduenture of this, that
thou thinkest, by subiecting thy selfe to a
Superiour, thou preiudicest thyne own liberty and honour? If thou be therefore
sory, and thy grief causeth a Repugnancy,
thou hast no occasion of being grieued, but
of being glad rather, seeing (as I said els
where) he who for loue of me submitteth
himselfe to a Superiour, submitteth himselfe to me, the Lord of all; and in this he
doth not a little increase his owne estimation and honour, because he doth a matter
worthy a generous & magnanimous mind.
And whiles he doth tread selfe loue, as it
were vnderfoot (which neither all, nor many do) he plainly declareth, what a regard
he hath of me, and of the loue of me. If I
the

the Lord of Maiesty did tor the loue of thee
put my selfe into subiection of men, and
obeyed them withall respectiue manner,
why shouldst thou be sory, whiles thou
subiectest thy selfe to thy Superiour my substitute?

3.   Consider Sonne, that this is to be
a subiect : consider that thou art come to
Religion, not to commaund, but to obey.
If thou wouldst in thy Superiours voyce
acknowledge myne, and if thou wouldest
consider, that to obey thy Superiour, is to
obey me, thou wouldst reioyce to haue any
thing commaunded thee, and thou wouldst
obey both feruently, and most willingly.
To thinke further, that in obeying thou
forgoest thy liberty, is a notable errour,
when as it is not only not lost, but also perfected : for as much as by the benefit of O-
bedience it is conformed and conioyned to
the diuine will, which is an infallible rule
of working well, and therefore as long as
mans will is conioyned with it, it cannot
but worke well. Neither is it to be doubted
but that, that liberty which relyeth vpon
good, is more perfect then that which is
otherwhiles accompanied with euil. That
is not lost, that is giuen to God, but it is
made more secure, that it may not be lost.

4.   Where-

4. Wherefore the Obedience of this second degree, that it may be pleasing vnto me, must be voluntary, and not forced. Some there be, who are afraid to be imployed by their Superiour, and therefore they seek sundry pretences, and euasions to auoyd it, one while by hiding themselues out of the way, anotherwhile by excusing themselues, and sometymes by pretending themselues to be busied in other matters; & if they be at any tyme sent any whither by their Superiours commaundment, they go with a very ill will. Others had rather obey one then another, as though I were not in all Superiours. But they plainly discouer, that they obey not for loue of me. He that in Obedience giuen to Superiours regardeth me, maketh no differéce between Superiors, but equally obeyeth all alike. O how much be they deceyued also, who make it no matter of conscience, if they contradict their Superiors will in spiritual matters, as in fastings, prayers, mortifications, and other thinges of that kind: for disobedience forgoeth not the name of disobedience in spirituall and good matters also.

5. Others againe there be, who obey promptly in any busines pleasing to their

owne

owne inclination and nature, and in other
things that pleafe them not, they find a
great auerfion, difguft, and repugnancy.
And this is imperfect and miferable Obedience, becaufe it is certaine, that it hath it
fource from the fping of felfeloue. The mifery is the greater for this, that where fuch
obey vnwillingly, they do not only loofe
their merit, but alfo by occafion of their
difguft, and repugnancy they make the act
of obeying the more difficult, and hard:
and the detriment and hurt which followeth, and fhould be vnto them moft fweet re-
fection, is through their owne default turned into bitter poyfon. For he that obeyeth
with a regreet, and vnwillingly, ordinarily
murmureth, is angry, and giueth an offence
to others; and in place of a reward that he
might haue deferued, if he had obeyed willingly, he doth voluntarily procure his
owne punifhment.

6.   Sonne, haft thou a defire to be freed
from thefe miferyes? Stir vp in thy felfe an
effectuall defire of obeying me promptly &
fincerely for the tyme to come, and craue
this gift of him who is able to giue it thee.
Next, exercife thy felfe manfully in al kind
of Obedience, both great and little, and
thinke, that he fufteyneth a great loffe of
                                                        fpiritual

spirituall gayne, who obeyeth with an ill
will. He that is neere to death, and dyeth
not willingly, maketh his paßage the more
painefull: euen so he who doth Obedience
but yet with a repugnancy of the will, is a
more torment to himselfe, and therefore
better it is of neceßity to make a vertue. He
that is able to carry his croße vpon his
shoulders, let him not trayle it vpon the
ground.

7. Some will indeed enter into the
way of Obedience, but with this condition
that they may go before their Superiour,
not follow him. And these be they, who
when they haue propoſed in their mind
any exerciſe, or buſines to do, they ſeeke by
ſundry wayes to draw the Superiour to
their owne mind, and therein they be ſo
anxious, and follicitous, as it they compaße
not their owne deſire, they are much troubled. Neither doth their imperfection ſtay
heere, but they further will do that exerciſe
after their owne way, and not after the
manner that is appointed by their Superiour; and ſo their will goeth before the wil
of the Superiour. He walketh not in ſecurity, who carryeth his light behind him.

8. The Superiour is he, who carryeth
the light wherwith he muſt ſhew thee thy
way

way, not thou him, and therfore thou muſt
follow him, and not go before him . Who
draweth his Superiour to his owne manner of doing , ſeeketh not to obey his Superiour, but that his Superiour obey him:
and he that endeauoureth to draw his Superiour to haue a will to that , which is in
his owne will, doth preferre his owne will
before his Superiours, & therfore his fruits
ſhall not be the fruits of Obedience , but of
his owne will, which he taſteth of himſelf,
and not I.

9. Another property of this ſecond
degree is , that Obedience be merry and
cheerfull, which ariſeth of the former. For
he that obeyeth willingly , obeyeth alſo
merrily : and he againe, who obeyeth with
an ill will, obeyeth with heauines & grief.
A little Obediéce donefor loue of me with
ioy, pleaſeth me more, then great Obedience done with an heauynes. He that obeyeth not merrily , declareth that he loueth
me not, becauſe ſad Obedience diſpleaſeth
me Moreouer he increaſeth his owne burden, euen as he who obeyth merrily maketh his burden of Obedience the lighter.
O in how great an errour is he, who accu-
ſtometh himſelfe to a ſad, and delaying O-
bedience, becauſe he ſatisfyeth neither me,
nor

nor his Superiour, nor his owne conscience; and within a while there creepeth vpon such an one, a loathing and disgust of Religious discipline, and after loathing there followeth a most vnhappy life. For he is miserable & vnhappy, who is not content with his owne estate.

10.   The third property is, that Obedience be feruent. Feruour ariseth of loue, and if thou loue Obedience, nothing will be commaunded thee that thou mayst not execute both with ioy and feruour. I know well inough, who serue and obey me feruently, and who coldly, and I know againe who they be, who can obey me with more feruour, then others. O if Religious men would consider me present in all their actions, and examine withall, how pleasing it is to me, and what a pleasure to see the subiects manfully, cheerfully, and feruently to satisfy the precepts of their Superiours. If they would also consider the blessings wherwith I preuent such obedient persons, no doubt but they would be most forward in performing the actions of Obedience.

11.   Sonne, where is that feruour and heate, that thou hadst in the beginning of thy conuersion? Where is now that exceeding great loue that moued thee t, desire,

that

that many difficult and hard matters might
be commaunded thee ? Can it possibly be,
that the greater knowledg thou hast had of
this very thing, the lesse thou shouldst do ?
The scholler, that is found more ignorant
at the end of the yeare, then he was in the
beginning, deserueth to be thrust out of
the schoole, and to be put to a more base &
contemptible manner of life.

Of the third degree of Obedience, apper-
tayning to the Vnderstanding.
CHAP. XXVII.

SONNE, this third and highest degree
of Obedience, appertayning to the Vnderstanding, requireth that a Religious man
thinke and iudge that to be the best, which
is determined and appoynted by his Superiour : yea, and it requireth that the subiect
haue neither a contrary, nor different iudgment from the Superiours iudgment. For
the diuersity of iudgments is the cause of
disquiet and trouble. The subiect, who in
will only conspireth with the Superiour,
vpon the very least occasion that may cause
a difference of iudgments, may differ in
iudgment from him ; but he that is once
conioyned both by will, & vnderstanding
vnto him, is not so easily separated in the

T   one

one, or the other from him. For the vnderstanding teacheth the will, that diuision is not conuenient, though sometymes in the execution of Obedience all be not pleasing to the subiects mind. But whiles by reason he approueth that to be well done, whatsoeuer is ordayned by the Superiour, he putteth the will in a quiet state. This coniunction and conformity of iudgments also profiteth to the perfect execution of that which is commaunded. He that not only willeth that which the Superiour willeth, but also iudgeth that to be done, which the Superiour shall commaud, obeyeth far more perfectly, then doth he, who in will alone imbraceth the Superiours commaundment. He that needeth spurrs, is more holpen with two then with one, and two cords do more strongly bind then one.

2. Lord, I do not well conceiue, how the subiect may conforme his iudgment to his Superiours iudgment in all things, as he may conforme his will. For sith the will is free, it may be bowed both wayes: but the vnderstanding, that is drawne from the knowne truth, and is not free, cannot bend it self, but that way wher the truth is: and therfore if the subiects vnderstanding, conuinced

conuinced by some reason, that representeth
a thing as true, consent vnto it, and the Superiours vnderstanding, conuinced by another different reason, inclyne another way
in the same thing, how can the subiect in
this matter conforme his owne iudgment
to the iudgment of his Superiour, when it
is not in his power to reuoke his vnderstanding from the truth formerly knowne?

3. Sonne, what thou sayst, is true, when
the truth is knowne; for then it so conuin-
ceth the vnderstanding, as it cannot be induced, or inclined to the contrary. But
when euidency and certainty is wanting,
the vnderstanding, holpen by the will, may
rather be inclined to one part, then to the
other, and then the Obedient, that he erre
not, ought to submit his iudgment to the
iudgment of his Superiour, so as that he
may not erre in will, he submitteth it also
to the Superiours will. Neither yet, because many subiects be of more sharp witt,
and of a more mature iudgment, then the
Superiour is, be they therefore exempted
from this subiection: for so long as they be
members, they must be subiect to the head.
But suppose, that those subiects be more intelligent for knowledge of learning, yet in
matter and manner of gouernement, God

T 2   euer

euer giueth greater light to the Superiour,
then to the subiects, and therfore his iudgment must be preferred & take place before
the iudgments of others, and greatly to be
reckoned of, sith I vse him in the gouerning
and conseruing of Religious.

4.   But admit, that the Superiour hath
not commaūded something aright, which
yet is not accompanyed with sinne, whether doth the subiect therefore erre therein,
if he obey? In no case. Is he depriued of
the merit of Obedience? Neither. Why the
should he not submit his iudgment in all
thinges to the Superiour? When I was in
subiection to my Mother, and to my foster-
father *Ioseph*, I obeyed them both readily,
euen in those things, which I knew would
fall out better, if they had beene done otherwise. It is not for the subiect to procure
that, that may be best which is commaunded by the Superiour, but only to attend
to this, that he execute in the best manner
whatsoeuer shall be commaunded, & suffer
the Superiour to appoint that which he
himselfe shall iudge and thinke to be best.
Neither must the subiect forbeare the executing of the Superiours commaundment,
though he be certaine, that he should do
better if he did not. For the subiect is not
iudge,

iudge, but only the putter of that in practise
which is commaunded, so there be no sin
in doing it. This indeed is a defect of them
who would that the Superiour should ordayne what were best, but yet they wil not
do it, though theseiues be otherwise bound
thereto.

5. That the Obedience of the Vnderstanding is most pleasing vnto me, is a matter out of all question, sith it giueth the last
perfection to the sacrifice that the Religious offereth, whilestogeather with the will
he offereth both his Vnderstanding and his
owne iudgment, which is the noblest faculty of man. Moreouer it is knowne to all
how vehement a propension nature it selfe
hath put into man to the following of his
owne iudgment, and yet a Religious man
restrayneth this propension so far, as for
loue of me he voluntarily subiecteth his
own iudgment to another, which I esteeme
highly of, and is very profitable to himselfe: for so he leadeth a quiet life, and
most agreeable to a true Religious man: &
on the contrary, he that relyeth vpon his
owne indgment, is neuer at repose in any
thing, and liueth vnquietly.

6. This third degree of Obedience
hath three propertyes. The first is called
T 3   Simplicity,

Simplicity, which considering me in the Superiour, causeth the Religious man to put his Ordinations in execution, without any examination, whether he should allow them or not. O how displeasing vnto me is the disputing Obedience, which in whatsoeuer thing that is ordayned by the Superiour, euer asketh wherfore, for what intent, for what end this or that is appointed? I haue not called thee out of the world to dispute, or to examine those things that be by the Superiour determined and commaunded, but to do them. And that they be done, it is nothing necessary to know for what cause, how, & for what end they be done. Wherefore let it be thy care to do so much of Obedience, as thou art bound vnto, and know thou, that it appertayneth not to the subiect to enquire, what end the Superiours haue proposed vnto themselues in their offices. If the Patriarke *Abraham* had demaunded of God, for what cause he would haue him sacrifice his Sonne *Isaac*, vpon whome relyed the benedictions of Nations, & many other promises formerly made, his Obedience had not bene so commendable, neither had he merited so much as he did by simply obeying.

7. The truly Obedient seeketh nothing, but

but to do the commaundment. O how
greatly did I fauour thofe Religious, who
in the commaund of Superiours would not
difcuffe and examine, whether they were
profitable or otherwife, conuenient or not,
or the contrary. Whence it hapned, that cō-
maūded by their Superiour, they laid hand
vpon moſt cruell & fierce beaſts, as Lyons,
leapt into riuers, watred dry ſtocks for
a long ſpace togeather, and did many the
like thinges, as ſtrang as thefe. And thefe
left behind them on earth noble examples
of Obedience, and for them they haue, for
their ſimplicity in obeying, obtayned moſt
glorious Crownes in Heauen. Sonne, deſireſt thou, that God ſhould haue a particular
care of protecting thee, as he had of thoſe
holy Fathers? Obey then with ſimplicity.

8. . The other property is Humility,
without which neither Obedience, nor
Chaſtity, nor Pouerty pleaſe me. For Humility is Obediences mother, and the one
may not conſiſt, and ſtand without the o-
ther. The Proud will not ſubiect himſelfe
to any, and therefore cannot be Obedient.
Pride, becauſe it calleth the ſubiect backe
from the execution of the Superiours commaund, both depriueth of all merit, and increaſeth the trouble.

The

The conclusion, of Religious Obedience .
CHAP. XXVIII.

SONNE, perfect Obedience requireth an abnegation of the owne iudgment, an entier resignation of the will, and an exact execution and performance of what is commaunded. The true obedient regardeth not the person of him who commaundeth, and whome he obeyeth, but in him he casteth his eye vpon God, for loue of whome he obeyth . The truly Obedient ceaseth not to obey, though he knoweth that an errour is committed in the manner of commaunding : neither relenteth he in Obedience, though the Superiour be imprudent , or subiect to any other imperfection . He is deceyued, who obeyeth , that his Superiour may esteeme much of him , or that he may obtaine something at his hands, because he is to obey for the loue of me .

2 .   The truly Obedient , at what tyme any thing is commaunded , runneth not away, nor withdraweth himselfe into corners , but rather offereth himselfe readily to what is commaunded , or to be commaunded . The true Obedient regardeth not, whether it be from his chief Superiour

or

or from a subordinate, but he doth with
a like promptitude imbrace the commaūd-
ments of both. He that had rather obey in
one thing, then in another, deserueth not
the name of a truly Obedient man. He that
more willingly obeyeth one Superiour,
then another, is not perfectly Obedient.
He that procureth that to be commaunded
him which he desireth, looseth rather then
gayneth.

3. The truly Obedient searcheth not
out, wherefore, or how this, or that is
inioyned him, but it is inough to him to
know, that it is commaunded. The truly Obedient, to make Obedience perfect,
leaueth not his workes at halfes, and imperfect. He that obeyeth the Superiour
for that he is wise, louing, kind, spirituall, dexterous, or liberall, is deceiued,
because he is to obey him only, in that he
is my Substitute, and holdeth my place.
Reuerence is not exhibited to my Image
and picture for the gold, or siluer whereof
it is made, but because it representeth
me: whence it is, that the like honour is
done thereto, if it be made of paper, or
wood, as there is when it is of siluer, or
gold. In like manner all respect, reuerence,
and Obedience ought to be giuen, and vsed

T 5   to

to the Superiour , not for the vertues
wherein he excelleth , but becaufe he fup-
plyeth my place, and reprefenteth
my perfon.

The end of the fecond Booke.

THE
THIRD BOOKE
of Religious Perfection .

Wherein is handled the principall Vertues of a Religious man : and wherin perfection moſt of all
conſiſteth.

Of *Religious Humility*.
CHAP. I.

ONNE, it is good to ſpeake of
Humility , but better it is to
exerciſe it by deeds. What profiteth it by ſpeaking, to deliuer
many notable ſayings, tou-
ching Humility , if in all that diſcourſe
thou ſeeke after vayne glory, and fondly
brag of thy ſelfe? The Humble, who thinketh lowely of himſelfe, buſieth not himſelfe

selfe in his owne commendable matters, but rather in remembring the praises of others. He that seeketh to seeme Humble, & hunteth after the glory of men, groweth in pride, and the more humble he would seeme, the more doth his prid increase within. An humble man, as he acknowledgeth all his spirituall goods, & gifts to proocced from God, so doth he conceale them as much as he can, and locketh them vp with the key of modesty in some secret place. He doth not only repute himselfe in all his workes vnprofitable, but the more he laboureth, the more he thinketh himselfe bound vnto me. For seeing he holdeth whatsoeuer good he doth, to be nothing worth, he attributeth all his good workes vnto me: yea he is ashamed before me, that I disdaine not to vse his seruice, that is, so vile and contemptible an instrument, as he thinketh himselfe to be.

2. O happy Religious men, who do within their breasts intertaine so pious cogitations of Humility: for by this they shew themselues the more precious in my sight, & the more deare vnto me, the more abiect and contemptible they make themselues for the loue of me. These be those, who haue found a fixed seate in my hart, whom

I

I most tenderly loue, and with whome I
treate and conuerse familiarily . These be
they, whome I raise vp and honour in my
court of heauen, in the sight of my eternall
Father, and in the presence of my holy Angels . In the Kingdome of heauen he hath
not the more honorable place who was
most honoured on earth, but he who was
the more humble : and therefore my spirit
doth not without cause repose vpon the
humble, because he is diffident of his owne
forces, & relyeth altogeather vpõ my grace.
I haue reason to communicate my grace to
the humble, because they do for the loue of
me renounce their owne honour , and estimation, so greatlyesteemed of in the world.
I do vpon good cause bestow a most noble
Crowne vpon the humble in heauen , for
that whiles they liued on earth, they tooke
the crowne from their owne head , and
layd it at my feet.

3 . Before I came downe from heauen
into the earth , I was most particularly affected to Humility, & therfore I chose an
humble Mother: & I was no sooner borne,
then that I began to exercise Humility by
deeds. For when as I was the Lord of glory,
I became a seruant , & subiected my selfe to
men : and in processe of tyme I did set vp a
schoole

schoole of Humility, and such as resorted
vnto it, I informed by deeds & by wordes
to Humility vntill my dying day. In like
manner my Disciples made a profession of
Humility. And this is the cause, wherfore
I had a perpetuall warre with Pride, for so
much as I euer hated Pride, the capitall &
sworne enemy to Humility, which I so
tenderlyloued. And sith the matter standeth
thus, let euery one that is wise, iudge whether it be conuenient, that there should in
Religion, that is in my Family, any proud
Religious man haue place, or that it were fitting that a proud scholer should be admitted
and receyued into the schoole of Humility.
Hence it is, that some Religious do not go
forwards in spirit, because they be not exercised in the booke of Humility, which is
the foundation of spirituall life, neither
do study to imitate me, who am their Maister. It little profiteth the scholler to frequent the schooles, if he follow not his
booke, nor exercise himselfe in those things
that be taught in the schoole.

4.   There be many amongst the Religious, who of theselues confesse, that they
be sinners, carelesse, dull, slouthfull, and
nothing at al: but if any other should say so
much of them, they are eftsoons troubled,
moued,

moued, & murmure for the matter, & feeke
to detend their own eftimation & honour:
and thefe men are far from Humility . For
a man in words to confeffe himfelfe to be
nothing, and yet in hart to hold himfelfe
for fomthing, is falfe and counterfait Humility . And to haue a defire to be efteemed
of others , is notable arrogancy . But the
greater gifts an humble man hath, the more
doth he abafe himfelfe before others.

5. Defireft thou to know, my Sonne,
what Humility worketh in a Religious
man ? Firft it inclyneth his mind to thinke
fubmiffiuely of himfelfe : fecondly, when
need is, it moueth him to manifeft his own
vtility & bafenes, euen by outward action .
He that is lowly in his talke , going, conuerfation, and other his actions, declareth
himfelfe to be a contemner of himfelfe.
Moreouer, true Humility caufeth a Religious man to endure with patience and ioy to
be contemned of others , & caufeth further
that he be not only not troubled thereby
or murmure, but alfo that he moft hartily
giue his Creatour thankes therefore, for as
much as he knoweth, that by fo doing he is
the more likned to me his Lord & maifter .
True Humility alfo inclineth to the fhun-
ning of humane prayfes, and to the attri-
buting

buting of all that is good, vnto God.
Moreouer the Religious, who laboureth to
the height of perfect Humility, must needs
desire, that he be contemned of all, and further with, that all may be throughly perswaded, that himselfe is truly worthy to be cō-
temned of all.

6.   Sonne, if in Religion thou art ashamed of an old, or patcht garment, or doest
not with any willingnes exercise thy selfe
in abiect offices, it is a signe, that thou doest
not serue vnder Humilityes Colours, but
art addicted to thy owne iudgment, and
wishest to be much esteemed of others. If
thou hold on this way, thou wilt soone repent thy selfe. He that deuoyd of vertue,
seeketh to be reckoned off, for that alone
sheweth himselfe blame-worthy. The religious man, who hunteth after credit and
reputation with the world, liueth in miserable state. Moreouer thou louest Humility, or louest it not. If thou louest it not,
thou shalt neuer be a cittizen of Haue, the
gate whereof, because it is narrow and
strait, receyueth not men proud minded.
And if thou louest Humility truly, wherefore contemnest thou an old garment, and
to be contemned of others? What other
thing is it to be contemned, then for a man

to

to exercife himfelf in Humility, to côuerie
with it, & by the benefit therof to make a
fpirituall gaine? If thou loueft it, as thou
beareft me in hand to do, thou fhouldft be
glad when any fuch occafion prefenteth it
felfe. No merchant is difcontented, when
any occafion offereth it felfe of traffique to
his gayne.

7. Who art thou, which wouldeft not
be contemned? Art thou greater then I who
am the fonne of God? Thou art not: & yet
I was contemned of a moft vile and bafe
people, and moft iniurioufly handled by
them. Art thou not borne in finne ? Art
thou not a facke of earth, full of infinit miferyes? Wherefore then art thou moued and
angry, if any one lay thy bafeneffe before thyne eyes, and who thou art, which
thou fhouldeft confeffe thy felfe? What doth
it, wretch, auayle thee to haue left the world
if in Religion thou continueft to be proud?
O blindnes! when thou wert in the darcknes of the world, thou thoughft pride of life
to be meer and damnable vanity, and thou
conceyuedft honour and eftimation with
men to be a childifh thing: and now in the
light of Religion thou apprehendeft the
fame for thinges of great worth, and of fingular regard. Is it not a figne of a good
V   fight,

sight, when a man seeth better in darcknes, then in the cleare light.

8. Know thou for certaine, that he cannot be a good Religious man, who hunteth after commendations from men. Neyther is any Religious man humble, who acknowledgeth not himselfe contemptible, and wisheth not to be so held and reputed of others. And this is so certayne, as if any thinke otherwise, he beguileth himselfe: yea I say more, if it should be for the good of peace, and for Gods glory, whether a religious man were contemned, or praysed and esteemed, he should conformably to the law of perfect Humility, wish contépt rather then honour, to be deemed rather a foole then wise, because by that meanes he is made more like to me. And this Humility greatly pleaseth me.

9. All do not rightly examine the mométs of thinges, or make an vpright esteem of them, and therfore my Prophet sayd to good purpose: The children of men are liars in ballances. Many there be, who for their Humility be of no weight at all or very little in the ballances of the world, because they be held for base and counterfait mettall, and those very men be of iust and perfect weight in my ballance. For men

measure

meafure all thinges by the outward fhew ,
but I caft myne eyes vpon the inward , and
vpõ that which lieth hid in the mind. And
therfore many are of men cõtemned as vile,
and reiected as little profitable, who notwithftanding be for many refpects in my
fight to be preferred before others, and fo
their Humility do, as precious ftones, fhine
beautifull in myne eyes .

10.   The world onely efteemeth the
rich & mighty, who hauing receiued their
ftipend of pride, are eftfoones puffed vp beyond themfelues, and do fill all things with
their infolencies, and loftynes of mind .
And thefe, though difturbers of peace,
do meruailoufly pleafe the world . But the
humble and peaceable pleafe me, whome I
fo much efteem, that I haue a particuler care
of them . And worthily, becaufe there is
not a vertue of more regard with me, then
is that of Humility : and more then that,
no vertue is pleafing to me, that is not founded in Humility . Heauen gates had not
beene opened to my Mother, who was euer
moft deare vnto me , if (notwithftanding
her virginity and excellent purity) fhe had
appeared without Humility . One may get
into heauẽ without virginity, but without
Humility none at all . And becaufe, when

she lyued vpon earth, she moſt of all practi-
ſed Humility ; and though ſhe were the
Mother of God, and the Queene of heauen,
yet ſhe called and reputed her ſelfe an hand-
mayd, ſhe merited not only to haue a place
in heauen, but alſo to be exalted aboue all
the quires of Angells.

11.   There be ſome Religious, who
complaine that they find not that tranquility and peace of mind, which they had in
their firſt entring into Religion: but if they
ſearch out the cauſe, they will impute the
fault to themſelues. The cauſe of their diſquiet is the defect and want of Humility.
The humble hath peace with God, he hath
peace with men, he hath peace with himſelfe, and which is more commendable, he
hath peace with his aduerſary. For none
may without breach of peace deale with a
proud perſon, but the humble. Yea the
proud himſelfe eſteemeth highly of Humility, becauſe, leaſt he may otherwhiles be
contemned, or ill dealt withall, he couereth
his pride and loftynes of mind with the
cloke of Humility. Sonne, haſt thou a wil
to liue a quiet life ? Shake off pride: for if it
troubled the peace of Angells in Heauen,
how much more will it diſquiet men on
earth?

12. Lord,

12 . Lord feeing thou haft created man for the obtayning the glory of heauē which thou art thy felfe, and haft bound him to feeke fo noble an end , whither nature alfo inclineth him; it feemeth nothing conuenient, that he fhould not humble himfelfe, yea and abafe himfelfe fo far, as he fhould contemne himfelfe, and repute himfelfe for nothing . True it is, Sonne, that man was created to a moft excellent end, but we are to fee & confider, by what meanes we muft come therto : and therfore they who haue raifed vp their throne too neere heauen, haue byn miferably thrown down into hel. For as the Wifeman fayth : Who maketh of another mans houfe his owne, feeketh ruine . Wherfore if thou defire to be rayfed to glory, whereunto thou art created, thou fhalt not vfe any either more fecure, or more commodious way and meanes for the attayning therof, then if thou practife Humility This way held I , this way followed the Apoftles, in this walked all the bleffed in heauen. He that fhall take another way, fhall furely miffe of his marke .

13 . Sonne, fuffer not thy felfe to be beguiled : attend now to the exercife of Humility, which of huble perfons maketh Angells ; as contrarife , Pride of men maketh

keth

keth Diuells . Other vertues take away particuler vices, that be the cause of some sinnes only, but Humility taketh away Pride , which is the roote and head of all sins. Humility causeth, that the humble are dearely beloued , & acceptable to all . True it is that I make no great reckoning, when the Religious man doth humble himselfe to those who yeald him honour & respect, for that is easy and done of all. But I hold it for a great matter, if he also submit himself to them, who afflict & persecute him. It is not a thing worthy of great prayse, if a man humble himselfe to others in his aduersityes, or whiles he is in great necessity & distresse, but that he be humble whiles all matters succeed, and prosper well with him .

14 . There was neuer any Religious man yet, who hath not wished the vertue of humility, but al do not possesse the same, because all do not labour for it as it deserueth, nor vse the best meanes for the compassing therof. How is it possible for thee to get Humility, if thou neuer , or seldome vse the company of the Humble , when thou well knowest, that examples worke greater effects, then do words? How canst thou be humble , if thou seldome humble thy selfe , sith the habits of vertues cannot be

be had without frequented acts? Sonne, haft
thou a defire of true Humility ? Then lay
before thyne eyes thy own defects, and bufy
thy mind rather in examining thofe things
that be wanting vnto thee, then in thofe
that be in thee ; for an humble perfon concealeth his own good to himfelfe . It helpeth alfo often to call to remembrance, that
thou art to dye . O how many haue there
been more noble and more honorable then
thou art, who be now nothing but duft &
afhes, which thou fhalt alfo be ere long . It
profiteth to contemne the dignity and honours of the world, and to hold them for
meere vanityes, as they be indeed. It is good
for them who be in place of dignity , not
to glory or be puffed vp , but to feare a fall,
for that it is not fo great a pleafure to climb
high, as it is dolefull, and hurtfull to fall
downe againe .

15 . Sonne, haft thou a defire to make
an experiment of thyne owne Humility ?
Thou fhalt know it thus. It is proper to the
humble to fhunne their owne prayfes, as it
is a manifeft figne of pride to feeke them .
The humble is fory to heare himfelfe pray-
fed, and the proud reioyceth at it . The
more excellent gifts the humble hath , the
more carefully he concealeth them, thin-

king himſelfe vnworthy of them : and he
earneſtly deſireth that they ſhould be attributed to God, and that himſelfe be reputed
vile, and contemptible. The humble giueth
place to all, & ſerueth all, as well his inferiours and Superiours. The humble con-
uerſeth willingly with perſons of the mea-
neſt condition.

16.　Sonne, wiſheſt thou for the tyme
to come to know, how much thou haſt
profited in Humility? Conſider the crowns
that Humility preſenteth her followers:for
ſhe is wont to giue three crownes to the
humble. The firſt, and that which is of
the loweſt price is, when a man truly, and
in his hart thinketh himſelfe worthy to be
contemned. The ſecond is of greater price,
when he beareth the contemning of himſelfe with patience. The third, and richeſt
crowne is, when he is glad he is contemned
and loueth him who contemneth him. And
now conſider, which of theſe three crowns
thou haſt deſerued.

Of a Religious mans Loue towards God.

CHAP. II.

SONNE, Charity is a fruit-bearing
plant, which the deeper roote it taketh
　　　　　　　　　　　　　　　　　in

in the Religious mans hart, the sweeter
fruite it bringeth forth . Two branches
do spring therout; the one mounteth vp-
wards, and imbraceth God, the other bow-
eth downewards, & imbraceth the neighbour : it imbraceth thee with both for the
sauing of thy soule. For thou by louing
God and thy neighbour, louest and gaynest
thy selfe, euen as by hating God and thy
neighbour thou hatest and vndoest thy self:
Of louing ones selfe much, there is a special
commaundment, as there is of louing God
and our neighbour: for he who loueth God
& his neighbour, loueth himselfe. Of these
two branches dependeth the whole Law,
yea they be a short summary of all that is
written, eyther by the Prophets, or Euan-
gelists. Charity is sayd to be a celestial vertue, and that not without cause, becaufe a-
mongst the Theologicall vertues, that only
mounteth vp to heauen, wheras other vertues only enioy the fruits, but Charity enioyeth both the fruit and tree togeather.
Charity hath a different effect from Humi-
For this being founded in the knowledge
of mans basenes & misery, so far depresseth
and humbleth a man, as it causeth him to
esteeme himselfe for nothing at all : but
charity relying vpon the maiesty of the in-
created

created goodnes, raiseth a man vp to heauen, and maketh him to enter into the very
bosome of his Creatour, the Ocean of infinit goodnes.

2.   My Scripture mentioneth many
prayses of Charity, thereby to induce all to
loue it. One while it is called the Band of
Perfection, because it so strongly bindeth
mans will with me, as we become as it
were one, for that is proper to loue, to
transforme him who loueth, into the beloued, & this is the greatest perfection that
a man can haue in this life. Another while
it calleth it the life of fayth, the forme of all
vertues, the prime fruit of the holy Ghost,
and (to comprehend all the praises of it togeather in a word) it sayth, that God himselfe is Charity, and he that is in Charity, is
in God, and God in him. And what excellency is to be compared with God? What
more security is there, then to be in God?
and what greater pleasure can a man haue,
then to haue God with him. Charity worketh great matters in a man that is possessed
of it, as contrarywise, when a man is without it, he sustaineth great detriments and
hurts, and occasion is giuen him of many
and sore falls. When the soule is by death
separated from the body, life instantly leaueth

ueth a man, and all the beauty of the body is gone: euen so charity is no sooner dead in a man, then that the spirituall life ceaseth, the actions of life euerlasting fayle, and the spirituall seemelynes so pleasing vnto me, perisheth cleane away. Without Charity I acknowledge none for my friend, neither be any vertues pleasing to me, if Charity hath not ordered them. If a man speake the language of all nations, and should haue the knowledge of all sciences, and yet be without Charity, it doth him no good. And though he should giue all that he hath to the poore, and yet shall not haue Charity, it profiteth nothing. And if a man should deliuer his body so as it may burne, if Charity be wanting, it is nothing.

3. Go to, tell me thou, who in Religion hast no regard or esteeme of Charity, what will it profit thee to haue renounced the world, and to haue left all that thou didst possesse therein, to haue giuen ouer all pleasures of the flesh, and to liue in subiection and command of another, if thou be without Charity? Dost thou peraduenture thinke, that all this is said of secular persons, and not of Religious? Thou art deceyued: yea thy payne and punishment shal be so much the greater, sith for this end I

haue

haue called thee to religion, that difrobed
of the worlds cloathing, thou mightft clad
thy felfe all ouer with charity . But if thou
now haft fo little regard to attend vpon my
table in thy wedding garment, know thou,
that to thine owne hurt, thou art one day
to be thruft down into vtter darknes for the
fame. If the fire that I brought down with
me from heauen, be not conferued in Religion, where will it be kept? If Religious be
not amongft the firft who warme thefelues
with it, who will be? To ftand neareft to
the fire, & not to receyue the heate therof,
is a bad figne. It doth not a little difpleafe
me, to fee a fecular man fet on fire with the
loue of God, and a Religious man to freeze
for cold . If a fecular man exceed a Religious in ftore of merits, becaufe he fhall haue
exercifed more acts of Charity, it manifefteth that a Religious man is worthy of
great reprehenfion.

4.   Sonne, thou haft an obligation of
louing me much, not in regard I haue made
and framed the world for thee, or for that I
haue giuen thee thy being, and whatfoeuer thou haft in this life, or els for that I
haue deliuered thee from the feruitude of
the Diuell, and from the perills & miferyes
of the world; but for that I haue tendred
thee

thee with so great loue vntill this present
houre. Loue is the first and greatest benefit of all, that hath beene conferred vpon
thee. For that I made the world for thee
& thy sake, proceeded from the fountaine
of loue: that I suffred and dyed to saue thee,
loue was the cause: that I drew thee out of
the stormes and miseryes of this world, loue
alone effected it. And wilt thou not deeme
it for a singular fauour, that I the Lord of
glory, and King of maiesty, haue preuented
thee, a poore worme of the earth, with my
loue, without any one desert of thyne?
What necessity moued me, or what vtility
and profit drew me to cast my loue vpon
thee? And therefore needs must thou be
more hard then the flint, if by me preuented with so louing a gift, thou louest me
not againe.

5. Lord, if I were to repay thee any
thing, that by right ought first of all to be
myne: for it is impossible, that I should
render thee any thing correspondent to thy
loue. When thou createdst me, thou gauest
me to my selfe: when thou redemedst me,
thou gauest thy selfe for me, and gauest me
to my selfe againe. If then, because thou
createdst me, I owe my selfe all vnto thee,
what shall I giue thee for repayring and re-
storing

storing me loft and vndone? What fhall I giue for thee, for hauing been offred vp for me: and if I were able to giue my felfe euery moment a thoufand tyms for thee, what am I compared with thee? And therfore I fincerely confeffe and acknowledge, that I am indebted vnto thee fo much the more, the more noble, and more deferuing thou art, then I.

6.   Lord, if it be true, as it is moft true, that my foule, body, life, works, and whatfoeuer good I haue in this wold, be al thyne, and that I am for a thoufand refpects bound vnto thee; I ought to cofeffe, that I acknowledge nothing in me to be myne owne but imperfections, defects, and finnes. But I fhould be moft iniurious vnto thee, if in requitall of my loue to thee for thy loue, I fhould offer them vnto thee, which be not only nothing pleafing vnto thee, but thou alfo extremely hateft, as contrary to thy holy will, and defire.

7.   So it is, Sonne, but yet fomething there is in thee, that is thyne, & to me moft acceptable, and that is thy loue, which thou canft & maift vfe at thy pleafure, fith thou art Lord and owner therof. For this is not only pleafing vnto me, but alfo maketh all thy actions acceptable to me, and

more

more then that, nothing can content me,
that goeth not accompanyed with it. And
meet it is, that sith I first haue loued thee,
thou againe loue me, seeing loue cannot be
requited but with loue againe. And though
I had done no more for thee, thē that I made
thee worthy of my loue, this one benefit
alone should haue beene inough to haue set
euen a frozen hart on fire with the loue of
me.

8.   It is true, Lord. O my soule, if thou
shouldest not be set on fire with Charity in
this glowing-hoate, and diuine fornace of
the loue of my Sauiour, I know not who
will deliuer thee from the euerlasting freezing cold? What father, or friend hath euer
so loued me, as hath my Redeemer? He hath
not loued me with the loue of seeking his
owne commodity, but with a sincere loue
because he had euer a regard to my saluatiō,
and not to any profit of his owne. For
when he was blessed in himselfe, and was
adored of the Angells in heauen, he came
downe into the world for me, and became
my brother and friend, and dranke vp the
bitter cup of his passion, that he might deliuer me from death euerlasting : wherefore
let me loue him, and though I cannot loue
him with an infinit loue, as he deserueth,
sith

sith he is infinitly good, yea and goodnes it selfe, yet let me at least loue him withall my hart. He is to be loued of me, as my father, and a most clement father, as a most munificent giuer of all that I haue, as my most compassionate comforter in all my distresses, as a most diligent steward and procuratour in all my necessityes, as a most abundant and liberall rewarder of all my good workes, sith neither eye hath seen, nor vnderstanding of man can conceyue, what God hath prepared in heauen for the that loue him. If he at any tyme chastize vs, we must loue him the more affectuously for it: for punishments inflicted of loue, hurt not. Euery one who chastizeth is not an enemy, as neither euery one is a friend that forgiueth. Wherfore seeing, euen when he punisheth, he is an amiable Father and a Father of mercies, it is to be thought that, if he do it, he doth it for our good.

9.   O my soule, not to loue God, as he is to be loued, is not to loue him at all. He ought to be loued respectfully, not for the good or euill he can or may do vs in this or the other life, but for himselfe: and all other things are to be loued in him, and for him. He must be loued strongly, for Charity putteth away all vayne feare, and ministreth

niftreth ability, & courage to ouercome all
difficultyes, and to beare all aduerfityes patiently. He is to be loued with all the hart,
with all the foule, with all the mind, and
with all the forces. And to loue with all the
actions inward and outward, is to loue
wifely, fweetly, feruently, and continually.
He is to be loued aboue all thinges, and fo
we fhall loue him, if we preferhim before
all creatures, if we would choofe rather to
dye a thoufand deaths, then to offend him
by one mortall finne.

10. Sonne, not all that thinke they
loue me, do fo : neither all who thinke they
intertaine Charity at home, do it. Charity
being the queene of all vertues, entreth into
no mans houfe, vnles be fhe intertayned as a
Queene, neither ftayeth fhe therein, vnles
he receyue her as a Queene, and honour
her for fuch. Moreouer I am to be loued,
not by words, but in deeds, and my will is
that loue be manifefted by workes, and not
by the tongue alone. How doft thou loue
me, if thou feldome thinkeft of me, & when
thou thinkeft of me, thou doft it only by
the way paffing, & in a languifhing manner? This is not to loue with all thy hart,
nor with all thy mind. How doeft thou
loue me, when whole dayes, weeks, and

X moneths

monethspasse, that thou speakest neither of me, nor of any thing appertayning to me, nor doest not willingly heare them who treate of good matters?

11.   Loue, shut vp within the breast, can neither forbeare to speake of me, nor stop the eares from hearing men talke of me: and how canst thou with truth affirme that thou louest me, if thou attend not to those thinges, that I speake vnto thee in thy hart? Or if thou be attentiue, wherfore dost thou not regard them? Who loueth truly, suffereth not any word of the beloued to fal in vaine out of his mouth, but layeth them vp within his hart in store, and there diligently examineth them and refleceth vpon them. How dost thou loue me, if when thou art able, thou dost it not, or giuest not with a ready mind, when any thing is asked or demaunded of thee for the loue of me? It is not hard for a true louer to repay lesse loue to the beloued, who hath giuen him his hart before, & more then that himselfe also. How louest thou me, if thou wilt not suffer any incommodity for my sake, nor expose thy selfe to any danger? Who loueth from the hart, will not sticke to dye for his beloued.

12.   How canst thou say, thou louest me,

me, if in obſeruing my commaundements thou findeſt ſo great difficulty, and art ſo negligent, as thou mayſt ſeeme not to keep them, but forced, and againſt thy will? Loue may not endure delay, neither is-it diſguſted at all, but doth with great alacrity the will of the beloued. How can it be, that thou loueſt me with al thy ſoule, when thou art ſo greatly deuoted to thyne owne eſtimation, and to other tryfling thinges, that agree very little with my will? He that loueth another beſids me, and not for me, either loueth me not at all, or loueth me not as he ſhould. How canſt thou aſ-firme, that thou loueſt me, if thou neither loue, nor reſpect thy Superiours, as they deſerue, who ſupply my place, when as I haue plainly declared, that the honour, or contempt, that is done to them, is done to me? He loueth not truly, who conformeth not himſelfe to his beloued.

Of the Religious mans Charity to his Neighbour.

CHAP. III.

SONNE, thou ſhalt find ſome in the world, who deſire not, that any honour be giuen them: thou ſhalt find thoſe, who

X 2   refuſe

refuse dignityes, and honours, thou shalt find also those, who receyue not the gifts, fauours, or presents that others giue vnto them, but thou shalt not find him, who desereth not to be loued of others, especially with due and respectiue loue, which for that it causeth vnto the beloued neither suspition, nor disgust, is wont naturally to please. Many loue their neighbour, but they know not how to loue, and therefore their loue is other whiles fruiteles, as also hurtfull. I gaue a commandment of louing thy Neighbour, and declared the manner of louing him. If thou loue thy Neighbour, because he is thy kinsman, or friend, or because he is thy Countryman, thou dost nothing, this is not Charity tending to Heauen, but naturall loue, creeping vpon the earth, and common to Infidells, and Barbarians. If thou loue him for any commodity or gayne that thou receyuest of him, or hopest from him, thou louest thy selfe, and not thy Neighbour, and this is called Loue of Concupiscence, neither is it of any longer continuance, then is the profit hoped for thereby. To loue our Neighbour for our owne commodity, is not Charity, but rather merchandize.

2.   Charity truly effecteth, that the
Neighbour

Neighbour be loued, becaufe he is created
to my likenes, and is capable of euerlafting
bliffe. True Charity difpofeth, that our
Neighbour be loued for God, and in God,
and he that loueth after this manner, loueth all, the poore equally with the rich,
the nobly borne, and the ignoble, he imbraceth all, and wifheth them life euerlafting. He loueth them as well in tyme of
aduerfity, as of profperity: for he who ceafeth to loue his Neighbour, in tyme of neceffity, manifefteth plainly, that he loueth
him not for me. All this I vnderftood,
when I commaunded a man to loue his
Neighbour as himfelfe, that is, that thou
fhouldft wifh vnto him, what thou wifheft
to thy felfe. And as thou muft loue thy felfe
in God, and for God by obeying his law on
earth, that thou mayft afterwards haue thy
reward in heauen : fo oughteft thou to loue
thy Neighbour, as capable of the fame bea-
titude with thee. O if the Religious would
obferue this manner of louing their Neighbour, there would not be feene fo many
partialityes in Religions and Churches.

3. Some be loued moft of all, becaufe
they are learned, and kind, others becaufe
they be rich, and in grace, others becaufe
they are gentlemen, or of noble bloud, and

X 3   those

tnose that be not such, they regard not. O
fraud, & deceit! What hath Charity cōmon
with learning and riches? as if a man that
is not rich, or learned, or well apparelled
were not to be loued? Charity hath in the
first place an eye to me, and for that cause loueth all in me. But there is another misery
more to be pittied, that some do therefore
loue others, because they haue the same
complexion of nature, and of bloud with
them. This is not Charity, but a carnall
affection, an enemy to true Charity. Charity dilateth it selfe far more wide: for it extendeth it selfe to all, because all be created
to eternall glory, and all be ransomed with
my bloud.

4.   Sonne do not put thy selfe in danger, both of hurting thee, and of offending
me, and therfore regard not the complexion
and inclination of bloud: if thou do, vnder
the pretence of Charity, thou wilt foster
sensuality, which will soone deceiue thee,
and will draw thee, and not thou it, into
a place, out of which thou shalt not find
meanes of getting out againe. Though the
whole Euangelicall law be myne, because
I made it, yet did I particulerly name that;
of louing the Neighbour, my commaundment, to
giue thee to vnderstand, how pleasing to
me

me was the sincere loue of the Neighbour.
I would also that Charity should be the
badge and cognisance, whereby my Disciples were to be knowne, in so much as ther
should not be any of my schoole, or of my
sheep, who loueth not his Neighbour, as
himselfe. Charity also is a signe of loue,
that a man carryeth towards me.

5. Thou art deceiued, my Sonne, if by
not loning thy Neighbour, thou thinkest
thou mayst loue me. He that loueth not
him whome he seeth (sayd my beloued
Disciple) how shall he loue him, whome
he seeth not ? It is true indeed, that the
loue towards God the creatour, must go in
the first place, out of which the loue to the
Neighbour may rise; but it is true with all,
that the loue of the Creatour is conserued
by the loue of the Neighbour, and therfore
if this languish, that must needs faint with
all. Many thinke they are my friends, and
yet are not, for the malice and little good
will they carry to their Neighbours. I am
not a friend of an hard and peruerse hart.
Not to loue, is a signe of a fierce mind, but
to hate is an argument of a wicked & cruel
hart. Loue if thou wilt be loued, and loue
all, if thou desire to haue me for thy companion; for that if thou except but one from
thy

thy Charity, thou shalt also thrust me out of thy hart with him. If thou being Religious, wilt not loue one, because he hath offended thee in some thing, what difference will there be betweene thee, and a secular man, who followeth the vanity of the world? My disciples did not so, who neither hated, nor hurt, by the least word those who had iniured them, but were very glad, if they had at any tyme occasion of suffering any thing for the glory of my name.

6. By what example canst thou be more stirred vp to loue thy Neighbour, then by that of my heauenly Father, who notwithstanding he had receyued most frequent and grieuous iniuries at the worlds hands, did neuertheles carry so tender affection towards it, as he gaue his only begotten sonne for it. And what did not I, being made Man, for my Neighbours, whiles I spent my whole life to do them good? Whiles I liued, I was their guide, and companion, and I spared no trauayle or paynes at all, that I might shew them the right way to heauen. And more then that, I layd vpon myne owne shoulders all their debts, that were obnoxious to the diuine Iustice, for which dying vpon the Crosse, I
satisfyed

satisfyed for all. Neither was there here
an end of my singular loue to my Neighbour. For at what time I was to depart out
of this life to my Father of heauen, I left
my self in the Sacrament of the Altar, both
that I might be mans meate, and that I
might vnite my selfe vnto him, and be euer
with him: and also, that he being strengthned by the vertue thereof, might one day
mount vp on high, where he might for e-
uer enioy those heauenly goods wherto he
was created.

7. By this euery one may iudge, whether the Religious, who be inuited to be
perfect, as my father of heauen is, and who
make profession of imitating me their maister, ought by their very works to loue their
Neighbours, and to help them in all they
be able. Let it be considered and weighed,
whether those Religious be worthy of my
loue, who take no care of louing their
Neighbour, or els in regard of some very
little incommodityes, which they feare,
neglect to help them, who craue their assistance. Let it be examined, whether the
iniuries, hurts, and trespasses done them
be any fit cause of not louing, or not helping
them, when as I suffered many far greater
iniuries, and yet did not for that withdraw

X 5 my

my loue, but spent my life and bloud to do
them good. All a Religious mans spiritual
gayne (who cannot patiently put vp iniuryes, and therefore will not do his Neighbour good) is conuerted into his own hurt.
For the iniury is domageable to him, who
doth another hurt, and auaylable to him to
whome it is done, if he beare it with patience. If then the iniury giueth a Religious man occasion of meriting, he hath in
truth no cause to be greatly moued against
him, who offereth the iniury. I neuer deliuered such kind of doctrine, I neuer gaue
my selfe an example in that kind, but alwayes taught, that good was to be rendred
for euill.

8.   Sonne, remember that thy selfe and
all thy forefathers do take their beginning
from one, that is from *Adam*, and for that
cause be bound to loue one another, as brethren. Call to memory my Apostle his
wordes, when he sayth : You are my members, and therfore there ought to raigne that
loue amongst vs, that is amongst the members of one body. And by this thou mayst
manifestly vnderstand, whether thou louest
thy Neighbour truly or no. He that either
little regardeth his Neighbour, or contemneth him, though in degree neuer so far
                                              inferiour

inferiour to himselfe, hath not true Charity. Neither the head, nor the eyes, which be the more noble members of man, do euer contemne the feet, though they be inferiour members, and lesse noble. He that is sory for his Neighbours good, or is glad of his hurt, sheweth that he loueth him not, for that one member either suffereth , or reioyceth in company with another . Charity deemeth the Neighbours either good , or ill, as proper to it selfe. He that out of enuy and malice either extenuateth, or traduceth the actions of his Neighbour, loueth not me . It was neuer seene, that the hands would hurt the feet. He that assisteth not his Neighbour, in what he is able, hath not Charity. The eyes neuer refuse to yeald vnto the other members the office of seeing. True Charity though it be preiudiced and hurt, is not moued to indignation , neither practiseth it reueng, but helpeth the Neighbour, and excuseth his fault.

Of the Religious mans gratitude towards God, for the benefits he hath receyued.

CHAP. IIII.

TELL me, Sonne, what Father or Mother euer did as much to their children

as

as I haue done to the Religious? And what
Sonne hath euer receaued so much from his
Progenitor, as haue the Religious from me
their Creatour and Lord ? Benefits loose
not the name of benefits, for that they be
common to many, neither doth their obligation cease, because many haue their shars
and parts therein. I haue created thee, and
made thee to myne owne image. And if, as
meet it is, thou wouldst consider & weigh
this, it would be inough to bind thee infinitly vnto me. For by creating thee of nothing, I gaue thee not whatsoeuer nature &
being, but a nature very noble, indewed
with reason, free, and a commaunder of al
creatures vnder heauen: yea I haue made
thee chief and Lord on earth, and haue subiected to thy commaund the fowles of the
ayre, the beasts of the earth, and all other
things created. And though all this be a
very great benefit, yet if it be compared
with the end wheruto I haue created thee, it
is none at all. Wherefore know thou, that
I haue created thee to a most noble, and a
most excellent end, then which there is
not any greater, nor can be in the world,
which is for all eternity to enioy the sight
of the diuine maiesty in heauen.

2.   Dost thou desire to see, my Sonne,
how

how exceeding great the benefit of Creation is, which is the foundation of all the o-
ther? Go to, tell me, if thou wert deftitute
of both hands and feet, what wouldft thou
not giue to haue them? and if thou wert
dumbe or blind, what wouldeft thou not
beftow for the recouering of both thofe facultyes againe? Thou wouldeft queftionles
giue the whole world, if it were thyne, &
thou wouldeft rather lead a moft poore life
with the vfe of thofe members and fenfes,
then to be a king on earth without them.
And heerehence thou mayft conceyue the
greatnes of the benefit of thy creation, by
which thou haft receyued a body, together
with all the members and fenfes thereof, a
foule alfo togeather with all the facultyes,
and life, with all things neceffary therunto.
Thou canft not be ignorant, that by the
greatnes of the benefit, an eftimate, or geffe
muft be made of the greatnes of the obligation.

3. Confider thou now, how much
thou art bound vnto thy Creatour for this
benefit alone, imparted vnto thee without
any deferuing on thy part at all. Confider,
how thou fhouldeft fhew thy felfe very vngratefull, if thou fhouldeft not imploy thy
life, thy health, the forces of thy body, and
whatfoeuer

whatsoeuer thou hast, towards the seruice
of thy benefactour. Consider, how grieuous a sinne it is to abuse the senses, and o-
ther the facultyes of the mind, to the offence and contempt of him, who hath gratiously bestowed all those thinges vpon thee.
And if the cryme of ingratitude be so odious
and great in secular men, how great wil
it be in Religious persons, who haue receaued greater light from me, and are obliged
vnto me for many more respects? O how
exact an accompt be the vnthankfull Religious to make, who not reflecting vpon the
greatnes of this benefit, do either quite forget, or little regard it. And what meruaile
that the vngratefull do not in this life receaue new benefits, but be sometymes be-
reaued of those they haue already receaued?
Ingratitude driueth away the Benefactour,
euen as gratitude inuiteth him to bestow
greater benefits.

4.   What I did after this for the conseruing of thee, is not inferiour to the afor-
sayd, neither bind thee lesse vnto me. I ordayned, that all creatures should serue thee,
some wherof serue for necessity, some for
recreation, some also for exercising both of
body and mind. The heauens go their cir-
cle for thee, whatsoeuer the sea and earth
bring

bring forth, it is for thy vſe. I haue ordained the Angells, ſo excellent creatures, to
guard thee. Neither doth any cogitation
ſeeme to preſſe me more, then of doing thee
good in all thinges, in ſo much as it may
be truly ſayd, that thou art the end & ſcope
of all this vniuerſe, ſith all is created for
thee, and prepared for thy vſe and ſeruice.
If thou aske me now, for what cauſe I haue
prolonged thy life till this very houre,
when as I haue dealt otherwiſe with many
both yonger and ſtronger then thou art;
certaine it is, that I haue not delayed it,
that thou ſhouldeſt hold on to offend me by
perſiſting in thyne owne ingratitude, but
that thou ſhouldeſt rather amend thy manners, and indeed ſhew thy ſelfe gratefull to
me, thy Benefactour?

5.   And all this I did for thee without
any thy labour, paynes, or trouble. But for
the redeeming of thee, & for the deliuering
of thee out of the miſerable captiuity of
ſinne, what did I not? When I was the
ſonne of God, and in ſupreme veneration
of all the court of heauen, for the ſauing of
thy ſoule I came downe from heauen into
earth, became man, and ſubiecting my ſelfe
to the infirmityes of man, I began to endure
exceeding great paynes, and trauayles for
thy

thy fake. How many miferyes did I fuftai-
ne, how many calumniations did I fuffer,
what abundance of teares, and bloud did I
fhed for thee? And more then that, I dyed,
that I might deliuer thee from death euerlafting, and free thee from the cruell tyranny of the Diuell. See, Sonne, how deare
a price I payed for thee. See, how by all
right thou art not thyne owne, but myne.
And know thou, that the benefit of thy re-
demption, though it be common to al men,
is not yet communicated to all, neither do
all enioy the fruites thereof, becaufe all
haue not receiued the light of faith, by help
whereof they may acknowledg & know the
way how to come vnto me. And becaufe
thou art one of thofe, who haue receaued
very great benefits at my hands, as hauing
beene borne within the bofome of holy
Church, and illuminated with my grace,
and light from heauen, fee thou be not in-
gate, but vfe thy receyued gifts, leaft thou
be depriued of thy felicity. He that feeth
fnares, and when he may auoyd them, putteth himfelfe rafhely into them, meriteth
to be punifhed : euen as he, who feeth not
the fnare, is worthy of compaffion, if he be
vpon the fodaine caught therein.

6.   I haue againe gone further with
                                    others

others in bestowing benefits vpon them, as
with those, whome I haue called to a more
high and more perfect state, and receyued
into the number of my most deare friends,
with whome I conuerse far more familiar-
ly then with others : & these be the Religious, whose obligation is greater, then thou
conceyuest, sith there is not a moment of
their life, that receyueth not a new increase
of one benefit or other. And if thou wilt
consider the matter well, they began to enioy a benefit, before they were borne into
the world. Doth it not seeme a benefit vnto thee, that I from all eternity haue without any their merit, out of my fatherly loue
cast myne eyes vpon them, to enrich them
with my heauenly gifts? And haue not I ,
since the tyme they were borne, had againe
a peculiar sollicitude and care of them ?
With how much patience haue I borne
with their imperfections? What meanes &
wayes haue I vsed to draw them out of this
deceiuing world , and to bring them into
the best way? From how many sinnes haue I
preserued them, one while by taking away
the occasion of sinning , another while by
giuing them hart and courage to shake off
tentations , at another tyme by auerting
their desires from hurtfull things . And

now, what Law commaundeth, or permitteth, that euill should be rendred for good?
What wild beast is so cruell, that would go
about to hurt his Benefactour? If ingratitude alone be worse then a wild beast, because it repayeth the Benefactour with ill;
if the forgetting of benefits be a thing infamous, and worthy of reprehension, what
will it be to offend the Benefactour? There
haue beene seene many Religious, who at
the tyme of their death haue much lamented their owne ingratitude, and haue made
a firme purpose, that, if it should be their
hap to recouer, they would be most thanke-
full, and would be most diligent in seruing
of God heere after. But these men became
wise, when it was too late.

7.   Sonne, hast thou a desire to auoyd
the detestable cryme of Ingratitude? Then
differre not thy good purpose, but begin
euen now to answere thy receyued benefits:
for this is to be gratefull. He is gratefull, who
is as much afraid to offend his benefactour
in the least thing, as he is of death it selfe.
He is gratefull, who imployeth his life,
health, strength, body, and whatsoeuer besids to his benefactours honour and glory.
He is gratefull, who is diligent in his deuotions, and in all his actions seeketh to

actor

accomodate and conforme himselfe to the
diuine will. Contrariwise, that Religious
man is vngratefull, who carryeth not himselfe towards his Religion, as towards his
mother and mistresse. The Religious that
respecteth not his Superiours, neither yealdeth them fit honour and reuerence, as vnto
my substituts, is vngratefull. And no lesse
is he, who prayeth not deuoutly for his benefactours, by whose help, meanes, and industry I prouide necessaryes for the intertaynement of the Religious. Finally gratefull is he, who desireth to shew himselfe
gratefull in all thinges.

Of Patience, necessary in a Religious man.

CHAP. V.

SONNE, sith this life is the vnhappy banishment of *Adams* children, a man cannot passe it ouer without much trouble and
many afflictions: and therfore my Church
calleth it the *Vale of Teares*, because there is
notany state therin, nor any place in which
there is not occasion of lamentation. Let a
man make an election of whatsoeuer state
he liketh best, and let him haue al temporal
goods and contentments at will, yet he shal
not want troubles, miseryes, and disgusts,

Y 2   and

and whence he least expecteth, thence will
molestations, and afflictions come vpon
him. For to excell in learning, to abound
in riches, to haue the fauour of all, to commaund others; do not exempt and free a
man from this banishment, and vale of
teares: and therefore as long as a man liueth, there is not wanting matter of sorrowing. All haue a will to fly from the
Crosse, but it hideth not it selfe from any,
neither is there one only Crosse in this life,
but they are infinite. No place, no tyme, no
state is without aduersityes, and therefore
better it is to seeke a remedy against them,
then to fly from them. Some, whiles they
put one Crosse by, do fal into another greater then the former, & where they thought
to haue found quiet of mind, they find perturbations and troubles both of mind and
body. The only, and present remedy of all
these calamityes is Patience, which preuay-
leth not by flying away, but by resisting.

2. And for the vnderstanding of the
office of Patience, thou must know, that of
the contrary accidents, that befall men in
the banishment of this life, there ariseth in
a mans mind so great an heauines and grief,
as it obscureth reason, and troubleth the
mind. And as a feuer in the sicke hindreth
the

the actions of the body, so doth sorrow disturbe & hinder not only the good actions
of the mind, but further openeth the gate
to many inordinate desires and sinnes. And
for this cause it is written of the Wiseman:
Sorrow hath killed many, not only by a
corporall death, but by a spirituall also.
And Patience is a vertue, that tempering &
moderating the grief and heauynes, that is
occasioned by tribulations, conserueth and
armeth Reason that she be not put from
her standing, and ouerthrown by the inordinate desires and passions of the mind. And
this is nothing els, then to stop the entrance
against many errors and defaults, that befall
whils the mind is vnquiet, and the Reason
troubled. And therfore in my Scripture it is
sayd, that Patience hath a perpetuall work,
for that when the sorrow, & grief of mind
is once moderated, all the hatred, indignation, reuenge, and other the euills which
are wont to rise of those perturbations, are
the more easily diuerted, and put by. And
when the Reason is once free from all perturbations, it hapneth, that a man executeth the workes of vertue after an entiere &
perfect manner. Hence it is, that some call
Patience the keeper and conseruer of vertues, and not without cause. For vertue

cannot

cannot exercise their power, when Reason
is troubled, and the mind disquieted, and
therfore they need the help of Patience, that
keepeth the reason free from perturbation,
and the mind from disquiet, & consequently the vertues be conserued also. The house
that hath not one within to keep it, is easily spoyled.

3.   For to cure the deseases of this present life, there be vsed three kinds of Antidots. The first is that which the Phisitians
prescribe, and this doth not alwayes cure
or help, yea sometymes it hurteth. For the
Phisitians often find not the cause of the
sicknes, and therfore they cannot well ap-
ply any cure vnto it. The second is prayer,
whereby recourse is made to the heauenly
Phisitian, who as most wise, hath a perfect
knowledg of all diseases, and being omni-
potent, is of power to take them away in an
instant. And this medicine, though it
doth euer good, doth not for all that restore
the health at all tymes. For the heauenly
Phisitian euer prescribeth a remedy, that is
expedient for the sicke person, but corporall health is not euer good for the sicke, &
therfore God doth not at all tymes giue it
him. The third Antido e is Patiéce, which
alwayes cureth, being healthfull both to
body

body and foule, and helpeth not the ficke
alone, but the ftanders by alfo for the good
example that is giuen them. And this third
Antidote is fo proper to Religion, as the
Religious, who either make little efteeme
therof, or vfe it not, be alwayes fore ficke.
The ficknes and infirmity is euill inough,
when the mind is difquieted by impatience.

4. Sonne, what is the caufe, when any
thing befalleth troublefome vnto thee in
Religion, when fome great labour is to be
vndertaken, or aduerfity to be borne, thou
doeft not vfe Patience, but art troubled,
murmureft, and afflicted? Haft thou not
giuen ouer the world to fuffer aduerfityes
for the loue of me? Haft thou not refolued
with thy felfe to endure all thinges, though
fore and painefull, for the good of thy foule?
Whence is it then, that when any occafion
offereth it felfe of accomplifhing thy fo pious defires, thou refifteft the fame, and art
troubled? Caft thyne eye a while vpon me,
and tell me, what finne I did commit in the
world? Whom I offended all my life long?
and yet from the tyme that I came into the
world, I euer fuffered fomething, & fwal-
lowed downe many a bitter morfell for thy
fake. How many contumelies were forged
Y 4 againft

against me, how many iniuryes were done
to me? which yet I endured patiently, to
giue thee an example of liuing conformably to thy vocation. And that thou haſt
now a will to practiſe Patience in bearing
reproaches with a contented mind, is a
thing, that beſeemeth not a man of the
world, much leſſe a Religious man, who
hath made profeſſion of vertue, and of imitating me, who did euer imbrace Patience
in ſo affectuous a manner.

5. Lord, I would very willingly endure
all thinges, for loue of thee: but when I
ſee ſome to perſecute me vniuſtly & wrongfully, I cannot a way with it, and therefore
am troubled and grieued. Thou art decci-
ued, Sonne, if thou thinkeſt, thou haſt any
iuſt occaſion of being troubled. Tell me,
was not I wrongfully perſecuted? Did not
I put vp and diſgeſt falſe accuſations, and
teſtimonyes againſt my ſelfe? Was I therefore troubled? Or did I make my cōplaint?
And how many Religious be there already
crowned in heauen, who ſuffered ſore per-
ſecutions whiles they liued on earth? If the
bad and wicked ſhould not iniure and perſecute any, the good ſhould not haue ſo exceeding ſtore of merits. To ſuffer wrongfully, is the crowne of Patience. But if
thou

thou suffer iustly , that is, for thyne owne
sinnes, it is rather a iust, punishment, then
any vertue of Patience sith Patience beareth and putteth vp iniuryes for the loue of
me . And therefore my Scripture pronoun-
ceth them for blessed, that suffer persecuti-
on , but yet for Iustice. Iniury to him, who
putteth it vp patiently, is a gaine, and to
him, that doth it, a sinne and losse .

6.   There be some Religious, that punish themselues diuers wayes, some by ta-
stings, others by wearing of haire-cloth, &
by disciplining themselues, which they suffer both willingly & patiently . But when
the same are imposed vpon them by Superiours, they fall to murmuring, & are troubled, and if they performe them, they do it
against their wills , with a repugnance of
mind, and so they loose all their merit. And
are they not manifestly, besids the offence it
selfe, deceiued herein ? Tell me, I pray thee
for what end thou shouldest punish thy body so cruelly, and with so great patience ?
Is it not to please me? If it be so, thou shouldest with a greater readines, and more patience receiue and performe the pennance
inioyned thee by thy Superiours, for then
thou shouldst do a worke far more pleasing
vnto me : for thou shouldest exercise three

moſt excellent vertues at once, namely, Humility, Patience, and Obedience. He that puniſheth himſelfe only out of his owne will, ſeldome becometh perfect.

7. O how much do the men of this world confound the Religious, who are the children of light? For moſt of them carryed away, either by ambition, couetouſnes, or ſome other bad deſire, ſpare not to take any paynes, ſuffer moleſtations, and put themſelues into whatſoeuer perills for the ſatisfying of their vayne deſires: and ſhould not a Religious man patiently ſuffer ſome tribulation for loue of me, and for the good of his owne ſoule? He that loueth not, is afraid to ſuffer. And more then this, the ambitious and couetous man if he ſuffer any incommodity at any tyme, is very carefull, that grief and heauines oppreſſe him not, or diſcourage him in the continuing of his negotiation, that he hath begon, but with a ſtout courage ſeeketh diuers and ſundry wayes, and meanes, for the repayring of his loſſes againe. But ſome Religious vpon the very leaſt croſſe, and trouble, ſuffer themſelues to be much diſquieted in mind, and are ſo ſore moued vpon the very leaſt word, as they looſe f om thenceforth all the fruit of the reſt of their works. My
Apoſtles

Apostles did not so, who went their wayes
reioycing, that they were held worthy to
suffer contumely for the glory of my name.
And the Martyrs endured most cruell torments with so great cheerfulnes of mind, as
some, who were by Tyrants commaunded
to go barefooted into the fire, did thinke
themselues in doing it, to walke vpon ro-
ses.

8. That a secular man suffereth iniuryes & aduersities with an impatient mind
is nothing to be meruayled, sith he thinketh
himselfe to be the maister of his owne honour and estimation, because he did neuer
renounce them, as do the Religious: and
therfore no meruayle, though being iniured, he be moued. Againe, a secular man,
because he hath neuer put himselfe vnder
the commaund of a Superiour, thinketh
himselfe to be wholy his owne man, and
to rely vpon himselfe, and therefore he cannot be much offensiue vnto others, if he
cannot with Patience put vp a disgrace, or
disgest a contumely. But that a Religious
man, who hath openly made profession of
renouncing all his owne honour and estimation, should take the iniury, that were
done him impatiently, is a thing vnworthy
his estate. And more then this, the Religious

ous being deliuered ouer to me, is no more his owne, but myne, and dependeth wholy and all in all of me, & therefore it may not seeme hard to any, if he be sometymes reproached, or be tryed by sicknes, or any other calamity. My seruant must only haue a care to serue me: but how he ought to serue me, either this way or that, that care he must leaue to me. I can vse his seruice, euen when he lyeth fast tyed to his bed, or when any other persecutiō is raised against him. For some serue me more perfectly, whiles they are sicke in their beds, or otherwise punished, then when they be in best health, & free from all aduersity. The Religious man is neuer a whit lesse regarded of me for his defects of body, but for his impatience, and other indispositions of his mind.

9. There be many Religious, who while they pray, thinke themselues of ability, patiently & constátly for loue of me to suffer all kind of torments, and to spend their bloud for me, and to dye martyrs: but within a while after, if they be but touched with a little word, or something be commaunded them that is accompanyed with some trouble and payne, they knit their browes, & can hardly forbeare (which

is

is worse) euen in the presence of others to
breake forth into words, & gestures of impatience. He that accustometh not himselfe
to beare with little things, will neuer with
patience away with great and hard matters. Sonne, hast thou a will and desire to
become a Martyr without the sword, and
without shedding of thy bloud for it? Conserue and keep thy mind in patience.

Of Meeknes, that ought to be practised by Religious men.
CHAP. VI.

SONNE, learne of me, for that I am
meeke & humble of hart. Meeknes was
the first vertue, that I taught in my Schoole,
and thereunto I exhorted my Disciples: for
it is both an easy and healthfull meanes for
the purchasing of the rest of the vertues. For
whereas it is the office of Meeknes to maintayne the peace of mind against the force of
anger, it causeth that the mind exerciseth
vertue, without any difficulty. And whils
it also defendeth the body against the in-
nordinate passions, it maketh the body a fit
instrument for the obeying of the soule in
the purchasing of vertues. And therfore the
Religious, who taketh no great paynes in
attayning

attayning Meeknes, is not truly one of my Schoole , and more then that, ſtoppeth vp the entrance againſt vertue , and Religious perfection .

2 .   There is not any ſo vnciuill & barbarous, who if he do but conſider the beauty, excellency, and propertyes of the vertue of Meeknes , would not extoll , and be in loue with it . Sonne, haſt thou a deſire to vnderſtand, how noble a vertue Meekneſis? Compare it with the contrary vice, namely with the intemperance of anger, which is bound to obey the reaſon of man , as to her Miſtreſſe whoſe handmayd ſhe is . For if it obey not reaſon, but go before it (as it ordinarily hapneth) it ſo diſtracteth the facultyes of the mind., and troubleth the angered perſon , as he may ſeeme to differ nothing from a foole and mad man , & from a beaſt poſſeſſed by the Diuell .

3 .   Anger, when it once getteth poſſeſſion, and commaund of the mind, firſt of al it effecteth, that the angred perſon remembreth neither God, nor his own conſcience. It depriueth the mind of all iudgment, that is , of the eye of the mind, whence blinded it is driuen into ſundry errours and falls. In the body it taketh away the equall temper and good proportion of humors, and giueth
cauſe

cause to sundry diseases. Moreouer it hurteth our Neighbours for the bad example.
To be short an angry mans life is most vnhappy , not only because none willingly
treateth with him, but also for that he will
haue al things done after his owne manner,
a thing that cannot be endured . Whereupon when a thing is not done according to
his mind, or he hath sustayned hurt in some
thing, or hath receiued some iniury, he eftsoones breaketh forth into flat rayling and
reuiling speeches , threatneth reueng, and
sometymes also by his intemperance of
mind turneth his fury and rage vpon himselfe.

4 . Meeknes remedieth all these euills ,
whose nature, and first office is to moderate
and stay the intemperance of anger, and to
restraine all other perturbations, arising of
it . First of all therefore it represseth , and
mittigateth the violence & fury of anger:
next it draweth the appetite of reueng to
the rule of right reason , for as much as in
the angry it is wont to transgresse and goe
beyond the bounds of moderatiō . Meeknes
in like manner conserueth all the facultyes
of the mind , euery one in his order, and
causeth them to do their owne functions.
Finally it reduceth the whole man to quiet
and

and maketh him fit, not only to acknowledge his Creatour, but also to conuerse in
familiar manner with him. And this gift
was peculiar to Moyses for his singular
Mecknes.

5. Neither doth the force and efficacy
of Meeknes stay heere, but it extendeth it
selfe further to the qualification and moderating of the anger of the Neighbours, for
that one benigne and gentle answere, or one
meeke action is inough to appease the fury
of any enraged beast, to say nothing of a
man incensed to anger. But (a thing much
more to be regarded) Meeknes is of so great
excellency and authority, as it mounteth vp
to heaué, auerteth the anger of Gods iustice
and obtayneth the pardon of most grieuous sinnes. Woe to him, who resisteth an
angry man, more mighty then himselfe.

6. Moreouer the life of the Meeke is
most happy, because it is most acceptable
not only to me his Lord, but also to all his
Neighbours. Hence it is, that euery one
willingly vseth the company of the Meeke,
and all desire to gratify him. Consider
therefore, Sonne, how profitable and pleasing the vertue of Meeknes is, and consider
thou, whether it be not conuenient, that
thou shouldest loue it, and labour with all
diligence

diligence to make thy selfe possessed of it.
Neither let it seeme any painefull matter
vnto thee to striue against the inclination
of nature, prone and propense to choller:
for it is proper to a Religious man to restraine his passions, to mortify his senses, &
to intertaine his inward peace of mind.
But admit, that Meeknes had nothing of al
this, yet this one thing should moue thee
to vse all diligence for the obtayning of
meeknes, for that it maketh a Religious
man like vnto me, his Lord and Maister.
Againe, is not all paine well taken in procuring that vertue, that is no lesse pleasing
to me, then it is profitable to the Religious
himselfe? Not for him to be Religious, but
to be indewed with vertue, maketh him
like to his Lord, and Maister. And for the
leading of a quiet & peaceable life, it is not
inough to haue forsaken the world, but a
man needeth further to bridle anger, and
the passions therof.

7.   Sonne, thinke not, because thou art
Religious, that thou art free from the darts
of thine enemyes, because the Diuell taketh
more paines in ouerthrowing of one seruant of myne, thē of many secular persons.
The same enemyes also, that is, the passions
and perturbations of the mind, when they

be not mortified, do giue the Religious very sore woundes, and therefore they need
a strong and sure buckler, for the receiuing
of so many of the enemyes blows. And this
shield is Mecknes, which no enemyes force
can possibly breake, but goeth away with
the victory by receiuing their blowes ther-
on. It causeth the Meeke also in all his aduersityes and crosses to place great confidence in me, and therefore while he continueth with a stout & vndaunted courage,
he doth not easily giue way, nor in prosperity please himselfe ouermuch: and this
is, to hold the place of a shield not only in
the tyme of warre, but of peace also. A Tar-
get profiteth him, who holdeth it fast, but
he that easily suffereth it to be stroken out
of his hands, is presently wounded. And so
is it with Mecknes, that defendeth him,
who holdeth it fast, and will not let it go.

8. Sonne, remember, that thou hast
bidden a farewell to the world, that thou
mightst rid thy selfe of the dangers of the
snares of it, and consecrate thy selfe wholy
to a spirituall life, and to my seruice: but
if thou be not Meeke, thou canst obtayne
neither. For if thou shalt in Religion be
subiect to anger and wrath, thou wilt easily therein contend also with others, and
so

so thou canst not but be troubled and difquieted. But if thou shalt be Meeke, thou
wilt not haue contention with any, and
with thy gentle and milde anſwers , thou
ſhalt appeaſe thoſe,that haue a will to con-
téd. Meeknes alſo helpeth, that thou mayſt
be affected to ſpirituall and heauenly matters, which do then ſet a man on fire with
the deſire of them, when they are well có-
ſidered and lookt into. But anger, when it
troubleth the mind, leaueth no place for
reaſon: but Meeknes, when it hath quieted
the mind, thruſteth out darknes, and bringeth light in place for the vnderſtanding of
ſpirituall things ; which being entred, the
vnderſtanding preſenteth vnto the wil the
imbracing of that, which it knoweth.

9. Amongſt the Euangelicall beatitu-
des I haue aſſigned the ſecond place next after Pouerty of ſpirit , to Meeknes, and for
the reward I added the Land of the liuing,
which is the heauenly countrey, where the
Meeke ſhall inioy my preſence for all eternity: and as I was heere in this life their
Maiſter,and an example of Meeknes; ſo wil
I be their hire and reward in heauen. I
ſhewed my ſelfe a meeke lambe for the loue
of men, and a lambe is a figure of me, and
therfore meet it is, that all thoſe, who haue

serued vnder this signe or banner, namely of Meeknes, and become lambes for my sake, should reioyce with me in heauen for euer.

10. How it beseemeth a Religious man to be Meeke and milde, and how vnbeseeming it is for him to be angry, is no hard thing to bevnderstood. The Religious state is peaceable and quiet, quite estranged from the spirit of indignation and contention. In all thinges it conformeth it selfe to the Diuine will, it neuer complaineth nor murmureth for any thing, it liueth cōtented with it owne, and taketh all that happeneth in good part. These and other conditions, seeing they be the fruits of Meeknes, cannot stand without it. Contrariwise, where the excesse of anger raigneth, nothing is heard but threatnings, iniuryes, clamours, and lowd outcryes, reuenge, and blasphemyes against God, his Saints in heauen, & all his creatures, which are not at the commaundment of the wrathfull person, whose actions, because they haue their origen not of reason, but of fury, are neither good, nor can possibly haue any good end. How then is it possible, that wrath can haue any community with religion, which is a certaine quiet Schoole of

of perfection, gouerned by the spirit of
Meeknes? How can a Religious man attend
to prayer, molested with the passion of anger? How can he be an help and example
to his Neighbour, who because of his im-
potency of anger, cannot haue any power
ouer himselfe? Sonne, thy nature is not the
nature of a serpent, but of a man: but if it
accustome it selfe to anger, it will become
so furious, as like a venomed serpent, it will
wound thee with the sting.

Of Mortification, necessary for a Reli-
gious man.

CHAP. VII.

SONNE, the kingdome of heauen suffereth violence, and the violent only carry it away. If thou thinke, that heauen
may be won by giuing thy selfe to idlenes
and ease, by pampering thy body, and by
yeilding vnto thy senses their pleasures in
euery kind, thou art greatly deceiued. For
this is not the ladder, whereby thou must
mount vp to heauen, neither be these the
armes, and weapons, wherwith thou must
fight, and ouercome, but thou must offer
violence to thy selfe, by mortifying the desires of the senses, and by resisting the flesh,

Z 3   as

as often as it seeketh and desireth after those
thinges, that haue no coherence, or corre-
spondence with the constitutions of thy
religious Institute. This is the way, that
bringeth to heauen. And though thou
mightst come to heauen without any contention with thy flesh going before, and
without suffering of any tribulations, yet
thou must neither desire, nor wish it. For
I the sonne of God, did not ascend into heauen, before I had suffered much, neither
would I go thither, but by the way of tribulation.

2. A Religious man therefore, if he resolue to win the kingdome of heauen, must
needs take vpon him so much strength, as
he may seeme to fight for three: for he, that
shall not fight for three, shall not go away
with the victory. First he must fight as
a man: for seeing he ought to lead a life,
correspondent to his nature, that is parti-
cipant of reason, he is also bound to liue
according to reason, which he cannot be
able to do, vnlesse he make warre against
his senses, which oftentymes resist their
maisters reason, & seeke to free themselues
from the gouernement therof. And Mortification is that, which subiecting the sense
to reason, causeth that a Religious man
                                        contayne

contayne himfelfe, and liue within the
bounds of vpright reafon.

3. Secondly, he muft fight, as a Chriftian, by the fword of Mortification, cutting off all that is forbidden by the Chriftian law . And therefore he muft not only
abftaine from rapine, from killing of men,
from fornication,& the like, but alfo from
a will of doing them, becaufe the one and
the other is prohibited by my law. And
herein thou muft needs exercife a certaine
violence, & mortification . For feeing man
in regard of concupifcence and his depra-
ued nature, is prone to the euill, by me forbidden , if he take not into his hand the
fword of my law ,and with it cut off, or
put to flight, whatfoeuer is contrary or repugnant to the law, it will neither be pof-
fible for him to triumph in heauen, nor on
earth defend and maintaine the honour of
a true Chriftian . Thirdly, he muft fight, as
a Religious man , who as he is bound to
many more thinges, then a Chriftian fecular man, fo hath he more and greater difficultyes, and therfore muft he the more be-
ftir himfelfe, and fortify himfelfe with the
armes of Mortification, & fight more manfully with the enemy.

4. That a Religious man may mortify
Z 4   his

his senses to liue conformably to reaso, it is good, but for the auoyding of falling into sinne, it is better to the accomplishing of the precepts of my law. But if he further bindeth himselfe to follow perfection togeather with obseruation of the counsailes of pouerty, chastity, and obedience, it is best of all: for that so doing he doth not only abstaine from all thinges vnlawfull, but for loue of me he also depriueth himselfe of many lawfull and good thinges, as of the dominion of temporall goods, of marriage, of the gouernement of himselfe, and all that is his, and the like. Herehence it followeth, that a Religious man ought to be so mortified, as he must be separated cleane from all creatures, yea and from himselfe also, and must haue his dependance on me alone. And this is to beare away heauen by mayne force. Sonne, he that conuerteth his eyes vpon the labours, and paynes that be in this combat, will thinke them to be many and great: but he that casteth his eyes vp to heaué, easily perceiueth, that they are not worthy of the future glory, that is there prepared for vs.

5. Mortification is nothing els, then a spirituall death, that depriueth a Religious man of all the life of his senses, and effemi-
nate

nate defirs, & cutteth the cleane off, with all
the bad acts arifing of the fenfual life: euen
as the death of body taketh away all the
forces of the naturall life, and the actions
therof. Wherefore that Religious man is
truly mortifyed, who is dead to his owne
loue. He that is dead to himfelfe, is dead
to the defires of the fenfes, and leadeth
a life conforme to the ftate of his Religion,
that maketh him Religious, and fpiritual.
The fpirit may not continue life, if the fenfuality be not firft dead.

6. There be fome Religious, who
mortify themfelues in fome one thing, and
not in another. Mortification, if it be not
whole, & vniuerfall in all things, nothing
pleafeth me, becaufe there is no being, nor
entrance for the fpirit, where all fenfuality
is not taken away. The bird, that is tyed
with many bands, is not free, & at liberty,
nor can fly her way, if there be but one
thrid, that holdeth her faft by the legge.
One defect may hinder a Religious man
from ariuing to the height of perfection.
Neither do thofe Religious leffe difpleafe
me, who begin indeed to mortify themfelues, but vpon the very leaft inducement
of the fenfes, or terrified by their owne
flouthfulnes, continue it not. Mortificatiõ

Z 5   that

that continueth not to the very end of life, looseth the reward. The victory is not gotten at the beginning of the fight, but in the end thereof.

7. Others there be, who thinke they discharge their duty, when they mortify their passions, and bad inclinations so far, as publiquely, and in the sight of others, they do nothing, that may not beseeme them. But this is not Religious mortification, for that such perturbations and motions of the mind be not truly mortified, but are only couered ouer, that their branches may not come to light and be seene. He that draweth not out the roote of the imperfections cleane, if it spring not forth to day, it will to morrow : and the Religious man will sooner giue ouer to cut off the peruerse branches, then will the roote to put them forth. Those Religious are very acceptable vnto me, who do not only cut off all outward bad workes, but do further endeauour by contrary acts to roote out the bad habits, and their inordinate affections, which be the rootes, and fountaines of imperfection. And this is true Mortification, which taketh away the bad actions togeather with their beginnings. Desirest thou to take away all the water?
                                                        then

then stop vp the spring head.

8. Sonne, I know right well, that this continuall warre betweene the flesh and spirit, and betweene the sense and reason, is very sore and troublesome vnto thee, but thou must know, that a man was not created with this discord. Neither was there this state in the terrestriall paradise, where when as the sense was obedient to reason, and man to his Creatour, there was exceeding great peace and concord; & sinne after it had stirred vp the inferiour part against the superiour, brake this peace. And if thou desire to be reduced, and to returne to this first peacable state, Mortification is to thee necessary, the office whereof is againe to bring the body in subiection to the seruice of the spirit, the lawfull Soueraigne, and the senses vnder the commaund of reason: for this is the way of renewing the peace. For the reducing of two souldiers, that be at variance, & do in hostile manner prosecute the one the other, necessary it is to peace & amity, that the one yeald to the other, the inferiour to the superiour: and therfore it is necessary, that the body yield to the spirit, sith it is a subiect to the spirit.

9. O how ill doth that Religious mã vnderstand the manner of his own vocation, who

who practiseth no true mortification, sith experience plainely teacheth, that whe c Mortification is not, there sensuality beareth sway. And what profitable fruit can grow from such a roote? What good can a Religious man do, that abaseth himselfe to the desires of men of the world? Of the many euils, that Sensuality produceth, this is one, that it is neuer quiet, vntill it hath drawne a Religious man into extreme misery both of body and soule. Contrariwise Mortification, forcing the passions to keep themselues within their own bands, greatly helpeth the Religious man towards the attayning of the perfection of vertues. For as it is impossible to come to perfection without vertues, so is it as impossible to compasse true vertues, without Mortification.

10. Lord, all that thou hast hitherto sayd, is most true, but sith there is in man so great a multitude and variety of inordinate desires, so many vnruly passions, so great a company of bad inclinations, how is it possible for a poore Religious man to resist so many contraryes? When shall he euer be able to tame so many wild and vnruly beasts? A man needeth to stand both day and night armed with a two-edged
sword

fword in his hand. And for this caule no maruell, though fome Religious be found not to mortify themfelues in all things, and others againe not to prefeuer in the care &c ftudy of Mortification.

11. Sonne, thou peraduenture thinkeft thy felfe the firft of them, who haue giuen themfelus to exercife mortification. Many indeed haue gone before thee, who haue laboured manfully and glorioufly in mortifying themfelues in this life, who now inioy the fruit of mortificatió in heauē. And there liue many in Religion at this day giuen to mortification, wherein they perfift not without their owne merit, and with great ioy to me. Neither muft it feeme ftrange, or hard vnto thee to be continually in armes. For if this life, as my feruant *Iob* well fayd, be a certaine continuall warfare on earth, what other thing is it to liue, thē to be euer in warres, and to fight without ceafing? When a Citty is befieged, if the enemy giue continuall affault day & night for the taking of it, neceffary it is for the befieged to be continually alfo in armes for the refifting of him. If then thou meane to defend and keep the Citty of thy foule, which is day & night molefted by paffions that be the enemys therof, it greatly imnor-

teth

teth thee day and night to be at defiance with them, and to fight against them. And if for the gayning of some fortificatiō men aduenture with the hazarding of their liues, wherefore should thy paynes of Mortification seeme hard vnto thee, for the gayning and winning of the castle of heauen, wherein thou shalt triumph for eternity? Thou shewest thy selfe ouer delicate. The souldiar, that is afrayd of paynes, soone fainteth and looseth courage.

12. Neither must thou be terrifyed with the multitude and variety of thy contrary passions: for though thou hast not forces inough in thy selfe to beare the violent impression of them, yet by the help of Gods grace, thou shalt be able not only to mayntaine thy selfe safe from their incursions, but also to put them to flight, and to take away the memory of them within thy selfe. All Religious haue a desire at the houre of their death to be found mortifyed, and yet but few haue a will to mortify theselues. If thou shunnest mortificatiō liuing, how wilt thou be mortifyed at the end of thy life, when thou cōmest do dye? Finaly the reward of Mortification is so excellent, as a man for the purchasing of it, should not forbeare to take any manner of paynes, though

though it were neuer so great. A good souldiar, to encourage himselfe to the paynes, that are to be taken in the fight, and to the victory, thinketh euer and anone vpon the reward.

Of *Discretion required in a Religious man.*
CHAP. VIII.

SONNE, he that vseth not an eauen payre of ballance, is easily deceaued in weighing: euen so he, who vseth not discretion and prudence in his actions, oftentymes committeth so great errour, as no remedy, or redresse is to be found, in either helping them, or taking them away. If thou exceed in chastening thy body, it will be weakned, lay down his burden, and refuse to discharge the seruice it oweth to the soule: againe if thou be ouer remisse in mortifying it, it will eftsoons rebell, and turne the heels against thee and kicke. For this cause Discretiō is necessary, which teacheth how to vse the ballance, and how to keep them eauen, that the one rise not ouer much nor the other be let downe too much. And this is the salt, that must season mans actions, that they may retaine the commendation of vertues, and may be pleasing vnto me.

me. They oftentimes come sooner to the a-
pointed races end, who hold on with a
moderate pace, then they who run in haft.
For he that hafteth with a moderation,
doth neither eafily fall, nor is foone wearyed, but he that maketh ouermuch haft,
though he fall not, is yet foone wearied, &
fo either commeth not at all, or with much
a do to the place, whither he intended.

2. O how great hurt, efpecially in Religion, worketh Indifcretion to the Religious, who vfe neither direction, nor cou-
faile in doing of pennances, and in continuing a more feuere courfe of life. They
thinke they pleafe me, when they mortify
their bodyes ouer much by faftings, difciplines, wearing of haire, and watchings:
but they are deceiued. For the good that is
done with Difcretion, hath the commendation of vertue, & pleafeth me: but what
is done without Difcretion, is a vice, and
defective, and pleafeth me nothing at all.
This their fpirit meriteth not the name of
feruour, but rather of indifcreet fury: for
as much as within a while they become fo
weake in body, as they neither profit thé-
felues nor others. He that fpurreth his horfe
ouer much vpon the way, is forced to ftay
in it, & this I iuftly permit for a punifhmét
of

of their pride of indiscretion . For if they
would submit themselues to the iudgment
of their Ghostly Fathers, or Superiours ,
that they might go the more securely on in
the way of spirit , they should neuer precipitate theselues into these inconueniences.
Pennance and austerity ought to be such, as
they may not ouerthrow, and destroy nature, but the vices therof .

3 . O how much better might they do,
and more pleasingly vnto me, if their pennances & mortification were euer accompanyed with two noble vertues: with Humility, I say, wherby they should submit
themselues to the iudgment of their spirituall Fathers: and Obedience, wherby they
might do, what they commaund them. For
by the direction of these two vertues, they
might the more securely enter into the
rough and vneauen way of Pennance, and
might merit much more before God. None
hath euer been a good guide, and iudge for
himselfe .

4 . Many of them commit another errour, who do in the spirituall way rely v-
pon their owne iudgment, and that is, that
while they obserue not the meane in mortification of their body , they ordinarily
are not solicitous about the extirpating of

the vices of mind. And though they should
not transgresse in any thingels, then that
in the way of spirit they would not be directed by them, whome I haue appointed
to gouerne in my place, should not this defect, arising of Pride, be a most dangerous
vice and fault of the will? Tell me, what
good will it do a Religious man to chastize and punish his body, and in mynd to
intertaine his owne will, and inordinate
affections? I omit to say, that such be oftentymes moued of vayne glory to do those
outward mortifications, that others may
see them, though the same be moderate,
more then to the inward, that are not seen
to men, which yet are not hidden from
myne eyes, and which I greatly esteeme,
because the austerity of life is not in so
great a regard with me, as is the mortification of the vices of the mind.

5. Moreouer the hurt, that the indiscreet do vnto others, is not little; for as
much as they who follow their example,
do also imitate their indiscretion, which is
vicious, and cause of many euills. Others
againe, obseruing the inconueniences, and
the infirmityes, that those men fall into,
who were ouermuch giuen to their pennances and mortifications of body, are
cleane

cleane and wholy auerted from thofe pious
and holy actions, fearing leaft themfelues
alfo by exercifing them, might preiudice
and hurt their owne health. Neither is it
in all, certainly to iudge, that thofe incommodityes will not follow of pennances,
but of the indifcretion, and pride of them,
who haue refufed to be aduifed by others.
He that feeketh not to auert the mifchiefe
and hurt, that is preiudiciall to himfelfe &
others, fhall be punifhed both for himfelfe
and for others.

6.   Lord, feeing our flefh is one of our
three capitall enemyes, and fo troublefome,
as it molefteth vs, both night and day,
wherefore is it, that thou wilt not haue it
afflicted and punifhed? I haue heard it faid,
that he who maketh ouermuch of his flefh,
doth nourifh & intertaine an enemy within his owne houfe, & giueth him occafion
of raifing warre againft him. Were it not
therefore a point of wifdome, and better to
make warre vpon it, then that it fhould firft
of all affayle vs? Neither feemeth there any
danger in punifhing it ouermuch, or in v-
fing of exceffe, fith the Scripture fayth, that
none euer hated his owne flefh.

7.   Sonne, my Scripture alfo fayth, that
the feruice done to me, muft be reafonable

and discreet, that may not exceed or go beyond the appointed bounds. It is indeed my will, that the flesh be mortified & punished, but yet with moderation. And though thy flesh be an enemy vnto thee, yet thou must remember with all, that it is the soules instrument, and therefore it must be in such sort handled, as it may not rebell against her spirit, and yet may serue the soule in her owne functions. But if thou exceed in punishing it, it will languish, and pyne away, and so it will not be able not only not to serue thee, but it will stand in need of the seruice of others it selfe. He that is to walke well, must shun the extremes.

8.   Some are openly tempted of the Diuel to multiply one sinne vpon another, and they be those, ouer whom he vsurpeth a full and absolute commaund. Others againe, because they be not yet caught in his snares, vnder pretence of good he induceth to sinne, as when he proposeth vnto them, that it is good for a Religious man, if he bring his flesh in subiection by long watchings, and other asperityes of body, as did the holy Fathers in the wildernes, who be now Saints in heauen, and are honoured in this militant Church for lights of the world. But the crafty enemy proposeth

not,

not, that thofe actions fhould be profitable to the foule, or pleafing to God, or exercifed by the rule of Difcretion : neither
doth he alfo declare, when the forces of
men be not equall, that it is not conuenient
for all to vfe the fame feuerity towards
themfelues : for what is mediocrity to one,
is ouermuch to another. Neither doth he
giue to vnderftand, that there needeth the
coũfell of fpiritual Fathers, without which
none may with fecurity walke on in the
way of fpirit. Sonne, feeing the Diuell deceyueth thee by himfelfe, if thou wilt not
be deceiued by him in thy pennances and
deuotions, follow not thine owne head,
nor truft thy felfe.

9. Finally, that a Religious man may
be difcreet in all his actions, it is therefore
alfo conuenient, becaufe he is regular, and
reafon requireth, that he direct all his actions to a certaine fquare and rule, & this is
to be difcreet. And more then all this, a
Religious mans actions muft be addreffed
to my glory : but what glory of myne can
it be, if the fame be vicious and indifcreet?
What pleafeth me not, procureth not either
honour, or glory. Confider now, Sonne,
if indifcretion in fafting, difciplines, and
in other good workes of that kind difpleafeth

seth me so greatly, how much thinkest thou
will it discontent me, if a Religious man
be indiscreet in eating and drinking, in
sleeping, and in the like actions, which be
not of themselues holy, but indifferent?
How much shal he displease me, if he exceed & be indiscreet in actions that be bad
in themselues? If indiscretion be ill of it
selfe, cōioyned to a bad thing it wil doubtles be worse, and will displease me more.

10.   Discretion is necessary as well for
Superiours, who gouerne others, as for subiects, who are gouerned. Discretiō, which
is the child of beneuolence, teacheth them
to be louing, and benigne Fathers, to be
compassionate to their subiects, nor to im-
pose heauyer burdens vpon them, then they
are able to beare. And it teacheth the subiect
to reuerence, honour, respect, & obey their
Superiours. O how displeasing a thing is
it to me to see a subiect indiscreet towards
his Superiour. Indiscretion, because it is
crueltyes daughter, and hardnes sister, causeth the subiect to afflict his Superiour, by
shewing himselfe froward in obeying, and
dissolute in discipline. I know very well,
how many sighes and deep groanes of the
poore & afflicted Superiours for their subiects hardnes of hart, ascend vp to heauen.

But

But woe to them, who shall haue giuen the
occasion. The contempt that is done to
Superiours, is done to me, and it appertaineth to me to examine and punish it.

Of Indifferency, necessary for a Reli-
gious man.

CHAP. IX.

SONNE, thou hast many a tyme and often heard, that Religion is the schoole
of perfection, & so it is : and therefore they
that enter into Religion, be not perfect,
but haue a desire to labour to the perfection
of Religious discipline. The scholler, that
hath begon to follow his booke, hath no
thing els proposed to him, but to learne to
speake & write Latin first, & after to passe
ouer to the higher Sciences. As touching
the meanes, whereby he may come to his
sayd end, he sayth not, I wil imprint these
rules in my mind, I must be conuersant in
this booke, and read it ouer & ouer, I must
heare such a lesson : but he is indifferent, &
submitteth himselfe wholy to the iudgmét
of his maister, to read, or heare whatsoeuer
shall to him seeme good. If a Religious
man doth not the same in the schoole of
Religion, he shall neuer write or read wel,
but

but shall comit many errours in Religious
discipline. His only care must now be to
aspire to perfection, but about the meanes
proper to Religion, let him be indifferent,
and leaue all to the iudgment of his Superiour, whatsoeuer is in that kind to be don,
And that Religious man is truly indifferēt,
whose will, put as it were into a payre of
scals, weigh not more to one part, or thing,
then to another, but is ready to do, what
the Superiour commaundeth.

2. Indifferency is Resignations daughter,
& this cannot be without that. Therfore
the Religious man, who is not, touching
his owne person, and those things that appertaine vnto him, resigned to my will, &
to that of his Superiours who supply my
place, neither is, nor can be sayd to be indifferent. O how little is that Religious
in grace and fauour with me, who when
any thing shall be by his Superiour commaunded him, answereth, that he is ready
indeed to obey, yet he had rather do this,
or that, & if that be not yealded vnto him,
he complaineth, or murmureth, and sometymes also neglecteth to do what is commaunded him. This is no indifferency nor
resignation, but is a kind of contract. He
that in accepting of obedience vseth this

But

But, hath a meaning that his worke should be but very slenderly rewarded. Who sayth, I will do it, but I would, or will, declareth that he is not yet dead to himselfe, nor hath renounced his owne will. In the world, when thou wert thyne owne maister, in dealing with me, didst thou not say, I wil, or I would? and therefore thou hast not yet either left the world, or it hath not left thee. This is no other thing, then to put one foot into two stirrops, and to haue a will to serue two maisters. The world doth not leaue them, who do not first forsake it.

3. Lord, if I be indifferent, and ready to performe all thinges that shall be commaunded me, who shall proue that to me to be better for my soule, and my quiet? Sonne if thou seeke to do that whereunto thyne owne affection swayeth thee, who may secure thee, that it is more expedient for thy soule, and for thy quiet? The good of soules proceedeth from me, and that I communicate to them who are conioyned with the Superiour, whom I haue assigned to gouerne : from whome, if thou, because thou art not indifferent, shalt separate thy selfe, thou shalt depriue thy selfe of all the gifts and graces, which I am accustomed to bestow vpon the subiectes, by

A a 5   help

help of the Superiours. Besides, if thou be
a true child of obedience, thou oughtst to
iudge and thinke that to be best, that thy
Superiour, where no sinne is, shall ordaine:
& if thou be indifferent, thou art bound
promptly to put it in execution. For if any
errour hap to be committed, it shal neither
be thyne, nor imputed vnto thee, neither
shalt thou loose any part of thy merit. A
good Religious man examineth not, whether it be better, or worse that is commanded, but it is inough to him, if it seeme better to the Superiour.

4.   Some there be, who can hardly be
induced to make their habitation in that
place, where Obedience would appoint
them, or to do the busines, that the Superiour iudgeth most conuenient for my glory,
and therfore they are troubled, and cannot
find any quiet or peace of mind, & they ascribe this their disquiet either to the place,
wherein they dwell, or to the company
with whom they conuerse, or to the office
that they execute, vntill they obtaine some
change in them. But that euill is hardly
cured, the cause wherof is not vnderstood.
This is no fit way of cure, and of remedying it: the origen of the euill is to be sought
into, which is an vnmortified passion, proceeding

ceeding of felfe loue. And of this it is, that
a Religious man is not indifferent, nor re-
figned in all thinges to the Superiours wil.
Thinkeſt thou, the place will effect, that
thyne inordinate paſſion, or proper loue
may be remoued, and taken away? The
change of bed doth not eaſe the ſicke man
of his feuer, but doth oftentymes increaſe
it. And though the change ſomewhat té-
pereth the hoat burning of it for the tjme,
yet within a while it tormēteth him more
ſore. So hapneth it to a Religious man,
who carryeth with him the cauſe of his
vnquietnes, and that is his inordinate paſſion : and vnles the axe of mortification be
vſed to the cutting away of this bad roote,
whatſoeuer change of place be made, it
will euer be worſe with him : for the longer the euill hangeth vpon him, the more
ſtrength it getteth, and the leſſe indifferent
it maketh him.

5. But tell me, if after the change of
place, or of office, thou find thy ſelfe as vnquiet, or more then before, as commonly it
is wont, what wilt thou do? Wilt thou wiſh
to remoue to another place? In no caſe: for
that were to play the pilgrim without a
ſtaffe, with thyn owne detriment, and the
bad example of others. Or wouldſt thou
rather

rather refolue to mortify thy felfe there, & to pull the caufe of thy difquiet vp by the roote? But that might be done as well in the place, to which obediéce had fent thee, and had beene done with edification of them, who knew thee to be vnquiet, little mortified, & leffe indifferent. He that hath not the fpirit of God, though he fhould find a place euen among Angels, will not ceafe to be vnquiet.

6. Others againe are fo tyed to one place, as when they vnderftand that the Superiour thinketh on fome change, they are tempted, and much troubled: and which is worfe, becaufe they thinke themfelues in that place, where they then are, to abide with the fruit, & increafe of Gods honour and feruice, they cenfure their Superiours for imprudent, and deftitute of zeale. Hence it is, that if they be againft their will remoued, and fent away to fome other place, they do not well accommodate thé-felues to any function or office, but do trouble others, and liue very vnquietly and dif-contentedly themfelues. Can it poffibly be, that fo little a regard fhould be had of In-differency, which is a Religious mans crowne? When I called thee to Religion, did I then promife, and vndertake to

place

place thee there , where thou wouldst, or
where I would ? Certes thou dost manifest,
that in seruing me thou relyest rather vpon
thyne owne sense , then my iudgment. O
misery! There is not a Religious man, that
would not thinke, & also affirme, that it is
good, yea and necessary, that my seruants
be indifferent and resigned, but when he
commeth to action , he findeth a repugnancy. What auayleth it an Horseman to
haue a generous and goodly horse, if he be
not tractable ? What helpeth it to haue a
seruant, though he be neuer so excellent, if
he suffer not himselfe to be gouerned, neither hath a will to do my will .

7 . Tell me, Sonne, is it not good for
a Christian to be indifferent in thinges ,
neither commanded, nor forbidden, and to
be ready to do what I shall command him ?
as to haue children, or not haue any ? to be
of an healthfull body, or of a sickly ? Euen
so , for seeing it is vnknowne vnto him ,
what is best for the good of his soule, there
is good reason he should stand to my iudgment. And this is to be indifferent . And if
this be true, as it is most true, wherfore dost
thou, that art Religious, choose out of thyn
owne will to execute this ministery and
office rather then that, to dwel in this place
                                        rather

rather then in another? How knowest thou, whether this or that be more for thy soules good, quiet, or perfection? He that is not indifferent, maketh the gouernement the more hard, laborious and paynefull. He that is not indifferent, seldome yealdeth to the iudgmēt of the Superiour, but ordinarily is inclined to performe those ministeryes, to the exercising wherof he is lesse fit, sith none is a good and impartiall iudge in his owne cause, in regard of an inordinate affectiō that deceiueth him. He that is not indifferent, peruerteth the order of right gouernement, for that, whiles he accommodateth not himselfe to his Superiour, as he ought, the Superiour is forced to accommodate himselfe vnto him. He that is not indifferent, can neyther be spirituall, nor deuout, and is ordinarily selfe-willd and heady.

Of Modesty, necessary for a Religious man.

CHAP. X.

SONNE, Religious Modesty is a silent Sermon, but such as penetrateth, and is efficacious, which like vnto a sharp pointed arrow, entreth into a mans hart, woundeth it, and worketh wonders therin, and the

more

more deepe wound it giueth, the more
plenteous fruit it bringeth forth: & it profiteth not only them, who heare the sermō,
but him also who maketh it. For Modesty
intertayneth a Religious mans spirit, and
maketh him so collected in mind, and present to himselfe, as all his actions breath
forth a most sweet sent of deuotion, and is
so excellent an ornament to a Religious
man, as it maketh him amiable, and most
deare to all who shall behold him. Againe
inward Modesty, whereof the outward
proceedeth, is so pleasing vnto me, as it is
a pleasure to me to vse the company therof.
And more then this, a Modest Religious
person is of so great authority with others,
as there is nothing, that he may not perswade them vnto. And if they do so many thinges in regard of a Religious mans
Modesty, what is it conuenient for me to
do, for whose loue he practised that Modesty? What should he not obtaine at my
handes, who is most deare vnto me, and
most acceptable?

2. It produceth also wonderful effects
in others. There is not any so incomposed,
so dissolute, and disordered, who would
not at the very sight of a modest Religious
man presently collect, and compose himselfe

selfe also to an externall Modesty, thinking
he should transgresse the bounds of Modesty, if before a modest Religious man he
should not demeane himselfe with the like
Modesty also. Moreouer Modesty woundeth the hart with a certaine other woūd,
and that a more healthfull one, and this is:
it sweetly draweth others to deuotion, and
to an imitation of good manners; neither
giueth ouer, vntill it shall haue drawne
them to a composition of the inward man,
wherein consisteth the true quiet and peace
of mind, then which nothing is more
excellent, or more to be wished in this life.
For Modesty produceth more plenteous
fruit, and profit, preacheth more effectualy
then doth the tongue. The Religious man
is not blamelesse, who shall not by his Modesty preach vnto others.

3.   Contrarywise the immodesty of a
Religious man woundeth the hart, but
the wounding therof doth great hurt, both
to him, in whome the immodesty is, and
to him, who obserueth it. Who euer saw
an immodest, & wandring Religious man
spirituall, and deuout? Immodesty goeth
euer accompanied with impudency, inso-
lency, and dissolution of manners. And
what spirit can there be of deuotion, where
there

there be found vices, so contrary to deuotion? The immodest not only wanteth all
authority with others, but also is further a
scorne to all: & which is more, obscureth,
and (not to say) taketh away the fame
and good name of his Religion, that had
formerly beene won by the vertue and modesty of others. Moreouer the immodest
not only offendeth & scandalizeth others,
but also inuiteth them to dissolution, especially the men of the world, who are easily
induced to thinke that to be very lawfull
for them to do, which they see done of
Religious men. Now then consider thou,
what punishment that Religious man is
worthy of, who when he was chosen out
to be salt, & the light of the world, for the
conseruing of secular men by his example,
doth by his loose manners put them forwards, and set them on fire towards all dis-
order and impudency of life. An immodest
Religious person is displeasing to all wise,
and spirituall men, who by his bad example be so sore offended, as they are confounded for very shame thereat. And how can
such a man be pleasing to me, who serueth
me, and dwelleth in my house? It is the
glory of a Prince of this world, if he haue a
modest, ciuill, and well ordred family: and
contra-

contrarywise it redoundeth to his ignominy and shame, if it be loose in manners, & giuen ouer to lasciuiousnes. Euen so, if the Religious, who be of my family, be modest, it redoundeth to my honour & glory: contrariwise it is my reproach & dishonour, if they be immodest.

4. Lord, I haue euer heard, that thou art contented with a mans inward vertue, and with an vpright hart. And if that be true, it cannot be altogeather displeasing vnto thee, if a Religious man be not at all tymes outwardly composed in manners, & modest, so his mind be aright & collected. Sonne, if thou thinkest me to be so delighted with the goodnes of the hart, as I regard not the outward conuersation and manners, thou art deceiued, because I require both. Though the Religious, who is of a good, and vpright mind, be ordinarily composed also in externall manners, and contrarywise, who is not well composed within, is commonly also dissolute and incomposed without: In like manner a Religious man is bound to giue edification to his neighbour. If he be only composed in mind, he cannot giue edification, because God alone is a beholder of the hart, and not the neighbour: and therfore necessary it is,

that

that he edify with his outward modesty,
whereby a gheffe & coniecture is made of
the inward modesty, and compofition of
manners . If then the Religious mans outward manners be not rightly compofed, a
man fhall eafily iudge, that the inward man
is ill compofed alfo, and fo in place of edification he fhould giue offence, and fcan-
dall .

5.   There be fome Religious men, who
indeed make a fhew of outward Modefty,
but are withall little follicitous about the
mortifying of the defires of the mind : but
this is not the modefty, that I requyre at a
Religious mans hands . For if he defireth
to feeme humble and modeft, that others
may commend him for it, he taketh vpon
him the Pharifaicall modefty, which is
fold at a good rate to men, but for the bafenes of the price, hath no reward at all in
heauen. But if he would feeme modeft,
that he may edify, or at leaft not fcandalize
his neighbour, he vfeth affected and an in-
forced modefty, which hath not any long
continuance . The modefty contenting
me, is that outward compofition, and de-
cency of manners, that groweth of the inward compofition, by benefit whereof all
the defires, and affctions of the mind, be

subiect to reason, and at the commaūd of it. And this Modesty procureth to a Religious man a certaine venerable seemlynes and authority. This is agreeing to the Religious state, and maketh it worthy the renerence, & respect of secular persons. This Modesty accompanieth a Religious man, both day and night, whether he be in the Church, or at home in his chamber, whether he sleepeth, or speaketh, is in iourney, or doth any thing els.

6.   Sonne, desirest thou an easy, but yet an effectuall meanes for the getting of Modesty? Conuerse in my presence and sight, that is, in all thy actions, either secret, or manifest, whether they be done by day, or by night, thinke me to be present, and a beholder of all, as I am indeed; and I doubt not, but thou wilt be ashamed to do any thing vnbeseeming, and vnworthy thy Religious state in my sight, and presence.

Of the Vertue of Prayer.

CHAP. XI.

SONNE, most true is that, which some affirme, that Prayer is to me a sacrifice, to the Diurll a scorge, and to him who prayeth a singular help. And that a sacrifice

fice may be offered vp for an odour of
fweetnes, neceffary it is, that it be pleafing
not fo much to him who offereth it, as to
him vnto whome it is offered, and therfore
that which may ftir thee vp to the defire
of prayer, muft be a pure defire of pleafing
me, and not others, nor thy felfe. And
doubtles, that prayer will be moft acceptable to me, if it anfwere my defire,
though thou fhouldeft not take any comfort thereof at all. The old facrifices were
made, as I had appointed in my Law, and
they that offered them, did not require of
the minifters any other thing, then that
their facrifices might be done conformably
to the diuine will. The Diuel doth not fo,
but he endeauoureth by diuers and fundry
wayes to hinder this pleafing facrifice of
Prayer. For one while he exaggerateth the
difficulty therof, that thou mayft giue it
ouer: another tyme he pretendeth that the
tyme is not commodious to do it, that thou
maift put it of: now he feigneth that it
would hurt thy health, that thou mayft
make light of it &c. And no meruaile, becaufe, as I fayd, Prayer is his fcorge, and
therfore he is moft of all afraid of it. And
the more he hateth it, the more reckoning
ought a Religious man to make therof, fith
it

it is the spirituall food, wherwith his soule
is refreshed, and strengthened.

2. The vertue of Prayer is so pleasing
to my Father of heauen, as he commaunded me, to come downe from thence, to
deliuer vnto my Disciples a manner and
forme of Prayer, wherein he would be named Father, that all might in their necessityes with a great confidence repaire vnto
him, and both prayse, and reuerence the
diuine Goodnes in this holy exercise of
Prayer, which is so pleasing vnto him, as
he sometymes differeth to impart the grace
that is required, and craued therein, that
the Prayer may be repeated, and sayd ouer
againe. Prayer was also no lesse pleasing
vnto me, then it was familiar vnto me, and
therfore I recommended it in the Ghospell,
and commended it vnto others, not by
words only, but by examples and deeds.
And when I had no leasure to attend to
Prayer by day, by occasion of the paynes of
my preaching, and of other works, done
for the good of my Neighbours, I spent the
night in it.

3. O how sore that Religious man
sinneth, and how strait an accompt is he
to yeild vp one day vnto God, who eyther
doth not bestow the tyme, that is by his

Religion

Religion allowed him for prayer, in that
holy exercise, or bestoweth it not in manner as he ought, and might, if he would.
And how great a shame is it to see, that
whē a signe is giuen to some recreation appertaining to the body, they come running
in all hast, and diligence: and when the
signe is giuen to Prayer, they come slowly
vnto it? If thou dost not performe, or very
negligently performe the taske of thy wonted Prayers, dost thou not consider, that
thou dost it with the preiudice of other Religious that haue a participation with thy
Religion? He that maketh no conscience
to depriue his owne soule of the fruit of
Prayer, will make lesse conscience to de-
fraud others. If the seruant be not affected
to that, which pleaseth his Lord, much
lesse will the Lord be affected to that
which is pleasing to the seruant.

4. Prayer is nothing els, then a talke, &
commerce of a reasonable creature with
his Creatour, to whome he confidently
proposeth both his owne necessityes, and
those of others, that as a Father of mercyes
he would vouchsafe to assist, & help his
children. But those please me much, who
being to deale in prayer with their heauenly Father, do inuocate some one of the

Saints,

Saints, to whome they are deuoted, that they would pleafe alfo to affift them with their prayers and petitions to God. They alfo pleafe me, who do not begin to pray, vntill they fhall haue craued grace of praying well: as do thofe alfo, who craue pardon for their imperfections and finnes; for as much as this is wont not a little to help and promote the fruite, and progreffe of Prayer. They alfo do well, who to pray with fruit, do not only exclude the cogitations of all other affayres, that are wont to diftract the mind, but alfo feeke to be well compofed, and to vfe fuch a fituation of body, as helpeth towards the faying of their prayers both attentiuely, and deuoutly. For feeing Prayer is a facrifice to God, it is not lawful to pretermit any thing in it, for the beft performing therof.

5. Some obtaine not at Gods hands what they haue craued in prayer, becaufe they craued not what was conuenient. He that asketh what is hurtful, or vnprofitable to the foule, asketh not that is conuenient for it, for as much as in prayer are to be craued thinges good, and profitable for the foule. Thinges indifferent, which may be vfed well or ill, fuch as be honours, riches, health of body, muft be asked with a condition,

tion, if they be good for the foule. Better
knoweth the Phifitian, thē the ficke, what
is more necéffary for his health, and therfore he doth neuer giue vnto the fick what
he demaundeth, but what may do him
good. I did not take from my Apoftle the
fting of the flefh, though by his prayer he
had more then once craued it of me, becaufe it profited him more to haue it ftill.
It is beft for the Religious, if his foule be
filled with merits, rather then that his will
fhould be fatisfied. He that is not humble
in his prayer, and acknowledgeth not his
owne mifery, obtayneth not what he cra-
ueth, becaufe he asketh not well. Who
prayeth not with confidence, fo as he firmely beleeue, that I am able to fatisfy his
petitions, obtayneth not grace, becaufe he
prayeth not, as he fhould. He that perfe-
uereth not in prayer, or giueth ouer his petition once begon, or els goeth forwards
after a languifhing & cold manner therein,
obtayneth nothing, becaufe he asketh not
well.

.6.   There are fome others, who fo foon
as they obtayne not the grace they craue,
giue ouer their prayer to their owne loffe,
for as much as I had determined to beftow
greater graces vpon them, then they asked

of me, but becaufe they might not endure
to be delayed, they loft all . Whiles I differ
the beftowing of my grace, and they yet
perfift and hold on in prayer, their defire of
praying waxeth hoater, and hauing obtay-
tained it , they imbrace it, and conferue it
with a greater feruour for the tyme to
come. Moreouer they côtinue their prayer,
which is a good action, & meritorious, &
they make themfelues the more apt for the
receiuing of the defired grace. For whiles
they are betwixt hope and feare of receiuing the grace they craue, they examine
themfelues, whether fome fecret finne , or
imperfection of theirs may peraduêture be
an impediment to the receiuing of fuch
grace ; and if they find any fuch, they become penitent for it, and therby they make
themfelues the more apt for the receiuing
of grace . Be not thefe diuers and different
priuiledges of graces, that I giue, whiles I
do not yeald vnto the petitions at the very
firft ? Why then do they giue ouer their
prayer ? Many things are obtained of God
by occafion of a vehement and continued
defire of the thing , which if it fhould not
be, they fhould not obtaine at all . Therefore as my Scripture fayth : *Better is the end of
Prayer, then is the beginning* . For no worke is
finifhed

finished, being but begon, but when it is
brought to an end. To one well disposed
God knoweth how, & when to giue more
then he is able to aske.

7. Others giue ouer their prayer, because they are dry, and find no deuotion in
their prayer at all, but this is no good remedy for the matter. If that aridity groweth through thyne owne default, as because thou comest to prayer without any
preparation going before, and with an
head distracted with many impertinent
cogitations, wherfore shouldst thou giue
ouer thy prayer for it? Let the cause of thy
aridity & distraction be rather remoued &
taken away. He that of his owne carelesnes
stumbleth vpon a stone, doth not therefore cut off his own foot, because he stumbled without any his owne fault, neither
omitteth he for that, to prosecute his iourney, but is more vigilant, that he may stū-
ble no more. Neither is prayer to be giuen
ouer, when the aridity commeth vpon thee
without any thy fault, for asmuch as I do
sometymes of purpose withdraw the grace
of consolation, that acknowledging thyne
owne insufficiency in thy selfe, thou mayst
for the obtaining of feeling, and deuotion in prayer, humble thy selfe, and confesse

felfe that it is one of the gifts, which I diftribute to whome I will, and when I pleafe. Befides, tell me, wherefore thou prayeft? If it be to pleafe thy felfe, there is no caufe, why thou fhouldft expect any other reward, becaufe thy payne of praying is acquitted, & that abundantly, with that pleafure, that thou feeleft in thy prayer: but if thou prayeft to pleafe me, it ought to content thee, that I accept of it at thy hands. He that inuyteth to good cheere, muft be contented, if his guefts like of it, though himfelfe taft not of it at all.

8. There are others, who neglect their prayer, becaufe they be therein molefted & troubled with diuers, and importune cogitations, and fcruples. He is no good fouldiar, who turneth his backe and runneth away at the firft found of the Trumpet, or fo foone as he commeth in fight of the enemy. What do bad thoughts hurt thee, if they come vpon thee againft thy will, neither haft any defire to intertaine them? I am fatisfyed, if when thou perceiueft and feeleft them, thou fhakeft them off, and if they come againe, thou do the fame, and though thou fhouldeft do nothing els all thy prayer tyme, thou fhouldft pleafe me as much, as if thou hadft made thy prayer

with

with greatest attention, and thou shouldst merit more at my hands, then if thou hadst receiued great consolation, and spirituall contentment in thy prayer. A good seruant taketh more pleasure of his Lords comfort, then of his owne, though he thinketh that of his Lords to be his. A very good remedy for scruples is, not to weigh them, at all but to haue a purpose only in prayer to prayse & extoll the diuine goodnes. He that regardeth scruples, looseth the fruit of many good workes.

9.   Some, because they see not the fruit of their prayer, do make a light reckoning of it, and therefore they contemne the exercising therof, as nothing profiting them: Sonne, it is no good consequence : I make no profit of my prayer, and therfore I do well, not to make any. For if thou dost not profit by it, the fault is thine owne, and not of prayer. For thou mightst, if thou wouldest, make most great profit thereof, sith Prayer is a most profitable thing. He that maketh a fire to warme himselfe, and goeth far from it, receiueth no heate at all from it. Prayer is a fire, whereunto if thou shalt forbeare to approach, thou shalt neuer be warme, or get any heate.

10.   O how do the Religiousmen please me,

me, who after they haue prayſed me, and done me all honour in their prayers that they can, do by the benefit of it lead a Religious and vertuous life, by abſtayning from vice, and imbracing vertue, whereon they meditated in their prayer. Neyther, though thou ſhouldſt find no profit in thy ſelfe at all, muſt thou therefore leaue of thy cuſtome of prayer, ſith that hath another fruit and commodity, that inſeparably accompanyeth it, and this is, for that by it great honour, and glory is giuen to me thy Creatour. Yet a good Religious man muſt not ſtay heere, but muſt proceed on to workes: for ſo doing he ſhall honour, and content me the more. Therfore he pleaſeth me not, who though he craue in his prayer Vertue, doth not afterwards take any paynes in purchaſing it, namely, by exerciſing ſome acts therof, for this is to tempt God. For thou muſt not expect all that from me, which thou art with my help to do and performe thy ſelfe.

11.   Lord, it is ordained and decreed by thy Law, that we pray alwayes, and without intermiſſion. And can that be poſſible, when we muſt needs ſometymes ſleep, ſometymes eate and drinke, ſometymes deale and trafficke with others &c.

with

with which actions it is impossible for vs
to pray. Son, that Law is not so to be vnderstood , as though it were necessary euery
moment to attend actually to prayer. For
that Religious person alwayes prayeth, and
prayeth truly without ceasing , who maketh his prayer at set tymes & houres : he is
also sayd alwayes to pray, who referreth al
that he doth to Gods glory. Also to lead a
good, and vertuous life, is to pray alwayes.
For he, who euer liueth in all thinges according to his vocation, obeying my will,
alwayes prayeth . And this is not impossible , nor very hard , that my Law commaundeth .

Of the Vertue of Perseuerance .

CHAP. XII.

SONNE, all the Angels were created in
heauen, but all stayed not there . All receiued many great gifts and benefits togeather with grace , but all conserued it not .
For some not perseuering in that most happy state, fell miserably, and lost all the fauour of God . But those that stood, were
confirmed in grace, and enioyed the priuiledge of euerlasting telicity . Who is not
content with his owne state & condition,
liueth

liueth vnquietly, and easily offendeth. Thy first Parents were formed of earth, but yet in the terreftrial Paradife, where they were enriched with fundry gifts, and especially with that of innocency: but after that, not content with their owne ftate, they had a defire to be as Gods, knowing both good and ill, and they were not only fpoiled of their innocency, but also with their extreme ignominy and hurt thruft out of Paradife, in fo much as thereby they brought themfelues, and all their pofterity into infinite miferyes. He that afpireth higher, & to more then his ftate permitteth, forgoeth that iuftly, which he had receiued before. O how many Religious perifh for want of perfeuerance! for they perfeuere not, who are not content with their ftate, & condition, that they haue in Religion, whereunto I called them. And how many of them be for a punifhment of their inconftancy and ingratitude found to lead a life in the world, vnworthy of a man? And that worthily befalleth them, becaufe they cotented not themfelues with their Angelical life in Religion.

2. Perfeuerance hath the dependance of conftancy, as hath the daughter of the mother. For he that is conftant in tolera-
ting

ting the troubles and trauayles, that be
preiented in the exercife of vertues, is fayd
to perſeuere in good, and where conſtancy
relenteth, there perſeuerance fayleth alfo.
O how much is inconſtancy in good works
vnbeſeeming to a Religious man, who
ſhould worthily be aſhamed, euen of the
only thought of inconſtancy. And no meruaile, ſith it is alfo diſhonorable to a man
of the world, who yet maketh no profeſſion of practiſing vertue, if he once leaue
off the good worke he had formerly begon, ſith it is not good to begin a good
worke, and to intermit it, and leaue it
vnperfected without iuſt cauſe. And
that Religious giueth it ouer to his greater
ſhame, who leaueth his vocation though
an inconſtancy, when as he is tyed vnto
it by the law of vowes, when he made a
profeſſion of vertue, and from the very in-
ſtant of his firſt conuerſion, began to labour to perfection. If a blind man, or
one who knoweth not the way, ſhould
go out of the fame, he were worthy of
excuſe: but if one illuminated, & by long
inſtructiõ intelligent of the ſpiritual way,
as the Religious be, ſhould ſtray out of the
right way, and by inconſtancy forfake his
former ſtate, what excuſe can he pretend

for

for himselfe? For it cannot be any iuſt excuſe, that he complaineth, that he cannot
be at quiet in Religion, and in concluſion is afraid of the perdition of his ſoule:
for as much as by this pretext he ſeeketh to
couer and conceale his owne inconſtancy.
But he laboureth in vaine, ſith he is vnquiet for none other reaſon, then for that
he hath a will to be vnquiet.

3. O how much is this poore man deceaued, thinking that he ſhould find more
quiet in the world, then he hath in Religion, as though in the world there were
no troubles, & croſſes, nor greiuous ſinnes
committed, or that in the world there were
more excellent remedyes and meanes for
procuring of quiet, and of the ſoules good,
then there be in Religion. It is nothing ſo,
my ſonne: but theſe be meere fanſyes of
thy, and owne ianglings and decyets of
the enemy. He that aſpireth to quiet, and
conſtancy in his vocation, which is as it
were a certaine pledge of ſaluation, muſt
be humble. An humble man, if any thing
happen hard, or heauy vnto him, ſayth:
This it is to be a Religious man, neither is
he troubled, becauſe he thinketh himſelfe
worthy to ſuffer more incommodityes,
then he doth. Perſeuerance alſo dependeth

on

on patience, which is the elder sister, without which Perseuerance cannot stand. For if there be not patience in suffering aduersities, Perseuerance eftsoones falleth to the ground, sith it consisteth in enduring troubles, paynes, trauells, & miseries vntill the liues end. Hence it is sayd, that Perseuerance crowneth the works, because it communicateth vnto them their last perfectiõ: for that without it they should be imperfect. For he is not happy who doth good, but he who perseuereth in good, neither is a reward granted to him who worketh well, but to him who persisteth in doing good vntill the very end. Many begin wel, but all do not end well.

4. Some forbeare to perseuere in the exercise of vertue, because they are afrayd of the paine. For when they consider that the payne is a sore thing, and very hard, & which they are scarce able to away with, they cast downe their burden, who when they might & were of power to ouercome, are neuertheles ouercome, and ouerthrown by their inconstancy. But Perseuerance repreth this feare, and animateth a man to persist manfully in the exercise of good workes, as much as is requisite. Sonne, if thou desirest to weare the crowne of Per-

seuerance,

seuerance, thou must shun two extremes
thereunto contrary. The one is called Ni-
cenes and ease, which easily yealdeth and
turneth the backe for some difficultyes,
that occure and present themselues in the
exercise of vertue. The other is a pertinacy,
and will, that adhereth ouer much to it
owne iudgment. But Perseuerance, that
keepeth the meane, neither permitteth the
good worke once begon, to be hindred by
any difficulty, nor to be put off, or differred
longer, then reason requireth.

5. Lord, I haue often heard, that Perseuerance in good is thy worke and gift,
and that it cannot be had, but by thy benefit, and that thou giuest it where, and to
whome it best pleaseth thee. And if it be
so, they seem free from al fault, as many
as perseuere not in a good worke begon,
sith they may for excuse of themselues say,
that they haue not receiued the gift of Perseuerance. Sonne, it is true, that Perseuerance in good workes is my gift, but yet
thou art bound to haue a firme purpose of
perseuering in good, as in a thing necessary
for thy soules health, and it is in thyne
owne power to go against that purpose of
thine, or also, with the help of my grace,
to keep and continue it. Neither, though
the

the gift of Perſeuerance commeth from me,
oughteſt thou therefore to be diſmaid : do
thou thyne owne part manfully, and I wil
diſcharge myne in aſſiſting thee with my
grace, where needis.

6, Tell me now, my ſonne, what there
is in Religion, that may make thee afraid
of not perſeuering? Be they perhaps, the
paynes, and troubles that be in Religion?
or becauſe all neceſſaryes of body be not
competently affoarded thee ? But neither
theſe, nor all things els can giue a Religious
man iuſt cauſe of giuing ouer his good purpoſe. I did my ſelfe from the firſt day of
my comming into the world, till my going out of it againe, ſuffer many and great
incommodityes: and my labours and paynes ſtill increaſed with my yeares. And if I
moued out of my loue to thee, perſiſted in
carrying my croſſe of paynes , and toyling
till my death, why ſhouldſt not thou for
the loue of me perſeuere in good, which by
my ſpeciall inſpiration thou haſt choſen ?
Why ſhouldſt thou without cauſe abandon
that, wheranto thou haſt voluntarily tyed
thy ſelfe ?

7. Conſider, ſonne , what ſentence is
pronounced touching this : That ſaluation
is promiſed **not to the beginners** , but
to

to the perseuerant till death . Consider also
that it is already defined, that he is not apt
for the Kingdom of heauen, who after his
hand once put to the plow, looketh behind
him . Consider, that the Diuell entreth togeather with thy will, that he may afterwards bring thee out with his owne. He
pretendeth the yoke of Religion to be heauy, that he may make thee to become an
Apostata , and a fugitiue of his campe. It
is not greiuous, that is endured for the loue
of me : and though thou mightst passe ouer
this life without paynes , and crosses , yet
that maner of life should not content thee,
because I thy Lord did euer liue in trauails
and carrying of my Crosse .

8.   He that perseuereth not in good
workes , iniureth me, because I haue inspired those good workes . He that without
iust cause neglecteth to perseuere in the
state that I haue assigned him, doth a work
pleasing to the Diuell, because he resembleth himselfe to him, who from an Angels
state fell downe to that of the Diuell. He
that by inconstancy giueth ouer the good
begon, ouerthroweth his owne deed, and
knoweth not , whether he shall do any
thing better .

The end of the third Booke .

THE
FOVRTH BOOKE
of Religious Perfection.

Wherein is treated, touching the Spirituall Actions of a Religious man :
wherby may be vnderstood, what
progresse, and profit he hath
made in the purchase of
Perfection.

How a Religious man must not take it ill,
though he be contemned of others.

CHAP. I.

ONNE, why art thou so much
afflicted and troubled, when
thou perceiuest others to haue
little regard of thee? Wherefore dost thou so earnestly seek
after honour, and the opinion of a great

name?

name? Art thou entred into Religion, that
thou mayst be esteemed of others, or rather
that thou mighst with more security come
to life eueerlasting? Hast thou renounced
the world for the pleasing of men, or that
thou mighst serue and please me? If thou
hast left it to please me, what skilleth it,
though thou be nothing regarded of o-
thers? Thinkest thou, that by this conceit
and opinion, either the good of thy soule is
hindred, or the seruice diuine which thou
hadst a desire to yeald vnto me? Truly no
such matter. If any thing were to be feared,
it should be this, least humane estimation
might worke thy ruine, when as the Apostle sayth: If he should still please men, he
should not be Gods seruant. Sonne, if thou
examine the matter well, he that esteemeth
thee not, profiteth thee much, because he
helpeth and furthereth thy separation from
the world, and to the making of thy recourse to me, who am to giue life euerlasting. He that maketh much of thee, and
recommendeth thee, stoppeth vp the way
of saluation against thee, and therfore my
seruants of old, who florished in former
tymes in their Religion, reioyced if they
were at any tyme contemned of others, &
were on the other side sory and grieued, if
any

any exceſſe were vſed in their commendations : and no leſſe do all thoſe Religious
men at this day, who haue their part in
the true ſpirit of God. He who liueth in
baniſhment, muſt little regard others, ſo he
be in the grace and fauour of him, of whom
he may be holpen.

2. The firſt rudiments to be learned
of a Religious man, be theſe, to contemne
himſelfe, to wiſh not to be eſteemed of o-
thers, to abnegate and deny himſelfe, to
deeme and hold himſelfe vnworthy of any
prayſe whatſoeuer, to do well, and to be
ill entreated and handled. Without the
practiſe of theſe rudiments and principles
no Religious man can profit in the ſpirituall diſcipline. Wherefore if after ſome
yeares ſpent in Religion, thou ſtill hunt
after honours, and the eſtimation of a great
name, it is a ſigne, that thou haſt not yet
learned the firſt principles, that be deliuered in Religions Schoole, and how then
wilt thou proceed and go forwards in ſpirit? What maruaile, though thou be troubled, when honour is not done thee? If
thou deſireſt to put all griefe out of thy
mind, begin in earneſt to make a little e-
ſteeme of thy ſelfe, for that he, who ſhall
once contemne himſelfe, ſhall not find any

diſguſt

disgust by others contemning of him. The greater opinion thou hast of thy selfe, the more shalt thou be grieued, when others yeald thee not the honour, that is due vnto thee, and thou expectest.

3. Tell me, is it not worse to be contemned, then not to be esteemed of? and is not he more confounded, who is shamefully handled, then is he, who is spoiled of the honour due vnto him? It is so indeed. Admit thou art not perhaps much esteemed: but I was of others despised, and laughed to scorne. Let the honour due vnto thee, be taken from thee: but I thy head was most ignominiously handled. Thou peraduenture art not courteously dealt with by thyne enemyes: but I was ill vsed euen by them to whome I had beene most beneficiall. And if I thy Lord, Head, and Maister, did with patience suffer so great iniuryes, vniustly done me, wherefore art thou dismayd, if at any tyme so much honour be not yealded vnto thee, as thou wouldst wish? Wilt thou be preferred before thy Lord, and Maister? Doth it seem vnto thee fitting, that vnder a thorny head and ignominiously treated, there should ly members hid, both delicate, and honorably regarded? The more a man resisteth

to

to be contemned, the more vnlike is he to
his Lord: and he that taketh not paynes to
resemble him on earth, shall not haue any
part with him in heauen.

4. Honour is the reward of vertue. If
thou desire to be honoured, thou must of
necessity be vertuous, elsthou wouldst wish
to haue that giuen thee, that is not thy due,
& he that should yeald it ynto thee, should
rather flatter thee, then prayse thee. And
what vertue is there in thee, for which
thou deemest thy selfe worthy of commendation, and veneration? True vertue euer
goeth in company with Humility, that is
the foundation of all Religious vertues. If
therefore there be not Humility in thee,
true vertue must needs be absent also. But
if there be Humility in thee, and thou be
truly humble, how can it be thou shouldst
desire honour, sith it is the property of Humility to fly from honours, and commendations of men? He that practiseth Humility, desireth to be despised of all, and is
glad that he is nothing reckoned of. Moreouer, what memorable, or noble act hast
thou done, wherefore shouldst thou desire
or seeke after such applause of men? Or
what hast thou suffered for the loue of me,
that thou shouldest receiue a reward at my
hands

hands in this life? Certainly thou haſt not
yet ſhead thy bloud for me, neither haſt
beene in bands, nor moſt ignominiouſly
haled and drawne through the ſtreets, nor
nayled to the croſſe, as I was for thy ſake.
And though thou hadſt ſuffered all this and
more for me, yet thou ſhouldeſt haue need
the help of my grace, without which no
good can be done, and ſo all the praiſe had
rather redounded vnto me, and not vnto
thee. Admitte it were true, that thou haſt
done many workes worth the rewarding,
thinkeſt thou it beſt to do ſuch thinges,
that they may be rewarded with an humane honour in this life, that is, with a
moſt contemptible price, if it be compared
with the diuine honour, prepared in heauen? He that ſeeketh for praiſe of the good
workes that he doeth in this life, muſt
not expect any other reward in the next
life.

5. Sonne, thou ſhalt neuer be reme-
died or cured of this euill, if thou find not
out the cauſe therof. The chief cauſe is the
magnificall and great opinion, thou haſt
of thy ſelfe, whereby thou perſuadeſt thy
ſelfe, that thou art worthy of honour, and
that he doth thee a great iniury, who ſhall
not haue the ſame conceit of thee. And
herehence

heer hence is the griefe, thou feelest, when
others make no great esteeme of thee. But
let vs examine, I pray thee, what there is in
thee, whereby thou shouldest deserue honours, and dignityes? For first whatsoeuer thou hast receiued of me, I do conserue the same, and if I should withdraw
my hand but a little from thee, thou
wouldest be brought to nothing. If all the
gnod in thee be myne, certainsy al honour
also is due to me, and not to thee. The miseries, imperfections, and finnes be thyne,
for which whether thou be worthy of
commendation, or rather of confusion,
consider well. O how many Religious men
be deceiued with the estimation, that
they haue of themselues, and will be the
iudges, and arbiters therof themselues. For
whiles they deeme themselues worthy of
honour, and yet see that they haue not got
the opinion of any good name, either with
their Superiours, or any other, they are
greatly troubled, and afflicted in mind. He
that layeth a bad foundation, maketh a
worse building vpon it.

6. Sonne, thou dost not yet know thy
selfe well, and therefore thou canst not be
a good iudge, nor iudge well of thy selfe.
If thou didst know thy selfe well, thou
wouldest

wouldeſt not raiſe ſo magnificall and ſtately a building vpon ſo weake and fraylea foundation. That a man be highly recommended, and held in great veneration, needs it muſt be, that there is an opinion, and eſtimation before in the mind, not of him who is to be honoured, but of them who are to giue the honour, touching his excellency and worthines. But if they ſee no vertue in thee at all, but imperfections rather, and leuityes, how can they haue a good opinion of thee, or ſpeake and report of thy prayſes? The good workes do cauſe a good opinion, and not the deſire of him, who ſeeketh his owne prayſes.

7. Deſireſt thou to ſee, how far thou art in this matter from the truth? Conſider what I am now to ſay vpto thee. Thou art either dead to the world, or not. If thou be not, thou art nothing worth for Religion, nor Religion for thee, ſith it receiueth and approueth none, but ſuch as haue from their hart renounced the vanityes of the world, and this is to be dead to the world. And amongſt the vanities of the world one is, to ſeeke after honour, and to deſire to be eſteemed for great. But if thou be dead to the world, why deſireſt thou to be honoured of it? A dead body careth

not,

not, whether it be placed on the right
hand, or on the left, in an honorable place,
or whether cappes and knees be giuen
it, or not . But if thou seekest for a more
honorable place, or a greater office, if thou
desirest that others should giue thee place,
how art thou dead to the world? Neither
doth it satisfy me, if thou sayst, thou desirest honour, for my glory and honour, that
thou mayst haue greater authority with
men, and by help thereof mayst be able to
do more good with others. For if it were
so, that appertained to me, and not to thee
to prouide ; and if there shall be any need,
I will not be wanting to my duty. In the
meane time it is my honour, and my glory,
if thou be humble, and not greiued, if thou
be at any tyme contemned: for so thou shalt
be like vnto me, thou shalt liue quiet in
Religion, and shalt receiue thy reward in
heauen. And know thou, that to be desirous
of prayse, is not the way to help others,
but to be a follower of Humility, Charity,
and other vertues, and most of all if thou be
wholy estranged from all ambition , and
auarice, and giue good example to others.

That

*That a Religious man must not be ouer-
much desirous of the commodityes
of his body.*

CHAP. II.

SONNE, to speake faire to a friend, to
pleate him, and to giue an occasion of
well doing, is very conuenient and com-
mendab e: but to fawne vpon an enemy,
who seeketh thine eternall ruine, and to
giue him oportunity of ill doing, is very
absurd and detestable. Thou art not ignorant, that of three capitall enemyes thou
hast, one is thyne own body: thou knowest also, that thy flesh, if it be not chasttised
and kept vnder, becometh so fierce and insolent, as it will cause thy soules ruine. Tel
me, what law hath appointed, that a Religious man should fawne vpon his body,
who is bound to restraine & kurbe it with
the bridle, and to mortify it? Wherefore
should the Religious attend to the care of
the bodyes commodityes, who is assured,
that the more he fauoureth and cherish th
it, the prouder it will become. My Apostle
by chastising his body, and intreat ng it
hardly, brou ht it to the duty it did owe
to the spirit. He therefore, who yealdeth
                                    vnto

vnto it ouer much, giueth an occasion vnto it of reuolt, and of rebelling againſt
the ſpirit.

2. Lord, thou haſt not made vs lords
of our body, that we may take life from it,
or mayme and mangle it, but thou haſt giuen vs a charge to preſerue the health of it,
as much as we can, and therefore we may
procure thoſe commodityes therof, that
make to the conſeruation of health, and ſo
much the more, for that we vſe not onely
the ſoule, but the body alſo for the doing
of thee diuine honour, and ſeruice.

3. Sonne, it pleaſeth me much, that a
Religious man conſerue and maintaine his
good health by fitt meanes, for the doing of my ſeruice, but this diſpleaſeth me,
that vnder pretece of preſeruing the health
of body he maketh ouer much of it. I like
not that Religious man, who will vſurpe
and take vpon him a Phiſitians office, and
iudge himſelfe what is for, and what is a-
gainſt his health. For of this it happeneth
that whatſoeuer pleaſeth his appetite, that
is good for him, & what agreeth not with
his taſt, that is hurtfull for his health. Neither doth he offend me leſſe, becauſe he
ſayth, he doth it for my greater and better
ſeruice. And indeed it is not to ſerue me,
but

but to serue his owne gust, and sensuality.
It is my seruice, when euery one mortifyeth his owne flesh, as much as is requisite,
and it needeth. O how many Religious
be there, who vnder a pretext of conseruing
their health, become the slaues of their own
desires? The health is better kept by parsimony, and moderation, then by the procuring of thinges apperrayning to the tast.
Yea by this the health is impayred, for
that there is excesse in all thinges commonly that haue pleasure with them.
Moreouer it is an obligation, proper to a
Religious person, to yeald no more to the
body, then what is needfull for intertayning of life, & not what is for the stirring
vp of the flesh.

4. If the Religious man would examine, whence ariseth that so great a care
he hath of himselfe, and of his body, he
would not be so anxious, and importune
in seeking after the commodityes therof.
In some it groweth of a superfluous cōmi-
seration and pitty towards themselues, because they could wish to yeald their body
some pleasure. In others it proceedeth of a
magnificall opinion they conceiue of their
owne estimation : for wheras they are perswaded, that it greatly importeth the cōmon

mon wealth, if they liue long, their care is
all in all about the preseruation of their
health . Both these, namely commiseration, and estimation, be selfe-loues daughters. And what good fruit can come of so
dangerous a roote? These men peraduenture thinke, that if they were gone, my
Church would come to decay, or their Religion would come to ruine. They are
greatly deceiued . Many other pillars haue
fallen, and yet both my Church, and Religion hold their owne : that care appertayneth to me alwell to conserue both, as to
prouide them of good workmen and la-
bourers. And I vnder take, that the Religiõ,
when such men are gon, shall not only not
come to ruine, but shall further receaue an
increase, because those commonly who
haue taken lesse paynes in Religion , and
haue most troubled it, be those who haue
beene most of all giuen to their pleasures,
and commodityes of body. And these be
they, who do by their example ouerthrow
Religious houses.

5. When thou becamest Religious,
didst thou t not with a mind of suffering
much for the sauing of thy soule, and for
the loue o me? Didst thou not purpose to
liue a poore life, and to beare with all in-

comme-

commodityes , that be incident to poore
perſons ? Whence then is it, that now,
when thou ſhouldſt haue greater light of
mind, and more charity, thou doſt not put
thoſe thy firſt cogitatiõs in effect by works?
O extreme bad iugling and deceite. Religion is inſtituted for the mortifying of the
body , and for the enriching of the ſoule
with ſpirituall riches, and thou thinkeſt
that a great care is to be vſed and had about
the cheriſhing of the body with the neglect
of the ſoules health? Tell me, I pray thee:
In the world hadſt thou thy commodityes
of body at will, or not ? If not, wherefore
deſireſt thou them in Religion , wherinto
thou didſt enter to ſuffer incommodityes
for Chriſts ſake? And if thou hadſt thy commodityes, and didſt therof voluntarily depriue thy ſelfe for the loue of me, that thou
mightſt pleaſe me the more, wherfore doſt
thou now in Religion ſeeke them, by thee
abandoned before, with an offence to me ,
and bad example to others ? Moreouer , if
thou haſt renounced the cõmodityes of thy
body for the loue of me, and now returneſt
vnto them againe , thou manifeſtly decla-
reſt, that thou wilt not haue any thing to
do with the loue of me . And what an e-
ſteeme ſhould I make of him, who is ſo fic-
kle,

kle, and inconstant in louing me? And if
peraduenture thou thinke, that thou mayst
both loue me, and seeke thy temporal commodityes withall, and that against my wil,
thou art greatly deceiued : for as much as
he cannot loue truly, who doth not conforme himselfe to the will of the beloued.

6. Sonne, if thou desirest to vnderstand,
how I handled myne owne body, runne
ouer my life from the day of my natiuity til
my death, and thou shalt easily see, how
few commodityes I vsed. For so soone as
I came into the world, a stable was my bed-
chamber, and the manger my bed. Within
a while after *Herod* persecuting me, I was
forced to flye into *Ægipt*. Consider thou
heere, what commodityes I found both in
my way thither, & in a countrey so far off
and barbarous, when as I had a poore
Mother, who also was to take her iourney
and to packe in all hast away in the night
tyme, so soone as she had newes of the matter. After that being returned from *Ægipt*,
I passed ouer the remainder of my life in
pouerty. In the thirtith yeare of my age
I retired my selfe into the desert, where I
punished my poore body with hungar,
thirst, watching, lying vpon the ground,
and the fast of fourty dayes and nights.

D d 3 After

After my leauing the deſert, I trauailed on foote from one towne & caſtle to another, and preached the kingdome of heauen in all places where I came, and liued continually by almes that others gaue me. In time of my paſſion, I did not only want all commodityes, but alſo one affliction ſucceeded in place of another. Finally, when I came to dy, a croſſe was my bed to lye on, and a crowne of thornes my pillow.

7. Now iudge thou, who art Religious, whether it be conuenient for thee my ſeruant, who haſt made profeſſion of imitating me, to handle thy body ſo nicely & delicately, ſince I thy Lord haue dealt with myne owne ſo roughly and hardly. And though my body were euer ſubiect to the ſoule, and moſt obedient to reaſon, yet I did neuer entreate it delicately, nor euer yealded vnto it any commodityes, or recreations at al. And wilt thou now affoard vnto thy body, that hath ſo often in a moſt inſolent manner inſulted againſt the ſpirit and reaſon, all kinds of contentements and pleaſures? I the Lord of maieſty euer contented my ſelfe with a poore and meane diet, and as meane cloathing, and other intertaynement: and wilt thou in Religion, not contented with the common, affect & deſire

defire fuperfluityes? This is not to be, or
to lead the lyfe of a Religious perfon, but
rather to couer and conceale a fecular life
by the habit of Religion.

8. An ouer great follicitude of temporall commodityes, is a thorne that pricketh
ouer fore, and greatly hurteth a Religious
man. For firft it maketh him a procuratour
for the body, yea and a bondflaue vnto it.
And who feeth not, how great an indigni-
ty it is for a Religious man of a punifher of
his body to become a Purueyour for it,
and infteed of whipping it, to yeald it all
manner of contentements? Againe, it holdeth and keepeth him fo diftracted in mind
as he taketh no guft., or pleafure at all in
matters of fpirit. And what other thing
is this, then to make him fenfuall, that he
may neither taft, nor mind thofe thinges
that be of God? Moreouer it maketh him
churlifh and harfh to thofe with whome
he liueth : for as much as he euer will in all
things haue what is beft, and moft commodious for himfelfe, neglecting the commodityes of others : yea he preferreth his priuate commodityes before the common,
not regarding what hurt may redound to
the Religion thereby, fo he may haue what
he defireth himfelfe. And what is this,

but

but to spoile a Religious man of charity, discretion, and all?

9. Neither is there heer an end of this importune & preposterous care of the body, but it further maketh the Religious querulous, idle, froward, surly, a murmurer, and of a peruerse and bad example. He would haue all moued to commiserate and pitty his case, all to shew beneuolence & good will vnto him, and therfore he attributeth euery least distemper of body, and indisposition of his health to the sore trauailes and paynes, he hath taken in Religion. And how can it be possible, that there should be either spirit, or Religious discipline in such mē? O vnhappy subiects, and as vnhappy Superiours, who permit such things in Religion, wherein they are pastours, and haue a charge, seeing this is nothing els, then to bring a certaine infection into it, & to shew a way vnto yong men for the quite ruining and ouerthrowing therof.

That

*That it is not inough for a Religious man to
mortify his body , vnles the mind
be restrained also.*

CHAP. III.

SONNE, that the Religious mã so mortify his body, & the senses thereof, as it
become not proud, & rise against the soule,
it is good and healthful, but yet Religious
perfection consisteth not therein, but rather in the inward vertues of the mind , of
which followeth the reformation of the
passions, and senses. Neither can the body
be directed by the soule, vnles the soule it
selfe, togeather with all it own facultyes
and powers, be first of all drawn out, and
fashioned to the right and straight rule. A
croked rule is not for the making of a thing
straight. The soule is then ruled straight,
when it is conformed to the diuine will ,
which is the first, and an infallible rule.
Let a man mortify his flesh, as much as he
will, and keep it in subiection as much as
possibly may be, if the affections be not reduced to a certaine rule, he shal neuer come
to that peace of mind, that is necessary for
the attayning of perfection . Againe , the
affections cannot be brought to a modera-

D d 5   tion,

tion, vnles the grounds of them , of which
they haue thei beg nnings , that is the vnderstanding and will , be brought in order
also .

2.   Thou knowest, that the vnderstanding is the principall power or faculty, on
which all the harmony, consent,& gouerne-
nement of the rest of the facultyes depend.
The will vnderstandeth not, and therefore
it cannot worke, vnles the light & knowledge of the vnderstanding put to the assisting hand. The rest of the inferiour facul-
cultyes, that execute the commaunds and
directions of the Superiour powers , depend also on the vnderstanding, which
sheweth vnto them, what euery one is to
do. But if the vnderstanding should chance
to be out of order, the whole frame & state
of the both inward and outward man must
needs be in trouble, and confounded. Selfe
iudgment doth indeed most of all preuent
and go before the vnderstanding, by which
it is so sore blinded , as it maketh no good
deliberation,& therof also frameth a worse
conclusion . Whence it is, that if thou desire to bring the vnderstanding to an vpright & true gouernemēt, thou must needs
spoile it of it owne iudgment.

3.   Proper iudgment I call that, which
is

is thyne owne conceit, thyne owne purpofe, and thyne owne opinion, that hath
not any correfpondence either with my
iudgment, or with that of thy Superiours,
and therefore is properly thyne, and peculiar to thee, diffenting from the common
iudgment of thy forefathers, of the wife &
vertuous. Wherefore when this thy iudgment is not agreable to myne, that is, to the
firft rule that neuer deceiueth, it cannot be
either right or good. For what rectitude,
and ftraightnes, or goodnes can there be of
that, which hath the origen of proud prefumption? Whiles thou cleaueft to thyne
owne iudgment, thou doft not only prefer
it before the iudgment of others, but alfo
thinkeft it better then the iudgment of o-
thers, that all be deceiued befides thy felfe,
that none vnderftandeth the matter but
thy felfe, and heereupon thou alfo becom-
meft proude in mind, contemning all o-
thers, as fooles, and leffe intelligent. And is
not this a notable prefumption, and pride?
What can be worfe, then for one man pre-
fumptuoufly to prefer himfelfe before all?
Hence it commeth, that being ouer deuoted to thyne owne iudgment, in delibera-
tions thou giueft no place at all to other
mens counfailes, which is nothing els, then

to become obstinate, willfull, stiffe, and stubborne.

4.   Who would now meruaile, if thou be exposed to be beguyled and deceiued by the Diuell? If thou fall into most grosse & palpable errours? For whence haue grown the Heresyes, Schismes, sects, discords, and other stirres not to be numbred, that were in tymes past, and be now in the world, but from men ouer much addicted to the conceit of their owne iudgment, & witt? The dearer thyne owne iudgment is vnto thee, the more it hurteth thee: for it separateth thee from thy Superiours: it maketh thee to seem wise in thyne owne eyes: to trust thy selfe ouer much, that it may the sooner bring thee to the height of pride, & in conclusion precipitate thee into that pit of cogitations, that thou wilt thinke thy selfe not to need any guide, or directeur in the spirituall way. O how much more vnderstanding, and more wise is that Religious man, who vseth his Superiours iudgment for his owne, nor seeketh any other thing: for by so doing he satisfyeth me, he heapeth vp his merit in heauen, and leadeth a quiet life on earth, then which nothing is more contenting, and pleasant.

5.   Another thing, that troubleth, and
peruer-

peruerteth the vnderstanding, is a certaine
curiosity of vnderstanding matters appertaining to God. For seeing the vnderstanding is addicted to learne and vnderstand
thinges, if curiosity also put it forwards, it
will wander vp and downe ouer so many
Countreys, as it doth in the end quite loose
it selfe. Matters of God do far exceed the
vnderstanding of man, and therefore impossible it is for his shallow capacity to cō-
prehend or conceiue them: and therefore,
he who would curiously search into their
mysteries, easily looseth his sight, and is
blinded with that infinite light. For if the
corporall eyes cannot without preiudice
of the sight behold the light of the Sunne,
how wilt thou haue, that human vnderstā-
ding, by nature limited, should be able to
comprehend that inaccessible light of God
which is infinite, & admitteth no circum-
scription, or limitation at all.

6. He that loadeth himselfe with a
burden that he is not able to beare, deserueth to be oppressed, and borne downe by
the weight therof. God should not be God,
if he should be conceiued of any created vnderstanding. Desirest thou to handle matters concerning God wisely? Accomodate
thy selfe to the vertue of Fayth, and seeke

no

no more: for it will in a very short tyme &
most certainly teach thee all, which is necessary for euerlasting saluation. Take thou
also away the curiosity of vnderstanding
such matters, as belong to Superiours, and
others that nothing concerne thee, because
they greatly disquiet and trouble thee, &
further hinder thee from comming to that
iust moderation and temper of vnderstanding, and knowing of others defects,
sith it is inough for thee to know thyne
owne, which if thou know well, and diligently amend, thy payne is not ill imployed. It is a vice of Curiosity to stir vp,
and put a man forwards to fish out, and to
learne other mens matters, and to be forgetfull of his owne.

7.   There is yet a other defect of the
vnderstanding, which is, to iudge rashly,
and if it be not taken away, the vnderstanding cannot be sayd to be squared straight.
And this default happneth, when without
any cause at all, no censure going before, an
vndoubted iudgment is pronounced and
giuen, touching others actions. And if a
man also interprete the intention of another in ill part, when he may interprete it
in good part, or excuse it, such a iudgment is very pernicious vnto him, because
it

it is against both Charity and Iustice. If
thou be not a iudge of the inward man,
nor yet knowest him, how darest thou
iudge and censure him? I am the searcher
of mens harts alone: euery mans intention
is manifest alone to me, and therefore the
office of iudging is due to me alone.

8. Moreouer for the directing of the
will, needfull it is to remedy three defects
most of all, no lesse troublesome, then dangerous. The first is, that the will is of it
owne nature blind, and obnoxious to a
thousand falles. The second is, sith the wil
is free, it can wander whither it list, whether it keep the good and right way, or the
bad, & by-way. As it is blind, that it stray
not and fall, it needeth a guide : and as it is
free, that it may not exceed, and go beyond
reasons bounds; it needeth a bridle. The
guide shall be the diuine will, declared and
explained by them, who exercise my place
in gouerning. The bridle shall be the feare
and dread of Gods iustice, which will direct it in the right way, and in security.
O happy is that Religious, who guided
with such a bridle, followeth so trusty and
faithfull a directour in his way. The third
defect is, that the will is wont to secke a
propriety in it selfe, from which vnles it be
deliuered,

deliuered, it will neuer be brought into order . To be Religious, and to retayne his owne will, can in no case stand togeather. For he is sayd to be a true Religious man, who folioweth me with his crosse . And it is already decreed in my Scripture , that none can follow me vnles he deny himself and forsake his owne will.

9.   Lord, is then a mans owne will to be left, if it be carryed towards pious and good things? Sonne, thou must abandone whatsoeuer thou desirest of thine own wil, whether it be temporall, or spirituall . I call that the proper will , that conspireth not with myne, or with that of thy Superiour, and is properly thyne: and becanse it is discordant from myne it cānot be good. Proper will is that, which proclaymeth warre against me: it I abhorre, it I hate: I haue laid the foundation thereof in hell: Hell intertaineth it , and it alone is most seuerely punished therein . O mad Religious man, who maketh more accompt of his owne will, then of Gods! I did not my selfe so . When my Humanity had an auersion from drinking the bitter chalice of my passion, I sayd to my heauenly Father: Not myne, but thy will be done . If I then would not in this life do myne owne will,

doth

doth it seeme fitting, and conuenient, that
thou shouldst do thyne ? Thinkest thou it
meet, that thou shouldest preferre thyne
own will before the will of thy Creatour,
and of thy Superiours? He that extolleth
himselfe by making a great esteeme of his
owne will, must needs expect a sore fall to
his vtter perdition for euer.

That a Religious man must shake off his in-
ordinate affection to his parents.

CHAP. IIII.

SONNE, vnles thou shalt forget thy
people, and the house of thy Father, I
will not loue and imbrace thee, nor deale
in any familiar manner with thee. It is
not inough once to haue renunced the
world, and thy parents, as thou didst in the
beginning of thy conuersion : but that thou
maist arriue to the height of perfection,
proposed thee, thou must needs persist and
continue in the same renunciation till the
very end of thy life. It little or nothing
profiteth the prisoner to be out of the prison
dores, vnles his yrons be also taken away,
which he had on his legs, when he was in
the prison. Euen so it w ll do the little
good to haue left thy Fathers house, vnles

thou shalt also cut off thyne inordinate affection to thy parents, sith this affection bindeth thee so strongly, as thou canst not forget them.

2.   It is true, that in holy Writ I haue promised to the Religious an hundred fold togeather with life euerlasting, but yet to them who out of a loue of seruing me, haue left father and mother, and whatsoeuer they possessed in the world. True it is, that I am the maister, and do teach, & haue also from the very beginning protested, that none can be my disciple, who shall not hate father and mother, his owne life, & what euer besids, that may keep him frō profiting in spirit. He is not a good scholler, neither can profit, who is not attentiue to what is read in the schoole. The lesson that I deliuer to my hearers is, that they dye to the world, that they maister & subdue their perturbations of mind that make a man vnquiet, that they spoile themselues of all carnall affection to parents, least they be excluded and shut out of the way to perfection. Dost not thou by thyne owne experience find, that the ouermuch affectiō thou carryest to thy parents, maketh thee vnquiet? Seest thou not also, that the same molesteth and troubleth others? Dost thou

not

not obferue, that whiles thy mynd and
care is on them, thou comeft to forget thy
felfe? And this in truth is not to reforto
my fchoole, but to runne rather out of it.
If thou be dead to the world, why doth the
care of parents trouble thee? If thou only
liueft to me, as thou oughteft, why art thou
not conioyned with me, and holdeft me in
place of Father and mother, & of all things
els? O how well did my beloued, and Religious feruant S. *Francis* vnderftand this,
when he fayd from his hart: *Deus meus & om-
nia*, and other my Religious Saints, who to
auoyd all occafions of dealing with their
parents, retyred themfelues into far remote
deferts, and as men dead to the world, hid
themfelues in caues vnder ground, as in
their fepulchres and graues.

3. Lord, haft thou not commaunded in
thy holy Law, that our neighbours fhould
be loued, yea & our enemyes to, & that they
are to be holpen in their neceffityes, and
wats. How the is it thou now exacteft, that
we fhould leaue, and hate our parents, who
hold the firft place amongft our neighbours? Sonne, I deny not, that the parents
and friends fhould be loued, whome thou
haft left behind in the world, but I fay they
are to be loued with a fpirituall affection,

and

and with that loue, which perfect Charity
reqnireth. And thou art not ignorant, I
know, that thou art more neere vnto thy
selfe, then thou art to parents, or friends:
and Charity requireth that thou loue them
so, as thou do not thy selfe any spiritual hurt for them. If then they trouble thee
in Religion, and be a disquiet vnto thee in
my seruice, and any impediment and let
also to thy spirituall profit, why shouldst
thou not forsake them? why shouldst thou
not get thy selfe far from them? Againe, art
thou not to hate those parents, who oppose
themselues against thee, and had rather
haue thee to liue out of Religion? & more
then that, labour also to draw thee out of
it, and to fly from them, as from the Diuels
instruments, and workes? Thou must not
hold him for father or friend, who seeketh
to put thy soule in ieopardy of damnation.
They are not thy neighbours, nor yet of
the number of those corporall enemyes,
whome the Christian law would haue loued: but they be the enemyes of thy spirituall good, they are the enemyes of my honour and glory, and to say in one word,
they be the baits of hell it selfe.

4. But when need is to releeue them
in their necessity, as well corporall, as spirituall,

rituall, how, and how farre, that thou art
to vnderstand from thy Superiours. And
know thou, that the Diuell hath by a feig-
ned and counterfaite shew of Charity and
piety towards parents, thrust many out of
their happy state of Religion. No Religiousman, vnles he be more then mortified,
and more then dead to the world, and to
selfe loue, may euer with security deale
with his parents. O how displeasing is it
vnto me, whiles I see some Religious to
haue a most earnest desire to vnderstand
something touching the state of their parents, and to receiue letters from them? For
what is it els, but to seeke an occasion of
trouble, and of distraction in their prayers?
It is not much to haue forsaken parents in
body, vnles thou also abandon them in
mind and cogitation. O how wisely did
some seruants of myne, who hauing receiued letters of their friends from far countryes, for the conseruing of their quiet and
peace of mind, threw them vnread into the
fire. O lamentable folly of some Religious
persons! Their parents by them left in the
world, haue laid a side all care and memory of them, whiles they againe be day and
night sollicitous and anxious about them.

5.   Neither do those Religious lesse of-

fend me, who do not only wish, but also
by all manner of diligence on their part
seeke to raise their parents or kyn to great
dignityes, and therefore they subiect themselues to the men of the world, that they
may gaine and wyn their fauour: & these
men do greatly preiudice both their owne
authority, and their Religion. Sonne, dost
thou not see, that is not to serue me, but
thy friends? Seest thou not, that is not to
furnish and enrich thy soule, but to make
others rich by many temporall commodityes? What rule perscribeth, that thou
shouldst play thy parents Procuratour?
Haue an eye to thy selfe, for I assure thee,
that in the latter iudgment I will not de-
maund of thee, whether thy parents were
great in this life, nor whether thou shewdst
thy selfe diligent in procuring them dignityes and honours, but will rather exact an
accompt of thee, whether thou hast busyed
and intangled thy self in such affaires. This
is not the way of Religious perfection,
but the way of loosing all spirit, and all
piety togeather.

6. Is it not an exceeding great madnes for a Religious man to be most cowardly and negligent in running the way of
perfection, whereto he was bound: and to
be

be most cunning, and to shew a great witt
about the raising of his friends vp to great
dignityes in the world? And what is worse
then it? It more displeaseth me, that there
be Religious, who take more care that
their parents and friends abound in temporall commodityes, then in spirituall.
Whence it is, that they very seldome, and
withall coldly, aduise them to the exercise
of vertues, but they often, and in very earnest manner excite them to the procuring
of earthly riches. Sonne, what will the
dignityes and titles of thy friends do thee
good, if thou be imperfect? What reward
expectest thou frō me, if thou trauailest &
takest paynes only for flesh and bloud?
Certes thou shouldst prouide better for thy
selfe, and for their soules good, if thou
wouldst direct them in the way of vertue,
and by so doing thy merit would be the
greater, and their soules good should be
the more securely promoted.

E e 4   *That*

That the Religious man ought to vse great
prudence, and circumspection in the
company of others.

CHAP. V.

SONNE, all the Religious with whom
thou liuest, be my beloued children, &
my charity wherwith I tender them, is
not partiall, but generall: for I loue all, &
I wish vnto all the true good. And I desire
that thou also by my example wouldst loue
all indifferently, and with vnto all perfection in this life, and euerlasting glory in
the next: for so perfect Religious Charity
requireth. O how much do the particuler
familiarityes of some Religious persons
displease me, who contract the charity that
they should extend to all, to two or three,
with whome they continually keep company, and by their bad example do greatly
offend others. And how is it possible, I
should not hate such conuersation? The
amity and friendship that hurteth the cō-
munity, was neuer good, neither had euer
a good ending, but euer brought forth
some euill, as murmurations, obloquies,
complaints, dissentions, wherby though
no other great mischiefe should follow,
these

thele conuerlations would be dangerous &
pernicious inough to Religion.

2. Sith thou art a member of a Religious community, thou art euery way and
by all meanes bound not only to loue it,
but allo for the loue of it to suffer lome-
thing not pleasing to thy liking. For we
lee that a man to be conlerued in health,
lome member therof is oftentymes either
tormented with cutting and learing, or
quite cut off from the body, for that the
mébers be naturally ordained for the con-
leruation of the whole body. If therefore
thou louest thy Religion, wherof thou art
a member, th u must haue a care, that it be
preserued whole and entire, & to remoue
all thinges from it, that may any way hurt
it, among which not without caule, is an
ouermuch familiarity with some particuler persons. He that loueth truly, is most
circumspect and carefull not to offend the
beloued in any thing. But we lee, that
Communityes be not a little offended &
hurt by priuate friendship, elpecially if the
lame be betweene persons delirou of a
more free life, who be held neither in the
number of the very spirituall, nor of the
well mortifyed. Wherefore it followeth,
that he, who forbeareth not from such like

conuer-

conuersation, that offendeth the rest of the company, is not a louer of the community, nor of his Religion. I know wel that some Religious person is otherwhiles found, who taketh very little or no care at all to loue his Religion, and little regardeth whether it goeth on well or ill, so he may not himselfe want his own commodityes. But euery Religious person must know, that Religion is his mother, and if he loue it not, and vseth it not as his mother, he shall not himselfe be dealt with, as with a sonne, but as ingratefull shall be one day punished, as he deserueth.

3. Neither am I ignorant, that there be not wanting of those, who excuse themselues, that they are of their own nature & complexion very melancholy, and for that cause do vse only the company of few. And whence hast thou learned, that the Religious must vse the direction and conduct of nature and complexion? If nature should incline thee to ease and ydlenes, or to pride, mighst thou giue thy selfe to ease and pride? But remember sonne, that thou art now become Religious, that thou mighst ouercome nature, and mortify the inordinate desires of bloud, or of complexion. Now then it appeareth, that the

affection

affection of particuler familiarity, sith it is not conforme to a Religious spirit, must needs be inordinate. Neither is it good, if thou sayst: That in this particuler conuersation there is no euill, nor any peruerse end intended : for it carryeth a shew of an euill great inough, when others are therby offended, and that the Superiours reprehend and find fault with it.

4. Lord, it is thy will, that all should profit in spirit, & vse those meanes, which may help to spirituall profit: I then find by experience, that I profit more in spirit by often conuersing with one, then by the talke of many, why wilt thou depriue me of such an help? Sonne, to conuerse, as it is meet with them, who may be able to promote thee in spirit, cannot be offensiue to the community: for this helpe thou mayst haue, all ouermuch familiarity being set aside, of which we heere speake. But if the community be offended, it is a signe, that thy conuersation goeth beyond the appointed bouds, neither is it so diuine and spirituall, as thou bearest thy selfe in hand. And though thou sometymes receiuest some spirituall fruit and good by that priuate familiarity and conuersation, yet this thyne owne commodity should not be

preferred

preferred before the common offence of thy Religion, but perfect charity requireth, that thou wouldst vse another way in procuring that spirituall fruit to thy selfe, without the offending of others.

5. And if ouer much familiarity among the Religious, and my seruants offendeth others, and therefore is worthy of reprehension, how much would it offend, if a Religious man should vse so often conuersation with a secular man, whereby an occasion might be giuen of bad suspitions? The conuersation of a Religious man with one of the world, ought not only to giue edification to them with whome he keepeth company, but to them also who see it, for as much as he is bound to be a good example to all. And if the wise & spirituall men censure so frequent conuersatiō with particuler persons not to be good, they ought to forbeare it. Neither is it inough, if he say, That he treateth of good & pious matters, that he laboureth about the mans conuersion, and that they do ill who censure him otherwise. I do not deny, but that thy neighbour should be holpen, but I affirme that it must be done by due and fit meanes: but ouer much conuersation with some one is no due meanes, neither ordred

by

by Charity. The Religious man, who in
helping others hath no care of his owne
good name, doth ill, but he that giueth an
occasion vnto others of thinking il of him,
doth worse, for so much as not only an euil
it selfe, but also the very shew of euill is
to be taken heed of.

6. Neither doth he satisfy who answereth, That he hath a good intention in
it, sith all our workes must of necessity be
both good, and remoued of all suspition.
Others do not iudge by thy good intention
which they see not, but by thy conuersation which they behold. And though they
should see thyne intention, yet they would
not excuse it, for that by thy ouermuch
familiarity thou bringest it in danger also?
O how many conferences haue amongst
Religious persons begon with the spirit,
and ended afterwards with the flesh and
bloud. The ouermuch confidence of our
selus hath caused many to fal. If many haue
beene caught but with one casting of the
eye, how many will be caught with long
conuersation, and often talking togeather? Our sensuality is very crafty, and
least her iugling should be found out and
discouered, otherwhils she concealeth her
self vnder pretence of helping some person,

and

& it beginneth indeed with spiritual talke,
but afterwards the speach full of affection
doth easily manifest whereto it aymed.
Sonne, beware of the Diuell, and that most
of all, when he transfigureth himselfe into
an Angell of gnt, and as death fly his cō-
pany to whome thou findest thy selfe sen-
sually affected. A little fire, vnles it be remoued far from straw, breaketh first into a
smoke, and afterwards into a flame.

7.   There be other Religions, who cotrary to their Superiours will, do seeke the
familiarity of great persons in the world,
not so much to promote and further their
soules good, as to gaine vnto themselues
their good will and fauour. And is not
this a thing most sorely to be lamented ?
Can it be possible, that a Religious man,
who hath renounced the world, should
seeke after the patronage of a Lord of the
world? Tell me, I pray thee, for what
cause dost thou seeke their fauour and help?
Is it to satisfy Religious discipline? or is it
to mortify thy selfe, as thou shouldst do ? or
also the more easily to come to perfection ?
But certes for this thou needest not the fauour or assistance of men of the world: but
if thou seekest help, thou hast many in Religion that can do it. Yet others be not so
simple,

simple, but that they eafily fmell out, tnat
thou doeft for none other caufe feeke their
good will and protection, then that thou
mayft withdraw thy felfe from Religious
difcipline, and that thy Superiour may not
commaund thee at his pleafure, that which
ftandeth not with thyne owne good liking. And what other thing is this, then
to put a Religious habit vpon fecular liberty? What is it, but vnder hand to liue
in the world, and to entertaine friendfhip
therwith, & in the cleare light to be at defiance with it? But I fee as well, and as
clearely by night, as by day, and I expect
them at a tyme, when they fhall be abandoned of all fauour, and help of others.
Then an accoumpt fhall be taken of their
pernicious wylineffe, & they fhall know
how much it hurteth, from my defence and
protection to degenerate and fall to the patronage of earthly Lords, and fhall to their
hurt cry aloud : *Accurfed is the man, who
trufteth in man.*

   *That a Religious man muft flye Eafe
         and Idlenes.*

CHAP. VI.

SONNE, Idlenes hath beene condemned euen from the tyme of the worlds
                                  creation

creation, as the origen of very many euils, and that was in such sort done, as none receiued it. Wherefore thy first Father *Adam* was placed in the terrestriall paradise in a place of pleasure, not to liue at ease, and to be idle therin, or to tryfle the tyme in recreating himself, but as the Scripture speaketh, to worke in it. And being thrust out of Paradise, that he might not be idle, the earth was deliuered him to manure and husband, that he might eate his bread in the sweat of his browes. And dost thou, who art made the heire of this thy first parents labours, thinke to eate thy bread without sweating? Thy Father *Adam* had also laboured in the terrestriall paradise, if he had continued therein, and wilt thou be ydle in thyne exile, that is a place of paynes taking? Wilt thou attend to thy pleasures in the vale of teares? Consider my sonne, that thou art not yet come to thy country, but art still a stranger and pilgrime, as all thy forefathers were. And if a pilgrime haue a desire to arriue at last home to his countrey, he must not giue himselfe to ydlenes, or stay vpon the way, but go continually forwards, least the darknes of the night come vpon him.

2.   My seruant Iob sayth, That man is
borne

borne to labour and therfore he that lo-
neth his eafe, and taketh not paynes according to his ftate, feemeth not to anfwere
the condition of man. And therefore fome
haue not without caufe called Idlenes the
buryall of a liuing man. O vnhappy Religious, whofe buryall is in his pleafures, the
ftench whereof, by reafon of an inueterate
cuftome he fmelleth not, but he fhall feele it
(alas) in his death, when he fhall alfo haue
a feeling of the hurt. For he muft of neceffity go depriued, and deftitute of good
workes, to another life, where the fewer
good workes a man fhall bring, the leffe he
fhall haue of happynes, and he that might
haue brought more, fhall be greatly forry
that he brought them not. O how true is that
which the Wifeman fayth, That a liuing
dog is better then a dead lyon. There be
fome Religious men excellently learned,
generous of nature, & enriched with many
talents by God, but fo giuen ouer to eafe &
idlenes, as where they are able wonderfully to promote the Chriftian caufe by
their paynes and trauaile, yet they do nothing, and what be they els, then dead
lyons? Certes a liuing dog, that is, that
Religious man doth much more, who
though but meanly and flenderly prouided

of

of learning, doth yet what he can, and is able, for the loue of me. And indeed he that doth little, when he can no more, pleaseth me more then doth he, who is of ability to performe much, and yet doth it not.

3. I was euer a capitall enemy of idlenes, and therefore meete is it, that thou, who makest a profession of imitating me, shouldst also be auerted from idlenes. Thou knowest well, that I began to take paynes from my very childhood, in helping one while my poore mother, another while my foster-father Ioseph in his trade; and wilt not thou, who art come out of the world to Religion to trauaile and take paynes, help the Religion thy mother in her labours, and thy Superiours who intertaine and gouerne thee? Remember, what my Apostle sayth, That an idle man is not worthy of his meate. To desire to eate, & not to haue a will to labour, is nothing els but to haue a will to consume and spend what is got by others: a thing vnworthy a man, not to say, a Religious man. Neither doth it satiffy, that thou sayst, I am ready to take great paynes, but my Superiour will not put me to those labours wherunto I haue an inclination, and which I am able to do with commodity and ease. This is

no

no iuſt excuſe, ſith it is not for thee to
chooſe the office, or thing that is to be ex-
erciſed or done . The ſeruant in ſeruing
muſt not follow his owne inclination, but
his Maiſters, and therefore the Superiour
ſupplyeth my place, to appoint vnto his
ſubiects, what is to be done to my greater
glory. Moreouer, whence art thou ſure,
that thou canſt performe that charge and
office well, whereunto thou haſt an inclination? Thou canſt not in this matter be
an vpright and indifferent iudge by reaſon of the paſſion that decciueth thee.
Euery one pleaſeth himſelfe in his owne,
but the paine and difficulty is, that the
ſame may alſo be pleaſing to others: and
though thou ſhouldſt content all, and yet
ſhould diſpleaſe me, what good would it
do thee? And therefore thou ſhalt neuer
free thy ſelfe from the fault of idlenes, vnles
thy trauayles be conforme to my will, declared vnto thee by thy Superiour.

4. O how pernicious a thing is idlenes
to a Religious perſon. For where idlenes
raigneth, there is no charity, which cannot
be idle, as my Apoſtle ſayth very well . If
therefore thou be idle, it followeth, that
thou wanteſt charity. And what will it
profit thee, poore and miſerable man, if

thou

thou haft receiued the gifts, and talents of all creatures, & be without charity? What merits canft thou heap vp for thy felfe, if thou laboureft not according to charity? Idlenes is no more repugnant to paines taking and Charity, then it is pleafing to the Diuell, to whofe tentations & affaults he giueth place, oportunity, and occafion. Where idlenes is, there the Diuell euer findeth ready entrance, for as much as idlenes is to him like a citty, vnprouided of the defence of walls. Hence it is, that thofe ancient holy Fathers, who made the deferts famous, did euer and anone admonifh their fchollers, for freeing themfelues from the impugnations & affaults of the Diuell, to haue a care to be euer in fome imployment or bufines, fith by fo doing an occafiō is taken from the Diuell of working his bad defignes.

5.   Idlenes further worketh another mifchief and hurt to a Religious man, & that is, that he falleth into many defeds, for as much as it maketh him curious, a breaker of filence, & detractour: it caufeth him to difturbe and hinder others in their good exercifes ; to go often abroad, and to wander vp and downe the Citty, and to feeke fundry recreations and paftimes for
the

the contenting of himielfe. This is not
the way of purchafing vertue, nor of labouring to perfection, wherunto thy forefathers ariued, and now do in a moft pleafant and contenting manner enioy the
fruit of their good works and labours.

6.   Finally idlenes is caufe of another
hurt, that it fpoileth the Religious man of
two moft precious thinges , namely tyme,
and life , and is not this a moft manifeft
madnes ? I haue giuen thee life, and do ftill
conferue it , that thou mayft enrich it by
meriting, and haft thou no regard of thyne
owne good , and commodity ? What profit or help can thy neighbour expect from
thee, if thou haft not any confideration of
thyne owne weale ? I haue granted thee
tyme , and oportunity of manuring and
cultiuating thyne owne vineyard, that is
thy foule , and thou fuffereft it , through
thyne idlenes, to grow wilde. What good
wilt thou do to thy Religion , who haft
fo little care of thyne owne foule ?

F f 3   *That*

*That a Religious man ought to be practised
in hearing, and talking of God, and
of spirituall matters.*

CHAP. VII.

SONNE, many be by Sermons drawn
to the faith, & to a better course of life,
and many by spirituall talke, and discourse
be stirred vp in the loue of God, and of vertues: whence it is, that to heare, or to speak
of matters of spirit, helpeth very much to
the attayning of perfection, for that the
one and the other findeth entrance into
the innermost receipts of the hart. Spirituall talke, whiles care is giuen vnto it, is
receyued into the hearers hart, as a good &
holy seed, that cannot but bring forth good
and answerable fruit. And because the
same commeth from out of the hart of the
deliuerer of spiritual matters, it must needs
also set his hart on fire, from whose mouth
such speach commeth. Conference therefore of pious matters profiteth both the
hearer, and the speaker.

2. All this is true, but yet if there want
loue in the hart, neither the tongue, nor
the eares will busy themselues much in
spirituall matters. Whence thinkest thou
doth

doth it come, that some speake so seldome,
and so coldly of spirituall matters, but of a
defect and want of feruent loue? Whence
thinkest thou, groweth the loathing and
disguft, when speach is had of pious things
and heauenly, but of a defect of the same
loue? If the fire of the loue of God, and of
vertues should burne within our harts,
they would vpon the very leaft talke of spirituall matters be so set on fire, as the very
flame would breake forth, and discouer it
selfe without: neither would there be talk
of any other matter, and nothing with
any greater defire heard, then of spirit, of
deuotion, of the loue of vertues: for not
only the tongue, but the very eares also do
moft readily follow the defires of the hart.

3. O how great a confufion is it of fome
Religious men, who though they make
the profeffion of Religious life, do yet either neuer, or very vnwillingly treate of
spirituall matters: whereas notwithftanding there is no man, that doth not willingly fpeake of the matters, that belong to his
owne function, or office, and also willingly
heare others, if they bring into their dif-
courfe matters, that appertaine to their profeffion. Sonne, doft thou long, and earneftly defire to fpeake of God often and with
F f 4 pleafure?

pleasure? Loue him, and the greater the
loue shall be in thy. hart towards him; and
the more deeply imprinted in it, the more
facility and pleasure shalt thou find in talking of matters concerning God. Hast thou
a desire to be often in company with them
who treat of spirituall matters? Be thou
earnestly affected to such talke: for to. him
that loueth, nothing can happen more contenting, then to heare others talke and
speake of the thing which he loueth.

4. The better the goodnes of euery
thing is knowne, the more it is esteemed,
and the more earnestly desired. That spirituall matters be not so well regarded, nor
so hartily desired, as they deserue, the fault
groweth of nothing els, then that their
goodnes, excellency, and worth is not
known. And among the vtilityes of spirituall talke this is one, that by the benefit
therof the dignity and excellency of spirituall thinges is discouered. An odiferous
thing, the more it is handled, the better &
stronger sweet smell it yealdeth: euen so
the more often spiritual matters be brought
into discourse, the more do the hearers receiue of the sweet smel of them, and for the
knowne and proued goodnes of them they
become the more hartily affected vnto thē.
But

But it happeneth much otherwise in corporal and worldly things, which the more they be examined, weighed, and proued, the more do they diſcouer & bewray their imperfections and faults, & therefore alſo leſſe beloued of the wiſe.

5. The Diuell extremely hateth ſpirituall conferences, & therfore he laboureth by all meanes to hinder it. For firſt, that they may not be brought in, he pretendeth they are troubleſome, hard, and nothing conuenient for the tyme: & if they be once brought in, that they may not be continued, he ſuggeſteth that they ſeem diſguſtfull, nothing pleaſing, and to be as it were without life, and pleaſure in them. And if the crafty enemy find any, who may trouble, and diſguſt the ſpirituall talke by laughter, or out of ſome leuity ſcoffe at it, it cannot be conceiued, how he reioyceth thereat. For he knoweth well, that there is no more effectual way to the ouerthrowing and taking away of the good cuſtome of talking of ſpirituall matters, then that. The helliſh ſerpent is not ignorant, how great a detriment, and hurt he is forced to ſuffer by ſpirituall conferences, wherein his ſnares, impoſtures, iuglings, and frauds are laid open and diſcouered, leaſt any may

through

through incircumspection and vnwarynes suffer himself to be caught and beguiled by them; and therfore as a theef shunneth the light, so doth he fly from, and detest spirituall talke. But the more they be displeasing vnto him, the more do they please me, and the more profitable be they to the Religious. And should not this, as certaine spurs, put them forwards to loue & serue me thy Lord & Sauiour? Moreouer if talke be had of vertue, and other spirituall things, their beauty, and splendour is layd open, which is such and so great, as it must needs procure the wonderfull loue of them, who cast but their eyes vpon it. And what can a Religious man require or desire in this life to do well, then that he be set on fire with the loue of vertues? What thing can befall more dolefull vnto the Diuell, then to see Vertue esteemed, and Vice to be contemned?

6. Tell me now, sonne, what iust cause mayst thou pretend, why thou art not more often delighted with spirituall talke? For, if thou be cold, therby thou mayst get thee an heat: if thou wantest deuotion, there is not a more compendious or shorter way for the procuring of it, then by conference had with a pious affection. Further, what is

is the cause, why thou dost not lend a willing eare to spiritual exhortations? Whence it is, that when there is discourse about the news of the world, or matters done by others that nothing belong to thee, thou art so attentiue thereunto : and when speach is had of pious and good matters, thou art either sleepy, or giuest eare with a certaine disgust and loathing? Some againe there be, who vouchsafe not to be present at a spiritual exhortation, vnles some subtil, & high conceit be therein proposed : and others there be, who in their familiar talke thinke, they should discourse and treate of matters far remoued from the common vnderstanding of men . But they are much deceiued : for I require no such matter in pious and familiar conferences . But I desire this especia ly, that whatsoeuer is in them sayd of deuotion, and other spirituall matters, it be easy, and accommodate to practise, and applyed vnto it, and therefore all must rather be directed to the affection, and to the promoting & putting forwards of the will, then to the feeding and delighting of the vnderstanding . Neither is there heere either tyme, or place of shewing wit, but of declaration of the desire, that euery Religious man ought to burne with, of
purchasing

purchasing vertue, and of attayning perfection.

7.   O how much hurt hath bad custome done, and still doth to Religion. This hath caused a Religious man to be prone and facil to heare vaine & light matters, and to speake idle & friuolous things, and on the other side slow and difficile to heare and speake of pious and good, and of such as agree with his vocation best. And of this those abuses, and defects for a great part haue their beginning, that are to be found in some Religious. It is an hard matter to temper the tongue, and vnles thou accustome thy selfe to speake of good things, it will hardly contayne it selfe from treating of vaine and idle matters. True indeed it is, that the fault heerof is not in the tongue, but al is in the hart, that should restrayne it, and keep it in. For the tongue vttreth no more, then what is first written in the hart, and as the harts trumpet, soundeth aloud whatsoeuer is in it. If there be vertue, deuotion, charity, and spirit in it, the tongue speaketh of them: if vanity, secular conuersation, wantones, and other the like; it resoundeth them also, and maketh them knowne vnto others.

That

That a Religious man ought to be
diligent in all his Actions.

CHAP. VIII.

SONNE, a feruant, that is diligent not
only in his miniftery and feruice, but
alfo in all things, that are appertayning
to his charge, cannot but be deare to his
Lord and maifter. And though he trefpaffe
and offend otherwhiles, yet becaufe he hath
not forgotten his former diligence, his
maifter diffembleth the matter and pardo-
neth him for it. That which caufeth the
maifter to loue his diligent feruant,
proceedeth not fo much of this, that he fa-
tisfyeth his office and duty, as that he feeth
him affected to his wonted feruice & doth
all, not out of a feruile feare, but of loue towards him : for loue is that, which maketh
him diligent . Contrarywife a negligent
feruant is difpleafing to the whole family
where he liueth : if any thing be committed vnto him, vncertaine it is, whether he
will do it, or not, and if he doth, whether
he will do it in tyme, and in good fort:
whence it is, that his maifter cryeth out e-
uery houre, and calleth vpon him, is troubled and moued with anger againft him,
in

in so much, as the negligent man is both
afflicted himselfe, and further giueth occasion of affliction to others. It happeneth
otherwise with a diligent and industrious
seruant : for he enioyeth exceeding great
peace and quiet , and because he doth his
office stoutly , he is cause , that all the family haue their part in the same peace and
quiet .

   2.   A diligent Religious man greatly pleaseth me also, as contrarywise an idle,
negligent and slouthfull man as much displeaseth me. Yet all those are not to be sayd
diligent, who make a ready dispatch eof
those thinges, that are committed to th m
to do, but those, who seeke after a perfect
manner to performe those things commaūded them , neither forbeare any labour in
doing them . He is diligent , who studieth
to do all thinges in their tyme, and as my
will is , they should be . He is diligent,
who what he hath to do, performeth with
a promptitude of will , and endeauoureth
rather to expect others, then to be expected
of them . But the negligent taketh a far o-
ther manner of way. For first his study is
to do what is commanded in the speediest
māner, so he may haue it out of hand, least a
disgust grow thereon , little caring how
                                                        well

well or ill the fame be done . He is negligent, who without any iuft caufe differreth
that from one houre to another that he is
to do . Againe, he is negligent and malicious alfo, who doth of purpofe bufy himfelf
in fomething , or feigneth himfelfe to be
bufied, leaft fome other thing be impofed
vpon him, of which he is afraid . Finally ,
that fubiect is negligent, who when he is
able and may, doth not for all that fo exactly and diligentiy difcharge what is commaunded him, as the Superiour expected ,
or would haue wifhed .

3. Sonne, it pleafeth me nothing, that
fome Religious be diligent there , where
there is no need, and out of negligence to
pretermit that which was neceffary to be
done. It is no great matter , if a man be
fometymes flow and negligent in outward thinges appertayning to the body
which is one day to be meat for wormes,
but if he fhew a neglect in matters which
concerne the mind, and the good ftate and
difcipline of Religion, wherby accuftomed
feruice and honour is yealded me, no little
domage and hurt commeth thereof . And
yet thofe Religious men offend me much
more grieuoufly, who fpare no paynes and
labours in procuring their commodityes of
body

body, and their recreations, and be drousy
and cold in promoting, and putting forwards the workes of spirit. Thou knowst
what my seruant Ieremy sayth, That accursed is the man, that doth Gods worke
negligently, and fraudulently. If thou canst
dispatch thyne owne affaires with expedition and diligence that make to thy profit,
wherefore dost thou it not? If the Angells,
heauens, elements, and the rest of the creatures be diligent in thy seruice, wherefore
art thou slouthfull & negligent in yealding
me thy Creatour, seruice and honour? If
for the fauour of men, whose good will
and loue thou seekest, thou art forward &
diligent in doing them some seruice, wherfore art thou so slacke in my affayres, for
the gayning of my good will and fauour,
who am thy Father & Lord? Iudge thou
now, whether that Religious man deserueth to be accursed, who doth my worke
after a remisse, languishing, and negligent
manner.

4.   If the Maister be diligent in procuring the commodityes of his seruant, euen
with the hazard of his life and goods, and
the seruant on the other side be backeward
and negligent in requiting him, will it
not be an vnworthy thing, & intollerable
withall?

withall? I suffered nothing on my part to
be wanting in the procuring of thy soules
good, and in increasing of thy merits,
though I were to endure many greiuous &
painefull thinges, to which neuertheles I
was not bound: and dost thou in working
well for loue of me, carry thy selfe slowly,
who art by thy vocation bound to serue
me? and whatsoeuer good thou dost, mayst
conuert to thyne owne good? Thou shalt
preiudice thy selfe very much, and greatly
iniure me thy Lord besids, if thou shalt neglect to be diligent in Religion, wherein
the honour of my Name, and Seruice is
in handling. Tell me, if thy Superiours
were negligent in procuring necessaryes
for thy meate, drinke, and cloathing, what
wouldst thou do? & if further they should
be slacke in seeking thy spirituall profit,
whereof thou hadst a great desire, what
wouldst thou not do? And if thou shouldst
with patience endure the one & the other,
it should appertayne to me to chasten both
negligences. And if it be so, what should
exempt thee from the like correctiõ, if thou
be careles, remisse, & slacke in obseruations
of the statutes of Religion?

5. More pleasing vnto me is one good
worke done with diligence, then many

G   negligently

negligently performed : for that Religious diligence proceedeth of loue, and euer accompaineth it, and negligence is a defect, growing of the imperfection of loue. And now none can but know, that no worke is acceptable to me, that is not proceeding from loue, and accomplished by it. Againe a worke done with ioy is much more pleasing vnto me, then a worke vnaccompanyed with ioy. He that in Religiō is diligent in the exercise of good workes, doth them commonly also with ioy, and for this respect the diligent is also more deare to me, then is the negligent. O how am I offended at the conditions of that Religious man, who only vseth a diligence and chearfullnes in doing those thinges, wherunto he is affected, & other things he doth and dispatcheth both drowsily, remissely, and imperfectly. For who seeth not, that in that former worke, though he loose nothing of his spirituall profit, yet he maketh no gayne thereof at all: for as much as he receiued the hire and reward of his good worke by the taste and pleasure he reaped thereby? And who againe obserueth not, that he looseth in his latter worke, sith certaine it is, that it is not inough to do a good worke, vnles it be well done withall?

And

And that Religious man doth it not well,
who goeth about it negligently, and as it
were with an ill will, and an vnwilling
mind.

6. Sonne, I haue feene many, who
though they paffed ouer their life very well
in Reiigion, were neuertheles at the houre
of their death very much troubled with
the reflecting on their owne negligence:
yea and great Saynts and holy men haue
for the fame fcruple beene greatly afraid
in that their laft paffage to another life.
And what wilt thou do, who art neither
an holy man, nor yet fure that thou fhalt
leade a life conforme to thy vocation, till
the end? And therefore it fhould be wifdome for thee, if thou often renew a diligence, and much more thy loue to God,
of which that diligence proceedeth, if thou
defire at thy death to be free from the fore-
fayd affliction of mind, and after death to
efcape the punifhments and paynes of the
other life.

That

*That a Religious man must not contend
with any, but must intertaine peace
with all.*

CHAP. IX.

SONNE, if thou longest in this banishment to haue a tast of the quiet of
the heauenly country, haue a care to conserue peace with three, with thy Creatour,
with thy neighbours, and with thy selfe.
Thou shalt intertaine peace with thy Creatour, if thou obey his precepts, and conserue thy soule free from sinne. Woe be to
thee, if thou takest armes against God : for
he that maketh warre vpon hope of victory, killeth himselfe. It is sinne, that moueth warre betwixt God and man, because
it induceth a man to repugne, & do against
the will of his Creatour. Take away sin,
and thou shalt haue peace with God.

2. Thou shalt intertayne peace with
thy neighbours, if thou be humble: for
Humility is Peaces mother, as pride is the
mother of discord. The humble liueth
peacebly with all, and conserueth peace a-
mongst the proud. And though he should
otherwhiles be forced to contend, yea and
to come to blowes, yet he shall not loose
                                        the

the opinion, and name of a peaceable man,
becaule his will would ayme at peace, and
necessity should cause the quarrell, contention, and fighting . Therefore be thou
possessed of humility, and thou shalt be loued of all, and not held peaceable alone .
Thou shalt keep peace with thy selfe, if
thou be mortifyed, and in what measure
thy mortification shall be, in the same wil
thy peace be also. Many peaces are wont to
be made between enemyes, but none goeth
beyond that which groweth of the victory
obtayned by warre . The vnruly passions
and desires be the enemyes that molest &
trouble thee, & therfore for the obtayning
and compassing of a stable and continued
peace, thou must needs weary them out by
making a rest es warre vpon them, and so
get the victory : for if thou shouldst giue
ouer the fight, they will not permit thee to
enioy any peace or quiet .

3 . I am in holy Writ called the prince
of peace, and worthily, because I was euer a
louer of peace, and therefore, when I came
first into this world, the Angells did sing,
Glory in the highest to God , and in earth
peace to men of good will . Againe, when
I was to go out of this world to my Father,
to my Disciples and their successours I left

G g 3   none

none other testament, & inheritance, then
Peace and Charity. Wherefore I acknowledge not that Religious person, who intertayneth not peace in his hart, for my
disciple and heire, but I thrust him out, &
exclude him from hauing any part in myne
inheritance. Now tell me, who hath
taught thee to contend in Religion, which
is my house, and the house of peace and
concord? Doth it seeme vnto thee reasonable, that thou, who hast forsaken the
world, that thou mightst lead a quiet life
in Religion, shouldst not only not liue in
peace, but shouldest further disturbe the
peace of others? Contentions, and discords
be most sore and bad Euills, and there
cannot be greater in the world. And if thou
thinkest it a great matter, that thou hast
left the world, thy friends, & all that thou
hadst, and bring-st contentions, debates,&
dissentions into Religion, thou art greatly
deceiued. For the Religion cannot do him
good, who liueth not in peace, and he cannot possibly haue peace, who in Religion
frameth and ordereth not his life according
to the institute and spirit therof.

4.   Lord, I sincerely acknowledge, that
contentions do in no sort beseeme a Religious person, but in this life there be so
                                      many

many toyes and controuersies, and men be
so contentious, as that he who will not
contend with them againe, often looseth
his right, and is contemned and trodden
vnder foot by others. Sonne, it is better
without contending to be borne downe by
men, then by contending to be trodden v-
pon by the Diuells. And though all others
should contend, yet none can compell thee
to contend : and if any would peraduenture
quarrell with thee, tell him with the Apostle : We haue no such custome. Neither
will there want meanes, whereby thou
maysthold, and recouer what is thy due,
and right.

5. O how much is that Religiousman
deceiued, who because he seeth equity to
stand for him, thinketh it lawfull for him
to contend and go to suite and Law with
another. It is nothing so. For though it
were lawfull, yet it should not beseeme
them, who make profession of perfection
of life, sith I haue taught in my Law, that
a man must rather, for the conseruing of
peace, yeald so, as to him, who should
seeke to spoyle him of his coate, for the a-
uoyding of contention, he should leaue his
cloake also. Yet there may be disputations,
so they be for defence of the truth, and for
the

the exercise of wits. A man may also co-
mence Ciuill and Ecclesiasticall suites a-
gainst others, so it be done by the prescript
of iust and vpright lawes. Those contentions be only forbidden, that haue repugnance with Iustice, which cause discord,
and giue an occasion of hatred: for if thou
vse them, thou plainly declarest thy selfe
to serue as a miserable souldier vnder the
colours of the infernall enemy, who is the
grand Captayne of all dissentions, and a
sworne enemy to peace and concord.

6.   Of a bad roote there cannot grow
but a bad tree, and of a bad tree, as bad
fruits. The roote of contention is pride:
for if one should yeald to another, there
would ensue no contention and fighting,
& not to haue a will to giue place & yeald
to another, is an argument & signe of pride.
But if enuy & malice be added to pride
which is contentios daughter, there groweth a more sore and more dangerous warre.
For it often happeneth in the heate of contention, that though a man see himselfe depriued of all reason, yet Enuy transporteth
him so far, as because he will not yeald the
victory to the other, he maketh no end of
contending at all. And if it hoppen, that
both of them be peraduenture more headstrong,

strong, and of a more impotent nature, or
haue patrons of their owne opinion present, or els stand vpon their honour and reputation, the flame and heat of contention goeth sometymes on so far, as no help
may quench and put it out, but with the
ruyne of them both.

7. The fruits of this tree be very pernicious to Religion, in gathering wherof,
if there be no vigilancy and diligence
vsed, it is to be feared least within a while
it become full of much infectious fruite, as
of hatred, dissentions, murmurations,
treacheryes, vnderminings, reuenges, and
other vices of that kind : neither shall
Religion be any longer the Schoole of vertue, but the sinke of vice, and a re-
ceptacle of Diuells, yea and for the scandall giuen to men of the world, more bad
then hell it selfe. And whereas hell is the
place of torments, and full of miseryes,
wherin sinners receiue their punishments,
it induceth no man to sinne, but rather ter-
rifyeth him from committing sinne : but
that Religiō in the bowels wherof raigneth
discord and hatred, for the scandal giuen
induceth secular men to sinne the more
greeuously. For if a secular man obserue
the Religious to be at contention and iars
amongst

amongst themselues, he will thinke, that it is much more lawfull for him to enter into such kind of contentions, & to continue them. But if it chance that secular men do intermeddle themselues, and take part in the contentions and debates of Religious men, then the Religion becommeth nothing els, then a house and habitation of diabolicall confusion. My Apostles had also contentions amongst them, which of them should be greater, & though their errour were not great, nor would haue done much hurt to the Colledge of my Apostles, yet I gaue them to vnderstãd, that such contention did not a little displease me, and by vsing correction I tooke away the seed of that discord, and taught them to practise Humility, which is Concords mother. And I further added this fearfull saying: Vnles you become as little ones, you shall neuer enter into the kingdome of heauen.

8. Sonne, if there be any found a louer of peace, and of vnion among Religious men, I am he: and if the contentions, and debates of them againe be displeasing vnto any, I am he most of all. And therfore that a quiet, and peaceable life might be led in Religion, besides that which I tooke from
them

them , Myne and Thyne, the beginning
of all difcords , I caufed further, that all
their conftitutiont and rules fhould be directed to the intertayning of peace and
côcord. But the Diuel hath fowen in them
the cockle of felfe eftimation, which if it
be not trodden vnder foote , is the femi-
nary of all contentions, fuits, debates, quarrells , and warres .

How a Religious man ought to carry him-
felfe in his Tribulations .

C H A P. X.

SONNE, if thou couldft go to heauen
without tribulation , or without the
fuffering of aduerfityes in this life, according to the lawes of loue, thou fhouldft not
wifh or defire it , confidering I thy Lord
entred into it by the way of the croffe, and
of tribulation . All the bleffed alfo, who do
now enioy moft perfect peace and reft, and
ioy in heauen, held the fame way . Wherefore if thou haft a defire to go any other
way, then that of tribulation , thou fhalt
neuer come to that place of quiet and ioy
thou feekeft , but of paynes and miferyes ,
fith affured it is, that none can haue his ioy
both in heauen and in earth togeather . If
thou

thou wilt in this life be an imitatour of the
rich Glutton, thou canst not liue in the o-
ther, in the company of *Lazarus*. My selfe
proued by many tribulations, carryed my
owne heauy Crosse vpon my shoulders, &
therby gaue thee sufficiently to vnderstand,
what way is to be kept to thy country. My
Apostle also declared it plainely inough,
that there is no getting into heauen, but by
many tribulations. And therefore to the
sonnes of *Zebedæus* my most deare disciples,
when they wished to sit one on the right
hand, and the other on my left in my kingdome, I sayd, That they knew not what
they asked, for that they were first to thinke
of their suffering of tribulations, and then
afterwards to speake of the reward therof.

2. Thou art therfore deceiued if thou
thinkest, that there is accesse for thee to heauē without thy crosse & tribulatiōs. Thou
art deceiued, if thou thinkest thou mayst
liue without the enduring of aduersityes:
thou art deceaued (I say) if thou thinkest
that thou canst be in Religion free and exempt from all affliction. If outward tribulations be wanting, the inward wil assayle
thee, for as much as the bad inclinations
passions and inordinate desires suffer not a
man

man to be at quiet, and free from his croſſe.
And though they were away, yet I will
not omit my ſelfe to ſend thee for thy ſouls
good and profit ſome affliction ,or other.
wherefore ſeeing it is certaine , and vndoubted , that in this exile the life cannot
poſſibly be paſſed ouer without croſſes and
tribulations, ſeeing the life it ſelfe is a continuall tribulation , euery Religious man
ſhould in earneſt do very well , and beſt
for himſelfe, if he would make a vertue of
neceſſity,& accommodate himſelfe to beare
the croſſe patiently, and with a ſtout courage . All labour, the more patiently it is
endured, the better and the more lightly is
it borne. Whoſoeuer refuſeth to follow me
with his croſſe, his croſſe will follow him.

3 . Sonne, what doſt thou, that thou
complayneſt in thy afflictions , and art
diſcouraged ? Doſt thou not ſee, that thou
makeſt them the more bitter vnto thee, and
that they torment thee the more ? Doſt
thou thinke, that for the afflictions that
thou beareſt , as thou art able, thou art the
leſſe beloued of me? I am not like vnto the
men of the world , who abandone their
friends, when it is their hap to fall into any
calamity, yea I ſend ſometyms tribulations
vnto ſome, that I may be preſét with them,
                                                    when

when they are in their troubles. I do in truth reproue and chastise my seruants the more, the better I loue them, that they may the more perfectly be purged from all the filth of their sinnes, their vertue may be the more strengthned, and beeing so corroborated may be manifested, and made known vnto others. If thou didst but see, in how great an esteeme a good and perfect Religious man is with me, when he is in affliction and misery, thou wouldst wonder, that I do not multiply more and greater afflictiōs vpon him. For he in that state looseth nothing of his spiritual gayne, & more then that he profiteth himselt exceedingly, & by his own exáple inciteth others wonderfully with a willing mind to imbrace tribulations, and to hold them, as a most singular gift, sent him from heauen. And therefore it often happeneth, that some pious, & Religious man, exercised by such tribulations, is able to effect more, and do more good, then many preachers. Patience manifested by worke, profiteth much more then when it is recommended and preached out of a pulpit.

4. O how much is that Religious man in my fauour, who when any affliction befalleth him, doth at the very first accept it,

as

as a particuler fauour of myne, and yealdeth me most harty thankes therefore, and
secondly seeketh to reape some profit therby for his soule, by crauing of my help
that he may for the loue of me beare it both
manfully and willingly. And can it be
possible, that I should not help such a Religious person? Why should I not lend him
my assisting hand in tribulation? Why
should I not free him, and glorify him?
Contrarywise, how much doth it displease
me to see a Religious man sighing deeply,
murmuring, and discontented in the very
least tribulation, as though he had pro-
claimed warre against me? Is not this a
palpable arrogancy? Is not this to take the
swords point in his owne hand? True it is
that tribulation is a sword, but it is to be
taken by the hilt: for he that shall lay hand
vpon the point, woundeth himselfe. A
good religious man, who taketh the sword
by the hilt, vseth and handleth it with profit in cutting off the imperfections and
superfluous desires, and also in driuing all
enemyes away from his soule.

5. It is to be confessed that tribulation
is bitter, but it is such bitternes, as is not il:
neither can it be properly ill, because it
cōmeth from my heauenly Father, whose
goodnes

goodnes is infinite, and leadeth to the supreme good, as it hath already brought all the blessed, that dwell now in heauen. And seeing I, the Sonne of God, was neuer without tribulation, it nothing beseemeth a Religious man to refuse it for the bitternes that is therein. He, that hath for the loue of me once spoyled himselfe of the pleasures of this world, must in Religion seeke not the pleasure of the senses, but to please the tast of his soule. For if I had refused the bitter cup of my passion, what a state would that haue beene of thyne, and of mankind besides? There are some, who thinke the affliction that they suffer, is ouermuch, yea and to exceed all the tribulations and crosses of the world. But it is nothing so, and more then that, by that conceit and opinion they greatly offend me, because they imagine & feigne me to be a cruell tyrant, who layeth more heauy burdens vpon men, then their forces may beare. I am not ignorant, how much euery one is able to beare: I know also, what may profit or hurt the: but it so hapneth, that to him who hath not been exercised in bearing affliction, the very least misery becommeth great, yea and intollerable also: and he, who hath not proued, or knoweth not

others

others calamityes or miferyes, thinketh his
owne greater then theirs.

6.　When a man hath not in this life
his part in affliction, and all things fucceed
vnto him as he would defire, it is no good
figne: for that whether he be iuft, or be a
finner, it is to be feared, that he is referued
for fome greater punifhment, and that the
profperity of this life is graunted him for a
reward onely of the good he hath done
heere. When the ficke perfons life is defpai-
red of, there is giuen him to tafte whatfoeuer he fhall defire. But when a man hath
his part in tribulations, it is a good figne.
For if he be good, by tribulations he is
made better, and as gold, the more it is
purged, the more it fhineth, and the more
perfect it beeommeth. If he be in the ftate
of finne, by tribulations he is awaked out
of it, that he may remember himfelfe, and
by fight of his owne mifery looke about
him, and repent. The Prodigall fonne,
when he was in his flourifhing ftate and in
his profperity, left his father, & when fortune after turned her whele, and want and
mifery oppreffed him, feeing the calami-
tous ftate wherein himfelfe liued, he returned home to his father. Tribulation
oftentymes caufeth vnderftanding, when
H h profperity

prosperity bereaueth a man of it. How many be there, who because they be not pressed with any thing aduerse, haue either layd aside all remembrance of me, or shew themselues like vnto those, in whose affection and loue I haue very little interrest? But when I shall but once send them the very least ague, or any dangerous infirmity or sicknes, they forthwith come running vnto me, and cry aloud, Saue vs we perish.

7. The necessity, that compelleth men to come vnto me, is healthfull, but yet desired of few, because it is vnknowne. Many be infirme, but they acknowledge not their infirmity, and though they know it, yet they know not what medicine is to be vsed for the remedying thereof. I am the domesticall Phisitian to Religious persons, and know exactly the complexions of all, as also the causes of their sicknes, and make a medicine fitting for the remouing and taking of them all away. Tribulation is a medicine, which with the more patience it is receiued, the more effectuall and soueraigne is it to cure. This medicine by me prescribed and willingly taken, not only purgeth and taketh away the bad effects of the disease, but also, if it be proportionably

tionably recciued, purgeth cleane the reli-
ques of all the antedent indispositions and
ficknes. It is a property of this antidote to
fearch to the root of the euill, and to take
it quite away, which is pride: in fo much
as by humblyng it cureth, and maketh the
froward, angry, and terrible, as meeke as
lambes. This medicine teacheth euery Religious man, how much he hath profited
in Religion, how folid he is in vertue, and
how conioyned he is with me, his Creatour and Redeemer. Finally tribulation
worketh fo, as whatfoeuer lyeth hid in the
foule, whether it be vertue or vice, it layeth
it open to the eye.

8. There is another property of tribulation, that it preferueth a man from future
mifchiefs. Many haue beene very neare to
moft grieuous falls, but by occafion of
fome calamity or other fent them, they
haue beene preferued from them. I like not
of that Religious man, who is grieued,
when any ficknes, or croffe befalleth him.
For he fhould thinke, that infirmity is no
leffe my gift, then is health: and how
knoweth he, that he could ferue me better
in good health then in infirmity? Whence
knoweth he, whether it would profit him
more to keep his bed, or to wander vp and

downe? How knoweth he, whether by
his sicknes he be to be deliuered from greater mischiefes and dangers, or not? And
therefore euery one should permit himselfe to my will, and gratefully to accept
whatsoeur I shall prescribe vnto him, and
not to seeke for any other thing then to
make some profit of his tribulations.

9. Sonne, resolue something, sith so
long as thy peregrination shall be of continuance in this mortall flesh, thou shalt be
subiect to tribulations. Be thou affected to
any place thou desirest, and to whatsoeuer
state of life that may most content thee,
thou shalt neuer want aduersity, till thou
come to thy country in heauen. Thou must
further vnderstand, that seeing tribulation
is a medicine, it worketh according to the
disposition it findeth, and therefore it may
sometymes do good, & sometymes againe
hurt. If thou take it with humility & patience, and thankesgiuing, it will profit:
if on the other side thou take it with an vnwilling mind, with indignation, & com-
playning against him who sendeth it to
thee, it will greatly hurt thee, and redouble
thy affliction besides. For to that which
hapneth and is felt from without, will
come another within, that is, that which
the

the inordinate defires cauſe and produce in
the mind, whiles a man becommeth inwardly moued, and angry for the tribulation, that hath a repugnance with his will.
The tribulation, that is taken with an ill
will, is not diminiſhed, but rather increaſed.

10. There be ſome, who when as they
cannot complaine of tribulation, as of an
ill thing, do transferre and lay all their cōplaint vpon the creatures whence it commeth, and ſay: I make no great reckoning
of the tribulation, but I take it in ill part,
that this man or that was the occaſion
therof, as though one might without my
will, and permiſſion, receiue tribulation
at anothers hands. It is nothing ſo: for as
much as all tribulations happen by my order, and I vſe creatures one while for
the puniſhing of ſome, another while for
the giuing vnto others an occaſion of meriting, and of exerciſing ſome vertue. And
their complaint groweth of none other
thing, then that they may not endure ad-
uerſityes. For where they are aſhamed ſin-
cerely to confeſſe it, leaſt they may ſeeme
deuoid of the vertue of patience and fortitude, they turne themſelues againſt the
creatures, and complaine that they be
ouer

ouer fore oppreffed therwith, not knowing
what way to turne themfelues. And fuch
men make it known, that they want both
patience and Charity.

11.　Tell me, my Sonne, why, when
thou lighteft vpon a very afflicted friend of
thyne, thou doft at the firft giue him fo
much good counfaile, and remedyes for his
euill, and yet if thou be thy felfe plunged in
the fame, or like affliction, thou vfeft it not
thy felfe? Thou knoweft how to tel others
that they beare all with patience, that they
conforme themfelues to Gods will, that
after tribulation they are to expect confolation, fith the Father of heauen doth not
fend his any affliction, but for their greater
good: And when tribulation vifiteth thy
owne houfe, wherfore doeft thou not wel-
come and receiue it with patience? Why
doft thou not conforme thy felfe to the diuine will? Why doft thou not reape fome
fpirituall profit by it? He is no good Phifitian, who applyeth not to himfelfe, what
he thinketh good for others. But this is
worft of all, that in tribulation thou art
moued with indignation, and fayft; what
haue I done? what, I fay, haue I done? Put
thy hand to thy breaft, and thou fhalt find,
that thou art a fonne of *Adam*, and conceyued

ued in finne, and nothing fo innocent, as thou thinkeſt. Thou ſhalt therefore do better, if thou ſayſt ; *Lord increaſe my ſorrow and payne , increaſe alſo my patience. Burne me heere , cut me heere, that thou mâyſt ſpare me for e-uer* .

That a Religious man ought to haue a care of gouerning his tongue .

CHAP. XI.

MY ſonne , the tongue is a little part of man, but yet of very great power to do much, either good or ill. I haue giuen a tongue to men , not only to conuerſe and treate one with another, but alſo, and that moſt of all for this , that by it they may prayſe me, celebrate & extoll my greatnes, and teach others the way to heauen . And therfore when a Religious man abuſeth it in diſcourſing vnproſitably, in murmuring againſt his Superiour, in cenſuring the life of another , in lying , in ambiguous ſpea-king, or with diſſimulation, it is a procee-ding much vnbeſeeming Religious profeſ-ſion, and no ieſſe diſpleaſing vnto me. And it may be ſayd of ſuch a one , that he car-rieth not himſelfe like a Religious perſon, and that, that is true, which my Apoſtle S .

Iames

Iames sayth: If any man thinke himselfe to be Religious, not bridling his tongue, but seducing his hart, this mans Religion is vaine.

2. But against this, o Lord, the same Apostle hath written, that none could euer tame the tongue, and that worse it is then a sauage and wild beast: whence it is, that the Scripture sayth els where, that to rule and moderate the tongue is a gift, that dependeth of thee. And if it be so, what fault is there on our part, when we permit it to breake forth into vnprofitable talke? It is indeed most true, my Sonne, that the tongue is worse thē a raging beast, because the hurt that such a beast doth, goeth no further then to the body, but the domage that the tongue doth, extendeth it selfe both to soule and body. The beast ordinarily doth no mischiefe to the maister who hath the handling and tending of him: but a bad tongue hurteth him whose it is first of all, and then others. It hath neuer beene heard, that one beast hath destroyed an whole prouince, but the tongue hath ruyned cittyes, and whole kingdomes: and as my scriptures say: More haue dyed by the tongue, then by the sword. True it is, that none can tame anothers tongue, but euery

one

ene may rule his owne with the help of
my grace: and further it is true, that the
Religious man, who is of power so to gouerne his tongue, as by it he offend not, meriteth at my hands great prayse, & no lesse
reward. But this perfection, besids that it
is hard, is almost impossible. It is only required, and necessary on thy part, that thou
endeauour to bridle & gouerne thy tongue
in the best manner thou canst, and so doing
thou mayst be assured, that thou shalt neuer
want the assistance of my grace. But if thou
giue it liberty & the raynes of thy own wil,
and permit it to vtter vpon euery occasion,
what commeth in thy mind, who should
endure the blame of these thy tongues faults
but thy selfe, and thyne owne neglect in
restrayning it?

3. And if thou desire in particuler to
know, touching what care a Religious
man should haue of his tongue, I say first,
that he must keep it from speaking much:
for so much as certaine it is, that there cannot want sinne, where speach is vsed. He
that speaketh much, considereth not what
he sayth, and by that occasion he speaketh
and vttereth many things to smal purpose,
and therewith vnprofitable also. And this
is that, which the Sage meant to giue vs to

vnderstand,

vnderstand, when he sayth, That fooles haue their hart in their mouth: because they speake whatsoeuer commeth in their mind, in so much as their hart seemeth to depend on their mouth. But on the contrary, the wise and circumspect hath his mouth in his hart, because he considereth, and premeditateth what he hath to say, & by that occasiō maketh the tongue to haue dependance on the hart, and not the hart on the tongue.

4. In the second place the Religious man must forbeare to speake ambiguously & doubtfully, or in a dissembling manner. For sith the life of a Religious man ought to be simple, and without fraud : euen so must his speach in like manner be round, open & without any dissimulation at al. It should be a matter reprehensible euen in a Pagan, much more in a secular Christian man to vse a doubtfull speach or Equiuocation to deceiue another, and to haue one thing in hart, and another thing in mouth: how much greater fault then should it be in a Religious man, vpon whome is imposed an obligation to labour to perfection. And more then this, he that vseth such manner of speaking, maketh himselfe ordinarily odious, if we beleeue the Wise man, who sayth :

sayth : He that speaketh sophistically, maketh himselfe hatefull to euery one. If then thou offendest me by this dissimulation or Equiuocation of speaking, how is it possible that I should loue thee, or giue thee any countenance? Or that I should yeald thee the assistance of my grace? And if this maketh thee hatefull to thy neighbour, how is it possible, that thou shouldst help him, or do him good? For none trusteth him with whome he hath lost his credit.

5. In the third place a Religious man must beware he speaketh not what is vntrue. Neyther must thou thinke it inough to forbeare lying that hurteth another, or that which is assuered or confirmed by oath, which be mortall sinnes, and whereinto not only many secular persons, but also many heathens would haue a care not to fall : But a man must further abstaine from all manner of lying that is spoken in iest, or for pleasure, to another, for that God is offended therwith : and euen the very least offence of God is to be auoyded with all possible diligence, though there should otherwise follow some great good, as is to saue the neighbours life or soule. We must neuer choose a bad means, wherby to come to a good end, and therfore euery Religious
man

man should rather endure whatsoeuer domage and hurt, euen death it selfe, then
that a lye should come from his mouth. He
is no good Religious man, who is not a
friend of truth, neither is he a friend
to truth, who maketh no scruple to lye,
euen in a light matter. Amongst secular
persons to tell a lye, is an act so base, & infamous, as for a lye they chaleng one another into the field. And lyars are commonly
held for vile, base and contemptible, and
for such, as are denyed vnworthy to be be-
lieued. What then may be thought touching a Religious man, that is a lyar?
To whome may we resemble him? It cannot be sayd, that he resembleth me, who am
the truth it selfe: it remayneth then, that
he be sayd to be like vnto Sathan, who is
in my Scriptures called a lyar, and the father of lyes.

6.   Moreouer tell me, my sonne, is it
not a great infamy to one, that credit is not
giuen him, though he speaketh the truth?
And yet this is the paine & punishment of
a lyar. For if he should lye but once, though
he loose not all his credit, yet he maketh
himselfe at least suspected, that euery one
may stand in doubt, and that with reason,
whether he speaketh what is true, or whether

ther he may beleeue him, or not. And if
it be a thing reprehenfible to lye, treating
about temporall matters with men, what
will it be to vtter what is falfe in thinges
fpirituall? What will it be to lye to his Superiour, or to his ghoftly Father, who
do hold my place?

7. O how much do thofe Religious
men difpleafe me, who hearing another
prayled, feeke to ftayne fuch his commendation fome way or other, or to obfcure it
by putting fome (But) in the way, or by
remembring fome one or other imperfection of his. And if fuch perfons would
diligently fearch out the roote of this fault,
& vnderftand whence it hath the origen,
they would endeauour, I am fure, to bridle
their tongue, and amend their fault. For
in fome this fault arifeth of a bad inclination they haue, and of a certaine pleafure &
contentment they take in cenfuring the life
and actions of another. In others it proceedeth of enuy, by which they are fory of
their neighbours good renowne, and therfore they feeke to obfcure it, or to diminifh
it by their bad reports of him. In fome a-
gaine it hath the fource of pride, and of a
perfwafion they haue, that by obfcuring
anothers praifes, they fhall increafe their
                                          owne,

owne, and make themselues to appeare greater, & better then thole, who be prayled. To abafe others, is not the way for a man to raife himlelfe: for it is no vice, but vertue that rayleth a man, in fo much as where the rootes be fo bad, & fo venemous, it is an eafy matter to thinke, that the fpeach which proceedeth thence, cannot be but bad, and venemous alfo. And therefore, my Sonne, thou muft haue a vigilant care neuer to diminifh the commendations or actions of another, as alfo not to exaggerate, and commend the fame with to mu.h amplification, for as much as the one and the other is a vice of the tongue, that difpleafeth me.

8. Thofe alfo are difpleafing vnto me, who in their fpeach take a contentment to bite and fting another, and to fay in one word, haue no fcruple to vexe, and moleft their brethren. Neither charity, nor the rules of Religious modefty teach, that any fhould take his pleafure with the difpleafur and moleftation of another. This is a thing worthy of blame euen in a feculer perfon, and therefore much more in a Religious man. A man may fometimes be mery and pleafant in his conuerfation, and vfe fome witty difcourfes, which yet muft be in time
and

and place, without the offence or discontent of any.

9. And the tongue, which is without the bridle of vertue, stayeth not it selfe there, but it passeth easily further to murmure, and to report ill of another: and it seemeth vnto it selfe oftentymes to haue found a sufficient and good excuse to say, that it is in a light matter, and that the sinnes be not grosse, that be spoken of. As though it were not any sinne to murmure of light matters, and that it were not an offence as well to God, as to the neighbour. O peruerse tongue, and worthy of double punishment! the one for speaking ill of another, the other for excusing thy fault, in saying, that it is no great matter. It is not any light matter, or such as importeth not much for a man to perseuere and continue in what is ill, though it be little. He that excuseth his sinne, hath not any care to amend himselfe. I haue not any where sayd, that a man might murmure in light matters, but I haue on the contrary forbidden it, when I commaund, That euery one should loue his neighbour, as himselfe. When another murmureth of thee, is it not true, that thou bearest it with an ill will? Thinke thou also, that others take it in ill part,

part, when thou murmurest of them, befides that thou offendest me, and therein
doest against my will.

10.   Moreouer the good opinion, that
is had of the perfons, and efpecially of the
Religious man, profiteth much to the helping of the neighbour: but the murmuring, and detracting tongue obfcureth this
good opinion, and confequently hindreth
the fruite of good example, and the light
of good edincation, that might be giuen
vnto others. And more then that, by fuch
difcouery of the defects and imperfections
euen of them, who haue the reputation of
good & vertuous perfons, is an occafioned
fcendall, being a thing vndoubted, that
thofe, who are yet feeble and weake, hearing mention made of the imperfections
of the good, come eafily to contemne them,
and which is more, are animated to commit greater faults themfelues. And if the
tongue that murmureth of fecular perfons,
be not-excufable, and greatly difpleafeth
me, how may that tongue be excufed, that
murmureth of my feruants? What will it
be to murmure of Superiours, who occupy my place? What will it be to impute
vnto one an imperfection, which he hath
not, therby taking an occafion to murmure
                                                  and

and speake ill of him?

11. The good Religious man doth restraine not only his tongue from all detra-
ction and murmuring, but also stoppeth
his eares, when he heareth the like from
another, and if it happen, that he heareth
any murmuring against his Superiour, he
defendeth him in what he can, seeking to
hide, & excuse the imperfectiõs that might
be in him. For thou must, my sonne, perswade thy selfe, that both the honour, and
the iniury thou dost to thy Superiour, redoundeth to me, and that I will be the
iudge either for thy punishment, or for thy
reward. O how much are those deceiued,
who hauing receaued some discontent at
the hands of their Superiour, do complaine
and murmure at him, affirming, that he
hath wronged them. Who hath made such
men their Superiours Iudges? What law
commaundeth them to reuenge themselus?
If the Superiour hath done amisse, in what
booke haue they found, that they may therfore murmure at him, and repay one euill
with another? Certes they haue not learned this lesson of me: for I do teach the
quite contrary, to render good for ill, & to
ouercome the bad-turne with a good one.

12. There is another vice of the tongue,

I i

no lesse pernicious, then be the precedent, and that is, to disclose some secret that a man should not, and which should be concealed. And what is worst of all in this kind, is, that there be some, who by a curious importunity, and wylie craft seeke to draw some secrets from another, that they may afterwards communicate the same with some other very familyar friend of their own. And in this the faults be many they commit. For first there is in it curiosity, secondly a sinne to induce another to discouer that which he should keep secret, thirdly another sinne in reuealing that which he hath receaued, as a depositum, to be kept secret. Finally, of it there groweth many debates, quarrells, hatreds, discontents, many ill and hard words, and other the like inconueniences. Seest thou now, my sonne, of how many euills a naughty tongue is the cause, and that it is not without ground, that my Apostle S. Iames calleth it an vnquiet and turbulent euill, full of deadly poyson, and a fire that consumeth all that it layeth hold on? But tell me, wherefore thinkest thou, that the tongue was shut vp within the mouth, as it were in a close chamber, & kept in with the teeth and lyps, as with a double rampire, if it be not

not to giue thee to vnderstand, that when
thou shouldst haue a will & desire to moue
thy tongue to speake, reason must first open
the gate, as one that hath the charge & cōmaund ouer it: and that when it should be
expected, that it be retyred and silent,
the same reason must shut vp the ports a-
gaine to keep it in : for els the tongue will
disperse the poyson, and do more hurt then
thou canst thinke, or imagine.

That a Religious man ought to make his
profit of all corrections and admonitions.

CHAP. XII.

MY sonne, what may be expected from
him, who being sore sicke, should
for want of vnderstanding his owne will,
refuse the medicine that might cure him,
or though he should take it, shouldnot keep
it any long tyme, but cast it vp presently
againe ? Such a one questionles should be
in great danger of his life. Correction is an
healthfull medicine, though few there be
that know it, and very few haue practise
of it : but because it is somewhat bitter and
troublesom , thereof it commeth, that it
is displeasant to them, who haue no desire
to perfect themselues, though it be to cure

them, and to promote them much in spirit
and in perfection. This medicine, as all o-
thers, must be proportioned to the complexion of the infirmed person, and is to be
giuen in tyme, when the humors be prepared, and when the sicke person shall be either at quiet, or lesse troubled. And to the
end the sicke person may take it with a
better will, he must first of all make himselfe capable of his euill, of the danger he
findeth himselfe in, and of the great ease he
may receaue by the medicine.

2. The Religion, that maketh no vse
of this sort of remedy, cánot long conserue
it selfe, and it is an exceeding great fault
in the Superiour to forbeare to correct his
subiects, and to permit them to liue at their
owne will, for feare of displeasing them.
The sicke, that liueth after his owne manner, becommeth rath r worse then amend-
eth. Since the corruption by sinne, human nature is so inclined to euil, as if there
be not an eye had to help and repaire it by
admonition and correction, it will soone
fall into some ruine, or other. O what
an accompt shall Superiours haue to make,
for feare of making themselues hated, or
for feare of discontenting, or for some o-
ther human respects, omit to correct their
inferiours.

interiours. They should perswade themselues, that the defects of their subiects,
which should haue been amended by their
correction, shal be imputed vnto them. But
much worse shall be the condition of the
inferiours, who being admonished by their
Superiours, become troubled and discontented, and do take the correction, which
is so profitable and soueraigne a medicine,
for an iniury done them : whence it commeth, that being vnworthy thereof, they
cease not murmuring against their Superiours: which is nothing els, but to murmure
against me, whose will it was, that such
correction should light vpon them . But
what hope is there of amendement in such
persons, when they become worse, and add
one fault to another? What good may be
expected from them , when they will not
acknowledge their fault, and eyther refuse
correction, or if they receaue it, they presently reiect it with a disdaine ? Vnhappy
is he, who hideth his wounds, and much
more vnhappy he, who hath no desire to
procure the cure of them.

3. Tell me, my sonne, whence is it,
that thou art so troubled, & so sore moued,
when thy Superiour blameth thee? Seest
thou not, that so to do, is to take the knife

by

by the edge, and therwith to giue thy selfe
a wound? Seest thou not, that by so doing
thou conuertest the medicine into poyson,
which I had ordained for thy good, and
for the healing vp of thy wounds, and thy
euill disposition? Is not this to say in plaine
termes to thy Superiour, that he aduise thee
no more, nor giue thee any correction, because thou wilt not beare it? And what
other thing is this, then to fauour thyne
owne euill, and to refuse cure? Not to haue
a wil to be reprehended, to speake properly,
is to haue a will to go from ill to worse:
which is neither thyne owne good, nor
the good of Religion, nor that which thy
Superiour may in conscience do, or suffer.

4.   But let vs consider a little, wherefore thou art so much troubled for being reprehended. Is it because thy Superiour blameth thee for a fault thou hast not done?
or that it is nothing so great a one, as thy
Superiour hath made it? or if for that thou
thinkest thy selfe to haue been wronged by
them, who haue made report of the matter
vnto him, and thou wou'dst peraduenture
haue the same examined, and proued by
witnes, and that finding it false & vntrue,
thou wouldst haue him punished; and to
make thee satisfaction, who hath made the
                                    report

report to thy Superiour? My sonne, this is
not the way to perfection, neither is it the
proceeding of Religious persons to examin
or to confront witnesses, nor to debate
matters by processe of Law. For so to proceed, were to multiply debates and contentions, to trouble & disturbe peace, to open
a gate to much hatred and discords: and
when I did in my Ghospell deliuer the
manner of fraternall correction, I did not
giue precepts or instructions of any such
manner of proceeding. It is a course both
better, and more beseeming the Religious
man, to ouercome by way of Humility,
then by way of debate, and contention. O
how much haue some of my seruants gayned and profited, who being reprehended
by their Superiours, euen for some fault
they had not done, receaued the reprehension as comming from me, and perswaded
that I was he who blamed them by the
mouth of their Superiour, humbled themselues, without further debating the matter
wherewith they were charged, and committing all to Gods prouidence craued pardon, yea by so doing much edified their
Superiour. And of this it came, that the
good opinion that was before had of them
was so far off from receauing diminution,

as it was thereby much increased, and they did continue withall much more enriched with merits. And notwithstanding this, it appertained to me to cause the truth to be after discouered, and to come to light for the manifestation of their vertue.

5. My sonne, it is in thy will to conuert correction much to thyne own profit, whether thou hast committed the fault, wherof thy Superiouraduiseth or blameth thee, or hast not done it. For if thou hast done the fault, this correction will serue thee for a purgation, and help to cancell & raze out the fault thou hast committed. If thou hast not done the thing, thou mayst vse it for a preseruatiue medicine, & it wil put thee in mynd to stand vpon thy guard more, and better then before tyme, giuing thee an occasion of conseruing thy vertue, & innocency. And this is the true meanes of making profit of correction, namely if thou receaue it as a medicine comming from me, and such as I haue ordayned for thy good.

6. There be others who complaine not so much of the correction, as of the manner wherewith it is vsed towards them, saying that the Superiour is ouer harsh in his reprehensions, and that he exaggerateth

teth anothers fault ouermuch . He that
would haue euery thing after his owne
fancy, hath many difcontentments, and liueth in much difquiet of mind . So the
medicine may do thee good , to what end
fhouldft thou trouble thyfelfe, whether the
potion be fweet, or fower ? My fonne ,
haft thou a defire to liue in peace ? Leaue
that, which concerneth thy Superiour, &
thinke of that alone, which toucheth thy
felfe . To haue an eye to this, that the correction be founded in Charity , that it be
done without choller, & without difdaine,
that it be proportioned to the fault, that it
be done in tyme, that the inferiour conceaue that which is done, be done out of a
defire of his good , all this appertaineth to
the Superiour, and not to the inferiour: but
to haue a care , that the correction be receaued humbly with patience , and a will
to make his profit thereof, that toucheth
the inferiour . But if the inferiour wil per-
uert this order , and haue his eye rather v-
pon the manner wherewith correction is
to be done, then how he ought to admit it,
it will not be well with him, no more then
it would be with the Superiour, if he
would haue an eye rather to the manner of
taking correction well , then to giue it,

in a manner fitting, and for the good of his subiects. He easily committeth an errour, who thinketh not often, and seriously on that, which concerneth and importeth him to do.

7. My sonne, if thou hast a desire to amend, loue correction, for so much as it is a good & assured meanes therunto. Thou knowest not thyne owne faults, or if thou doest, thou knowest them not, as thou shouldst. Thou perceiuest not how offensiue they be to anothers eye, how is it then possible, thou shouldst amend them? And correction is that, which giueth thee vnderstanding, and knowledge both of the one, and the other. The Diuell hateth correction, and in the Religious labourerh to worke an auersion from it, for that he well knoweth the great good which they may receaue thereby towards their aduancement & progresse in perfection. O how do those Religious men pleafe me, who do not only willingly receaue correction, and seeke to make their profit therof, but do also desire some one or other of their friends to put them very often in remembrance of their faults, and imperfections, whereinto they may hap to fall. He that desireth not correction, nor that he be told

told of his faults, giueth to vnderstand, that he hath not any forward disposition to amend himselfe.

8. Others there be, who may not endure to be admonished, or reprehended by him who is not their Superiour, and they do not only not take it in good part, but do further conceaue an indignation against him; and deeme him for a man troublesome and importune. Consider I pray thee, my Sonne, how far Pride leadeth a man, when it causeth him to be discontented, and angry with them who exercise towards him an office of Charity, in putting him in mind of his faults, for which he hath iust cause to render him thanks. But it may be, that such persons thinke themselues irreprehensible, and be o conceited of themselues, that all they do, is well done, or that they are discontented to be reprehended by their equalls, though in the mean while they know wel inough, that themselues are faulty. The one and the other cannot proceed of any thing but pride, and to say truly, he is such a one, and of the number of those Religious mē, who haue no will to practise either Humility or Mortification. The poore man, who knoweth his own need and necessity,

taketh

taketh willingly the almes of any one, whosoeuer it be, that giueth it, be he maister or seruant, and humbly thanketh him for it : the very same doth euery Religious man, who hartily desireth perfection, and loueth euery one, who helpeth him to the attayning therof.

9.   Correction and reprehension is an act of Charity : and as Charity is common to all, so may euery one vse a modest reprehension, and he who omitteth to do it, when he ought, and hath an hope of doing good by it, though he be not a Superiour, doth not well, & displeaseth me also. How much then shall I be displeased, and how much greater shall that mans sinne be, who knowing an imperfection of his brother, doth not only not admonish him touching it, but also commendeth him for it, saying that he hath done very well, and that he did as he should do, therby inducing an imperfect Religious man to become more bold, and to confirme himselfe the more in his imperfection. And this we may affirme to be the pestilent oyle of sinners, wherof the Prophet speaketh : and vnhappy is that Religious man, who hath his head annoynted therwith. I do my selfe the correction otherwhiles, and send inspirations, to the

the end my feruants may by that occafion
find out and difcouer their owne imperfections, and amend them : fometymes againe I admonifh them by fome affliction
or other, that they may enter into themfelues, and correct what is amiffe : fometymes I permit one whole order of Religion to be afflicted & perfecuted, that the
negligent and bad Religious men, that are
or may be in it, may become good, and the
good better: but the end indeed is, that they
haue a defire to be holpen. They want not
the helps, and meanes of doing well fo
much, as a firme refolution to put thefelues
into a courfe of doing well, and to hold on
the fame, as they ought. My fonne to differ
and put that off till the morrow, that may
profit thee to day, is not an argument or
figne of a man well aduifed. And the more
thou fhalt neglect to amend thy felfe, and
to differ this happy refolution, the more,
and the greater will thy loffe be.

*How a Religious man ought to carry
himfelfe in his fcruples.*

CHAP. XIII.

MY fonne, thou knoweft well, that
to pleafe me, and to receiue a recompence

peace from my hands, it is not inough to
do a good work, but it must be done well.
That one, for feare of offending me, standeth vpon his gard, and endeauoreth to do
all the best he can, this is to do prudently:
neither must he thinke this to be a scruple,
but a filiall feare, a iust feare, and an holy
and meritorious feare. They be scruples,
when one is in his actions perplexed, and
full of anxiety, without hauing any lawfull cause thereof, but only by light con-
iectures and suspitions ill founded, and that
he feares that he sinneth in the thing that
he doth, or that he hath done, or that he
ought to do: whence it commeth, that he
afflicteth himselfe, and continueth altogeather troubled in mind. These scruples,
which be no other (to say truely) then
vaine and carefull imaginations, displease
me very much, and be in the soule of him
who is seazed and taken therewith, as it
were with an hoate and burning feuer,
which tormenteth him both night and
day.

2. Wilt thou vnderstand, my Sonne in
few words, what is the nature of scruples?
when he, who is molested with them, retayneth them in mind, and stayeth vpon
them, when he should contemne them,
they

they are vnto him as many ropes, by which
the Diuell bindeth him, and draweth him
which way he lifteth: but when he contemneth them, he ftandeth firme and ftable,
and the enemy hath no power ouer him at
all.

3. Lord, thefe fcruples difpleafe me:
I defire nothing more, then to be rid of
them, but it is not in my power. I know
right well, my Sonne, that it exceedeth
thy power to fhake of the fcruples that a-
rife of a melancholy complexion, & which
continue as long, as continueth the caufe
whereof they proceed, and that is the melancholy humour it felfe. Againe thou art
as litle able to free thy felfe from thofe fcruples, that I fend thee, or permit thee to fall
into, to the end thou mayft enter into a
true knowledge of thy felfe, or for the hu-
bling of thee, or for the better purging of
thy foule, or for thy greater merit: for as I
fend thefe fcruples, fo it is in me to remoue
them, and I take them away, when it beft
pleafeth me. But thou mayft well (affifted
with my grace) eafe thy felfe of thofe
fcruples, that haue their beginning of proper loue, when by occafion of the ouer
great affection to thy felfe thou becomeft
ouer anxious, and art more afraid, then
                                          thou

thou shouldst, least some inconuenience, or impediment may befall thee, for the doing of what thou hast, or oughtst to do. The good Religious man ought to be circumspect, and haue an eye to himselfe, yet rather by a desire to please me, then for feare of any trouble, or paine to himselfe. In like manner it is in thyne owne power to discharge thy selfe of these scruples, that are occasioned by the suggestiō of the enemy, to the end thou mayst be there afraid, where no cause is of feare at all: and these scruples be nothing els, but a vaine apprehension proceeding from meere fancy.

4. O how much domage do scruples cause, and how much good do they hinder? For first they depriue the person, who is molested with them, of that inward peace, which euery one ought so much to desire, seeing without it a man can neither haue any true deuotion, no do any meritorious act. And more then this, they marre, and ouerthrow the complexion of nature, and trouble the humours of the body: whence it hath hapned, that many by such scrup es, haue broken their braynes, and some haue made themselues vnprofitable both for themselues, and for Religion. Scruples cause a man to loose his tyme, that might
otherwise

otherwise be imployed in profitable things
and in good workes. For how much tyme
doth a scrupulous man loose in saying one
prayer, or in reading of a psalme? He beginneth againe and againe, he repeateth what
he hath formerly sayd, and neuer maketh
an end, and which is worse, when he hath
all done, he remaineth lesse satisfyed, then
he was at the very first : and if it happen ,
that notwithstanding all this, he maketh
no more repetitions, it is rather in regard of
a certaine yrksomenes, and loathing he findeth, then out of any perswasion to himselfe, that he hath satisfyed what he should
do . Againe the scrupulous doth not only
loose his tyme himselfe, but he further causeth the losse thereof to his Superiour, or
to his Ghostly-father, with whome he con-
ferreth touching his scruples, and if they
yeald him the hearing, it will be long before he make an end, and the more a man
condescendeth to a scrupulous person, the
more and greater will be his hurt.

5 . Scruples make the scrupulous
man stiffe and obstinate: for where a vayne
feare of offending , and of not satisfying
predominateth & beareth ouermuch sway
in him , thence it commeth , that he yealdeth not, nor obayeth very easily , and that
K k he

he will not condescende to his Ghostly
Father, or Superiour, & so he becommeth
headstrong, and euer retayneth these his
scruples. Scruples cause the scrupulous
man not to consider his Creatour, as a good
and louing Father, as he should do, but as a
seuere exactour, and a rigorous iudge of his
actions: and this consideration of his fil-
leth him with so many vayne feares,
and so great, as he seemeth to himselfe to be
already in the very torments of hell. My
sonne, thou dost very iniuriously to deale
with me in this sort: I haue not created
thee for thy damnation, but for the glory
of heauen, and I desire nothing els, but thy
good, and thy saluation. I haue for the sauing of thee endured a thousand paynes &
miseryes all my life long, and therfore my
will is, that thou bid adieu to this vaine
feare, and that thou from henceforth conceiue of me, as of a good, and mercifull Father, desirous of thy soules good.

6. And if thou hast a desire to rid thy
selfe of this malady, and not be scrupulous,
there be three thinges for thee necessary.
The first is, that thou be not thyne owne
phisitian, and be resolued to giue credit to
thyne owne aduise and iudgment. A Phisitian, be he neuer so learned, and experienced,

enced, is nothing fit to ordaine a medicine
for himſefe , when he hath any ſicknes,
and much leſſe ſhall the ſcrupulous man be
fit: whoſe paſſion and imagination being
ſtronger , and more vehement then any
feuer, or paine of body, troubleth him in
ſuch ſort, as it robbeth him of all his iudgment, and cauſeth him to ſee and take one
thing for another.

7. The ſecond thing neceſſary, is,
that thou follow the aduiſe of thy ſpiritual
father, or of thy Superiour, though thou
be otherwiſe of a contrary opinion . And
to the end thou maiſt accommodate thy
ſelfe with the more facility thereunto, thou
muſt perſwade thy ſelfe, that I am he who
gouerne the Religious in their ſcruples,
and that I gouerne them by the mediation
of their Superiours , and therefore thou
muſt be perſwaded and hold for aſſured ,
that the counſaile , which they ſhall giue
thee in thy ſcruples, commeth from me.
And indeed I could not well deale with
them in any other manner. For if the Religious man haue , out of a deſire to ſerue
me , forſaken both parents & friends, very
reaſonable it is , that I ſerue them alſo for
father and mother , for kin and friends. If
flying from the world, they haue caſt thé-

Kk2   ſelues

selues into my armes, reason it is, that I
imbrace and receiue them, and serue them
for their refuge. If they haue made their
election to depend of me for the confir-
ming of themselues all in all to my will,
meete it is, that I assist them with my direction, and counsaile, and that they admit
it, as comming from me, what they shall
aduise them in that behalfe.

8.   The third thing that thou must obserue, is, to obay thy sayd spiritual Fathers,
and to execute and do with a promptitude
what they shall say, & this is so necessary,
as if it be not kept, all the rest will not
profit thee a whit. For what would it
help to ordayne a medicine, and farther
to be perswaded, that it is prescribed by an
excellent Phisitian, if the patient and infirme person will not vse it? My sonne,
take heed of Sathan who for the hindring
of many of thy good workes seeketh to
trouble thee with many scruples, and to fill
thy head with infinite anxietyes, and
vnstayed and running thoughts. I know
that he maketh thee anon to say, or thinke
in thy mind, who knoweth whether my
spirituall Father be not deceaued in commaunding me to do this, or leaue that? It
may be, he hath not vnderstood me, or that

I

I haue not sufficiently explicated my selfe.
I am in doubt, whether this counsaile
which he giueth me, be not rather to comfort me: and which is more, that in himselfe he thinketh not, that I haue offended
God, and that I shalt be damned. All such
thoughts arise of a vaine and false feare caused by the enemy, who troubleth the water, for feare thou shouldst see the truth.
But seest thou not, that though thy spirituall Father should deceiue thee, thou art not
for all deceaued in obaying him, for that
thou oughtst to obay him in all thinges,
where there is not apparence of any manifest sinne. And more then that, to thinke
that he hath not well vnderstood thee,
ought not to trouble thee, sith it ought to
be inough for thy satisfactiō, if he say, that
he hath vnderstood thee well: for thou art
bound to beleeue him. In like sort to
thinke, that thou hast offended me by
thy scruples, and that I will damne thee
for them, is a thing, that must be far remoued from thy imagination. He that hath
so many pledges and testimonyes of my
loue and benignity, as thou hast, hath a
good occasion to put his trust in me. If
thou hast a firme purpose not to offend me,
and rather to dye, then to commit a mortal
sinne

sinne, this being a true signe of thy saluation, and of my amity, wherefore fearest thou? And he who feareth this, is not afraid to offend me.

9.   Neither must the desire that thou feelest in thy selfe, of making a generall confession, for feare, or doubt, that thou hast not made it well, trouble thee. If thy spirituall Father iudge it neither necessary nor profitable, but rather domageable, thou must content thy selfe with that, which he telleth thee, and obay him : for if there should be any fault, it should not be imputed vnto thee . For a man to repeate his confession without necessity, is to multiply his scruples. The Confessour who yealdeth vnto the scrupulous, by his importunity what he should not, doth not well dischargehis office, and hurteth the scrupulous, as being an occasion by that means vnto him of more scrupulosity then before. For the more, doubtles, is taken away in so doing, the more do they still entertaine & increase the scruples. So to moue and turne the earth without sowing seed thereon, is to cause that bad weeds spring vp in the place. Tell me, when thou madst thy last generall confession, didst thou not then satisfy thy conscience? If thou sayst thou didst, and that

the

the Prieſt gaue thee Abſolution of thy
ſinnes, wherefore makeſt thou any doubt
now, if thou didſt then confeſſe all ? If
thou madſt thyne examine as thou oughſt?
If thou hadſt a ſufficient ſorrow for thy
ſinnes? For a man may iudge better of his
confeſſion then when he made it, then he
can a long tyme after . If there had beene
any default in it, thou ſhouldſt rather haue
perceaued and found it out then, then
now .

10. My ſonne, remember that it is long
that thou haſt been troubled with ſcruples
and that becauſe thou hadſt a will to gouerne thy ſelfe by thyne owne fancy, thou
art not yet cured and eaſed of them, but findeſt thy ſelfe more diſquieted and troubled
then euer before, and therefore euen human
prudence would require, that thou ſhouldſt
change the remedy, and that ſith thou art
ſicke, thou be not a Phiſitian to thy ſelfe.
And therefore thou muſt reſolue, that for
the curing of thy ſcruples, the beſt remedy
is to beleeue and obay thy ſpiritual Father .
And in that thou muſt diligently take heed
thou come not vnto him with a certaine
artificiall skill, and an intention to draw
him to thyne owne will by importunity,
or otherwiſe ; for that were euer to returne

to the same, and to haue a will to be thyne
owne phisitian in thy scruples, and to procure to be gouerned by thy spirituall Father conformably to thyne owne fancy,
wherein there should be a double fault: for
that besides thyne, thou shouldst cause thy
spirituall Father, or Superiour to fayle in
the discharge of his office. Thy spiritual
Father is a meanes wherof I serue my selfe,
and he is myne instrument, not thyne, and
therefore he must be moued by me, and not
by thee. The thing which appertaineth
vnto thee to do, is to leaue him in his liberty, and considering him, as one who
holdeth my place, to haue an hope, that by
meanes of him I will not fayle to direct
thee for thy greatest good.

That a Religious man must flye Curiosity.

CHAP. XIIII.

MY sonne, I see thee ouer diligent and
curious in searching out the knowledge of noueltyes and strang things of
the world, wherein thou giuest to vnderstand, that thou hast not yet giuen ouer
thy affectiō & loue to it, in so much as thou
art not yet wholy dead vnto it. If thou hast
so abandoned it, as thou shouldst not haue
any

any thing to do with it, whence is it that curiofity maketh thee to inquire after what is therein done, and what is fayd and paffeth? What haft thou to know and vnderftand that, which concerneth thee not, and that bringeth not any good to thy foule, but domage rather? Thou haft more then often tryed, that the news of the world which thou haft heard, occurreth to thy mind in thy prayer, in the tyme of Maffe, and other good exercifes. How much better courfe did thofe good Hermites take, who becaufe they might not vnderftand, or know what paffed in the world, withdrew themfelues into the wildernes, and there hid themfelues in holes vnder the ground?

2. Curiofity, fith it is an inordinate defire to know, is reprehenfible, & repugnant to the rule of right reafon, but much worfe is the roote whence it commeth. If a Religious perfon were well affected to matters diuine and fpiritual, he would not be curious to fearch into thinges humane, that touch him not at all. Curiofity ordinarily arifeth of the little affection, that men haue to the works of vertue, and therfore it greatly importeth the Religious mã at all tymes to haue imployement in fome

profitable

profitable and commendable thing or o-
ther, though the same be not inough to
withdraw him wholy from curiosity. For
as it is attractiue, it causeth a man oftentimes to leaue euen profitable occupations,
and therfore the Religious must not only
busy himselfe in things of profit, and such
as agree with his profession, but also ap-
ply his mind and affection therunto, and
so doing he shall shut vp the dore against al
curiosity, and therewithall free himselfe
from many disquiets and troubles of mind.
But when curiosity is in the Religious
man accompanyed with idlenes, or light
imployments, then she keepeth holy day,
because she well knoweth how to find entrance, when she listeth, being the property
of idlenes to set open both his dores and
windowes: & she no sooner getteth in, but
that she forthwith setteth the senses at liberty, which be her messengers, and sendeth
them forth to search out noueltyes, on
which she afterwards causeth the inward
powers of the soule to reflect, and to buyld
their iudgments, and castles in the ayre:
wherby it appeareth, how much curiosity
is repugnant to the Religious state, which
requireth that all the senses be brought in
subiection and mortifyed, and that they
haue

haue not the liberty to wander where
they fhould not, and when it appertaineth
vnto reafon to guide, and direct them, and
not curiofity.

3. Marke my fonne, the craft and policy
of Sathan, whereby he induceth the Religious man to open the gate of curiofity.
Firft he putteth in his thoughts, that it is
good for him to vnderftand the difafters &
tepefts of the world, to the end he may render vnto me the more condigne thanks for
hauing brought him into the quiet & fafe
harbour of Religion: and to the end, that
hauing a better & more perfect knowledge
of the finifter, and miferable euents of the
world, he may the better vnderftand the
felicity of the ftate whereunto he is called,
and from how many troubles and dangers
he is deliuered: finally to the end, fayth he,
he may haue a compaffion, and be moued
to pray for the poore of the world, who
are fo fore oppreffed, and afflicted in
the world, as euery good Religious man is
bound to do. But to take all this at the beft,
it is nothing els, but to deceiue vnder the
apparence of good: and what is of it felfe
vicious and bad, cannot be a meanes to the
producing and doing of good workes.
Therefore curiofity being a finne, it is nothing

thing conuenient to make vſe of it for the doing of good. And my Apoſtle hath plainely and expreſly ſayd, that no euill is euer to be done vnder the hope and pretence of any good. But that which the Diuell pretendeth, is to induce the Religious man to affect and giue himſelfe to curioſity, knowing right well (as he is wylie, and crafty) that hauing once drawne him to curioſity, he will neuer compoſe himſelfe, neither to the exerciſe of the ſayd good works, nor of any other. And in this lyeth his deceit, to make ſhew to haue a will to induce thee to the doing of good, to the end he may go away with the victory to thy domage and loſſe.

4. A iuſt man muſt euer hold the loue and beneuolence of an enemy ſuſpected: & for the rendring of thankes vnto God for the happy ſtate of Religion, and praying for thoſe of the world, is it not neceſſary to enquire curiouſly about that which paſſeth in the world. For without it a man knoweth inough touching the ſtormes, & miſeryes that the poore ſecular perſons endure: for as much as ſuch miſeryes began not to day, but haue been heretofore, and ſhall alſo may be. And more then this, Religion hath ſo many gifts, priuiledges and graces,

graces, as of it selfe it giueth a sufficient
knowledge thereof, without necessity, for
the attayning & getting of such knowledg
to enquire curiously about the news, and
miseryes of the world.

5. Harken my sonne, now to another
deceite, wherof Sathan serueth himselfe by
meanes of curiosity. In the beginning he
is contented, that the curious loose his time
in reading, or hearing read vaine and curious bookes, in vnderstanding the news
that passe in forraine countryes that touch
him nothing at all, in hauing I know not
what faire and curious thing, and the like,
but he stayeth not there. For passing further, he laboureth to induce and draw him
to know, & see what is not lawfull, & euen
that wherin there is danger, be it a thing
that prouoketh to the sinnes of hatred, reuenge, or impurity, and in fine he seeketh
to moue him to do all openly without any
shadow or pretense at all. And this is
then, when the curious person, for the vnderstanding of secret and hidden things demaundeth and enquireth them of the Diuell, or of some other who hath commerce
with him. And what good doctrine can
one learne of the Father of lies? Or what
fruite or learning can be drawne or gotten
out

out of so vnhappy a schoole?

6.   Curiosity is a vice, which cannot so
be easily shaken off, as a man would thinke.
The elder a man is, the more increaseth his
curiosity, and thence it is, that a man is neuer weary in hearing of news. Curiosity,
that moueth a man to enquire of anothers
affayres, causeth him to forget his owne,
and himselfe also: & he who runneth to the
houses of others, and leaueth his owne, is
in danger at his returne not to find all that
he left at his going forth. The curiosity,
that proubketh the senses to fasten themselues vpon curious & impertinent things,
maketh the curious to stumble and fall, &
that oftentymes very fowly. Who is apt to
fall of himselfe, he will fall much more easily, being thrust by another. And sith mans
nature is so debilitated by sinne, as we see, &
experièce in our selus, the very least occasiõ,
as may be this of curiosity, is inough to
precipitate it. My sonne, hast thou a desire,
that curiosity should not giue thee any occasion of ruine by thy senses? Let there not
on thy part any occasion be giuen of abu-
sing them. For if thou seruest thee of thy
senses for thy pleasure only, and not for necessity, or for profit, it will be an inuitation
to curiosity, and an occasion vnto it of abu-
sing

fing them in vanityes. If thou lend thy
hearing to all, and lookeft vpon all that
commeth in thy mind, who feeth not, that
fo to do is to put the bridle of thy fenfes into curiofityes hands, that it may turne and
wind them which way it pleafeth? Haue
a care to thy fenfes if thou defire, that they
fhould be follicitous to preferue and keep
thy hart from all vanity.

That a Religious man ought to flye from
all manner of Ambition.

CHAP. XV.

MY fonne, a good Religious man, and
prudent, doth euer and anone lay
before his eyes the end, for which he hath
left the world, and entred into Religion,
which is to ferue me, who am his Lord,
in a more perfect manner, then he did in
the world, and thereby the better to affure
the fauing of his foule. And more then
that, he thinketh vpon the meanes of attaining this end, which be vertues, mortification of the paffions, abnegation of
himfelfe, contempt and hatred of all,
which the world loueth and imbraceth.
Befides this, he thinketh on that, which is
an impediment of comming to this end,
and

and such be vices, of the number wherof is
ambition Prids daughter, which doth not
only diuert the Religious man from my
seruice, but also maketh him to entertaine
an opposition against me . And therefore
where ambition is an inordinate appetite
and desire of woridly honour, necessary it
is, that it be quite banished out of Religion,
because Religion is a schoole opposite to
that of the world . And if the Religious
man be come out of the world, and hath
already beene at defiance with it, is it beseeming vnto him to seek worldly honour
in Religion? None can be a scholler in
two contrary schooles .

2 .   Heare my sonne, what ambition
teacheth in the schoole of the world . It
teacheth the schollers to seeke after honour
and reputation, to desire preheminences &
dignites, to procure great charges , offices,
and titles of greatest honour . But in the
schoole of religion the custome is to teach
the contrary, and I am the maister thereof,
as willingly & patiently to put vp wrongs,
to beare reproaches, dishonours, infama-
tions, ignominyes, to shunne preheminences and dignityes . This is my liuery, this is
the doctrine, that I haue alwayes both
taught , and practised . When the Iewes
                                          came

came with scepter and crowne vnto me to make me their King, I ranne away : but when they came into the garden to apprehend me, and to bind me as a theef, to conduct me before an earthly Iudge, I did not only not runne away, but I also went forth vnto them, & willingly deliuered my selfe into their hands. The seruant is knowne by his Maisters liuery, and the scholler by that which he learneth.

3. O my soule, what shal we do heere! Thou seest that thy Sauiour is wholy contrary to the world, as the world is cotrary to him. Thou seest that their schools be altogeather opposite, their liuery, & the way which they trace & hold, most different, & therfore either the world must needs be deceyued in seeking after honours, or our Sauiour in flying and contemning them. And because our Sauiour, who is the wisdome of the eternall Father, cannot be deceyued, it followeth, that it is the world that deceyueth it selfe in it owne ambition, & all those who take pleasure in the vainity of such smoakes. And therfore if we haue not a will to be of the number of them, and not to be deceiued with them, we must tread all vaine,& worldly honour vnder foot, and with the ignominy of the

L l   Crosse

Crosse follow our sweet Sauiour, who is our conductour and guide to true glory.

4. But tell me, my Sauiour, if thou hast created me for glory euerlasting, that is accompanyed with the greatest glory and honour that can possibly be, wherefore dost thou forbid me to seeke after honour, and glory in this world? If thy Apostle hath left written, that he who desireth a Bishoprike, desireth a good worke, wherfore should it not be lawful for me to desire titles of honour?

5. My sonne, remember, that thou wert not created for an earthly glory, but for a celestial, & none can hinder thee from purchasing this. On the contrary, I am displeased to see, that any should busy is mind with the glory of the world, for that of heauen. As touching that saying of my Apostle that thou alleadgest, thou must know, that to desire a Bishopricke, to trauaile & take paines for the sauing of soules, is a commendable thing, and an act of charity: but to desire it for the honour and dignity that is annexed vnto it, or for the temporall commodity which a man may receaue thereby, is neither good, nor expedient. In the primitiue Church the Bishoprikes were without honour, and riches and

and were accompanied with much paine
and trauaile, in so much as he who desired
a Bishoprike at that tyme, desired by that
occasion to trauayle and take paynes in the
Churches behalfe, and to become a martyr
for my sake: and therefore then to desire to
be a Bishop, was a good and holy desire.
But since the time, that the Bishopricks began to haue preheminences, honours, and
riches annexed vnto them, such a desire
cannot be without many dangers: & therof it commeth that my Apostle, to giue to
vnderstand, that it was not lawfull for e-
uery one to aspire to such dignityes, added
presently after, that a Bishop must be irreprehensible, not contentious, but sober,
chast, and charitable. Thus thou seest, my
sonne, that these dignities haue more burden, then honour, and thou shalt do a great
matter, if thou canst guide thyne owne
soule without medling with the gouerning of anothers. For if there should not
be any other thing besids this consideratis-
on to say, that a Bishop must be irreprehensible, it would be inough for the instru-
ction of any man of meane iudgment.

6. Moreouer the difference, that is
betweene him who becometh Religious,
and him who taketh the charge of a Bishoprike,

prik, manifesteth the same. For he who entreth into Religion, entreth in for the attaining of vertue and perfection, but a Bishop entreth into his charge to exercise perfection, and to teach vertue vnto others, not only by words, but much more by example of good life, and therefore he must euen then be perfect, and he must haue vertues not only in expectation and hope, but in effect also. My sonne, suffer not thy selfe to be misled, and abused by the enemy, when he putteth into thy head, that when thou shouldst be promoted to any dignity, or prelacy, or when thou shouldst be a Superiour, thou wouldst serue me better, and wouldst do many more and better good workes: for as much as in such dignityes both the obligation bindeth more, and the occasiōs of falling be much greater in those conditions, then in other. And if thou mayst not acquite thy selfe in lesser obligations, how wilt thou discharge thy band in greater? If one little and light occasion maketh thee to fall easily, what will it be in a greater? Remēber, that it is a lesse euill to fall from a low place, and that he must not presume to take vpon his shoulders a great & heauy burden, who seeth himselfe apt to fall vnder a light one. But if thou
hast

haft a will not to be deceaued in this cafe,
obferue what I fhall tell thee. Firft neuer
intrude, or prefent thy felfe to any dignity
or prelacy: fecondly neuer defire nor feeke
them, but rather fhunne them, vnles thou
be cõmanded by him who may bind thee
to accept them, or that the neceffity were
fuch, as in the iudgment of thy fpirituall
Father, charity fhould bind thee to admit
them for the common good, and my greater feruice.

7. A man may eafily know by the propertyes of Ambition, how repugnant it is
to a Religious ftate. There is not a vice
that diffembleth, or difgufteth, as doth
Ambition, and therof it proceadeth, that
it is worthily called hipocrifies and adu-
lations mother. Ambition, for the attayning of any office or dignity, maketh
a femblance and fhew, that it is poffeffed of
many vertues, wherof it hath not the very
leaft part, or any thing at all. With how
many colours fetteth it forth her owne
actions, to make them to be efteemed worthy of that it defireth? To whome doth
it not crouch, & bow the knee, that it may
haue audience, and treate with him, at
whofe hands it ftandeth in hope of fauour?
It euer liueth betweene feare and hope

of

or compassing that, which it pretendeth, and thertore needs must it be alwayes
vnquiet: the sleep is euery houre interrup-
ted and broken with cares: the repose is by
peece-meales, it still eateth with anxiety,
it is in despaire, when he at whose hands it
expecteth fauour, shew it a bad counte-
naunce, or looke awry vpon it: it is puffed
vp and sweileth with pride, when he looketh merily vpon it, or giueth it a good
countenance, in so much as there is not a
sea so troubled and tossed, as is the hart of
an ambitious person. He honoureth all
the world, he maketh a thousand promises
to euery one, he maketh semblance of louing all. And what haue these, and the
like ceremonyes, which be nothing but
vanity, to do with the Religious state,
which exacteth true Humility, sincerity,
and entiere Charity, which be capitall enemyes to ambition? What hath the Religious man, who retyreth himselfe from the
world, for the leading of a quiet life, to
meddle with ambition, that is accompanyed with so many troubles, and disquiet,
and putteth the soule into so great danger?
O how much better vnderstanding haue
some of my Religious had thereof, who
that they might not be constrained to accept

eept of dignityes and prelacyes, that were
presented them , got them out of the cittyes into some desert or wildernes, yea &
some of them hid themselues in sepulchres,
that they might not be found. And if they
came thither to seek them out, & that they
forced them to take and accept of such dignityes, they gaue to vnderstand by the a-
bundance of teares, that fell from their
eyes, with how ill a will they amitted the.

8. But Ambition stayeth not heere: for
being come to one dignity, it must aspire
and mount vp to a greater, vntil it get vp to
the last, and highest of all. And this is that,
whereof I reprehended the Pharisyes, who
for the glory of the world desired the first
seat's in the Synagogues & feasts, & all honorable salutations in the streetes. This
is not the way that leadeth to Religious
Perfection, but rather to blind a man with
the smoke of the world , and that in such
sort, as he become starke blind, that he
neither see any more the end of the iourney
which he intendeth , nor the way how to
come to it. So the Religious man must be
attentiue to that , which their Superiour
shall commaund them, and they must perswade themselues, that he who preacheth,
or teacheth in chaires of more note, be not

those,

those, who do what pleaseth me best; neither profit their neighbours most, or merit the most for them, but he who laboureth well with most humility, and greatest charity. He that taketh paynes for loue of me, seeketh nothing els, but what may contēt me, but he who taketh paynes to get himselfe fame, & reputation among men, hath selfe-loue the proper motiue vnto himselfe for the getting of the highest seate, and the places of most honour. And when it happeneth, that matters succeed not with so much honour to them, & applause as they desired & expected (as it often falleth out) a man may see such manner of men afflict themselues, to be vexed, & to cast the fault I know not vpon whome, & they consider not, that it is a punishment of God, sent vnto them for their ambition and pride. The sinne of Ambition doth not consist in enioying the preheminence of places but in desiring to haue them, & afterward to liue very proudly therein.

FINIS.

CERTAINE

ADVERTISEMENTS

to Religious men,

For the leading of a vertuous life in Religion, and for the better obseruation of their Rules.

OD sayth by the mouth of the Prophet Ieremy: What is it, that my Beloued hath in my house done much wickednes? As though he meant to say more expresly: I haue good occasion to complain, in seeing that my creatures haue so sore offended me, but that those whome I loue most, and whome I nourish in Religion, as my house-hold seruants, and familiar friends haue so highly offended me, and make no reckoning neither of their institute they haue imbraced, nor of the Vows whereunto they be bound, nor of the obseruation of their Rules, nor of profiting

and

and going forwards in the way of perfection, is a thing intollerable, and not to be borne withall. And if God may not endure to see this abuse, meet is it that we be fory also, and therwith also endeauour to find out a way & meanes for the remedying of so great an euill by all possible industry. And to this purpose it will profit vs to meditate and often to reuiew these points following.

1.   Consider first, my sonne, how rigorously God did punish the sinnes, that were committed in the holy places: as in the person of Lucifer, who was for his pride thrust out of heauen and cast downe into hell: in the person of Adam & Eue, whom he banished out of the terrestriall paradise for their disobedience: in that of Dathan & Abyron, whome the earth swallowed vp aliue: in that of Ananias & Saphyra, who fell downe dead at S. Peters feet for lying vnto him. Consider these examples, and feare thou also, least he punish thee in body or soule, or at least for the sinnes thou hast committed in Religion, he abandon thee cleane. Therefore make thou from hence forth this resolution, & firme purpose, that thou wilt keep all thy rules and lawes of Religion, for feare least God lay his heauy

and

and rigorous hand vpon thee.

2. Secondly confider, what our Sauiour fayth of the tree, that did not beare any fruit : Cut it down, to what end occupieth it place in the ground ? He comaunded it to be cut down, being againſt reaſon it ſhould take the place of another tree that would beare fruite. If our Sauiour would giue ſo rigorous a ſentéce vpon an vnfruitfull tree , what would he haue done, if it had borne fruit infectious, impoyſoning, and deadly? Thou art that barren tree, that in Religion doſt in vayne occupy the place of another that would ſerue God truely, and as it ſhould beſt beſceme a Religious man. Thou art the vnfruitfull tree, that beareſt none, but the fruits of death, & of many ſinnes: and for this thou haſt cauſe to feare, that God will with the axe cut thee down, & remoue thee from the place, where he hath ſo mercifully ſet thee, and plant another for thee, who ſhall ſerue him Religiouſly, and ſhall beare fruit to life euerlaſting. Therefore my ſonne, read thy Rules often, obſerue them exactly, be feruent in thy vocation, and endeauour to go forwards from one vertue to another, to the end our Lord may gather the fruit, that he deſireth, of thee, whome he hath by ſo

ſingular

singular a priuiledge planted in the vine-yard of holy Religion.

3.   Thirdly consider, that all the holy inspirations, spirituall helps, and all the ordinances & rules of Religion be giuen by God for this, that the Religious seeke to perfect themselues in his seruice: and therfore thou must thinke, that doing the contrary, thou wrongest God, and iniurest thy selfe very much, and hast iust occasion to feare, least he will pronounce this dread-full saying, mentioned in his Prophet Esay, against thee: In the Land of the Holy he hath done wicked things, and he shall not see the glory of our Lord. As though he should say: I haue giuen thee a place, in an holy place, amongst Holy ones, to the end thou shouldst become like vnto them. I haue for the same end prouided thee of all possible commodityes, and so many good inspirations, lawes, ordinances, and rules for thy better help, and the more perfecting of thee in my seruice, and all these helps thou hast abused, and hast been so far from profiting & going forwards in my seruice, as thou art become worse. And what will be the end of all this? Because thou hast abused al these helps that I haue giuen thee towards thy increase in vertue, thou sha't

not

not haue any part in my eternall glory.

4. Fourthly confider, that the finne which is committed againft any Vow is much greater, and difpleafeth God more then do other finnes. A Vow impofeth a greater and ftraiter obligation of feruing God, and therfore when the fault is made in that behalfe, the finne is the greater a-gainft God. And more then this, thou muft perfwade thy felfe, that al which thou vfeft for thy meate and drinke, cloathing or o-therwife, whether thou haft it of the Reli-gion wherof thou art an vnworthy mem-ber, or otherwife by way of almes of well difpofed perfons, turneth to the finne of fraud, becaufe thou defraudeft & deceaueft thy Religion on the one fide, in not obfer-uing the rules therof, and on the other fide thou art vnworthy, and incapable to pray for them, who beftow fuch almes vpon thee. For our Lord vouchfafeth not to heare thy prayers, fo long as thou fhalt o-mit to obferue what thou haft promifed him.

5. Laftly confider, how feruent and earneft a defire thou hadft to ferue God, when he did firft call thee vnto Religion. And if euen now notwithftanding thou be intangled in fo many finnes, and affections

of

of the world, thou yet feelest in thy selfe so harty and earnest a desire to aspire to perfection, whence is it, that being in so holy a place, amidst so many and excellent helps and meanes of profiting to perfection, thou art so miserable, cold, and negligent? And if thou answer me, that thou art indeed a grieuous sinner, but thou entredst into Religiō to be good, whence commeth it, that after so long tyme of thy being, & of trayning vp in this schoole of vertue, thou seemest to be so far off from thy first desires, and from that which appertayneth to thy profession? And therfore my sonne, be ashamed that thou art so imperfect, & make a firme resolution to returne to thy first feruour, and to an exact obseruation of thy rules, & of thyne Institute, that thou mayst from this tyme forwards serue God in all loue, and holynes, as meet is thou shouldst do.

Certaine Considerations, that may help to the obseruing of the Rules in Religion.

THE first is, to read them often, and to meditate the forementioned points euery moneth once, or more often, to the end by such meditation thou mayst stir vp in thy selfe a desire of obseruing them. And to conceiue a firme purpose neuer to infring

or

or breake any Rule whatsoeuer, vnder pretence that it importeth little, or is not of any consequence, will help much thereunto.

2. The second is, to desire thy Superiour, and all the other Religious persons of the house to reprehend and admonish thee freely, as often as they shall see thee to trasgresse against the Rules, or to commit any other fault, which thou seest not thy selfe.

3. The third is euery moneth to do some voluntary penance, either in secret, or in publque by the permission of thy Superiour, for the faults that moneth committed against the Rules, and good desires and purposes that God hath inspired thee with, accompayning it with a good desire and firme resolution to obserue them better for the tyme to come.

4. The fourth is, that thou haue a particular affection to the obseruation of thy foure vowes of Pouerty, Chastity, Obedience, and Enclosure, keeping them with more care, then thou wouldst most precious stones. And to the end thou mayst the better affect them, read or meditate the aduertisements following.

Of the vowes, which the Religious make,
and first of Obedience.

THou must obey thy Superiour perfectly for the loue of God, & consider
that hauing the vertue of Obedience, thou
shalt togeather with it haue the other also: and especially for this, that by it our Sauiour did redeeme the world, that was ru-
ined by the contrary vice of disobedience.
And therfore cease not to make petition to
his diuine Maiesty, that he please to grant
thee, to know and vnderstand the impor-
tance, merit, efficacy, and perfection of
this vertue, that knowing it thou mayst be
the more stirred vp to plant it, and procure
it to increase in thy soule.

    The Religious man that desireth to
be perfect in the vertue of Obedience, must
be perswaded, that the voice of the Superiour, when he or she commaundeth any
thing, is nothing els, but the very voyce of
God, and when he vnderstandeth the signe
of doing any thing, he must thinke that it
is God who calleth him. And then he must
leaue off all other busynes, and instantly go
about that whereunto he is called: namely
when he is called to the Quire, to Masse, to
prayer, and to other the like spirituall exercises.

cifes. The good & obedient Religious examineth not whether that which is commaunded him, be well or ill commaunded,
but obeyeth promptly, readily, and without any murmuration in all thinges where
there is not any manifest finne.

Of the Vow of Chaſtity.

I Need not to tel thee of the vow of Chaſtity, ſith it is cleare and manifeſt, how
perfectly it ought to be kept, & ſith it hath
two côpanions & ſiſters, that neuer depart
from her ſide. The former is a certaine holy Baſhfulnes, which may worthily be called the keeper and intertayner of Chaſtity,
as that which defendeth and preſerueth it
againſt all ſtayne of diſhoneſty. The office
of this Baſhfulnes is to cauſe that the eyes
be kept downe, and caſt vpon the ground,
and to cauſe the Religious perſon to conceiue an horrour of ſeing, & of being ſeen.
And if peraduenture ſhe ſhould be to ced to
ſpeake, or to ſuffer her ſelfe to be ſeene, ſhe
eftſoones couereth her face with an honeſt
bluſh, the teſtimony of the care which ſhe
hath of the purity of her ſoule. To be ſhort,
this Baſhfullnes cauſeth her to be modeſt
in her geſtures, in her going, and in all that
ſhe doth, and by that occaſion conſerueth

M m　　　　　　the

the vertue of Chaſtity in her perfection.

The other ſiſter of Chaſtity is a Purity of hart, by meanes whereof the ſoule becommeth ſo exceedingly affected to this vertue, as it conceiueth not only an horrour at the very leaſt diſhoneſt thought, but alſo at euery inordinate affectió to whatſoeuer creature, euer carrying a chaſt hart to her Spouſe, and holding it for ſpirituall adultery neuer ſo little to ſeparate her affection from him.

Of the Vow of Pouerty.

AS touching the Vow of Pouerty, I would haue thee to be carefull to cótent thy ſelfe with the only vſage of things that ſhall be vnto thee neceſſary, and to make a conſcience of vſing them as thyne owne, for feare leaſt vnder the colour of neceſſity thou become in tyme a Proprietary. Therfore thou muſt not giue any thing vnto another without licence of thy Superiour, nor in like manner take any thing without leaue, though it ſhould be otherwiſe neceſſary. Thou muſt neuer haue any money at thyne own diſpoſition, whether it be in thyne owne hands, or in anothers, leaſt the Diuell deceaue thee, and vnder the pretence of neceſſity induce thee to violate

thy

thy vow of Pouerty, and by so doing cause
thee to incurre the danger of eternall damnation for not keeping thy promise made
vnto God. And because this vice of propriety is wont to raigne in the negligent, and
carelesse Religious, thou must marke certaine points, which may serue as antidots
for the dryuing of this affection far from
thyne hart.

    Consider first, that this is a greater
sinne, then it is to cast off the habit, or to go
from one Couent to another, which yet is
held for a very scandalous thing. It more
importeth the Religious to keep the three
essentiali Vowes thereof, and in particuler
the vow of Pouerty, which is as the wall
and rampier therof, then to weare such an
habit, or to liue in such a monastery. If
then it be so great a sinne to returne to the
habit of the world, and to cast off that of
Religion, or to runne from one monastery
to another: what then thinke we, shall it be
to vse any thing as our owne, and to breake
the vow of Pouerty, which conserueth Religion in her integrity.

    Consider secondly, how great a scā-
dall thou giuest thy Religious sisters, yea &
secular persons, and how thou defamest thy
Religion in as much as is in thee, besides

that, in so doing, is to robbe and steale, by keeping, or giuing that which is not thyne. For that which the Religious may gaine by her industry and paynes, or that which is giuen her, whatsoeuer it be, is not hers, but the communityes. And this theft is so much the greater, because it is committed in that which apperstayneth to the Church, to an holy place, to the poore, and to Gods seruants : and of this it commeth that the sinne of propriery is called sacriledge, and consequently worthy most grieuously to be punished.

Consider thirdly, that the pretious stone, whereof our Sauiour maketh mentiō in the Ghospel, is nothing but Pouerty, and that thou hast bought it with the price of all thy goods, in forsaking Father and Mother, brethren and sisters, and all thyne other friends, all thy pleasures & commodityes, and more then all this, thy owne selfe also. And draw out of this an holy confusion, that thou giuest all againe for a thing of nothing, which thou doest when thou vsest the things, that are giuen thee as though they were thy owne. Acknowledge thy owne fault herein, and remember, that thou canst not haue any greater treasure, then holy Pouerty, for that in it

is

is found the Creatour , and Lord of all
thinges .

Consider fourthly, how foolish and
ill aduised that man should be, who being
escaped out of the dangers of the sea, by the
help of a good ship wherinto he had got
himselfe, he should fill it with water by
little and little : for so doing he should in
coclusion sinke the ship, & drown himselfe
withall . Thinke then thou dost the same .
For being escaped out of the sea of this
world, and got into the ship of holy Religion, and resuming the thinges which
thou hadst formerly forsaken, for the satisfying and fulfilling of thy own will, is nothing els, but more shamefully to ruyne thy
selfe, then thou wouldst haue done in the
world . And therfore acknowledge thyne
owne blindnes herein, & haue nothing to
do with this so dangerous a vice of propriety : lay hold vpon thy most sweet Sauiour,
dying naked vpon the Crosse, and to that
purpose renew thy vow of Pouerty, which
thou hast formerly presered vnto him, with
all possible feruour and affection , as thou
didst when thou first madest it .

THAT thy Enclosure which thou keepest may be pleasing to God, & profitable to thy selfe, thou must keep it of a pure
and free will, for that the Religious person
who keepeth it not but in body, & in will
runneth all the world ouer, besides that,
that she neuer inioyeth true repose, looseth
all the fruite and benefit of her Enclosure.
Consider my child, how many graces thou
hast receaued by the meanes thereof: how
many occasions thou hast auoyded of offending God: yea & into how many sinnes
thou wouldst haue fallen, if it had been in
thy liberty to go forth at thy pleasure: and
it may be, that if thou hadst not been de-
barred of thy liberty in this behalfe, thou
hadst been peraduenture euen now torme-
ted in hell fire for all eternity. God hath
deliuered thee from these, and other like
dangers not to be numbred, by the meanes
of this thy Enclosure: & for this thou hast
most iust cause to loue it. And seeing thou
hast made a promise of it to God, thou
must keep it exactly, to the end thou
maist merit, and make thy profit therof.

Of

Of the Ioy, which the Religious ought to make vpon the day of their Conuer-sion, and what ioy it ought to be vnto them.

IT would be good to haue a particuler deuotion of thy Vows, that is to say, that euery yeare thou make a festiuity of the Day that thou didst enter into Religion, and madest thy vowes. For as we euery yeare celebrate the day of the dedication of a materiall Church : so ought we in like manner, and with more iust reason keep solemne the day of the dedication of our Soule, which is the liuing Temple of the Maiesty diuine. And for the well effecting thereof, thou mayst practise, and do these three thinges.

1. In the first place, thou must make a generall Confession of all the yeare past.

2. In the second, thou must offer thy selfe anew to God, to serue him in perpetu-all Pouerty, Chastity, Obedience, and En-closure, being sory for not hauing, for the tyme past, perfectly kept that which thou hast promised him, and for hauing profited so meanely in vertue, and in his holy ser-uice.

3. Lastly

3.　Laſtly thou muſt take new hart, &
new forces, renewing thy holy purpoſes,
and thy firſt deſires and feruours, returning
to thy exerciſes intermitted, and endea-
uouring to perfect thy ſelfe in them. Further, thou muſt ſee if thou canſt by the grace
of God, find out any other meanes, more
proper, and eaſy for helping of thee to put
in execution all that which thou art to do,
and in particuler thou muſt haue at al tyms
this deſire to renew thy ſelfe in the vertue
of prayer, and in the exerciſe of all other
vertues. O how would this feſtiuity, and
celebration of this thy Conuerſion, & day
of entring into Religiō, haue profited thee,
if thou hadſt done it as thou ſhouldſt. But
thy own ſiouth and negligence hath beene
an occaſion, that thou haſt omitted to vſe
the meanes, and helps, that God hath affoarded thee. And therefore pray thou
inſtantly, that he would pleaſe to pardon
thy paſſed faults, and to giue thee grace to
do thy endeauour better for the tyme to
come.

F I N I S.

THE
RELIGIOVS MANS
LOOKING-GLASSE,

Or a short way of attayning to Perfection in Religion.

I

The principall study of a Religious man.

1. TO deny himselfe.
2. To roote out Vices.
3. To plante Vertues.
4. To dye to himselfe, and to the world.
5. To loue God.

II.

*What is necessary to obtaine peace
of the mind.*

1. To desire and seek what is most humble and abiect.
2. To keep silence.
3. Not to contradict.
4. Not to intrude himselfe.
5. With indifferency to accept all things at Gods hand.

III.

A Religious man must exercise himselfe
continually.

1. In Humility, and Charity.
2. In Patience, and Mortification.
3. In Reading, and Praying.
4. In Meditation of the life of Christ.
5. In Communication with God.

IIII.

Thinges specially to be auoyded by a
Religious man.

1. The familiarity of Women.
2. Singularity and proper iudgment.
3. Selfe-will, and selfe-loue.
4. Idlenes, and the care of the belly.
5. Pride, and Vaine-glory.

V.

What a Religious man must do at home,
and in his Cell, or Chamber.

1. To thinke God to be present, and to see
    all thinges.
2. To withstand the suggestions of the Di-
    uell.
3. To read, and study how to do, and
    liue well.
4. To stir vp himselfe to Prayer and Medi-
    tation.

5. To

5. To arme himselfe, that he may go forth
   with safety, and profit.

VI.

The office of a Superiour towards his subiects.

1. To loue all alike.
2. To be watchful, that Religious discipline
   be obserued.
3. To be exemplar himselfe vnto al.
4. To instruct, and correct in spirit of lenity
   and mildenes.
5. To pray to God for all.

VII.

The office of a subiect towards his Superiour.

1. To loue him, as his Father.
2. To honour him, as his Lord.
3. To heare him, as a Doctor or Teacher.
4. To obey him, as Christ himselfe.
5. To pray to God for him.

VIII.

A Religious mans office and duty towards his brethren.

1. To loue them all in our Lord.
2. To hold them all for his betters.
3. To admonish them in Charity.
4. To support them with Patience.
5. To edify them by good Example.

IX

IX.

What is to be done in the morning early.

1. To arise speedily at the tyme appointed.
2. Forthwith to present himselfe in Gods sight, and seruice.
3. To giue him thanks for that nights preseruation.
4. To conceiue good purposes.
5. To craue help and grace for the due execution thereof.

X.

What is to be obserued about Prayer, and Meditation.

1. To prepare the mind, and the matter.
2. To expell Thoughts which diuert, or hinder vs.
3. To perseuere therein with Constancy.
4. With an humble hart to follow the inspirations of the Holy Ghost.
5. To be sorry for the defects committed therein, and to giue thankes for the good successe, if any hath beene.

XI.

What thinges are often to be handled, and thought vpon in Prayer.

1. The Knowledge of our selues, and sorrow for our sinnes.

2. The

2. The foure laſt thinges of man .
3. The benefits of God .
4. The life , and paſſion of Chriſt .
5. Conuerſation with God, and his Saints.

XII.

What is to be obſerued about Confeſſion.

1. To examine our Conſcience well .
2. To be hartily ſorry for our ſinnes.
3. To confeſſe our ſinnes entierly .
4. Earneſtly to purpoſe amendment of our life.
5. Forthwith to fulfill the pennance inioyned vs.

XIII.

What is to be obſerued about the Sacrifice of the Maſſe .

1. To clenſe the Conſcience firſt by Confeſſion.
2. To come vnto it with an humble , and contrite hart ,
3. With reuerence and deuotion to offer it vp to the glory of God, for himſelfe , and for the Church .
4. To communicate with a ſpirituall hungar , and Charity .
5. To go away with thankeſgiuing .

XIIII.

What is to be done after Maſſe .

1. In hart to hide himſelfe with Chriſt .

2. To

2. To offer himselfe all that he is, or can to Chrift.
3. To lay open his owne, and others neceſſityes vnto Chrift.
4. To aſke of Chrift many thinges for himſelfe, and for others.
5. To deſire & long after eternal Happines.

XV.

What is to be obſerued in ſaying Office.

1. To purge the hart from whatſoeuer other thoughts.
2. To procure deuotion.
3. To attend to the ſenſe of the words, and to God:
4. To ſpeake the words diſtinctly, and perfectly.
5. Not to make haſt to come to an end.

XVI.

What is to be done about the Examen of the Conſcience.

1. To aſke light of God.
2. To giue thankes for his benefits.
3. To diſcuſſe and examine well the Conſcience.
4. To be ſorry for our ſinnes.
5. To purpoſe amendment.

XVII.

XVII.

What is to be pondered in the examination of the Conscience.

1. The transgression of thy Vowes.
2. Thy tepidity & coldnes in Gods seruice.
3. The distraction of thy mind.
4. The bad motions of thy mynd.
5. Detractions, and Murmurations.

XVIII.

What is to be obserued in the Refectory.

1. To be silent.
2. To seeke mortification.
3. To eate and drinke soberly.
4. To be attent to that which is read.
5. To feed the soule spiritually.

XIX.

How to behaue thy selfe abroad without dores.

1. Diligently to guard and keep the gates of thy senses.
2. To obserue and keep Grauity, and Religious Modesty.
3. Not to giue eare to Vanityes or Noueltyes.
4. To speake and treat of spiritual matters.
5. To dispatch quickly, and soone returne home.

XX.

X X.

To be obserued in thy bed.

1. To commend thy selfe to God , to thy
    Angell Guardian, and other thy holy
    Patrons.
2. To thinke of Death, and of thy graue.
3. To arme thy selfe againſt temptations,
    and ſuggeſtions of the Diuell.
4. To call vpon God, as often as thou awa-
    keſt
5. Not to lye longer thē thou muſt needs.

FINIS.

to be obserua